George Payn Quackenbos

Advanced Course of Composition and Rhetoric

A Series of Practical Lessons on the Origin, History, and Peculiarities...

George Payn Quackenbos

Advanced Course of Composition and Rhetoric
A Series of Practical Lessons on the Origin, History, and Peculiarities...

ISBN/EAN: 9783337203467

Printed in Europe, USA, Canada, Australia, Japan

Cover: Foto ©Paul-Georg Meister /pixelio.de

More available books at **www.hansebooks.com**

ADVANCED COURSE

OF

COMPOSITION AND RHETORIC:

A Series of Practical Lessons

ON

THE ORIGIN, HISTORY, AND PECULIARITIES OF THE ENGLISH LANGUAGE, PUNC-
TUATION, TASTE, THE PLEASURES OF THE IMAGINATION, FIGURES, STYLE
AND ITS ESSENTIAL PROPERTIES, CRITICISM, AND THE VARIOUS
DEPARTMENTS OF PROSE AND POETICAL COMPOSITION:
ILLUSTRATED WITH COPIOUS EXERCISES.

ADAPTED TO SELF-INSTRUCTION, AND THE USE OF SCHOOLS AND COLLEGES.

"True grace in writing comes from ART, not chance."—POPE.

BY G. P. QUACKENBOS, A. M.,

PRINCIPAL OF "THE COLLEGIATE SCHOOL," N. Y.; AUTHOR OF "FIRST LESSONS IN
COMPOSITION," "ADVANCED COURSE OF COMPOSITION AND RHETORIC,"
"ILLUSTRATED SCHOOL HISTORY OF THE UNITED STATES," ETC.

NEW YORK:
D. APPLETON & CO., 443 & 445 BROADWAY.
1866.

TO

THE REV. DR. FERRIS.

CHANCELLOR OF THE UNIVERSITY OF THE CITY OF NEW YORK,

AS A TRIBUTE OF PROFESSIONAL RESPECT

FOR SOUND SCHOLARSHIP AND UNWEARIED LABORS IN THE CAUSE OF EDUCATION
NO LESS THAN AS A MEMORIAL

OF

PRIVATE ESTEEM AND FRIENDSHIP,

THIS VOLUME

Is Respectfully Dedicated

BY

THE AUTHOR.

"No man seeks a reason for believing what he sees or feels; and, if he did, it would be difficult to find one. But, though he can give no reason for believing his senses, his belief remains as firm as if it were grounded on demonstration. . . . The statesman continues to plod, the soldier to fight, and the merchant to export and import, without being in the least moved by the demonstrations that have been offered of the non-existence of those things about which they are so seriously employed. And a man may as soon, by reasoning, pull the moon out of her orbit, as destroy the belief of the objects of sense."—REID, Essay ii. chap. xx. pp. 278-4.

PREFACE.

THE favor with which the public have kindly received the Author's "First Lessons in Composition", and the frequent calls made by Colleges and higher Academies for a more advanced work on the same plan, with which to follow it, have led to the preparation of the present volume. The elementary book to which reference has just been made, was intended to initiate the beginner by easy steps into the art of composition; the work now offered to the public has a wider scope, embracing a variety of subjects worthy of the attention of advanced pupils, and presenting much important matter heretofore scattered through a number of different text-books. Claiming to give a comprehensive and practical view of our language in all its relations, this "Advanced Course" views it as a whole, no less than with reference to the individual words composing it; shows how it compares with other tongues, modern and ancient; points out its beauties; indicates how they may best be made available; and, in a word, teaches the pupil the most philosophical method of digesting and arranging his thoughts, as well as the most correct and effective mode of expressing them.

The volume commences with a condensed history of our tongue prefaced by a consideration of the origin of language in general, both spoken and written. Attention is first paid to the successive steps, by which, with Divine aid, man was enabled to develop a system of spoken language, to frame that elaborate and wonderful fabric without which civilization would be blotted from the globe. The invention of letters and the various systems of writing form the next subjects in order. The primitive language of Britain is then traced through successive modifications, produced by as many political changes, until at last the German invaders banished it to wilds and fastnesses, and introduced the sturdy mother-tongue of our own English. The history of the latter is then traced, from the days of Hengist and Horsa, through lines of Saxon kings, Scandinavian usurpers, and Norman conquerors; until, modified, enriched, and improved, by the foreign elements with which it was brought in contact, it became a new tongue, that was soon embodied by poets in undying verse, and was destined to give birth to the noblest and most valuable literature of modern times.

The formation of the English language having been thus considered, its words are treated of, both with reference to their origin and the parts they respectively perform in a sentence. The memory of the pupil being then refreshed by a condensed review of the leading topics of grammar, a chapter on false syntax, and an exhaustive view of the principles relating to the use of Capitals, the too generally neglected subject of Punctuation is next taken up. As this art, when considered at all in educational text-books, is treated only in the most cursory manner, it was regarded as a desideratum to present in this volume a complete and thorough system, which should cover exceptions as well as rules, and provide for every possible case, however rare or intricate. Such a system, it is claimed, is here set forth.

Rhetoric proper constitutes the next division of the work. Here, by means of strict conciseness, space has been found to treat with due attention and minuteness of every important subject connected with the art. The student is led to consider successively Taste, its elements, characteristics, and standard; the pleasures of the imagination; its sources,—the novel, the wonderful, the picturesque, the sublime, and the beautiful; sublimity and beauty of writing; wit, humor, and ridicule; figures their use and abuse; style, its varieties and essential properties; and criticism. A thorough preliminary course on these important subjects was thought necessary before requiring the student to write original exercises.

Thus prepared, the pupil enters on the subject of prose composition. The process of Invention, which furnishes the thoughts to be clothed in a dress of words, and which constitutes the most difficult if not the chief branch of the art, is first considered. The young composer is shown how to analyze his subject, and to amplify the thoughts successively suggested into a well-connected whole. The different parts of an exercise are taken up in turn various forms and models of introductions are presented; description, narration, argument, &c., are treated, and the peculiarities of each pointed out, as well as the styles which they respectively require. The varieties of prose composition follow; and, with carefully selected models before him, the student is required to prepare original compositions on the same plan,—such previous instruction having been given, and such aids being presented, that the process of composing, no longer a dull, routine, performance, becomes a highly intelligent and, improving mental discipline. Thus made acquainted successively with Letters, Narratives, Fiction, Essays, Argumentative Discourses, and Orations, and furnished with subjects in each department and suggestions as to their proper treatment, the student is next led to the consideration of Poetry, its feet, measures, rhymes, pauses, and different varieties.

The subject last referred to is not treated with the view of making poets. A claim to this high title must be founded on something more than a mere ability to versify or rhyme correctly. But, while it is admitted that no rules can make a poet of one whom nature has not constituted such, it is sincerely believed that a knowledge of the principles here set forth will have a tendency to produce more correct and better poetry, as it certainly will enable the reader to have a higher appreciation of its merits. Not every one who goes through a course of syntax can write good prose; yet this does not alter the fact that a thorough acquaintance with syntax is essential to the good prose writer.

If it be asked, what constitute the distinguishing features and advantages of the volume here presented to the public, the author would reply: In the first place, *clearness* and *simplicity*. Though the work was prepared for pupils of an advanced grade, and has been written in a style adapted to their comprehension, yet it was deemed of primary importance to set forth every point perspicuously and intelligibly. Secondly, it embraces in small compass a variety of important subjects, which have a common connection, and mutually illustrate each other; but which the pupil has heretofore been obliged to leave unlearned, or to search for among a number of different volumes. In the third place, it is eminently practical. Exercises have been introduced throughout the work, wherever admissible, which will ensure that what has been learned is properly understood, and impressed on the mind.

It remains for the author to acknowledge his obligation to the various sources from which he has received assistance in the preparation of the present work. His object throughout having been to produce a useful book, he did not feel at liberty to reject aught that could be turned to practical use. He has, therefore, as far as was consistent with his own plan, carefully gleaned whatever he has found of value in the works of those who have preceded him. Particular reference is here made to the text-books which for years have been regarded as standards on the subjects of which they respectively treat; to Blair's Lectures, Burke on the Sublime and Beautiful, Alison's Essay on Taste, and other books of a similar stamp, from which ideas, and occasionally language, have been freely drawn. Nor have more modern English publications been overlooked. In a word, it is believed that, while originality of plan and execution have been strictly maintained, whatever may have been elsewhere contributed to the elucidation of the subject, will not be wanting here: at the same time it has been the author's aim, in drawing from others, to improve upon their language, to adapt their style to the comprehension of all, and to avoid the errors of fact, grammar, or rhetoric, into which they may have fallen.

The author is aware that an objection to the use of a text-book on Composition exists in the minds of some, who prefer that their pupils should prepare written exercises from given subjects without aid or instruction of any kind. Of such he would respectfully ask a careful consideration of the question whether something may not be gained by pursuing a regular, consistent, plan. As, in the various departments of industry, much more can be accomplished, in a limited time and with a given amount of labor, by those who work according to a definite enlightened system, than by men of equal energy, who, with an end alone in view, without regard to a choice of means, go blindly to their task, directed by no higher principle than chance; so, it is claimed, an equal advantage is gained by those students of composition who pursue a well-digested plan, matured by experience, and elaborated by careful thought. Those who have tried both courses must decide whether this position is not as consonant with fact, as it certainly is with reason.

Repeating his thanks for the patronage extended to the little volume which preceded this, the author can only express the hope that the work now sent forth may meet with an equally kind reception.

NEW YORK, *Sept.* 11, 1854.

CONTENTS

PART I.

HISTORY OF THE ENGLISH LANGUAGE.

I. Media of Communication,
II. Origin of Spoken Language,
III. Written Language,
IV. Alphabetic Writing,
V. Formation of Language,
VI. Origin of the English Language,
VII. Origin of the English Language (*continued*),
VIII. Origin of the English Language (*continued*),
IX. Analysis of the English Language,
X. Characteristics of the English Language,
XI. Parts of Speech,
XII. Sentences,
XIII. Capital Letters,
XIV. Exercise on Capitals,

PART II.

PUNCTUATION.

XV. Principles of the Art,
XVI. The Period,
XVII. The Interrogation-point.—The Exclamation-point,
XVIII. The Colon,
XIX. The Semicolon,

CONTENTS.

LESSON		PAGE
XX.	The Comma,	104
XXI.	The Comma (*continued*),	108
XXII.	The Comma (*continued*),	113
XXIII.	The Comma (*continued*),	118
XXIV.	The Comma (*continued*),	123
XXV.	The Comma (*continued*),	128
XXVI.	The Dash,	131
XXVII.	Parentheses.—Brackets,	136
XXVIII.	Apostrophe.—Hyphen.—Quotation-points,	141
XXIX.	Exercise on the Apostrophe, the Hyphen, and Quotation-points,	147
XXX.	Other Marks used in Writing and Printing,	149
XXXI.	Grammatical Inaccuracies,	155
XXXII.	Exercise in False Syntax,	160

PART III.

RHETORIC.

XXXIII.	Province and Objects of Rhetoric,	168
XXXIV.	Taste.—Its Universality and Cultivation,	169
XXXV.	Elements and Characteristics of Taste,	173
XXXVI.	Standard of Taste,	178
XXXVII.	Pleasures of the Imagination,	183
XXXVIII.	Sources of the Pleasures of the Imagination.—The Novel.—The Wonderful.—The Picturesque,	188
XXXIX.	The Sublime,	194
XL.	The Sublime in Writing,	201
XLI.	The Sublime in Writing (*continued*),	206
XLII.	The Sublime in Writing (*continued*),	211
XLIII.	The Beautiful,	214
XLIV.	Gracefulness.—The Beautiful in the Human Countenance, in Sound, and in Writing,	221
XLV.	Wit,	225
XLVI.	Humor and Ridicule,	231
XLVII.	Figures of Orthography, Etymology, and Syntax,	235
XLVIII.	Figurative Language,	239
XLIX.	Exercises on Figurative Language,	245
L.	Figures of Rhetoric,	246
LI.	Exercise on Figures,	253
LII.	Rules for the Use of Rhetorical Figures,	254
LIII.	Exercise on Figures,	260
LIV.	Style and its Varieties,	262

CONTENTS.

LESSON
LV. Exercise on the Varieties of Style,
LVI. Essential Properties of Style.—Purity.—Propriety
LVII. Exercise on Purity and Propriety,
LVIII. Precision,
LIX. Clearness, or Perspicuity,
LX. Exercise on Clearness,
LXI. Strength,
LXII. Harmony,
LXIII. Exercise on Harmony,
LXIV. Unity,
LXV. The Forming of Style,
LXVI. Criticism,

PART IV.

PROSE COMPOSITION.

LXVII. Invention.—Analysis of Subjects,
LXVIII. Amplification,
LXIX. Revision and Correction of Compositions,
LXX. Exercise in Amplification,
LXXI. Exercise in Amplification,
LXXII. Exercise on Plain and Figurative Language,
LXXIII. Exercise in Extended Simile,
LXXIV. Exercise in Extended Simile,
LXXV. Exercise in Metaphorical Language,
LXXVI. Exercise in Allegory,
LXXVII. Exercise in Hyperbole,
LXXVIII. Exercises in Vision and Apostrophe,
LXXIX. Exercise in Personification,
LXXX. Exercises in Climax and Antithesis,
LXXXI. Parallels,
LXXXII. Exercise in Parallels,
LXXXIII. Exercise in Parallels,
LXXXIV. Exercise in Defining Synonymes,
LXXXV. Exercise in Defining Synonymes,
LXXXVI. Exercise in Paraphrasing,
LXXXVII. Exercise in Paraphrasing,
LXXXVIII. Exercise in Abridging,
LXXXIX. Exercise in Abridging,
XC. Exercise in Abridging,
XCI. Exercise in Criticism,

CONTENTS.

LESSON
XCII. Exercise in Criticism,
XCIII. Description of Material Objects,
XCIV. Description of Natural Scenery, and Persons,
XCV. Narration.—Argument.—Exposition.—Speculation,
XCVI. Letters,
XCVII. Letters (*continued*),
XCVIII. Narratives,
XCIX. Exercise in Biography,
C. Fiction,
CI. Essays,
CII. Exercises in Essay-Writing,
CIII. Theses, or Argumentative Discourses,
CIV. Orations.—Sermon-Writing,

PART V.
POETICAL COMPOSITION.

CV. Verse.—Quantity.—Feet.—Metres,
CVI. Stanzas.—Sonnets.—Heroic Verse.—Blank Verse,
CVII. Rhymes.—Pauses,
CVIII. Varieties of Poetry,

Specimen Proof-Sheet,
Explanation of Marks used on the Specimen Proof-Sheet,
List of Subjects,
Table of Abbreviations,
Index,

ADVANCED COURSE

OF

COMPOSITION AND RHETORIC.

PART I.

HISTORY OF THE ENGLISH LANGUAGE.

LESSON I.

MEDIA OF COMMUNICATION.

§ 1. MAN is distinguished from the brute creation by the possession of reason. Brutes are governed by instinct; man, by his reasoning faculties. The senses of both are the same, and on these senses material objects produce similar impressions. But from these impressions brutes cannot reason any further than their natural instincts enable them, and their necessities require. Man, on the other hand, being possessed of intellectual faculties, is capable of drawing inferences; and thus from the impressions made on his senses by a single external object, receives many different ideas, which, producing others in their turn, may be multiplied to infinity.

---

§ 1. How is man distinguished from the brute creation? By what are brutes governed? By what, man? How do the senses of men and brutes, and the impressions produced upon them, differ? How, then, do men receive more ideas from these impressions than brutes?

§ 2. Men, being endowed with social dispositions, naturally desire to interchange the ideas received in the manner above described. Brutes, also, particularly those of gregarious habits, are at times actuated by a similar impulse to make known their feelings to each other. Now in both these cases some medium of communication is necessary; and we find that the ingenuity of man has devised four means more or less adapted to the purpose, the first two of which the instinct of the lower orders of creation has led them also to employ. These are as follows:—

I. *Gestures.* By these are meant the movements of the body or its members. In the case of brutes, they are often so expressive as to leave no doubt as to the predominant emotion. Thus, in the billing of doves we see love exemplified; in the lion lashing his sides with his tail, and the cat raising her back at the sight of an enemy, we have unmistakable evidences of anger; and in the horse depressing his ears backwards, of fear. Man, having generally other and better means of communication, seldom uses gestures alone, though he often employs them to illustrate and enforce what he says. When other means, however, are wanting, he is able with their aid alone to express his sentiments; as in the case of the sick who have lost the power of speech, or of one attempting to make himself understood by those with whose language he is unacquainted. It is surprising, indeed, to see how perfectly persons practised in the use of gestures can communicate even complicated trains of thought and long series of facts. Good pantomimists will make the plot of a theatrical piece just as intelligible to an audience as if it were developed by dialogue.

---

§ 2. What desire results from man's social disposition? Is this desire confined to the human race? How many means of communication has man devised? How many and which are employed by brutes also?

What is the first medium of communication? What is meant by gestures? Give instances of the use of gestures by brutes, and mention the emotions they indicate. For what purpose does man generally use gestures? Do they ever serve alone to express his sentiments? Give instances. What may be communicated by gestures? Give an instance. What is said of the action of the Greeks and Romans? How far was it carried on the stage? What point was debated by Cicero and Roscius

This fact was known and appreciated by the ancient Greeks and Romans, whose action was much more vehement than we are accustomed to see at the present day. On the stage this was carried so far that two actors were at times brought on to play the same part; the office of one being to pronounce the words, and that of the other to accompany them with appropriate gestures, a single performer being unable to attend to both. Cicero informs us that it was a matter of dispute between the actor Roscius and himself whether the former could express a sentiment in a greater variety of ways by significant gestures, or the latter by the use of different phrases. He also elsewhere tells us that this same Roscius had gained great love from every one by the mere movements of his person.* During the reign of Augustus both tragedies and comedies were acted by pantomime alone. It was perfectly understood by the people, who wept, and laughed, and were excited in every way as much as if words had been employed. It seems, indeed, to have worked upon their sympathies more powerfully than words; for it became necessary, at a subsequent period, to enact a law restraining members of the senate from studying the art of pantomime, a practice to which it seems they had resorted in order to give more effect to their speeches before that body.

When, however, the Roman Empire yielded to the arms of the Northern barbarians, and, as a consequence, great numbers of the latter spread over it in every direction, their cold and phlegmatic manners wrought a material change as re-

---

* "Ergo ille corporis motu tantum amorem sibi conciliârat a nobis omnibus."—Pro Archia Poeta, VIII.

What does Cicero tell us with respect to this actor? In the reign of Augustus, how were both tragedies and comedies represented? How did some of the senators seek to give effect to their speeches? What law was passed on the subject? What effect did the conquest of the Roman Empire by Northern barbarians have on the gestures and tones of the people? How do the tones of the people of Southern Europe now compare with those of the North? Of what nations, in particular, is this true?

gards the gestures, no less than the tones and accents, of the people. The mode of expression gradually grew more subdued, and the accompanying action less violent, in proportion as the new influences prevailed. Conversation became more languid; and public speaking was no longer indebted for its effect to the art of the pantomimist. So great was the change in these respects that the allusions of classical authors to the oratory of their day were hardly intelligible. Notwithstanding these modifications, however, the people of Southern Europe, being warmer and more passionate by nature, are, at the present day, much more animated in their tones and more addicted to gesticulation than the inhabitants of the North. This is particularly true of the French and Italians.

II. *Inarticulate Sounds*, or cries used by man, particularly during infancy, and by all other animals, to express strong and sudden emotions, such as fear, love, sorrow, and the like. In the earlier periods of man's history, before a perfect system of language was developed, it is probable that these natural interjections were used more frequently than at present. Grammarians consider them the earliest elements of speech. Among these inarticulate sounds may be classed sighing, groaning, laughing, and screaming, each of which is a key to the prevailing sentiment of the mind.

III. *Spoken Language*, or an assemblage of articulate sounds, which are individually the type of certain ideas, and by a combination of which thoughts may be expressed. This means of communication, as well as that which follows, is employed by man alone.

IV. *Written Language.* By this is meant a combination of arbitrary characters, which convey to the mind the ideas they represent through the medium of the eye.

What is the second medium of communication? What is meant by Inarticulate Sounds? When were they most frequently used? How do grammarians regard them? What may be classed among these Inarticulate Sounds?
What is the third medium of communication? What is Spoken Language? By whom is it employed?

It will be seen that, as the ideas generated by man's reflective faculties infinitely outnumber the emotions of brutes, so his means of communication are at once more numerous and precise.

Gestures and inarticulate sounds our subject does not lead us to consider any further; of language, spoken and written, we shall now proceed to treat.

LESSON II.

ORIGIN OF SPOKEN LANGUAGE.

§ 3. It is a question that has been much and ably discussed, whether spoken language is a divine or human institution: whether God gave it to man, as He gave the mental faculties; or man invented it for himself, stimulated by the desire of communicating with his kind.

Those who think language is a human institution believe, with the ancient philosophers and poets, that men were originally "a dumb and low herd"; * that they were in all things rude and savage, totally ignorant of the arts, unable to communicate with each other except in the imperfect manner of beasts, and sensible of nothing save hunger, pain, and similar emotions. Cicero, alluding to the human race in primeval ages, says: "There was a time when men wandered every where through the fields after the manner of beasts, and supported life by eating the food of beasts." Diodorus, Lucretius,

---

* "Mutum et turpe pecus."

What is the fourth medium of communication? What is meant by Written Language?

How do man's ideas and means of communication compare with those of brutes?

§ 3. What question has been much discussed? What did the ancient philosophers and poets regard as the original state of men? What does Cicero say of the human race in primeval times? What ancient writers agree with him in this opinion? What

Horace, Pliny, Juvenal, and other ancient writers, agree with Cicero in this opinion, and hold that it was only after a long and gradual improvement that men came to their present enlightened state.

Lord Monboddo, who, in his work on "The Origin and Progress of Language," labors to prove that man is but a higher species of monkey, thinks that originally the human race had only a few monosyllables, such as HA, HE, HI, HO, by which, like beasts, they expressed certain emotions.

Dr. Murray gives it as his opinion that all language originated in nine monosyllables, AG, BAG, DWAG, GWAG, LAG, MAG, NAG, RAG, SWAG. "Each of these," says Dr. M., "is a verb and indicates a species of action. Power, motion, force, ideas united in every untutored mind, are implied in them all. They were uttered at first, and probably for several generations, in an insulated manner. The circumstances of the action were communicated by gestures and the variable tones of the voice; but the actions themselves were expressed by their suitable monosyllables."

Rousseau represents men as originally without language, as unsocial by nature, and totally ignorant of the ties of society. He does not, however, seek to explain how language arose, being disheartened at the outset by the difficulty of deciding whether language was more necessary for the institution of society, or society for the invention of language. Maupertius, however, overcomes this difficulty by holding that "language was formed by a session of learned societies assembled for that purpose.

§ 4. But we must leave these absurd theories. Language is, beyond doubt, a divine institution, invented by the Deity and by Him made known to the human race. If language was

---

Is the title of Lord Monboddo's work? What does the author try to prove in it? How does he think that the human race originally expressed their emotions? In what does Dr. Murray think that all language originated? What part of speech, according to him, was each of these monosyllables? What ideas does he think were implied in them? How does Rousseau represent the original race of men? What difficulty disheartened him at the outset of his enquiries? What does Maupertius hold?

devised by man, the invention could not have been at once matured, but must have been the result of the necessities and experience of successive generations. This, however, does not accord with the facts of history; for, however far we go back, we cannot arrive at any period when even the most unenlightened portions of mankind did not possess a system of language. Scripture informs us that this means of communication was employed by the first man and woman, as well as their immediate descendants; and we are hence forced to the conclusion that it was the result of a direct revelation from on high.

Nevertheless, while the elements were thus imparted by God, it is natural to suppose that much was left for man to perfect; and that, just as a mind was given to him which he is required to cultivate and fit for the performance of its duties by a long course of training, so the mere elements were imparted, out of which he had to form by successive improvements a perfect means of communication. "Three things," says Scaliger, " have contributed to enable man to perfect language,—necessity, practice, and the desire to please. Necessity produced a collection of words very imperfectly connected; practice, in multiplying them, gave them more expression; while it is to the desire of pleasing that we owe those agreeable turns, those happy collocations of words, which impart to phrases both elegance and grace."

We are confirmed in this supposition by the fact that the history of many languages shows a gradual progress from imperfect beginnings to a finished state, and that there is hardly any cultivated tongue, which, if traced back to its earlier ages, will not be found either defective in some of its parts or wanting in those characteristics which are a source of beauty and

---

§ 4. Leaving these theories, by whom must we conclude that language was invented? If it was devised by man, what would we find on looking back at the history of early times? Was this the case? What does Scripture inform us with regard to the first man and woman and their immediate descendants? What follows from this? Was any thing left for man to perfect? According to Scaliger, by what was man enabled to perfect language? What did necessity produce? What did practice impart to them? What do we owe to the desire of pleasing?

strength. The language of a nation, traced through the successive eras of its existence, will be found to have undergone a series of improvements in all respects analogous to the advances which have been made in the institutions and social condition of the people who speak it. In the first great antediluvian language similar changes must have occurred.

It may be added that the divine origin of language is maintained by a number of our best writers. Locke, in his "Essay on the Human Understanding," Book III, chap. 1, sec. 1, says: "God, having designed man for a sociable creature, made him not only with an inclination and under a necessity to have fellowship with those of his own kind; but furnished him, also, with language, which was to be the great instrument and common tie of society."

LESSON III.

WRITTEN LANGUAGE.

§ 5. IDEAS may be communicated by written, as well as spoken, language. The latter represents ideas by articulate sounds; the former employs certain arbitrary characters to represent these articulate sounds, and thus through a double medium conveys the ideas themselves. It is written language alone that gives permanence to thoughts.

§ 6. Written language was devised by man. The exact period of its origin is unknown; but it is supposed not to have been invented until several centuries after men were in

---

What fact confirms us in the belief that in language much was left for man to perfect? What is Locke's view of the origin of language?

§ 5. What else besides spoken language enables us to communicate ideas? How does spoken language represent ideas? How, written language? Which gives permanence to thoughts?

§ 6. By whom was written language devised? When is it supposed to have been

possession of a complete system of spoken language. The systems first employed were necessarily rude and imperfect; but, as men increased in experience and knowledge, successive improvements were made, until at last the present simple method was devised. Four systems have been employed in different ages and countries; the Ideographic, the Verbal, the Syllabic, and the Alphabetic.

§ 7. *Ideographic System.*—The earliest method of conveying thoughts by means of written characters is called Ideographic. It represented material objects and facts by means of pictures; and what was not material or visible, but was merely conceived in the mind, and could not, therefore, be thus depicted, by symbols. Thus the idea of a battle was conveyed by a pictorial representation of two men engaged in fighting; while the abstract idea of eternity was denoted by a circle, which, being without beginning or end, was an appropriate emblem. It represented things themselves, and not their names.

The hieroglyphics* of Egypt constituted one kind of Ideographic writing. The Mexicans, also, used it at the time of Cortes' invasion; their king was informed of the arrival of the Spaniards and their ships, by pieces of white linen on which were painted objects resembling vessels, and men in Spanish garb. Ideographic writing is also said to have been employed by some of the North American Indians.

§ 8. *Verbal System.*—The Verbal system is second in point of antiquity. It appropriated a peculiar character to each

---

* This word signifies "sacred carvings," being derived from the Greek words ἱερος, *sacred*, and γλύφω, *to carve*.

Invented? What was its character at first? What change took place as men increased in knowledge? How many systems have prevailed?

§ 7. What is the earliest system called? How did it represent material objects? How, what was not material or visible? Give an example. Did it represent the objects themselves, or their names? To what system do the hieroglyphics of Egypt belong? What other people used this system? How was the Mexican king informed of the Spaniards' arrival? By what other race has Ideographic writing been employed?

§ 8. What is the second system called? How did it represent material objects and

object and idea, without reference to the word by which such object or idea was represented. This was an improvement on the Ideographic system, but was objectionable on account of the great number of characters required. Chinese, at the present day, is written in a measure according to this system. Old authorities inform us that it employs no less than 80,000 characters; later researches, however, prove the number to be considerably smaller. As each character represents an object or abstract idea, and not merely a sound, it follows that any thing written according to this system is understood by all that are acquainted with the characters, although their own spoken languages may be totally different; just as the value of figures in their various combinations is universally known to the nations of Europe, notwithstanding the difference in their respective tongues. The written language of the Chinese Empire, accordingly, is read and understood by the people of Japan, Corea, Loo-choo, and Cochin China, as well as by various other tribes who are unable to hold the slightest oral intercourse with each other.

It is proper to add that this is denied by some, who contend that Chinese is written mainly according to the Syllabic system, a description of which follows. If any Japanese or Coreans are found to understand written Chinese, it is, according to these authorities, from their having studied it, or else on account of its resemblance to their own written systems. Our present greatly increased facilities for obtaining information respecting the people of the Celestial Empire and their peculiarities, will soon dissipate all uncertainty on this subject; and we shall probably find that each opinion has some foundation in truth. It is likely either that the characters are partly Verbal and partly Syllabic, or else that there are two distinct systems, originally perhaps used by different classes, but now employed indiscriminately at the option of the writer.

---

abstract ideas? What rendered it objectionable? In what language is it still employed? How many characters are required in this language? Need one understand the spoken language, in order to understand a written language in which the Verbal system is employed? Give an example. In illustration of this, what is mentioned with regard to the written language of the Chinese Empire? What account do other authorities give of written Chinese? How do they explain the fact that some Japanese and Coreans are found to understand it? What is probable with regard to these different opinions?

§ 9. *Syllabic System.*—By the two systems above described, things themselves were represented without reference to the sounds by which they are denoted. But the frequent recurrence of the same syllables in the names of things soon led men to see the advantages that would be gained by representing the sound instead of the thing signified; and hence originated a third method, commonly called the Syllabic system. In this, certain characters were employed to represent, not objects, but syllabic sounds, by a combination of which the names of things were denoted. Thus the word *agriculture* would be expressed by four characters only, one representing each syllable. Though this was a great improvement on the Verbal System, it was also objectionable on account of the number of characters required. It is thought at one time to have been used by many Asiatic nations; and is still the basis, though in a somewhat modified form, of the written language of the Ethiopians and that of the Siamese.

§ 10. *Alphabetic System.*—The defects incident to the systems described above finally taught man the necessity of inventing some new method of conveying his thoughts; and hence resulted the introduction and ultimate perfection of Alphabetic writing, which is used in almost all languages at the present day. This may be regarded as the greatest of human inventions, and has contributed more than any thing else to the progress of civilization. According to this system, the simple sounds of the human voice are represented by appropriate marks or letters, by combining which syllables and words are formed; and that with such precision and completeness that not only can all material objects be denoted and described,

---

§ 9. How were ideas represented by the two systems already described? What system was next invented? According to the Syllabic system, what did each character represent? How were words denoted? How many characters would this system require to express the word *agriculture?* How did the Syllabic compare with the Verbal system? What rendered the Syllabic system objectionable? By what nations was it at one time employed? In what written languages is it still used?

§ 10. By the defects of these systems, what was man finally taught? What system was next invented? How may it be regarded? What are represented by the charac-

but also abstract ideas, the emotions of the mind, and every variety of thought.

LESSON IV.

ALPHABETIC WRITING.

§ 11. *Derivation.*—The word *alphabet* is derived from ἄλφα, βῆτα, the first two Greek characters, and signifies the letters of a written language disposed in their regular order.

§ 12. *Origin.*—The inventors of alphabetic writing are unknown. According to the Jewish Rabbis, it is of divine origin. "God," says one of their number, "created letters on the evening of the first Sabbath." Adam Clarke also inclines to this opinion, although he places the revelation at a later date, maintaining that God taught Moses the use of letters by writing the Ten Commandments with His own finger on the tables of stone. Eusebius, Clemens of Alexandria, Cornelius Agrippa, and others, attribute this noble invention to Moses himself; Philo, to Abraham; Irenæus and others, to Enoch, who is by some thought to have been the author of a work still extant, to which there is an apparent allusion in the 14th and the 15th verse of St. Jude's Epistle. Bibliander considers Adam entitled to the honor of the invention; and the Sabians actually produce a book which they pretend was written by this patriarch. If, however, letters were known at this early period, it can hardly be explained why men, in spite of the vastly superior facilities they afford, should have gone back to the ideographic or the syllabic system.

---

ters employed in the Alphabetic system? By combining these characters, what are formed?

§ 11. From what is the word *alphabet* derived? What does it signify?

§ 12. What is said of the inventors of alphabetic writing? To whom do the Jewish Rabbis attribute its invention? What is Adam Clarke's opinion? To whom do Eusebius, Clemens, and Cornelius Agrippa attribute it? To whom, Philo? To whom, Irenæus? What reason is there for supposing Enoch to have been acquainted with

Among the Greeks and Romans, the invention of letters was generally attributed to the Phœnicians.* For the Greeks this was natural, as they received the greater part of their alphabet directly from Cadmus, a native of Phœnicia, and would therefore be likely to think that the honor of the invention belonged to that country. Yet it is clear that some of the most learned of the Greeks regarded Cadmus in his true light; not as the inventor, but merely as the introducer, of letters. Plato expressly says that Thaut, the Egyptian, was the first to divide letters into vowels and consonants, mutes and liquids. An individual of this same name, Thaut or Taaut, is also mentioned by Sanchoniathon, the historian, as the inventor of letters, but is claimed by him as a Phœnician, living in the 12th or the 13th generation after the Deluge. To reconcile these conflicting accounts, Jackson, in his "Chronological Antiquities," holds that letters were invented by Taaut or Thoth, the Phœnician, a son of Misraim, about five centuries after the deluge, but were introduced into Egypt four hundred years afterwards by a second Taaut; whom he supposes to have been identical with the celebrated Hermes Trismegistus of the Greeks, the inventor, according to Diodorus, of grammar, music, letters, and writing. Whether this supposition is correct or not, we may fairly conclude that, whichever of these nations first employed letters, they were not long in becoming

---

* "Ipsa gens Phœnicum in gloria magna est literarum inventionis." 'The race of Phœnicians themselves enjoy the great glory of the invention of letters.'—PLINY, Book v., chap. 12.

"Phœnices primi (famæ si credimus) ausi
Mansuram rudibus vocem signare figuris."—LUCAN.

---

this system? By whom does Bibliander think it was invented? What evidence of this is furnished by the Sabians? What objection is there to the supposition that letters were known thus early?

To whom did the Greeks and Romans attribute the invention of letters? What led the Greeks to this opinion? How did some of the most learned Greeks regard Cadmus? Whom does Plato mention in connection with the classification of letters? Who else alludes to this Thaut? What does Sanchoniathon say of him? How does Jackson explain this inconsistency? With what Greek personage does he suppose this second

known to the other; as the commercial relations of the Egyptians and Phœnicians were intimate and likely to make their respective inventions common property.

According to some late writers who are versed in Oriental literature, the claims of the Indians to the honor of having devised letters are not without some weight. The Sanscrit, which is the most refined of the Indian languages, is supposed to have been one of the most ancient now existing, and is the parent of almost every dialect of Southern Asia. The Hindoos assert that they were acquainted with letters before any other nation on the globe; and that, in their ancient books, sages from Egypt and other countries are represented as coming to India, to inform themselves respecting alphabetic writing and other inventions for which the Hindoos were at that early period distinguished. As, however, none of these ancient books have yet made their appearance in Europe, and as national vanity has led the Orientals generally to exaggerate their ancient standing in literature, art, and science, we can hardly weigh these unsupported statements against the positive testimony presented from other quarters.

Modern scholars seem to be divided in opinion as to whether this great invention is due to the Phœnicians or the Hebrews. Mr. Astle, whose essay on " The Origin and Progress of Writing" displays great research, and is justly regarded as high authority, on the evidence of the ancients, pronounces in favor of the Phœnicians. It must be remembered, however, that while the Greeks were well acquainted with the latter nation on account of their intimate commercial relations, to the Hebrews they were almost entire strangers; and

---

That to have been identical? What is said of the relations that subsisted between the Egyptians and the Phœnicians?

What other people claim to have invented letters? What is said of the Sanscrit language? What do the Hindoos assert with regard to their ancient books? Have we any reason to believe their statements?

What are the views of modern scholars on this point? In whose favor does Mr. Astle decide? What reason is there for supposing that the Greeks may have been mistaken in attributing the invention of letters to the Phœnicians? From what alphabet

hence, though their evidence may be reliable as regards the claims of the Phœnician alphabet to an antiquity greater than either the Egyptian or the Syrian can boast, they must still have been unqualified to pronounce between it and the Hebrew. From the latter, indeed, the Phœnician alphabet is now generally thought to have been derived. It is at least well known that writing was practised among the Jews long before we have any evidence of its having been in use among the Phœnicians. The Pentateuch itself is a living proof that alphabetic writing was known to Moses, while the frequent allusions to that art which it contains shows that this knowledge was not confined to the legislator alone.* The injunction contained in the 9th verse of the 6th chapter of Deuteronomy, that the people should write the words of the law on the posts of their houses and on their gates, proves such a general acquaintance with the art as to justify the inference that it was then no recent invention, but had been known and used for years. The suggestion urged by some that the writing here alluded to, as well as that in which the five books of Moses were originally composed, may have been according to the hieroglyphic or syllabic system, is inadmissible; for we have not the slightest trace of the existence of these sacred books in any other form than that which they now bear.

Nor are we by any means driven to the inference which some have drawn from the passage, that the Deity himself communicated to Moses, and through him to the human race, a knowledge of the alphabetic system. Had so important a revelation been made, we have every reason to suppose that

---

* See Exodus, xxiv., 12; xxxii., 15, 16; xvii., 14 · xxxiv., 1, 27: Numbers, xxxiii., 2: Deuteronomy, xxvii., 8.

Is the Phœnician supposed to have been derived? How early was alphabetic writing known among the Jews? What leads us to suppose that the people generally were acquainted with the art? What precludes us from supposing that the writing here alluded to was according to some earlier system? What inference has been drawn from these passages? What renders it unlikely that this was the case?

it would have been recorded in distinct terms by the Jewish legislator.

§ 13. *The Greek Alphabet and its Derivatives.*—Whatever alphabet may have been the most ancient, one fact is clearly established; that Cadmus introduced sixteen letters from Phœnicia into Greece, to which Palamedes subsequently added four, and Simonides, at a still later period, four more.

The Phœnician language was written from right to left. The Greek at first followed it in this respect; but was in course of time written from right to left, and from left to right, alternately, as land is ploughed. The Laws of Solon were engraved in this style, about 600 B. C., as also were many inscriptions still to be seen on ancient monuments. Soon after this period, however, the present manner of writing, from left to right, came into general use. It had been introduced many years before by Pronapides, who, according to some, was a teacher of Homer's.

From the Greek alphabet, the Etruscan, Oscan, Latin, Coptic, and others, were formed. The Latin alphabet contained twenty-five letters. From it, ours is derived. The number and form of the Latin letters are retained in English without any further change than the addition of *W.*

§ 14. *Comparison of Different Alphabets.*—As letters are merely arbitrary marks used to denote the elemental sounds of which spoken language is composed, the number of letters in the alphabet of any people ought to correspond exactly with the number of such sounds which they employ. Yet in no language do we find this to be the case. In some the alphabetic characters are the more numerous in consequence both of the admission of more than one letter to express the same sound, and of the introduction of characters to denote com-

---

§ 13. Who introduced letters into Greece, and how many were there? How many were subsequently added, and by whom?

How was the Phœnician language written? What other language was written similarly to it? What change was afterwards made as regards the Greek language? What laws were written in this style? By whom was the present method of writing introduced? What alphabets were derived from the Greek? How many letters did the Latin alphabet contain? What alphabet was derived from it? How do the two correspond?

§ 14. What are letters? With what ought the number of letters in the alphabet of any people to correspond? Do we find such a correspondence? What is the reason of this inconsistency? How do the different alphabets compare in the number of their

pound sounds which could otherwise be perfectly represented by combinations. In other languages some sounds are entirely unrepresented, and consequently in these there is a deficiency of alphabetic characters. Hence, though about the same number of elemental sounds are in use among different nations, there will be found no little difference in the number of letters composing their various alphabets.

Thus, the English alphabet contains 26 letters; the French, 23; the Italian, 20; the Spanish, 27; the Russian, 41; the Hebrew, Samaritan, Syrian, and Chaldean, each 22; the Arabic, 28; the Persian and Egyptian, each 32; the Turkish, 33; the Georgian, 36; the Armenian, 38; the Sanscrit, 50; the Abyssinian, 202; and the Indian, or Brahmanic, 240

LESSON V.

FORMATION OF LANGUAGE.

§ 15. THERE is every reason, as we have seen, to believe that, while in the invention of language man was assisted by the Deity, it was still only after many years of gradual development and improvement that it arrived at its present perfection. As it is impossible for us to ascertain how far divine assistance was vouchsafed, we shall consider the steps of formation as it is most likely they would be taken by man, independently of a direct revelation, under the stimulus of necessity and the desire of pleasing.

The first words were, no doubt, Interjections; for it would be natural for men, however savage or ignorant of the use of words, to employ exclamations for the purpose of expressing

---

sounds, and how in the number of their letters? How many letters does the English alphabet contain? The French? Italian? Spanish? Russian? Hebrew, Samaritan, Syriac, and Chaldean? Arabic? Persian and Egyptian? Turkish? Georgian? Armenian? Sanscrit? Abyssinian? Indian, or Brahmanic?

§ 15. Is it probable that a complete system of language was given to man? How has it been brought to its present perfection? What words, is it supposed, were first

their sudden emotions. The words that next came into use did not probably denote the name of any particular object; but were such as expressed a whole sentence, indicative of desires or fears, or intended to convey some important news or information; as, *the enemy is coming, the victory is ours.*

Individual objects next engaged attention. The savage lived, we will say, in the midst of a forest. Inasmuch as he derived his means of subsistence partly from certain trees which it contained, he was soon compelled, in his intercourse with others, to allude to them, and represent them by some name, or, as grammarians would say, Noun. This appellation he at first probably applied to all similar objects. It was not till experience taught him the difference between oaks, cypresses, cedars, &c., and their respective peculiarities, that he gave them specific names. As it often became necessary to allude to more than one, it was not long before a distinct form was adopted to denote the plural number.

Before all the visible objects of creation had been thus arranged into classes and distinguished by general appellations, and before experience and observation had assigned particular names to the various species, it must have been necessary for men occasionally to allude to a specific object in contradistinction to the rest of its class. To identify it, therefore, intelligibly to another, they would have to distinguish it by stating either its distinctive qualities or the relations in which it stood to other objects. Thus, if they desired to allude to a tree of particular size, or one standing by a spring, instead of characterizing it as the fir or the elm, they would naturally say, *the large tree, the tree by the spring.* In this way were formed Adjectives, which generally express quality, and Prepositions, which indicate the relations subsisting between Nouns (often called substantives) and other words.

---

employed? Explain the reason. What words next came into use? Give an example Describe the way in which Nouns were formed. When were specific names coined? What distinct form was afterwards adopted, and why? Describe the necessity which called for the Adjective. Give an example. What other class of words had the same

FORMATION OF LANGUAGE.

Though several important steps had by this time been taken towards the formation of a complete system of language, yet the means which it afforded of distinguishing objects were still imperfect; for, when any substantive was used in discourse, as tree, river, horse, how was it to be known which of the many individuals embraced in the general class, which tree, river, or horse, was meant? When the thing alluded to was within the range of sight, it could without difficulty be pointed out by a movement of the hand; but, when this was not the case, it became necessary to invent words by which the particular object intended could be specified. Hence arose the Adjective pronouns *this* and *that*, and the Article *the*.

Verbs must necessarily have been coeval with the first attempts towards the formation of language, as no affirmation can be expressed without the assistance of this part of speech. We seldom speak except to express our opinion that something is or is not, that some act does or does not take place; and the word which affirms the fact or state is always a Verb.

Thus, then, we have seen Interjections, Nouns, Adjectives Prepositions, Articles, Adjective Pronouns, and Verbs, successively called for by the wants of men, and consequently invented as component parts of language. Personal Pronouns were probably the creation of a later age. A young child, it has been observed, almost invariably repeats the noun instead of using the substitute. Speaking of himself, a child would be likely to say, "Give Johnny Johnny's whistle", and not "Give *me my* whistle." So great, indeed, seems to be the disinclination of youthful minds to multiply terms that it is often found quite difficult to teach them the use of the pro-

---

origin? Give an example. Give an account of the origin of the Adjective Pronouns *this* and *that*. What Article originated in the same way? What class of words is required for the expression of affirmations? When did they come into use?

Of what class of words have we thus far traced the origin? What part of speech was the creation of a later age? Are children generally inclined to use the personal

noun. Such was the case, in all probability, with man in th. infancy of his being; and it is not likely that he added this new species of words to his primitive and necessary stock, until sufficient advance had been made in the formative process to show their great advantage as regards brevity of expression and pleasantness of sound.

Among the early races of men, it seems probable that there was much less said than at the present day. Their sentences were at once fewer, shorter, and simpler, than ours As successive advances, however, were made, and it was found that mutual intercourse was a source of pleasure, men did not confine themselves simply to what it was necessary to communicate, but imparted freely to each other even such thoughts as had no practical bearing. The original brief mode of expression was gradually laid aside; longer sentences were used; and a new class of words was required to connect clauses so closely related in construction and sense as not to admit of separation into distinct periods. This was the origin of Conjunctions; and the same cause, when man's taste was still further improved and he began to think of beautifying language while he extended its power of expression, led to the invention of the Relative Pronoun.

To tell how, when, and where the action expressed by the verb was performed, and also to indicate the degree in which any object possessed a certain quality, as for instance how tall a tree was, man's inventive faculties were not long in perceiving that a new species of words was required and in forming them accordingly. Adverbs were thus introduced; and with them the elements of language, or Parts of Speech, as they are termed, were complete. Man now had the means of expressing fully and intelligibly all that came into his mind;

---

pronoun? What do they employ in its place? What is gained by the use of the Personal Pronoun? What was the character of the sentences used by the early races of men? What change took place in the course of time? What kind of sentences came into use? What new class of words was thus required? What parts of speech originated in this way? Describe the origin of Adverbs. What are the elements of lan-

and his future efforts were to be directed, not to the creation of new elements, but to improving and modifying those already devised, to harmonizing the whole and uniting them in a consistent system. Up to this point necessity had operated; the improvements subsequently made must be attributed to the desire of pleasing.

§ 16. In thus tracing the origin of the Parts of Speech, we have based our theory and deductions on the supposition that man's starting-point was a state of utter ignorance. It is believed by many that this ignorance was entailed on the human race at the same time with death, as a punishment for the first disobedience; that, immediately on their expulsion from Eden, our first parents lost that enlightenment with which they had been originally endowed by the Deity. Others think that this sinking to savagism was gradual, and was the result of the moral degradation which, as the Bible informs us, characterized most of the descendants of Adam at the time of the Deluge. In either of these cases, or if there was no direct revelation from on high, the successive steps in the formation of language were probably similar to those described above, for such would be their natural order. If God did assist men directly, it is likely that He merely put them in possession of such elements as barely enabled them to communicate with each other what was absolutely essential, and that much was left for human ingenuity to devise; in which case, also, we may conclude that the steps of formation were successively taken in the order described above.

In what condition men were as regards their language at the time of the Deluge, cannot be ascertained. Different communities probably spoke different dialects, of greater or less comprehensiveness and power of expression, according to the various circumstances of their position and history.

---

guage, or classes of words, called? After the formation of the parts of speech, to what were man's efforts directed?

§ 16. On what supposition is this theory of the origin of words based? According to some, when was this ignorance entailed on man? What is the opinion of others on this subject? In either case, what seems probable with respect to the steps of formation? To what extent is it likely that the Deity assisted man? What is said regarding the different dialects spoken at the time of the Deluge?

LESSON VI.

ORIGIN OF THE ENGLISH LANGUAGE.

§ 17. *Britain before the Roman Conquest.*—The earliest authentic account that we have of the inhabitants of Britain is from Julius Cæsar, by whom the southern part of the island was conquered in the year 54 B. C. The Roman general informs us that he found the people of Kent far more civilized than the rest, and adds that there was no great difference between their customs and those of Gaul.* This is not to be wondered at, as the southern part of the island was unquestionably peopled directly from Gaul; that is, from the northern districts of what is now called France, which lay directly opposite and were separated from it by a strait so narrow as to prove no obstacle to emigration. The historian Tacitus, who, in his Life of Agricola, takes occasion to describe the ancient British, confirms this account. He remarks that many points in the personal appearance of the Silures, or inhabitants of South Wales, together with their proximity to the Spanish coast, afford sufficient foundation for the belief that they were a branch of the Iberi, or first settlers of Spain; while there was little question that the parts opposite to Gaul had been seized on by the people of that country, their respective languages, religious rites, and general characteristics, bearing a marked resemblance to each other.†

---

* Ex his omnibus longe sunt humanissimi qui Cantium incolunt: quæ regio est maritima omnis; neque multum a Gallica differunt consuetudine.—CÆSAR, *de Bello Gallico*, Lib. V., c. 14.

† In universum tamen æstimanti, Gallos vicinum solum occupasse credibile est. Eorum sacra reprehendas, superstitionum persuasione: sermo haud multum diversus: in deposcendis periculis eadem audacia,

---

§ 17. Who furnishes us with the earliest authentic account of the people of Britain? What part of the island did Cæsar conquer, and when? Which of the inhabitants did he find most civilized? Whom did they resemble in their manners and customs? How is this accounted for? Who confirms Cæsar's account? Where did the Silures live? From whom, according to Tacitus, did they derive their origin? By whom does he think that the parts opposite Gaul were peopled? What great race had

The great Celtic race was at this early period scattered over the whole of Southwestern Europe; and no doubt successive bodies had found their way to Britain, either directly, or after a temporary residence on the opposite coasts of the continent. At the time of Cæsar's invasion, therefore, in Britain, as well as in Gaul and Spain, dialects of the great Celtic tongue were spoken; but it was not to this original vernacular that our English of the present day owes its origin. We allude to it here because it is important that the student should be acquainted with its history and be able to trace its connection with our language, in the formation of which it has had its share, in a measure directly, but more particularly through the medium of its derivatives, the Latin and Norman French.

Ireland appears to have been originally peopled by colonies from Carthage, and through this channel to have received its language from the Phœnicians, to whom also the Celts seem to have been indebted for theirs. Their own historians declare this to have been the case; and the Irish language was originally called Bearni Feni, or the Phœnician tongue. No inscription, however, is to be found in Ireland in Phœnician characters; and it is therefore probable that the colonies which emigrated thither from Carthage started after the First Punic War. for it was at this period that the Carthaginians gave up their own alphabet for that of the Romans. Subsequently to this settlement, there was probably a considerable influx of Iberi from Spain; who carried with them their Celtic dialect, and, grafting it on the Phœnician before in use, produced a tongue which, though not identical with that of ancient Britain, bore a close resemblance to it.

---

et, ubi advenere, in detractandis eadem formido.—TACITUS, *Julii Agricolæ Vita*, XL.

---

settled in Southwestern Europe? What language prevailed both there and in Britain, at the time of Cæsar's invasion? Is Celtic the groundwork of English? What share has it had in the formation of our language?
Whence does Ireland seem to have been peopled? From whom did it receive its language? What was the Irish language originally called? At what period is it probable that the Carthaginian colonies emigrated to Ireland? What reason is there for this supposition? What other element, besides the Phœnician tongue, had a share in the formation of ancient Irish? By whom was the Celtic language introduced into Ireland? What islands, also, were colonized by the Spaniards? What was their ancient name? For what were they renowned? What people carried on an extensive

The Spaniards, also, we are informed by Dionysius,* colonized the Scilly Isles, those famous Kassiterides, renowned among the ancients for their exhaustless stores of tin. The Phœnicians seem, from a very early date, to have carried on an extensive commerce with these islands, for the express purpose of supplying the nations on the Mediterranean with this useful metal. For a long time they succeeded in keeping the position of the islands a secret; and we are informed that a Phœnician trader, perceiving himself to be watched by a Roman merchantman, ran his vessel ashore rather than betray their locality, and was recompensed for his loss from the treasury of the state. The successive attempts of different nations to discover these valuable islands were, however, at last successful; and the Kassiterides, as well as the large islands to which they were adjacent, were soon peopled by the restless Celts.

§ 18. *Celtic Language.*—The Celtic Language derives its name from the word Κελτοι, the appellation given by the Greeks to the primitive inhabitants of Western Europe, who came originally from the same stock as the Greeks and Romans themselves, but had pushed their migrations further. The name was afterwards assumed by an individual tribe, who after various wanderings, settled in Gaul immediately south of the Loire. Celtic is regarded by etymologists as the parent of most of the languages of Southern and Western Europe, of some African tongues, and the various dialects of the two Tartaries.† Latin and Greek are also reckoned among its derivatives.‡

* Τοθι κασσιτεροιο γενεθλη
Αφνειοι ναιουσιν ἀγανοι παιδες ’Ιβηρων.
DIONYSIUS, *Perierg.*, v. 563.

† La langue celtique dans son sens le plus extendu, est la langue que parlerent les premiers habitans de l’Europe, depuis les rives de l’Hellespont et de la Mer Egée, jusques à celle de l’océan; depuis le cap Sigée aux portes de Troie, jusques au cap de Finisterre in Portugal, ou jusques en Ireland.—GEBELIN, *Disc. Prélim.*, art. 2.

‡ Lingua Hetrusca, Phrygia, Celtica, affines sunt omnes; ex uno fonte derivatæ. Nec Græca longe distat; Japheti ge sunt omnes ergo et ipsa Latina.—STIERNHELM.

---

trade with the Kassiterides? What incident is related in illustration of the value which the Phœnicians set upon their exclusive trade with these islands? By whom, at last, were the Kassiterides peopled?

§ 18. From what does the Celtic language derive its name? From what stock did the Κελτοι spring? By whom was the name afterwards assumed? What tongues have been formed from the Celtic? From what language was Celtic an offshoot? What resemblance confirms this fact?

Celtic was itself an offshoot from the Hebrew or Phœnician tongue; thus etymology, as well as profane history, confirms the account given by Moses of the peopling of the earth from one parent family. A marked resemblance may still be observed between the Hebrew and Welsh of the present day; and we can only wonder that thirty centuries, involving so many political revolutions, should not have produced a greater difference between them.

As we have said that the original British was derived from the same stock as the language of Greece and that of Rome, it may seem strange that there was not sufficient resemblance between it and the latter to be observed and recorded by Cæsar when he invaded the island. It must be remembered, however, that centuries had elapsed from the time of their formation; that all languages at that early day, being spoken rather than written, were particularly liable to mutations; and that, after separating from each other, all intercourse between the kindred tribes ceased, and their dialects must therefore in a great measure have lost their affinity. The radicals common to both must have assumed distinct forms, and the new objects and inventions peculiar to each must have originated new terms to which the others were strangers. As they did not advance towards civilization with the same degree of rapidity, so their respective languages could not have been equally copious or polished; for words multiply with ideas and successive advances in art and science. In process of time, these causes, added to the difference in the natural features of their respective countries and in the objects with which they were surrounded, must have obscured the common roots, and produced such accessions of new words to each dialect as to make them seem entirely distinct from one another.

Even the temperature, soil, and atmosphere of a country have a great effect on its language. "It is commonly observed," says Rowland,

---

What connection had Greek and Latin with the original language of Britain? How, then, is it to be explained that there was not sufficient resemblance between them to be observed and recorded by Cæsar? What changes must have been made, and why? What natural circumstances produce changes in the language of a country?

the learned author of "Mona Antiqua Restorata", "that different cli mates, airs, and aliments, do very much diversify the tone of the parts and muscles of human bodies; on some of which the modulation of the voice much depends. The peculiar moisture of one country, the drought of another (other causes from food, &c., concurring), extend or contract, swell or attenuate, the organs of the voice, so that the sound made thereby is rendered either shrill or hoarse, soft or hard, plain or lisping, in proportion to that contraction or extension. And hence it is, that the Chinese and Tartars have some sounds in their language that Europeans can scarcely imitate."

It is probable that the Celtic spoken in Britain and Gaul before their conquest by the Romans bore a much closer resemblance to the parent tongue than the dialects that prevailed in the Southeast of Europe; for the obvious reason that the former countries had paid less attention to literature and science, enjoyed fewer opportunities of intercourse with other nations, and suffered less from invasion, war, and conquest.

§ 19. *Branches of Celtic.*—Of the Celtic stock there are two branches; the British or Cambrian, and Gaelic or Erse. The former was the dialect that anciently prevailed in Britain and Gaul; embracing the Cornish, spoken till a recent period in Cornwall, and the Armorican of the French province of Bretagne. It is represented by the Welsh of the present day. To the second or Erse branch belong the ancient and present Irish, the Gaelic of the Highlands of Scotland, and the Manks of the Isle of Man.

In the first class is placed, as we have seen, the language of Bretagne or Brittany, on the north-west coast of France, generally called Armorican. An astonishing resemblance exists between this tongue and Welsh, which proves them to have had a common origin and to have suffered very few subsequent modifications. So similar are they that

---

What does Rowland say in this connection? Which resembled more closely the parent tongue, the Celtic cf Gaul and Britain, or that of Southeastern Europe? What reason is assigned for this?

§ 19. How many branches are there of the Celtic stock? Name them. Where did the British or Cambrian prevail? What dialects did it embrace? By what is it represented at the present day? What languages belong to the Erse branch? To which branch does the language of Brittany belong? What is it generally called? What tongue does Armorican resemble? What does this prove? Relate an incident illus-

when a Welsh regiment passed through Brittany some years since, after the conquest of Bellisle, they could converse with the inhabitants and were readily understood by them. When and how this district was settled is not known; but the inhabitants are manifestly of British, and therefore primarily of Celtic, origin. Some suppose that a body of British were driven by the Saxons across the Strait of Dover and settled on the French coast; others give credit to a tradition which prevails among the Armoricans, that they are descended from some British soldiers who were summoned to Italy as auxiliaries to the Roman army and who, on their return, seized on this district for a home in consequence of having learned that the Saxons had become masters of their native land.

§ 20. *Peculiarities of Celtic.*—Of the ancient Celtic we can form a tolerably correct idea by examining the modern Welsh and Irish. Its peculiarities seem to have been,

I. A lack of inflection in its nouns; that is, they did not undergo any change of termination to indicate a change of case. The modern Irish has a peculiar form for the dative plural; but with this exception there is no change in the terminations of nouns either in Irish, Welsh, or Armorican.

II. A system of initial mutations, by which the noun alters its first letter or receives a prefix, according to its relation to other words in the sentence.

It must be remembered that we are now speaking of the original language of Britain, and not of the English of the present day. The formation of the latter was the work of a later date. Yet it contains some traces of the old Celtic, introduced either directly from the remains of that language,

---

trative of the resemblance between Welsh and Armorican. When and how was Brittany settled? How do some account for its settlement? What tradition prevails among the Armoricans on the subject?

§ 20. How may we form an idea of the ancient Celtic? What peculiarity belonged to its nouns? How do modern Irish, Welsh, and Armorican agree with ancient Celtic in this particular? How was the relation between the noun and other words in the sentence indicated?

Is Celtic, the original language of Britain, the groundwork of our present English? What connection is there between them?

still preserved in their greatest purity in the British Isles, or at second-hand from the Norman French or some other derivative from the same stock.

§ 21. *Period of Roman Supremacy.*—Britain was subjugated by the Romans about 50 B. C., and remained in possession of its conquerors for four centuries. It was an invariable point of policy with the Romans to introduce their own language into conquered states, as the most effective means of removing their prejudices and reconciling them to their bondage. Latin, consequently, supplanted a number of aboriginal tongues, just as English has superseded the vernaculars of the native Indians of America. In some countries, where a war of extermination was carried on, this change was immediate; in others it was more gradual. The Celtic of Britain, however, does not seem to have received much modification during the period of Roman supremacy. Our language has, it is true, many derivatives from the Latin; but these came through the medium of the Norman French, and were not introduced in the days of Cæsar or his immediate successors. Though numerous Roman garrisons were stationed in the island, and though many of the British youth were drafted into the armies of the Empire, while others were sent to Rome for their education, yet, either from their inaptness at learning or their aversion to those who had deprived them of liberty, the mass of the people continued firm in their attachment to their ancient language and in its exclusive use. Many, however, of the higher classes became acquainted with Latin, and through their means some words were introduced from it which are still found in modern Welsh. English, also, contains a few terms introduced from the language of the

---

§ 21. At what date did the Romans subjugate Britain? How long did it remain in their possession? What policy did the Romans pursue in the states they conquered? What was the consequence? Does the Celtic of Britain appear to have received much modification during the period of Roman supremacy? How, then, are we to account for the Latin derivatives in our language? What opportunities did the British youth have of learning the Roman tongue? Why did they not embrace these opportunities? What class remained firmest in their attachment to their ancient language? Through

Romans at this period; such as the word *street*, from the Latin *strata*; and names of places ending in *coln*, a contraction of *colonia* (a colony), and in *cester*, derived from *castra* (a camp). Hence the origin of Lin*coln*, Lei*cester*, Glou*cester* &c.

LESSON VII.

ORIGIN OF THE ENGLISH LANGUAGE (CONTINUED).

§ 22. *The Saxon Conquest.*—In this state of comparative purity the language of the British Celts remained until the beginning of the 5th century. About this time, the whole of Southern Europe began to be overrun by Goths, Huns, and other Northern barbarians; who, allured by the advantages of a milder climate and more productive soil, emigrated from what was then called Scandinavia, answering to our modern Norway and Sweden, and wrested province after province from the Roman Empire. Their conquest was so complete as to effect a radical change in the customs, laws, and of course dialects, of the districts they subjugated. The languages spoken by the Northern tribes were mostly of a common origin, and belonged to the great Gothic stock; yet, though resembling each other in their main features, they were distinguished by many minor points of difference. The Huns and Lombards, overrunning Italy soon corrupted the Latin language and originated the modern Italian. The Franks and Normans, grafting their vernacular on the Latin-Celtic of Gaul, produced

---

what class were a few Latin words introduced at this early period? Give some Latin derivatives of this date, with the words from which they were formed.

§ 22. How long did the Celtic of Britain remain comparatively pure? About this time, what incursions began to be made in Southern Europe? Whence did the Northern barbarians come? What was the result of their conquests? To what stock did their languages belong? Which of these tribes overran Italy? What language originated in their corruptions of Latin? What tribes grafted their vernacular on the

Norman French. Spanish and Portuguese arose from a similar combination of the language of the Visigoths with the half Celtic and half Roman patois of the Peninsula, subsequently modified by the introduction of some Arabic elements during the supremacy of the Moors in Spain.

Nor did Britain escape invasion. While the attention of Scandinavian nations was directed principally towards Southern Europe, several German tribes fixed their eyes on this isolated province of Rome; and, either allured by the hope of plunder, or induced to send out colonies by the denseness of their population, despatched thither successive expeditions. Prior to this period, indeed, German colonies of greater or less size had been planted in Britain; for we read that this was done by the Emperor Antoninus, at the close of the war with the Marcomanni. These early settlers, however, were too few to effect much change in the customs of the inhabitants. It may have been through these colonists that their kinsmen on the continent obtained a knowledge of the island, and were induced to emigrate thither in such numbers. Other accounts state that they went on the invitation of the British themselves, who solicited their assistance against the Picts, a fierce race occupying the northern part of the island; and that, having succeeded in vanquishing the latter, they were tempted to remain by the fertility of the soil and the pleasantness of the climate. However this may be, the first expedition of which we have any authentic account was led by Hengist and Horsa, and effected a landing on the shores of Kent, A. D. 449. It was in this county, therefore, that the original British was first superseded by the mother-tongue of our present English.

Latin-Celtic of Gaul? What tongue was thus produced? How did Spanish and Portuguese arise? What elements were subsequently introduced?

To what part of Europe was the attention of Scandinavian nations principally directed? What tribes fixed their eyes on Britain? What induced them to send expeditions thither? By whom, and after what war, had German colonies been previously planted in Britain? Had these early settlers effected any change in the customs of the inhabitants? How did the Germans come to send expeditions to Britain in the fifth century? Why did they remain in Britain? Who led the first expedition? Where

Two traditions are handed down with respect to the stratagem by means of which Hengist procured sufficient land for his first settlement. Geoffrey of Monmouth, a Welsh historian of the twelfth century, states that he purchased for a nominal sum as much land as could be inclosed with an ox-hide; and that then, having cut it into narrow strips, he surrounded with it an extent of ground sufficient for the erection of a castle. This is a familiar story, found in the traditions of various nations. The other version is given by the Saxons. They say that their great leader bought from the inhabitants a lap-full of earth at wha seemed to his companions an extravagant price; but that he proceeded to sow this soil over a large tract, and then, since it could not be distinguished from the other ground, laid claim to the whole, and made good his pretensions by force of arms.

A second expedition from the north of Germany followed in the year 477, under the command of Ella. This chieftain established himself in what is now called Sussex (that is, South Saxony). The kingdoms of Wessex (West Saxony), lying in what is now known as the County of Hants, and Essex (East Saxony), were next settled by successive expeditions, in the years 495 and 530 respectively. After this, large bodies of Germans were constantly arriving. It is unnecessary to trace any further the history of their emigrations.

As soon as they found themselves possessed of sufficient strength, the new comers formed the determination of seizing upon the whole island, or at least all those parts of it that were specially favored by Nature. In this they finally succeeded; and the original inhabitants, to avoid extermination, were obliged to flee to the mountains of Wales and Cornwall, where they maintained their independence for many centuries, and have preserved their language, with but little alteration to the present day. In the rest of the island, however, a radical change both in language and customs immediately took

---

did they effect a landing, and when? What tradition is preserved by Geoffrey of Monmouth respecting Hengist's stratagem for procuring land? What is the Saxon account?

In what year did a second expedition follow? Under whose command? Where did this chieftain establish himself? What kingdoms were next settled, and in what years? What determination did the new comers soon form? Did they succeed in carrying it through? Whither were the original inhabitants obliged to flee? What

place. There was no engrafting of one tongue on another, as was the case in Southern Europe; but an immediate substitution of the language of the conquerors for that of the vanquished. The tongue spoken by these German invaders is therefore the real groundwork of our language; a fact well established by history, as well as by the etymological analogies subsisting between English and the various dialects of Gothic origin.

§ 23. *The Invaders.*—By which of the German tribes the expeditions alluded to were fitted out, was formerly a subject of doubt, but seems now to be satisfactorily established. The Saxons, Angles, and Frisians, appear to have been the principal ones concerned in them. Of these, the first occupied the valley of the River Weser, their territory, as far as we can now locate it, corresponding with the Kingdom of Hanover, the Duchy of Oldenburg, and part of Holstein. They were a powerful people, and constituted the chief body of the invaders. This is inferred from the fact that the ancient Britons knew their German conquerors by no other name than that of Saxons; and still further because this is the appellation which the Welsh, Armoricans, and Gaelic-Celts universally apply to the English of the present day. Yet, though the Saxon element originally preponderated, the Angles were evidently strongly represented; for they enjoy the distinction of having given their name permanently to the island, *England* being nothing more than a corruption of *Angleland.*

Who these Angles were, is by no means certain. Tacitus and Ptolemy allude to them; the former, indefinitely, in connection with other tribes, while the latter locates them in the central part of the valley of the Elbe. They seem at one time to have been a distinct and powerful tribe, and were per-

---

change took place in the rest of the island? What tongue is the real groundwork of our language? How is this fact established?

§ 23. What German tribes seem to have taken the principal part in the invasion of Britain? Where did the Saxons live? With what modern countries did their territories correspond? Whence do we infer that the Saxons constituted the chief body of the invaders? What other tribe was strongly represented? What reason have we

haps allied by birth to their Saxon neighbors. Having become reduced in number by war or some other calamity, they were incorporated with the latter, and found their way to Britain along with them. While on the Continent, they were far outnumbered by the Saxons, and played so unimportant a part that little mention is made of them in history: the influence of the two nations in Britain was more nearly equal; and the Angles may at length have preponderated over their kinsmen and allies, and thus succeeded in giving name to their new habitation and its language.

The Frisians are not generally thought to have formed part of the German settlers of Britain; but that they were concerned in one or more of the expeditions seems probable from the following considerations:—

I. Occupying the whole coast from the Zuyder Zee to the mouth of the Elbe, they must have been situated between the Saxons and the sea, and are therefore likely to have joined the latter tribe, to a greater or less extent, in their maritime expeditions.

II. The historian Procopius, speaking of Britain, expressly mentions the Frisians as composing a part of its population.* Hengist himself is represented as a Frisian by some authorities. The Saxon Chronicle, also, alludes to Frisians in Britain.

III. The Frisian language, as now spoken in Friesland, bears a closer resemblance to English than any other known tongue.

---

* Βριττίας δὲ τὴν νῆσον ἔθνη τρία πολυανθρωπότατα ἔχουσι, βασιλεύς τε εἷς αὐτῶν ἑκάστῳ ἐφέστηκεν, ὀνόματα δὲ κεῖται τοῖς ἔθνεσι τούτοις Ἀγγίλοι τε καὶ Φρίσσονες καὶ οἱ τῇ νήσῳ ὁμώνυμοι Βρίττωνες.—PROCOPIUS, B. G. IV. 20.

for supposing this? What early historians allude to the Angles? Where does Ptolemy locate them? What seems to have been their early history? On the Continent, how did they compare in power and influence with the Saxons? How, in Britain? What other tribe seem to have taken part in these incursions? Explain how their position renders this supposition probable. What historian and what work mention Frisians as forming part of the population of Britain? What warrior is by some repre-

Dr. Latham, whose researches have thrown much light upon this subject, and whose "Hand-book of the English Language" is replete with scholarship and learning, thus sums up the whole matter: "It was certainly from the Anglo-Saxon, and probably from a part of the Frisian area, that Great Britain was first invaded."

§ 24. *The Saxon Language.*—The language which thus suddenly superseded the Celtic of the ancient British was, as has been remarked, an offshoot of the great Gothic stem, which itself dates as far back as the Celtic. The nations that spoke the various Gothic dialects lived in the northern part of Europe, having probably emigrated at an early date from Southwestern Asia, or been driven out by more powerful tribes. Their bards, whose business it was to recite the exploits of their heroes, agree in assigning to their race an Eastern origin; and Herodotus mentions the Germans among other tribes of ancient Persians.* The Gothic stock is divided into two great branches: the Scandinavian, including the dialects of Norway, Sweden, Denmark, and Iceland; and the Teutonic, or Germanic. To this latter division Anglo-Saxon belongs.

§ 25. *Norse or Danish Element.*—The first introduction of a foreign element into the pure Saxon of England was occasioned by the invasion of the Scandinavian nations during the ninth and the tenth century. The pirates who effected the conquest of the island are generally called Danes; but the Norwegians seem to have played the principal part in these expeditions. Their supremacy must have caused, to a certain

---

* "Άλλοι δὲ Πέρσαι εἰσὶ οἵδε, Πανθιαλαῖοι, Δηρουσιαῖοι, Γερμάνιοι.—HERODOTUS, *Clio*, 125.

---

nted to have been a Frisian? What additional evidence have we in the language now spoken in Friesland? What does Dr. Latham say on the subject?

§ 24. From what great stock did the Saxon language spring? Where did the Gothic dialects prevail at this time? From what part of the world did the nations using them originally migrate? What evidence have we of this? Into how many branches is the Gothic stock divided? What are they? What dialects are included in the Scandinavian branch? To which division does Anglo-Saxon belong?

§ 25. What occasioned the first introduction of a foreign element into the pure Saxon of England? What name is generally given to the pirate-conquerors? What nation

extent, a temporary admixture of foreign terms. To decide what words we owe to this era is extremely difficult, on account of the analogy subsisting between the Scandinavian and German dialects, both of which, it will be remembered, were derived from the same Gothic parent. It is certain, however, that very few Danish terms were ultimately incorporated; as he island suffered a change of masters, rather than of people, customs, or laws. The Norsemen have left in our language but little trace of their invasion; and this chiefly in the names of places on or near the coast.

LESSON VIII.

ORIGIN OF THE ENGLISH LANGUAGE (CONTINUED).

§ 26. *First Introduction of Norman French Elements.*— Not perceptibly affected by the invasions of the Norsemen or even by their temporary usurpation of the throne, Saxon continued to be the language of the island until the Norman Conquest, 1066 A. D. During the six hundred years that elapsed between its introduction and this event, it underwent, indeed, some modifications of greater or less moment; and these are particularly noticeable in the century immediately preceding the battle of Hastings. It was at this period that the first importation of Norman French words took place, under the auspices of Edward the Confessor. Educated in France and prejudiced in favor of all that belonged to that country, this prince, on returning to England and assuming the throne, surrounded himself with Norman favorites, and sought to introduce French customs into his court and French idioms into

---

had most to do with the invasion? What effect did their supremacy produce on the language? Were many new terms incorporated? As regards the names of places, where have they left the principal traces of their invasion? What renders it difficult to determine the words introduced by the Norsemen?

§ 26. How 'ong did Saxon, in comparative purity, continue to be the language of

his language; much to the disgust of his subjects, whose affections he estranged by this injudicious course. Inconsiderable as were the changes thus brought about, they served to pave the way for those fundamental modifications which the Norman Conquest was destined to produce.

§ 27. *Norman Conquest and its Effects.*—William, Duke of Normandy, invaded England 1066 A. D., and, having won the battle of Hastings, seated himself without delay upon the throne. Resolved to wean the people from their ancient institutions, he endeavored, as the most effective means of accomplishing this object, to make them forget their language. With this view, he ordered that in all schools throughout the kingdom the youth should be instructed in the French tongue; and this ordinance was generally complied with, and remained in force till after the reign of Edward III. It was also required that the pupils of grammar-schools should translate their Latin into French, and that all conversation among them should be carried on in one of these two languages. Anglo-Saxon was banished from the tribunals of the land, and pleadings were required to be in French; deeds were drawn and laws compiled in the same language; no other tongue was used at Court; it was exclusively employed in fashionable society; and the English nobles themselves, ashamed of their own country, affected to excel in this foreign dialect. The lower classes, however, at first vigorously resisted these attempts; and for fifty years all that was done towards changing the language was effected by the hand of power. Yet in spite of this feeling on the part of the people, even during the very period in question, the intercourse necessarily carried on with the Normans introduced not a few of their terms into common conversation. Thus undermined, popular prejudice

---

England? What was the principal modification it had previously undergone? Who was the author of these changes? For what did they pave the way?.

§ 27. By whom was England invaded 1066 A. D.? What battle decided the fate of the empire? What was its result? How did the Conqueror endeavor to alienate the people from their ancient institutions? In what were the youth instructed? What was made the language of the courts? By what class were these attempts resisted?

gradually became less violent. The superior versatility of the language of their conquerors and its peculiar adaptedness to poetry were soon acknowledged by the educated. The treasures of the early ballad and romantic literature of Normandy were eagerly sought for; and, within a hundred years after the Conquest, we find the people as willing to learn the Norman tongue, and engraft its beauties on their own, as their fathers had been opposed to speaking or even hearing it.

This willingness, however, extended only to a modification of their vernacular; the determination was still as strong and unanimous as ever against allowing the introduction of Norman French at the expense and to the exclusion of the latter. To improve its constructions and enlarge its vocabulary would be to increase its usefulness; and for these purposes they freely drew on the language of their conquerors. But the latter was rendered odious by too many unpleasant associations to allow of its substitution for a tongue which the use of centuries had rendered sacred in their eyes. Of effecting this, the power of William and his successors was totally incapable. The people carried their point; and within two hundred years these very kings and nobles from across the channel were compelled to learn the Saxon, at first so much contemned, now converted into ENGLISH by the important changes just alluded to, which commenced as early as the middle of the twelfth century. In 1362, the new language thus formed was introduced into the courts and allowed to be used in pleading; all classes of society spoke it; poets employed it as the vehicle of their choicest thoughts; and English literature may be said to have had its origin.

Did they succeed in keeping their vernacular unalloyed? How were Norman words gradually introduced? In what qualities did the educated Saxons find that the Norman language surpassed their own? What was the state of feeling among the Saxons a century after the Conquest? How far did this willingness extend? For what purposes did they draw on the language of their conquerors? Did the kings or the people carry their point? Two hundred years after the Conquest, what do we find? Into what was Saxon by that time converted? In 1362 what took place? In what localities were these changes soonest effected?

These changes, though covering in the kingdom at large a period of two hundred years, were in some parts much sooner effected. The greater the number and influence of the Norman inhabitants in any given locality, the sooner did Anglo-Saxon prejudices give way and the distinctive features of the French become blended with those of the vernacular.

§ 28. *Conversion of Anglo-Saxon into English.*—Marks of the successive changes to which allusion has been made are evident in the few extant writings of the twelfth and the succeeding century. In the case of some of the productions of this transition period, critics have found it difficult to decide whether they should be classed among the latest specimens of Saxon, or the earliest of English, literature, bearing, as they do, the characteristics of each; they have, therefore, introduced the word SEMI-SAXON, which they apply to all writings between 1150 and 1250 A. D. Passing over a few works of minor importance, the Travels of Sir John Mandeville, written in 1356, may be called the first English book. Wicliffe's Translation of the Bible followed twenty-seven years afterwards, and did much towards fixing the unsettled forms of the new language.

The English of these early times, however, differs much from that of the present day. Even the poetry of Chaucer, who wrote in the latter part of the fourteenth century, cannot be understood without the aid of a glossary. Our language has not, to be sure, since the Norman invasion suffered any shock from the intermixture of conquerors, and their dialects; but its appearance is much changed in consequence, not only of manifold simplifications in the spelling, but also of the disuse of many Saxon terms (one fifth of those current in Alfred's time being now obsolete), and the continual introduction of new words from the dead languages, as well as from the French, Italian, and Spanish. For scientific terms resort has generally been had to the Greek; and, as new discoveries have been constantly making since the Middle Ages, the additions from this source have been considerable. Commerce has also

---

§ 28. In what writings have we marks of these successive changes? What writings are classed as Semi-Saxon? What may be called the first English book? When was it written? What work followed twenty-seven years afterwards? How does this early English compare with that of the present day? What is said of Chaucer's poetry? Whence arises this difference? What part of the Saxon words current in Alfred's time

widely extended; and commodities formerly unknown have been introduced into common use, retaining in most cases their foreign names. Thus we have obtained the words *camphor, arsenic*, and many others. The changes and additions just mentioned, as well as a variety of modifications which are found to have affected, not only our own, but also every other modern tongue, have so altered the appearance of the later English that a close examination is necessary to convince the reader of its identity with the language of Chaucer.

§ 29. *Changes by which Anglo-Saxon was converted into English.*—The principal changes by which Anglo-Saxon was converted into English, were,

I. Modifications and contractions in the spelling of words.

II. The introduction of French terms, phrases, and idioms.

III. The use of less inversion and ellipsis, especially in poetry.

V. The omission of inflections or changes in the termination of the noun, and substitution of prepositions to express its relations to other words. This last-mentioned change is the only one of sufficient importance to authorize us in considering the new derivative as an independent tongue. It is an alteration which time very often brings about; and is, perhaps, to be attributed rather to the natural efforts of the people to simplify their grammar, than to the effects of the Norman Conquest or the new dialect it introduced. Observation shows that this tendency has by no means been confined to English. It seems to be a universal principle, that, the further we go back in the history of a given language, the more terminational changes we find in its nouns and verbs, and the fewer prepositions and auxiliaries.

---

are now obsolete? Whence have we obtained most of our scientific terms? How have we received the words *camphor, arsenic*, and many others? What is said of the affect of these alterations and additions?

§ 29. Mention the four principal changes by which Anglo-Saxon was converted into English. Which of these is the most important? How is it often brought about? To what is it attributable? Is this tendency confined to the English language? The further we go back in the history of a tongue, what do we find?

LESSON IX.

ANALYSIS OF THE ENGLISH LANGUAGE.

§ 30. To recapitulate and enlarge on what has been said in the preceding lesson, it appears that our language, as it now stands, is composed of the following elements:—

1. SAXON.—Of the forty thousand words contained in our fullest dictionaries, twenty-three thousand are from this source; as are, also, our chief peculiarities of construction and idiom. Some of these it may be interesting to particularize. The inflection of our pronouns; the terminations of the possessive case and plural number, as well as of the second and third person singular of verbs; the syllables *er* and *est*, and the words *more* and *most*, by which we form the comparative and superlative of adjectives and adverbs; the suffix *ly* (derived from *like*); which enters into the formation of a large proportion of our adverbs,—all these are derived from the Saxon. As to the words we have received from it, they are those which occur most frequently and are individually of the greatest importance: such as the articles *a, an, the;* all our pronouns; the adjectives oftenest used, especially such as are irregularly compared; the commonest adverbs of one syllable, *how, now, then,* and the like; nearly all of the numerous irregular verbs, as well as the auxiliaries, *have, be, shall, will,* &c.; and the prepositions and conjunctions, almost without exception.

Irregular nouns, adjectives, and verbs, are in every language among the oldest words, and are very likely to be those most used in common conversation; to which fact their deviation from regularity may often

---

§ 30. How many words are contained in our fullest dictionaries? Of these, how many are Saxon? What terminations have we received from this source? Which of our words are Saxon? Mention some of them. What is said of the irregular nouns, adjectives, and verbs in every language? What striking objects have received Saxon names? Whence come most of our abstract terms? Whence, the specifications under them? Give examples. What rich fund of words is almost entirely Saxon? Mention

be traced. These, as we have seen, our Saxon ancestors gave us; to them, also, we owe the names of the striking objects which constantly meet our view, of *sun* and *moon*, *land* and *water*, *hill* and *dale*. While, moreover, we borrow from the Latin or French most of our abstract terms, the specifications classed under them are for the most part Saxon. Thus Latin supplies us with the general term *color*; but to Saxon we are indebted for the particular varieties, *white* and *black*, *blue* and *yellow*, *red* and *brown*: from the former we get the comprehensive term *to move*; from the latter, the different kinds of motion, *walking*, *running*, *leaping*, *springing*, *gliding*, *creeping*, *crawling*, &c. Hence, too, the rich and necessary fund of words by which we express our feelings and passions as well as the relations which call them forth. These emotions the Saxons shared with all others of the human race, and the words which they employed in expressing them have come down to us almost without alteration. To this class belong the words *love* and *hate*, *hope* and *fear*, *smile* and *tear*, *sigh* and *groan*, *weeping* and *laughter*, *father* and *mother*, *man* and *wife*, *son* and *daughter*. Our common business terms, the language of the shop, the market, and the farm, have the same origin. Saxon, therefore, besides dictating the laws and furnishing the particles by which our words are connected, yields the most available terms for expressing the feelings, describing the objects of sense and imagination, and conveying the facts of every-day life.

2. NORMAN FRENCH.—From the time of the Conquest till the days of Chaucer, a period of three hundred years, this element played an important part in the formation of our tongue. First introduced by royal authority as the language of law, chivalry, and feudalism, and unwillingly received by the masses, it finally found its way into their affections, and was largely drawn upon for words in which the Saxon vocabulary was deficient. From this source it is estimated that at least five thousand words were added. Besides covering the abstractions and generalities of every-day life, they often convey slight distinctions and delicate shades of thought. We find them particularly useful, when we wish to express disap-

---

some. What other terms have the same origin? What portion, then, of its syntax and vocabulary does English owe to Saxon?

Between what periods did Norman French play an important part in the formation of our tongue? How was it first introduced? In process of time, how was it received by the people? How many words have we taken from this source? What do they convey with peculiar accuracy? When do we find them particularly useful? How is this explained?

probation without wounding the feelings of another. The natural courtesy of the Normans led to the creation of a fund of words applicable to this purpose, for which the energetic and too often rough expressions of the Saxons were totally unsuited.

3. MODERN FRENCH.—From this offspring of the ancient Norman our authors have, at different periods, taken many useful words; which, either with very slight changes in their spelling or without any modification at all, have, after a time, by common consent, become incorporated into the language. A taste for French expressions as well as French opinions has from time to time prevailed in England, and of course led to the introduction of many foreign terms from this source; whence, also, numerous additions have been made through the medium of trade, many fabrics which owe their invention to the artists of France having come into general use and retained their foreign names.

4. LATIN.—Under this head must be classed those elements which have come directly from the Latin, and not through the medium of any other tongue. Between the two classes it is not always easy to draw a dividing line, particularly in the case of the later derivatives. The earliest additions from this source (if we except proper names and a few military terms, introduced into the original vernacular of Britain during the period of Roman supremacy, and thence received and naturalized at a later date by the Saxons) were ecclesiastical words, such as *monk, saint, cloister, mass*, and the like, necessarily employed wherever the Church of Rome carried its doctrines, institutions, and ritual. Next follow the Latinisms introduced in the thirteenth century, at which time a taste for classical studies began to revive in England

---

What is said of the additions from modern French? Through what medium have they mostly been received?

Into what two classes are the Latin elements of our language divided? Is it easy to distinguish between them? What additions were made from this source during the period of Roman supremacy? What Latin terms were next introduced? Give examples. What Latinisms next followed? Towards the close of the eighteenth cen-

as well as elsewhere. Thenceforth, as necessity required, occasional additions were made from the same source, especially by theological and scientific writers; until, towards the close of the eighteenth century, Johnson and his imitators, having coined largely from Latin roots and naturalized a variety of classical idioms, succeeded in making their high-sounding derivatives fashionable, at the expense of the less pretending Saxon.

It has been questioned by those who compare the simplicity of Addison with the pompousness of Hume and Gibbon, whether this wholesale latinizing was any improvement to our language and literature; if, however, it resulted in no other advantage, it has at least secured us an array of synonymes (that is, words that have the same or a similar signification) unequalled by those of any other modern language.

5. CELTIC.—Next in importance are the Celtic elements, some of which were introduced into our language at or shortly after the period of its first formation, while others have been added in modern times, either by antiquarians or in consequence of intercourse with the Welsh and Irish. As examples of the latter, may be mentioned the words *tartan*, *plaid*, *flannel*, &c. The former class may be arranged under two subdivisions :—

I. Those elements which came directly from the Celtic itself; embracing a great number of geographical names, such as *Thames*, *Kent*, &c., as well as a variety of common nouns in every-day use, among which are *bran*, *darn*, *flaw*, *gruel*, *mop*, *tackle*, &c.

II. Such as originated in the Celtic, yet were received into English, not directly from that tongue, but through the medium of Latin or Norman French, into which they had previously found their way.

---

tury, what taste became fashionable? How does the style of Addison compare with that of Hume and Gibbon? What question has been raised with regard to this wholesale latinizing? What great advantage has resulted from it?

What elements are next in importance? When were the Celtic additions introduced? What is the first class into which the ancient elements are divided? Give examples. What, the second? How have Celtic words found their way into English in modern times?

6. GREEK.—To this language we are indebted largely foi scientific terms, but little or none for words of every-day life The elements thus derived are all of recent addition. If we except the words *phenomenon, criterion, automaton,* and a few others, they have all been introduced within the last hundred and fifty years. New discoveries of science having rendered an enlargement of our technical nomenclature necessary, recourse was had to the Greek as affording the greatest advantages for this purpose. Hence our numerous words ending in *logy* and *graphy*, and their derivatives.

7. MISCELLANEOUS ELEMENTS.—Under this head fall the few isolated words added from time to time, through the medium of business, or as occasion has required, from Eastern and North American dialects, or the modern tongues of Europe not before alluded to.

Dr. Latham, in his "Handbook," p. 56, furnishes us with a variety of examples:—

ITALIAN, virtuoso.
RUSSIAN, Czar.
TURKISH, coffee, bashaw, scimitar.
ARABIC, admiral, assassin, alchemy, alcohol, and a variety of words beginning with the Arabian article *al.*
PERSIAN, turban, caravan.
HINDOO, calico, chintz, curry, lac.
MALAY, bantam, gamboge, rattan, sago.
CHINESE, nankeen, tea, and its varieties, bohea, hyson, &c.
N. AMERICAN INDIAN, squaw, wigwam.

§ 31. From what has been stated, however, with regard to the numerical proportion of the elements composing our language, no correct idea can be formed respecting their rela-

---

What terms do we owe to the Greek language? When were they introduced? Within this period, what has called for an enlargement of our scientific vocabulary? What terminations in English indicate Greek origin?

How have a variety of miscellaneous elements crept into our language? Give examples from the Italian; Russian; Turkish; Arabic; Persian; Hindoo; Malay; Chinese; North American Indian dialects.

§ 31. From what has been stated with regard to their number, can a correct idea be formed of the relative importance of the elements that compose our language? Why

tive importance. Some words, for instance, (and this is the case with many of our Saxon derivatives) are constantly recurring, while the use of others is rare and limited to certain styles or subjects. To determine what part of our language, as commonly written, is really Saxon, various passages from the authorized version of the Scriptures and from standard writers of different eras have been analyzed. The result, as given in Turner's Anglo-Saxons, shows that when the words were classified under the languages from which they were respectively derived, more than four fifths of the whole were found to be of Saxon origin. The individual passages compared were found to differ widely from each other as regards their proportion of foreign elements. The translators of the Bible wrote by far the purest Saxon, only $\frac{1}{30}$ of their words being derived from other sources; of Swift's words, $\frac{1}{6}$ are not Saxon; of Milton's, $\frac{1}{8}$; of Shakspeare's, $\frac{1}{8}$; of Spenser's Addison's, and Thomson's, about $\frac{1}{5}$; of Johnson's, $\frac{1}{4}$; of Pope's and Hume's, $\frac{1}{3}$; of Gibbon's, much more than $\frac{1}{3}$.

LESSON X

CHARACTERISTICS OF THE ENGLISH LANGUAGE.

§ 32. Before proceeding to consider the different classes of words, and the parts they respectively perform in a sentence, we may with advantage look at our language as a whole, and observe its leading characteristics.

Derived, as we have seen, from so many different sources,

each of which has contributed some of its own peculiar features, it naturally follows that English, like every other compounded language, is full of irregularities. We must not expect entire consistency in its parts, or that complete analogy of structure which is found in simpler tongues that have been built on but one foundation. Our words, naturalized from widely different dialects, "straggle," as Blair says, "asunder from each other, and do not coalesce so naturally in the structure of a sentence as the words in the Greek and Roman tongues." Our orthography is anomalous; the same combination of letters may be pronounced in half a dozen different ways : * and our syntactical constructions are so arbitrary that it often perplexes the best grammarians to account for them. We have introduced foreign idioms and modes of construction; and our sentences too often look like patchwork, composed of divers pieces, handsome enough in themselves, but of such different colors and qualities that the eye cannot help being struck with the variety in passing from one to another.

Composite languages, however, have advantages as well as drawbacks. The very variety alluded to above is preferable to sameness, and often imparts vivacity to what might otherwise seem monotonous and dull. Such tongues, moreover, are generally enriched with copious vocabularies; and particularly is this true of English, whose abundance of historical, political, moral, and philosophical terms, leaves little to be desired by the writer. Nor are we less amply provided with distinct and peculiar poetical terms. With us poetry differs from prose, not only in having a certain arrangement of syllables and feet, but

---

* For example, *ough* in *through, though, cough, tough, lough, hiccough, plough.*

---

ent sources? What must we not expect? What says Blair respecting our words? What is the character of our orthography? Give an example. What is said of our sentences?

What advantage, on the other hand, do composite languages possess? With what are such tongues generally enriched? With what kind of terms are we amply provided? In English, how does poetry differ from prose? Whose writings prove this?

in the very words that compose it; so much so that the writings of Ossian, though they have neither rhyme nor metre, are classed by many among poems. In this respect we enjoy a great advantage over the French, whose poetry, without rhyme, would be hardly distinguishable from their prose; and with whom, as a consequence, blank verse is never attempted. For this richness we are indebted to the fact that our language, originally made up from several others, has borrowed from them all; and thus has supplied from one what was wanting in another, and even in some cases appropriated duplicate terms and expressions to denote the same thing. These are of great use to the writer in every department of composition, enabling him to diversify his style and avoid unpleasant repetitions.

§ 33. Every language is supposed to take, in a greater or less degree, its predominant tone from the character of the people that speak it. Though it cannot, of course, exactly represent their customs, manners, powers of mind, and habits of thought, yet it must necessarily be in some measure, if ever so little, affected by their national characteristics. The vivacity of the French, the thoughtfulness of the English, and th gravity of the Spanish, are unmistakably impressed on their respective tongues.

From the character of those by whom our language was originally formed, and from whom it has received most of its subsequent additions and modifications, we would expect to find it distinguished by strength and energy; and this is the case, notwithstanding the numerous small particles and auxiliary verbs which we are constantly obliged to employ, with a decidedly weakening effect. Though our constructions are by no means compact, and our thoughts are diluted with a superabundance of words, yet, in spite of these disadvantages, since it abounds in

---

What is said of French in this respect? What kind of verse is, therefore, never attempted in that language? To what fact is English indebted for this richness? How is this quality of use to the writer?

§ 33. From what does every language take its predominant tone? What is the sharacteristic of the French and their tongue? What of the English? What of the Spanish? Judging from the character of the formers of our language, by what would we expect to find English distinguished? Is this the case? What words, however,

terms adapted to the expression of the strongest emotions, and presents superior facilities for forming compounds, and thereby briefly representing complex ideas, our language is admitted by all nations to be eminently nervous and energetic.

Flexibility, or susceptibility of accommodation to different styles and tastes, so as to be either grave or gay, forcible or tender, simple or imposing, as occasion may require, is one of the most important qualities that a language can possess, as regards both writing and speaking. To ensure flexibility, three characteristics are essential; copiousness, capacity for changes of construction and arrangement, and strength and beauty as regards individual words. The first two of these qualities we have seen that English possesses in a high degree; in the last it is not deficient. While, therefore, it is inferior in flexibility to Latin and Greek, and of modern languages perhaps to Italian, it is still capable of being used with success in any style; as must be apparent to all who examine the master-pieces which our literature has produced in the various departments of prose and poetry.

It has been said above that our tongue is not deficient in harmony; and this is proved by the fact that it is capable of being formed into poetry without the aid of rhyme. Vowel sounds abound, and please the ear with their variety. The frequent recurrence of the hissing consonant *s*, however, has an unpleasant effect, which we have only partially removed by assigning to that letter, in certain positions, the sound of *z*, as in *is, these, ears, loves, resolves*, &c. The melody of our periods is also materially affected by our tendency to throw the accent of polysyllables back towards the beginning; to which tendency we are indebted for such awkward words as *tempo-*

---

have a decidedly weakening effect? What is said of our constructions? How are our thoughts diluted? Notwithstanding this, what is the general character of our language? To what features does it owe this character?

What is one of the most important qualities a language can possess? Enumerate the characteristics essential to flexibility. How does English rank as regards those three essentials? How does it compare in flexibility with Latin, Greek, and Italian? What proves its adaptation to all styles?

rarily, mischievously, mercenariness, miserableness, and many others similarly discordant.

Whatever may be said of the English language in other respects, in simplicity it undoubtedly surpasses the rest of European tongues. It is free from intricacies of case, declension, mood, and tense. Its words are subject to but few terminational changes. Its substantives have no distinctions of gender except what nature has made. Its adjectives admit of such changes only as are necessary to denote the degrees of comparison. Its verbs, instead of running through all the varieties of ancient conjugation, suffer few changes. With the help of prepositions and auxiliaries, all possible relations are expressed, while the words for the most part retain their forms unchanged. We lose from this, no doubt, in brevity and strength; but we gain vastly in simplicity. The arrangement of our words is, in consequence, less difficult, and our sentences are more readily understood. The rules of our syntax are exceedingly simple, and the acquisition of our language is easy in proportion.

LESSON XI.

PARTS OF SPEECH.

§ 34. Having traced the history of our language, considered the sources from which it is derived, and noted its chief characteristics, we shall now proceed to treat of its words,

---

What proves that English is not deficient in harmony? What consonant has an unpleasant sound? How have we attempted to remove the difficulty? What tendency in accentuation interferes with the melody of periods? Mention some inharmonious words thus accented.
In what does English surpass all other European tongues? What features are mentioned, which conduce to its simplicity? How are the different relations of nouns and verbs expressed? In what respects do we lose in consequence of this? In what do we gain?

viewed with reference to the respective parts they perform in a sentence. A knowledge of grammar being presupposed in the pupil, we shall here, by a brief summary, merely recall to his mind its leading principles, with such definitions and illustrations only as are absolutely essential to the proper understanding of the succeeding lessons.

The classes into which words are divided with reference to their use and mutual relations, are called PARTS OF SPEECH. They are nine in number.

I. NOUNS, or names of things. They are divided into two classes: COMMON NOUNS, or names that distinguish one class of objects from another,—as, *man, city, river;* and PROPER NOUNS, or names that distinguish one individual of a class from another,—as, *Moses, Brooklyn, Rhine.*

The term SUBSTANTIVE is frequently used as synonymous with *noun.* Besides nouns, it embraces whatever may be used as such; that is, pronouns, verbs in the infinitive, and clauses.

II. PRONOUNS, or words that may be used instead of nouns.

They are comprised in the following classes:—

1 PERSONAL, or such as show by their form what person they are; that is, whether they represent the person speaking, the person spoken to, or the object spoken of. The Personals are, *I, thou, he, she, it,* and their compounds, *myself, thyself, himself, herself, itself.*
2. RELATIVES, or such as relate to a substantive going before, called an Antecedent. The relatives are, *who, which,* and *that.* *What, whatever, whoever,* and *whichever,* include the antecedent, and are called compound relatives.
3. INTERROGATIVES, or such as are used to ask questions. The interrogatives are, *who, which,* and *what.*

¶ 84. What do we mean by parts of speech? How many are there? Which is the first? What are nouns? Into what classes are they divided? What are common nouns? What are proper nouns? What term is often used as synonymous with *noun?* What else besides nouns are included under the general head of substantives?

What is the second part of speech? What are pronouns? Enumerate the classes into which they are divided. Define the term *personal pronoun.* Mention the personals. What are relative pronouns? Enumerate them. What are interrogatives? Mention them. What is meant by adjective pronouns? Mention the principal ones.

I. ADJECTIVE PRONOUNS, or such as on some occasions take the place of substantives, and on others are used with them, like adjectives. Under this head fall the words, *this, that, each, every, either, neither no, none, any, al., such, some, both, other, another.*

III. ARTICLES, or words placed before nouns to show whether they are used in a particular or general sense. We have two articles: *the*, called DEFINITE, because it defines or points out a particular object; and *an* or *a*, called INDEFINITE.

IV. ADJECTIVES, or words which describe or limit substantives; as, "The *five good* emperors".

V. VERBS, or words that express an action or state; as, "He *is* sure *to succeed.*" That respecting which the action or state is primarily expressed is called the SUBJECT of the verb; thus, in the preceding example, *he* is the subject of the verb *is*.

Verbs are divided into two classes: TRANSITIVE, or such as express an act done to an object; and INTRANSITIVE, or such as express a state, or an act not done to an object. "James *reads* Latin", "James *can read*", "James *is* asleep": in the first sentence the verb is transitive; in the last two, intransitive.

To show the relation which the subject bears to the action expressed, transitive verbs have two distinct forms, called VOICES. The ACTIVE VOICE represents the subject of the verb as acting; as, "Cæsar *conquered* Pompey." The PASSIVE VOICE represents the subject of the verb as acted upon; as, "Pompey *was conquered* by Cæsar."

A verb is said to be FINITE when it is limited by person and number. This is the case in every part except the infinitive mood and the participles.

By the REGIMEN of a verb or preposition is meant the substantive it governs with all the limiting words belonging thereto; as, "A good citi-

---

What is the third part of speech? What are articles? Mention them, and give their names.
What is the fourth part of speech? What are adjectives? Give an example.
What is the fifth part of speech? What are verbs? What is meant by the subject of a verb? Into how many classes are verbs divided? What are they? What are transitive verbs? What, intransitive? Give examples. How many voices are there? What are they called? How does the active voice represent the subject of the verb? How does the passive represent it? When is a verb said to be finite? What is meant by the regimen of a verb or preposition? Give examples.

zen obeys *his country's laws.*" "The age of *miracles is past.*" "A company of *wicked and profligate men.*"

To verbs belong

PARTICIPLES, or words which, partaking of the nature of adjectives and verbs, describe a substantive by assigning to it an action or a state. Transitive verbs have six participles three in the active, and three in the passive, voice; as, *loving, loved, having loved,* and *being loved, loved, having been loved.* Intransitive verbs, admitting of no passive voice, have but three participles; as, *walking, walked, having walked.*

VI. ADVERBS, or words added to verbs, participles, adjectives, and other adverbs, to express time, place, degree, comparison, manner, &c.; as, *now, here, very, so, gracefully.* Adverbs of manner for the most part end with the letters *ly.* This class of words must be carefully distinguished from adjectives, which also express manner or quality, but are always joined to substantives.

VII. CONJUNCTIONS, used to connect words, sentences, and parts of sentences. The most common ones are,

and,	or,	either,	because,	except,
as,	nor,	neither,	since,	whether,
for,	yet,	than,	though,	lest,
if,	but,	that,	although,	unless.

VIII. PREPOSITIONS, which show the relations between substantives and other words in a sentence. The following list contains the principal:

about,	behind,	during,	out of,	touching,
above,	below,	except,	past,	towards,
across,	beneath,	for,	regarding,	under,
after,	besides,	from,	respecting,	underneath,

What are participles? How many participles have transitive verbs? How many have intransitives? Give examples of each.

What are adverbs? With what syllable do adverbs of manner generally end? From what must adverbs be carefully distinguished? What is the difference between them?

What are conjunctions? Mention the most common ones.
What are prepositions? Enumerate the principal ones.

against,	between,	in,	round,	until.
along,	betwixt,	into,	save,	unto,
amid,	beyond,	notwithstanding,	since,	up,
among,	but,	of,	through,	upon,
around,	by,	off,	throughout,	with,
at,	concerning,	on,	till,	within,
before,	down,	over,	to,	without

IX. INTERJECTIONS, or words used to denote a sudden emotion of the mind; as, *ah! alas! O! oh! fie! hist* &c.

EXAMPLE.—The following sentence contains all the parts of speech, the words falling respectively under one of the above classes, as denoted by the numbers placed over them:—

"But alas! he soon fell before the malignant tempter."
(7)   (9) (2) (6) (5) (8) (3)   (4)   (1)

§ 35. Of these parts of speech, the noun, pronoun, and verb, alone are inflected; that is, undergo changes in termination to denote different cases, numbers, persons, &c.

§ 36. That we may determine to which of the above classes a word belongs, we must examine the relations it sustains to the rest of the sentence; and, as in different connections the same word often performs very different offices, it follows that in one sentence it may be one part of speech, and in another another, according to its application. The same word often appears, as

I. Noun and verb. Example, HEAT. "The heat is great"; here, being the name of something, it is a noun. "Heat the plate"; in this case it expresses an action, and is therefore a verb.

II. Adjective and noun. Example, DAMP. "A damp cellar"; in this expression it describes *cellar*, and is conse-

---

What are interjections? Give examples.

Give a sentence containing all the parts of speech, and mention the class to which the words respectively belong.

§ 35. Which of these parts of speech are inflected? What is the meaning of the term *to be inflected*?

§ 36. How are we to determine to which of these classes a word belongs? How may the same word be used in different sentences? As what, for instance, does the word *heat* appear? Give examples, and state what part of speech it is in each. As what two parts of speech does the word *damp* appear? Give examples. To what

quently an adjective. "Misfortune casts a damp over the spirits"; here, being the name of something, it is a noun.

III. Adjective and verb. Example, DRY. "A dry climate." "Dry your cloak."

IV. Adverb and conjunction. Example, AS. "As bright as the sun." The first *as*, being joined to the adjective *bright*, to express comparison, is an adverb; the second *as*, connecting parts of the sentence, is a conjunction.

V. Adverb and preposition. Example, UP. "Look up." "Up the hill." When followed by a noun or pronoun as its object, it is a preposition; when not, an adverb.

§ 37. Difficulty is often experienced in parsing the words *that* and *but*.

THAT, according to its use, may be a relative pronoun, an adjective pronoun, or a conjunction. When *who* or *which* can be used in its place, it is a relative; "He *that* (*who*) has a guilty conscience is not to be envied." When it points out a particular object, it is an adjective pronoun; "*That* fact can not be doubted." When it connects parts of a sentence, it is a conjunction; "I hope *that* you may succeed."

BUT is employed as an adverb, a preposition, and a conjunction. When *only* can be used in its stead, it is an adverb; "*But* (*only*) three were there." When equivalent to *except*, it is a preposition; "No one *but* (*except*) Napoleon could have conceived such an idea." In other cases it is a conjunction; "Cæsar was great intellectually, *but* not morally."

---

classes does *dry* belong? Give examples. As what two parts of speech does *up* appear? Under what circumstances is it a preposition, and under what an adverb?

§ 87. As what three parts of speech does the word *that* appear? How can we determine which it is? Give examples. As what is the word *but* employed? How can we determine what part of speech it is?

ORAL EXERCISE.

Mention what part of speech each of the following words is, and how you know it to be so:—

1. A violent storm at sea is often succeeded by a calm. 2. Calm your agitated mind. 3. How calm, how beautiful, comes on the still hour when storms are gone! 4. With dulcet songs the mothers still their babes. 5. The still of midnight is at hand. 6. Still water runs deep. 7. A still is a vessel used in the distillation of liquors. 8. Still one was absent. 9. My cheeks no longer did their color boast. 10. Fie! color not a glaring falsehood with feigned and specious excuses. 11. A little mind often dwells in a great body. 12. Little did the French Emperor anticipate the overthrow that awaited him in Russia. 13. Man wants but little here below, nor wants that little long. 14. The Dutch till their fields with such care that the whole of Holland resembles a highly cultivated garden. 15. Occupy till I come. 16. It is no worse to rob a man's till than to despoil him of his fair reputation by spreading slanderous reports. 17. The Arctic adventurers were imbedded in ice till the ensuing spring. 18. Past twelve o'clock, and yet the hermit sighs. 19. While the body was still hanging on the gallows, the queen and her train rode gaily past. 20. Past time never returns. 21. Spirit of the Past! look not so mournfully at me with thy great tearful eyes. 22. For me, for all, Death comes alike. 23. Men are never so ridiculous for the qualities they have as for those they affect to have. 24. Fenelon, hearing that his library was on fire, exclaimed, " Ah! God be praised that it is not some poor man's dwelling!" 25. No man should think so highly of himself as to imagine he can receive but little light from books, nor so meanly as to believe he can discover nothing but what is to be learned from them.

LESSON XII.

SENTENCES.

§ 38. ALL language consists of sentences.

A sentence is such an assemblage of words as makes complete sense; as, "Truth is eternal."

§ 39. Every sentence consists of two parts, subject and predicate.

The subject is that respecting which something is affirmed,

---

§ 38. Of what does all language consist? What is a sentence?
§ 39. Into what is every sentence divisible? What is meant by the subject? What,

asked, or exclaimed, or to which a command, an exhortation, or an entreaty is addressed. In the above example, *truth* is the subject.

The predicate is that which is affirmed, asked, or exclaimed, respecting the subject; or the command, exhortation, or entreaty addressed to it. In the above example, the words *is eternal* constitute the predicate.

The subject of a sentence may be ascertained by putting *who* or *what* before the leading verb. The answer to the question thus formed will be the subject, and the rest of the sentence the predicate. Thus:— "Truth is eternal." *What* is eternal? Answer, *truth*. *Truth* is therefore the subject, and *is eternal* the predicate.

In imperative sentences, that is, such as express a command, an exhortation, an entreaty, or permission, the subject is often understood; as, "Look not upon the wine when it is red." *Thou* understood is the subject; all the words expressed constitute the predicate.

§ 40. There are two kinds of subjects, grammatical and logical.

The grammatical subject is the name of the person or thing respecting which the affirmation is made, the question asked, &c., (see § 39) without any limiting terms. It usually consists of but one word, and is nominative to the leading verb in the sentence.

The logical subject consists of the name of the person or thing respecting which the affirmation is made, the question asked, &c., together with all the words that limit or describe it.

"The worst kind of lie is a half truth." *Kind* is the grammatical subject; *the worst kind of lie* is the logical subject; *is a half truth* is the predicate.

When there are no limiting words, the logical subject corresponds with the grammatical. Thus in the sentence, "Truth is eternal," *truth* is both the grammatical and the logical subject.

---

by the predicate? How may the subject of a sentence be ascertained? What is said of the subject of imperative sentences? Give an example.

§ 40. How many kinds of subjects are there? What are they called? What is the grammatical subject? Of how many words does it generally consist? What is the logical subject. Give an example of the two kinds of subjects? In what case does the logical subject correspond with the grammatical?

§ 41. Some sentences are susceptible of division into two or more leading parts, entirely independent of each other in construction and having distinct subjects and predicates. Such parts are called Members. The following sentence consists of two members: "A friend exaggerates a man's virtues; an enemy magnifies his crimes."

§ 42. Sentences may contain adjuncts, phrases, and clauses.

An Adjunct consists of a preposition and its regimen; as, "The appearance *of evil*"; "The blessings *of a kind God*".

A Phrase is a combination of words which separately have no connection, either in construction or sense, with other words in the sentence, but which, when taken together, convey a single idea and may be construed as a single word. *In short, in a word, on the contrary,* are phrases.

A Clause is a combination of words for the most part independent in construction of other words in the sentence, and by themselves incomplete in sense, generally introduced for the purpose of asserting some additional circumstance respecting the leading proposition.

§ 43. The clauses in most common use are eight in number; viz., Relative, Participial, Adverbial, Vocative, Adjective, Appositional, Causal, and Hypothetical.

A Relative Clause is one that contains a relative pronoun; as, "He *who lives to nature* rarely can be poor."

A Participial Clause is one that contains a participle; as, "*Awakened by the morning sun*, the birds carol their songs of gratitude."

An Adverbial Clause is one that performs the office of an adverb, generally expressing time, place, or manner; as, "There is a pleasure *in the pathless woods*."

---

§ 41. What is meant by the members of a sentence? Form a sentence containing two members.

§ 42. What may sentences contain? What is an adjunct? Give an example. What is a phrase? Give examples. What is a clause?

§ 43. Mention the clauses in most common use. Define each in turn, and give an example.

A Vocative Clause is one that contains the name of an object addressed; as, "Go to the ant, *thou sluggard!*"

An Adjective Clause is one that contains an adjective, as, "*Firm in his attachments*, Lafayette never forgot a friend."

An Appositional Clause is one that contains a noun or pronoun in apposition with some other substantive, that is, which refers to the same object and is similarly construed; as, "Down they go, *the brave young riders.*" *Riders*, referring to the same persons and being in the same construction as *they*, is in apposition with it.

A Causal Clause is one that indicates the motive with which, or the end for which, an action is done; as, "*To perfect his education*, he went to France."

A Hypothetical Clause is one that embodies a supposition; as, "*If thou hadst been here*, my brother had not died."

§ 44. These clauses, when used by themselves, do not make complete sense, as will be seen by making the trial in the sentences given above as examples. They are therefore called Dependent Clauses.

The leading clauses on which they depend, make sense by themselves, and are therefore called Independent Clauses Thus, in the sentence, " To perfect his education, he went to France ", *to perfect his education* is a dependent, *he went to France* an independent, clause.

§ 45. As regards their signification, sentences are divided into four classes; viz., Declarative, Interrogative, Imperative, and Exclamatory.

A Declarative Sentence is one that declares something, as, " It rains."

Declarative sentences constitute the greater part of written language.

---

§ 44. What general name is given to these clauses? Why? What is meant by an Independent clause? In the sentence, "To perfect his education, he went to France" select the dependent and the independent clause.

§ 45. As regards their signification, how are sentences divided? What is a declarative sentence Give an example. What is an interrogative sentence? Give an example

An Interrogative Sentence is one that asks a question; as, " Does it rain ? "

Interrogative sentences are generally introduced by the interrogative pronouns, *who, which,* or *what;* or, by the auxiliaries, *do, am, have, shall, may,* &c.; as, " Who is there ! " " What is truth ! " " Am I right ! " " May we go ? "

An Imperative Sentence is one that expresses a command, an exhortation, an entreaty, or permission; as, " Let it rain.'

Imperative sentences are generally introduced by a verb in the imperative mood, *let* being often used for that purpose; as, " Go in peace; " " Let him arise."

As already remarked, the subject of an imperative sentence is often understood; thus, in the above sentences, *thou* understood is the subject.

An Exclamatory Sentence is one that exclaims something; as " How it rains ! "

The adverb *how* and the adjective pronoun *what* are often used to introduce exclamatory sentences; as, " How dead the vegetable kingdom lies ! " " What a bereavement ! "

It is a nice point, in the case of some sentences introduced by or containing the word *what*, to determine whether they are exclamatory or interrogative; as, " Unhappy man that I am, what have I done ! " In such cases, judge from the context whether an answer is expected: if so, the sentence is interrogative; if not, exclamatory.

§ 46. As regards their construction, sentences are divided into two classes, Simple and Compound.

Simple Sentences are such as have but one member. (See § 41.)

Compound Sentences are such as have two or more members.

How are interrogative sentences generally introduced? What is an imperative sentence? Give an example. How are imperative sentences generally introduced? What verb is often used for this purpose? What is said of the subject of these sentences? What is an exclamatory sentence? Give an example. With what words are exclamatory sentences often introduced? With what are they sometimes liable to be confounded? What is the rule for deciding when a sentence is exclamatory and when interrogative?

§ 46. As regards their construction, now are sentences divided? What are simple sentences? What are compound sentences? What may a simple sentence contain ?

A sentence may be simple, and yet contain any of the above dependent clauses. It may have two grammatical subjects connected by a conjunction, or a compound predicate, and yet be a simple sentence; as, "Humility and modesty are cardinal virtues, and cannot be too much cultivated." A compound sentence must have two members wholly independent of each other in construction, each having its own subject and predicate. A slight change in the above example will make it a compound sentence, the difference between the two consisting not in meaning, but simply in form; thus, "Humility and modesty are cardinal virtues; they can not be too much cultivated."

ORAL EXERCISE

Point out the sentences which compose the following extract, and state with regard to each, whether it is declarative, interrogative, imperative, or exclamatory; also, whether simple or compound. If simple, state what is the subject (both grammatical and logical), and what the predicate. Analyze the compound sentences into their members, and state the subject and predicate of each.

Point out and name any of the above clauses that may occur, and mention the leading clause on which each depends.

EXAMPLE.—The first stanza given below constitutes a simple imperative sentence. The first line is an independent clause, inasmuch as it makes sense by itself. The second line is a participial clause, since it contains the participle *filled*. The last two lines constitute an adverbial clause, in which is embraced the relative clause *that beat the murmuring walks like autumn rain*. *Thou* understood, being nominative to the leading verb *let*, is the grammatical subject; and the logical also, inasmuch as there are no limiting terms. The whole stanza, as it stands, is the predicate.

THE CROWDED STREET.

Let me move slowly through the street,
　Filled with an ever-shifting train,
　Amid the sound of steps that beat
　The murmuring walks like autumn rain.

What must a compound sentence contain? Give an example of a simple sentence, and show how, by a slight change, it may be converted into a compound one.

How fast the flitting figures come!
   The mild, the fierce, the stony face;
Some bright with thoughtless smiles, and some
   Where secret tears have left their trace.

They pass, to toil, to strife, to rest;
   To halls in which the feast is spread;
To chambers where the funeral guest
   In silence sits beside the dead.

And some to happy homes repair,
   Where children, pressing cheek to cheek,
With mute caresses shall declare
   The tenderness they cannot speak.

And some, who walk in calmness here,
   Shall shudder as they reach the door,
Where one who made their dwelling dear,
   Its flower, its light, is seen no more.

Youth, with pale cheek and slender frame,
   And dreams of greatness in thine eye,
Goest thou to build an early name,
   Or early in the task to die?

Keen son of trade, with eager brow,
   Who is now fluttering in thy snare?
Thy golden fortunes—tower they now,
   Or melt the glittering spires in air?

Who of this crowd to-night shall tread
   The dance till daylight gleams again?
Who sorrow o'er the untimely dead?
   Who writhe in throes of mortal pain?

Some, famine-struck, shall think how long
   The cold, dark hours, how slow the light;
And some, who flaunt amid the throng,
   Shall hide in dens of shame to-night.

Each where his tasks or pleasures call,
   They pass, and heed each other not.
There is who heeds, who holds them all
   In His large love and boundless thought.

Those struggling tides of life that seem
   In wayward, aimless course to tend,
Are eddies of the mighty stream
   That rolls to its appointed end.

4

LESSON XIII

CAPITAL LETTERS.

§ 47 Letters are divided into two classes, known as Small Letters (a, b, 𝒶, 𝒷) and Capitals (A, B, 𝒜, 𝐵). The former constitute the great bulk of all kinds of printed or written matter. Capitals, however, are employed in certain cases at the commencement of words, for the purpose of attracting special attention.

It was formerly the custom, both in writing and printing, to begin every noun with a capital, and such is still the practice in the German language. This custom, however, conducing to no useful end, has very properly been laid aside; and at the present day the use of capitals is confined to such cases as fall under the following rules.

RULES FOR THE USE OF CAPITAL LETTERS.

§ 48. RULE I.—Begin with a capital the first word of every sentence.

§ 49. RULE II.—Begin with capitals all proper nouns, and titles of office, honor, and respect; as, *Rome, Myrtle Avenue, Mr. Chairman, Dr. Franklin, Gen. Washington, dear Sir.*

§ 50. Under this head fall adjectives, as well as common nouns, when joined to proper nouns for the purpose of expressing a title; as, Alexander the *Great,* Charles the *Bald, King* William, *Good Queen* Bess.

---

§ 47. How are letters divided? Which constitute the greater part of all printed matter? Where and for what purpose are capitals employed? What custom formerly prevailed?

§ 48. Repeat Rule I.

§ 49. Repeat Rule II. Give examples.*

§ 50. What adjectives and common nouns fall under this rule?

---

* NOTE.—Hereafter, when an example is given in illustration of a definition or rule, the student is requested to repeat it without its being required by a special question.

§ 51. When the title is employed without the proper name, if used in addressing a person, commence it with a capital; if not, in which case it will be preceded by the article *the*, commence it with a small letter. Thus: "O *King*, live forever!"—"The *king* soon after resigned his crown." When used without reference to a particular individual, such titles become common nouns and must commence with small letters; as, "A *king* is no better than his subjects."

§ 52. The same principle applies to the words *mountain, river, gulf*, &c. When joined to proper nouns, either with or without a preposition between, they must begin with capitals; as, *the Rocky Mountains, the Mississippi River, Hudson's Bay, the Gulf of Guinea, the Cape of Good Hope, the Isle of Man*. When used by themselves, though with reference to particular objects, they must commence with small letters; as, "These *mountains* are covered with snow."

§ 53. The words *North, East, South*, and *West*, and their compounds *North-east*, &c., when nouns, referring to certain districts of country or the people that inhabit them, begin with capitals; when nouns, referring to a point of the compass, and generally when adjectives, they commence with small letters. Thus: "The *South* generally opposed the bill."—"The wind is from the *south*."—"Florida is *south-west* of New York."

§ 54. *Heaven*, used in the singular and signifying the abode of the blest, must commence with a capital; as, "Let *Heaven* be your goal." In the plural, it signifies the sky and begins with a small letter; as, "The *heavens* were overcast."

§ 55. The names of the months and the days of the weeks must commence with capitals; those of the seasons, with small letters; as, *May, Sunday, summer*.

§ 56. RULE III.—Begin with capitals all adjectives formed from proper nouns; as *Roman, Spanish, Elizabethan*.

---

§ 51. What rule applies to the title when used without the proper name? When used without reference to a particular individual, what do such titles become, and how must they commence?

§ 52. To what words does this same principle apply?

§ 53. State the rule that applies to the words *North, East, South, West*, and their compounds.

§ 54. How must the word *Heaven* commence? In the plural number, what does it signify, and how must it commence?

§ 55. How must the names of the months, the days of the weeks, and the seasons, commence?

§ 56. Repeat Rule III. What is said of the usage of the French language on this point?

In this respect the usage of the French language differs from ours.

§ 57. Under this head fall adjectives denoting a sect or religion, whether formed from proper nouns or not; as, *Catholic, Protestant, Universalist.*

§ 58. A few adjectives derived from proper nouns, used merely to express a quality, without reference to the names from which they are derived, begin with small letters. Thus, *stentorian*, though derived from Stentor, a fabulous personage noted for the strength of his lungs, is now used as simply synonymous with *loud* and does not commence with a capital. The word *heavenly* is another case in point. When used in the sense of *very great, more than earthly*, it must begin with a small letter; an initial capital is proper only when it means, literally, *pertaining to Heaven.* We speak of the "*heavenly* beauty of a landscape"; but, " the *Heavenly* rest in store for believers".

§ 59. RULE IV.—Begin with capitals common nouns when spoken to, or spoken of, in a direct and lively manner, as persons.

In these cases, usage is by no means uniform. In the inferior kinds of personification, for instance where sex merely is attributed to inanimate objects, a small letter must be used; as, " The *sun* sheds his beams upon the earth." A capital is proper only in the more vivid and glowing personifications.

§ 60. RULE V.—Begin with a capital the first word of every line of poetry; as,

"Swans sing before they die; 'twere no bad thing,
Should certain persons die before they sing."

§ 61. The only exception to this rule is in the case of humorous poetry, when a word is divided at the end of a line, and a portion of it is carried to the beginning of the next verse: in this case the syllables thus carried over must not commence with a capital. As,

"Pyrrhus, you tempt a danger high,
When you would steal from angry lioness her cubs."

---

§ 57. To what other adjectives does this rule apply?

§ 58. State the rule applicable to a few adjectives derived from proper names, but now used merely to express a quality. Illustrate this principle in the case of the words *stentorian* and *heavenly.*

§ 59. Repeat Rule IV. In what cases is it not applicable?

§ 60. Repeat Rule V.

§ 61. What is the only exception to this rule?

§ 62. RULE VI.—Begin with capitals all appellations of the Deity, and the personal pronouns *he* and *thou* when standing for His name.

Under this head are embraced adjectives which form part of the titles applied to the Deity; as, "the *Eternal* One", "the *Supreme Being*"

§ 63. It must be observed that several of the divine appellations are also used as common nouns, and in that case, of course, commence with small letters. This principle is illustrated in the following sentences by the use of the words *god* and *providence:* "The *gods* of the heathen bow before our *God.*"—"Trust in *Providence.*"—"The *providence* [foreseeing care] of God directs every event."

§ 64. RULE VII.—Begin with a capital the first word of a direct quotation; that is, one that forms a complete sentence by itself and is not connected with what precedes by *that, if,* or any other conjunction, as, "Remember the old maxim: 'Honesty is the best policy.'"

In such a sentence as this, "He has come to the conclusion that 'honesty is the best policy'", it would be wrong to commence *honesty* with a capital, because the quotation is introduced by *that.*

§ 65. RULE VIII.—Begin with a capital every noun, adjective, and verb, in the titles of books and headings of chapters; as, "Hervey's '*Meditations* among the *Tombs*'".

In advertisements, handbills, &c., it is customary to begin with capitals the names of the principal objects, to which it is desired to draw attention.

§ 66. RULE IX.—Begin with capitals words that are the leading subjects of chapters, articles, or paragraphs.

Thus, when a word is being defined, it is proper to commence it with a capital; as in § 42.

This rule leaves much to the judgment of the writer. It is not well

---

§ 62. Repeat Rule VI. What adjectives fall under this rule?

§ 63. How are several of the divine appellations also used? In this case, how must they commence? Illustrate this principle.

§ 64. Repeat Rule VII. If the quotation is introduced by *that*, how must it commence?

§ 65. Repeat Rule VIII. What is the custom in advertisements, hand-bills, &c.?

§ 66. Repeat Rule IX. What is said about interpreting this rule too liberally? When there is doubt, what is the safest course?

to interpret it too liberally, as has been done by some transcendentalists and imitators of German philosophers, who speak of the *Me* and the *Not Me*, *Entity*, the *Good*, the *Beautiful*, and the like, checkering the page with plentiful capitals as if it were a turgid advertisement. This is bad taste. Wherever there is any reasonable doubt, use a small letter.

§ 67. RULE X.—The pronoun *I*, and the interjection *O*, must always be written with capitals.

§ 68. Observe the difference between the interjections *O* and *oh* The former is used only before the names of objects addressed or invoked, is not immediately followed by an exclamation-point (!) and must always be a capital; the latter is used by itself to denote different emotions of the mind, has an exclamation-point after it, and begins with a small letter, except at the commencement of a sentence.

§ 69. RULE XI.—Begin with capitals words denoting well-known events, historical eras, noted written instruments, extraordinary physical phenomena, and the like; as, the *American Revolution*, the *Middle Ages*, the *Magna Charta*, the *Gulf Stream*, the *Aurora Borealis*.

The object of beginning such words with capitals is to enable the reader to distinguish at once between the individual objects they represent and common nouns of the same form and appearance. This must be done in all cases where there is liability of confusion. Thus in the sentence, "Then cometh the Judgment", if we mean the Day of Judgment, *judgment* must begin with a capital, or the writer's meaning may be misunderstood.

§ 70. Use a small letter in all cases where one of these eleven rules does not apply. When in doubt, use a small letter.

§ 71. In printed matter, a style of character formed like capitals, but smaller, is employed for running titles, captions of chapters and paragraphs (see § 212), &c.; as, A, B, C. These are known as SMALL CAPITALS.

---

§ 67. Repeat Rule X.

§ 68. What interjections must not be confounded? What must be observed with respect to *O*? What, respecting *oh*?

§ 69. Repeat Rule XI. What is gained by following this rule? Illustrate its application in the sentence " Then cometh the Judgment."

§ 70. When none of these rules apply, what must be used?

§ 71. In printed matter, what style of character is used for running titles, &c.?

LESSON XIV

EXERCISE ON CAPITALS.*

In the following sentences, apply the rules given in the preceding lesson. Where a capital is improperly used, substitute a small letter.

UNDER § 48. act well thy Part. avoid the appearance of Evil. watch and Pray. labor Conquers all Things. what a heart-rending Scene! has honor left the world? thou art mortal. truth Is mighty. whither can I fly? what a disappointment!

UNDER § 49. charles martel defeated the saracens. what has become of the mohegans, the pequots, the iroquois, the mohawks, and the hundred other powerful tribes that lived east (*see* § 53) of the mississippi when our fathers landed at plymouth and jamestown? iceland belongs to denmark. sir william herschel was born in 1738, at hanover, in germany.

UNDER § 50. edward the elder succeeded his father, alfred the great, on the throne of england. john lackland usurped the crown of his Brother, richard The lion-hearted, during the absence of the latter in the holy land.

UNDER § 51, 52. great king, forgive me. the king hastily took horse and fled to london. An emperor, after all, is but a man. dukes, earls, counts, and Knights, flocked to the crusades (*see* § 69). The amazon is the largest River in the World. mountains and oceans shall waste away. The pyrenees form the Boundary between france and Spain. These Mountains are infested by daring Banditti.

UNDER § 53, 54, 55. as far as the east is from the west, as far as heaven is from Earth, so far is Vice from Virtue, Truth from Falsehood. our winter consists of three months, december, january, and february. The senator has spoken for the west; let him understand that the west is capable of speaking for itself. an east wind often brings a Storm. Last tuesday the wind was north-west.

UNDER § 56, 57. most of the french peasants belong to the roman catholic church. The reign of queen anne is generally admitted to have been the augustan age of english literature. in civilization and Refinement, christian lands far surpass mohammedan and pagan countries.

UNDER § 58. The north-american indians endure the tortures of their

---

* NOTE TO THE TEACHER.—The portions of this book headed EXERCISE can be either recited orally or written out, as the teacher may prefer. The latter method, however, in the author's opinion, is attended with great advantages over the former, which will more than make up for the additional time it may consume. When required to write these tasks, the student is not only likely to receive a much more durable impression of the principles illustrated, but is at the same time exercised in orthography and penmanship, and forms, from the close observation of words thus required, an invaluable habit of precision.

Enemies with Stoical fortitude. beau brummell's tastes were decidedly epicurean. a Platonic attachment subsisted between petrarch and laura. A long face and puritanical demeanor are no proofs of a man's piety. diesbach discovered the process of making Prussian blue.

UNDER § 59, 60. Fiercely grim war unfolds his flag. The moon can infuse no warmth into her rays.

> honor, thou blood-stained god (§ 63)! at whose red altar
> sit war and homicide, oh (§ 68) to what madness
> will insult drive thy votaries!

> humility herself, divinely mild,
> sublime religion's meek and modest child.

> peace, thy olive wand extend,
> and bid wild war his ravage end,
> man with brother man to meet,
> and as a brother kindly Greet.

UNDER § 61.

> Her cheeks were ros-
> y, and so was her nose;
> And her hat
> Was of sat-
> in, and dirty at that.

UNDER § 62, 63. how comprehensive is the providence of god; he orders all things for his Creatures' Good. those who trust in providence He will not desert. omnipotent creator, all-wise, eternal being, thou keepest us from day to day! In the latter days the comforter shall come.

UNDER § 64. What sound advice is conveyed in Bion's Maxim: "know Thyself." If "a tree is known by its Fruit", as our saviour said, what must we think of uncharitable christians?

UNDER § 65. Burke's "philosophical inquiry into the origin of our ideas of the sublime and beautiful", and alison's "essays on the nature and principles of taste", are standard text-books on the subjects of which they respectively treat. sismondi's "historical view of the literature of the south of europe" is a work well worthy of careful study.

UNDER § 67, 68. i banished—i, a roman senator! beware, o treacherous people! i have reasoned, i have threatened, i have prayed; and yet thou art not moved, o hard-hearted man. oh for a lodge in some vast wilderness! whither, oh whither can i go?

UNDER § 69. the wars of the roses desolated england between the years 1455 and 1485. the invincible armada, fitted out by the spaniards against england was the largest naval armament that europe ever saw. the flight of mohammed from mecca, known in history as the hegira, took place 622 A. D., and is the era from which the arabians and persians still compute their time. the norman conquest was the means of introducing chivalry and the feudal system into England.

PART II.

PUNCTUATION.

LESSON XV.

PRINCIPLES OF THE ART.

§ 72. PUNCTUATION is the art of dividing written language by points, in order that the relations of words and clauses may be plainly seen, and their meaning be readily understood.

In spoken language, these relations are sufficiently indicated by the pauses and inflections of the voice; but as written language has no such aids, it is necessary to supply the deficiency with arbitrary marks.

§ 73. The ancients originally wrote their manuscripts without marks or divisions of any kind. Points are said to have been first used about 200 B. C., by Aristophanes, a grammarian of Alexandria, but did not come into general use for several centuries. The modern system of punctuation was invented by Manutius, a learned printer who flourished in Venice at the commencement of the sixteenth century. To him we are indebted for developing the leading principles of

---

§ 72. What is Punctuation? How are the relations of words and clauses indicated in spoken language?

§ 73. How did the ancients write their manuscripts? When and by whom were points invented? How long before they came into general use? By whom was the modern system devised? When and where did the inventor live?

the art, though in some of their details they have since that time undergone considerable modification.

§ 74. Punctuation does not generally receive in educational institutions the attention its importance demands; and hence, in the case of otherwise well-informed persons, there is too often a lack of accurate and practical information on this subject. Even those who have made literary pursuits a profession, have regarded this important art as altogether beneath their notice, and leave their manuscripts to be supplied with points entirely at the discretion of the printer. As there is no man at whose hands business or friendship does not require an occasional letter, so there is none that ought not to be able, by a proper use of points, to make his meaning intelligible; particularly since the art is simple in itself, is founded on the principles of grammar, and often admirably illustrates the latter science.

§ 75. Punctuation not only serves to make an author's meaning plain, but often saves it from being entirely misconceived. There are many cases in which a change of points completely alters the sentiment.

An English statesman once took advantage of this fact, to free himself from an embarrassing position. Having charged an officer of government with dishonesty, he was required by Parliament, under a heavy penalty, publicly to retract the accusation in the House of Commons. At the appointed time he appeared with a written recantation, which he read aloud as follows: "I said he was dishonest; it is true; and I am sorry for it." This was satisfactory; but what was the surprise of Parliament, the following day, to see the retraction printed in the papers thus: "I said he was dishonest; it is true, and I am sorry for it!" By a simple transposition of the comma and semicolon, the ingenious slanderer represented himself to the country, not only as having made no recantation, but even as having reiterated the charge in the very face of Parliament.

§ 76. It is frequently objected to the study of Punctua

---

§ 74. What is said of the general neglect of punctuation? Why ought a knowledge of the art to be possessed by all?

§ 75. What does punctuation often prevent? How may a complete change of sentiment frequently be made? Repeat an anecdote illustrative of this fact.

tion that good usage differs widely in this respect, and it is therefore impossible to lay down any fixed rules on the sub ject. To a certain extent it is true that usage differs. Punctuation is an art in which there is great room for the exercise of taste; and tastes will be found to vary in this, as well as in every thing else. Yet it is equally true that, as an art, it is founded on certain great and definite principles; and that, while considerable latitude is allowed in the application of these, whatever directly violates them is wrong and inadmissible. As well might it be argued that the study of rhetoric is unnecessary, because different authors use different styles of expression; or, that there are no grammatical principles from which to deduce rules, because even in celebrated authors we have frequent instances of false syntax. The faults of others, whether in grammar or Punctuation, should not be seized on by any one as an excuse for his own ignorance; but should rather lead him to redoubled diligence, that he may avoid the rock on which they have split.

§ 77. Old grammarians taught that points were used merely as aids to reading; and that, when the pupil came to a comma, he should stop till he could count *one*, when to a semicolon, till he could say *one, two*, &c.; and some writers, in accordance with this principle, use points, without reference to sentential structure, wherever they wish the reader to pause, determining what mark is to be employed solely by the length of the pause required. From such a system grave errors necessarily result. However convenient it may be to give such instructions to a child when beginning to read, it will soon be found that, if he remembers them and carries them out, he will not only constantly violate the principles of elocution, but will for the most part fail to understand the meaning of the sentences he enunciates. Punctuation is entirely

---

§ 76. What objection is frequently made to the study of punctuation? Does usage differ? For what is there great room? On what, nevertheless, is the art founded? Is there any ground for the objection?

§ 77. What did old grammarians teach with regard to points? What will result from carrying out such a system? What connection is there between punctuation and

independent of elocution. Its primary object is to bring out the writer's meaning, and so far only is it an aid to the reader. Rhetorical pauses occur as frequently where points are not found as where they are; and for a learner to depend for these on commas and semicolons would effectually prevent his becoming a good reader, just as the use of such marks wherever a cessation of the voice is required would completely obscure a writer's meaning. This may be seen by comparing a passage properly punctuated with the same passage pointed as its delivery would require.

PROPERLY PUNCTUATED. The people of the United States have justly supposed that the policy of protecting their industry against foreign legislation and foreign industry was fully settled, not by a single act, but by repeated and deliberate acts of government, performed at distant and frequent intervals.

PUNCTUATED FOR DELIVERY. The people of the United States, have justly supposed, that the policy, of protecting their industry, against foreign legislation and foreign industry, was fully settled; not, by a single act; but, by repeated and deliberate acts of government, performed, at distant and frequent intervals.

From a paragraph punctuated like the last, little meaning can be gathered.

§ 78. Let the following principles with regard to Punctuation be constantly borne in mind.

I. Points must be placed without reference to rhetorical pauses. In the expression *yes, sir*, if we consulted delivery we would place no point after *yes*; grammar, however, requires a comma there.

II. The principal use of points is to separate words and clauses, and indicate the degree of connection between them. Thus, clauses between which the connection is close must be separated by commas; those in which it is more remote by semicolons.

III. Points are also used to indicate what part of speech

---

elocution? How does a passage properly punctuated compare with the same passage pointed for delivery?

§ 78. What must not be consulted in the use of points? What is the principal use of points? What else are they employed to indicate? Illustrate this with the word

a word is. Thus, *shame* is in most sentences a noun or verb; if used as an interjection, it has an exclamation-point after it, to denote the fact—*shame!*

IV. Another office they perform by showing to what class a sentence belongs. Thus, "George is well," followed by a period, is a declarative sentence, asserting that George is in good health: followed by an interrogation-point, it is an interrogative sentence, and implies belief that he is well together with an inquiry whether it is not so; in other words, it is equivalent to "George is well; is he not?" This important difference of meaning can be conveyed in no other way than by the use respectively of the period and interrogation-point.

V. Points are also employed to indicate a sudden transition or break in the construction or meaning. Thus, where a sentence is suddenly interrupted or broken off, a dash is placed; as, "Woe to the destroyer! woe to the ———."

VI. Finally, they are used to denote the omission of words. Such is the office of the commas in the following sentence: "Reading maketh a full man; conference, a ready man; writing, an exact man." The verb *maketh* being left out in the last two clauses, commas are inserted to denote the omissions.

VII. Never introduce a point unless you have some positive rule for so doing. Whenever there is any reasonable doubt as to the propriety of employing the comma, do not use it. The tendency of punctuators at the present day is to introduce too many points.

VIII. Be guided by rules and principles, no matter how many or how few points they may require. Sentences may be so constructed as to need points after almost every word; while others, even of some length, require no division at all.

---

shame. What other office do they perform? Show this with the sentence, "George is well." What do they frequently indicate in the construction or meaning? What else are they used to denote? When there is doubt as to the propriety of employing a comma, what is the safest course? What is the tendency of punctuators at the present day? What is stated under the eighth head respecting the frequency and paucity of

IX. Remember that "circumstances alter cases"; and that, therefore, a mode of pointing which is accurate in a short sentence may not, in a long one, be either tasteful or even strictly correct. We shall revert to this subject from time to time hereafter.

§ 79. The characters used in Punctuation are as follows:—

PERIOD,	.	SEMICOLON,	;
INTERROGATION-POINT,	?	COMMA,	,
EXCLAMATION-POINT,	!	DASH,	—
COLON,	:	PARENTHESES,	( )
		BRACKETS,	[ ]

We shall proceed to take these up in turn. Careful attention to the rules, and particularly to the examples that illustrate them, will, it is believed, enable the writer to punctuate with propriety every sentence that can occur. If, after diligent trial, he finds himself unable to do this in the case of any sentence of his own composition, he is advised to look over it carefully, to see if he has not violated some principle of rhetoric or grammar. Punctuating often leads to the detection of such errors.

LESSON XVI.

THE PERIOD.

§ 80. The word PERIOD is derived from the Greek language, and means a *circuit*. This name is given to the full stop (.), because it is placed after a complete *circuit* of words. The period is found in manuscripts of a comparatively early date, and was in use before any other point.

---

points in a sentence? According to the ninth head, what is to be regarded in punctuating a sentence?

§ 79. Name the characters used in punctuation. What advice is given to the writer, when he finds difficulty in punctuating a sentence of his own composition?

§ 80. Give the derivation and meaning of the word *period*. Why is the full stop so called? When did the period come into use?

§ 81. RULE I.—A period must be placed after every declarative and imperative sentence; as, "Honesty is the best policy."—"Fear God."

These sentences having been defined in § 45, it is presumed no difficulty will be experienced in recognizing them, or in determining how much of a paragraph must be taken to compose them. As soon as a passage makes complete sense, if it is at the same time independent of what follows in construction and not closely connected with it in meaning, the sentence is complete; and, if it be declarative or imperative, must close with a period.

§ 82. The degree of closeness in the connection is a matter which must be left somewhat to individual judgment; and this degree, it may be remarked, is often the only criterion which a writer has to guide him in deciding between periods and colons, colons and semicolons, semicolons and commas. No rule can be laid down that will cover every case; but one or two principles may be stated, as applicable to most of the cases that occur in practice.

I. Words, clauses, and members, united by a conjunction, are regarded as more closely connected than those between which the conjunction is omitted. Thus: "Truth is the basis of every virtue. Its precepts should be religiously obeyed." It is not improper to divide this passage into two distinct sentences, and to separate them with a period. If, however, we introduce a conjunction between them, we make the connection closer, and cannot use a higher point than a semicolon. "Truth is the basis of every virtue; and its precepts should be religiously obeyed."

II. A clause containing a relative pronoun is more closely connected with the one containing the antecedent, than the same clause would be if a personal or demonstrative pronoun were substituted for the relative. "At this critical moment, Murat was ordered to charge with his indomitable cavalry; which movement having been performed with his usual gallantry, the issue of the battle was no longer doubtful." By changing *which* to *this*, we diminish the connection between the two parts, and may punctuate differently. "At this critical moment, Murat was ordered to charge with his indomitable cavalry. This movement &c."

---

§ 81. Repeat Rule I. How is it determined when a sentence is complete?

§ 82. What is said of the degree of closeness in the connection? What effect does the omission of a conjunction between words, clauses, and members, have on the closeness of the connection? Does a relative or a demonstrative pronoun institute a closer connection between the parts of a sentence. Illustrate this. How does a portion of a

III. A portion of a sentence that has a distinct subject of its own is less closely connected with the rest, than such a part as depends for its subject on some preceding clause. Thus, in the sentence, "Truth is the basis of every virtue; and its precepts should be religiously obeyed," a semicolon is placed after *virtue*, because a new nominative, *precepts*, is introduced into the final member. If we keep *truth* as the subject, the connection will be closer, and we must substitute a comma for the semicolon after *virtue;* as, "Truth is the basis of every virtue, and should be cherished by all."

It follows from the above remarks that it is not proper to place a period immediately before a conjunction which closely connects what follows with what precedes. This is frequently done in the translation of the Scriptures, where we have verse after verse commencing with *and;* but it is not authorized by good modern usage. In such cases, either the passage so introduced ought to form part of the preceding sentence, and be separated from it only by a colon or semicolon; or else, if this is impracticable on account of the great length or intricacy it would involve, the following sentence should be remodelled in such a way as to commence with some other word. These remarks apply to all conjunctions that *form a decided connection* between the parts; such as merely signify *to continue the narrative*, and imply no connection with what precedes, may without impropriety introduce a new sentence.

As the substance of the preceding paragraph, we may lay down the following general rule, remembering that there are occasional exceptions:—
A sentence should not commence with the conjunctions *and, for*, or *however;* but may do so with *but, now*, and *moreover*.

EXAMPLES.

"Friendship is not a source of pleasure only; it is also a source of duty: and of the responsibilities it imposes we should never be unmindful." Here *and* intimately connects the two members, and a period must not precede it.

"There is only one species of misery which friendship cannot comfort, the misery of atrocious guilt; for there are no pangs but those of conscience that sympathy does not alleviate." Here *for* implies so close a connection that a period is inadmissible before it.

---

sentence containing a distinct subject of its own compare in closeness of connection with one that depends for its subject on some preceding clause? Give an example.
Where is it improper to place a period? In what book do we frequently find sentences commencing with *and?* What two remedies are suggested for such cases? To what conjunctions do these remarks apply? What conjunctions may with propriety commence a new sentence? Is it ever proper to begin a sentence with *and?* In what case?

'Then cried they all again, saying, Not this man, but Barabbas Now Barabbas was a robber." In this sentence it is right to precede *now* with a period, because this word does not imply connection, but means simply *to continue the narrative, to go on.*
"Domitian was a low, cruel, and sensual wretch, whose highest pleasure consisted in maiming helpless flies, whose mind was paralyzed by sloth, whose soul was surfeited with disgusting gluttony, whose heart was dead to every generous impulse, and whose conscience was seared by crime. And this was the emperor of Rome, the controller of the world's destinies." Here a period may be placed before *and.* Sentences in which, as in this, *and* does not closely connect, but is simply equivalent to *now,* as used in the preceding example, constitute an exception to the general rule, and admit a period before *and.*

§ 83. From Remark II. it follows that a period must not separate a relative clause from its antecedent. It would, therefore, be wrong to substitute periods for semicolons in the following sentence: "There are men whose powers operate in leisure and in retirement, and whose intellectual vigor deserts them in conversation; whom merriment confuses, and objection disconcerts; whose bashfulness restrains their exertion, and suffers them not to speak till the time of speaking is past."

§ 84. RULE II.—A period must be placed after every abbreviated word; as, *Dr. Geo. F. Johnson, F. R. S.*

§ 85. The period in this case merely indicates the abbreviation, and does not take the place of other stops. The punctuation must be the same as if no such period were employed; as, "My clerk put the letter in the P. O.; there can be no mistake about it." "Horace Jones, jr., M.D., LL.D."

§ 86. When, however, an abbreviated word ends a sentence, only one period must be used; for an example, see the close of the preceding paragraph.

§ 87. Under this head fall Roman capitals and small letters, when used for figures; as, "Charles I. was the son of James I."

§ 88. An important exception to this rule must be noted. When an abbreviated word is of such constant occurrence that, without reference to the word from which it comes, it is itself considered as a component part of our language, no period is placed after it. Thus, it would be wrong to put a period after *eve* abbreviated from *evening*, or *hack* from *hackney.*

---

§ 83. What must a period in no case separate?
§ 84. Repeat Rule II.
§ 85. In this case what does the period indicate? Must it take the place of other stops?
§ 86. In what case, however, is there an exception?
§ 87. When must the Roman capitals and small letters be followed by periods, under this rule?
§ 88. What large class of abbreviated words constitute an exception to this rule?

§ 89. So, when the first syllable of a Christian or given name is used, not as an abbreviation of the latter, but as a familiar substitute for it, no period must be employed; as, "Ben Jonson."

For a comprehensive list of abbreviations, see Table at the close of the volume.

EXERCISE I.

Insert periods in the following sentences, wherever required by the above rules:—

A graphic description of this scene may be found in Gibbon's Hist of the Dec and Fall of the Rom Em, vol ii, chap 5

Mrs Felicia Hemans was born in Liverpool, Eng, and died at Dublin, 1835, A D

Messrs G Longman and Co have received a note from the Cor Sec of the Nat Shipwreck Soc, informing them of the loss of one of their vessels off the N E coast of S A, at 8 P M, on the 20th of Jan

James VI of Scotland became Jas I of England

EXERCISE II.

In the following extract all the stops are inserted except periods. The pupil is required to introduce these points wherever they are needed, and to begin each new sentence with a capital.

THE GROTTO OF ADELSBURG.

"This great natural curiosity lies about thirty miles from the Adriatic, back in the Friuli Mountains, near the province of Cariola we arrived at the nearest tavern at three in the afternoon; and, subscribing our names upon the magistrate's books, took four guides and the requisite number of torches, and started on foot a half hour's walk brought us to a large rushing stream, which, after turning a mill, disappeared with violence into the mouth of a broad cavern sunk in the base of a mountain, an iron gate opened on the nearest side; and, lighting our torches, we received an addition of half a dozen men to our party of guides, and entered we descended for ten or fifteen minutes through a capacious gallery of rock, up to the ankles in mud, and feeling continually the drippings exuding from the roof, till by the echoing murmurs of dashing water we found ourselves approaching the bed of a subterraneous river. We soon emerged in a vast cavern, whose height, though we had twenty torches, was lost in the darkness the river rushed dimly below us, at the depth of perhaps fifty feet, partially illuminated by a row of lamps, hung on a slight wooden bridge by which we were to cross to the opposite side.

"We came after a while to a deeper descent, which opened into a magnificent and spacious hall it is called 'the ball-room', and is used as

---

§ 89. What exception refers to certain Christian or given names?

such once a year, on the occasion of a certain Illyrian feast. The floor has been cleared of stalagmites, the roof and sides are ornamented beyond all art with glittering spars, a natural gallery with a balustrade of stalactites contains the orchestra, and side-rooms are all around where supper might be laid and dressing-rooms offered in the style of a palace. I can imagine nothing more magnificent than such a scene a literal description of it even would read like a fairy tale.

"A little farther on, we came to a perfect representation of a waterfall the impregnated water had fallen on a declivity, and, with a slightly ferruginous tinge of yellow, poured over in the most natural resemblance to a cascade. After a rain we proceeded for ten or fifteen minutes, and found a small room like a chapel, with a pulpit in which stood one of the guides, who gave us, as we stood beneath, an Illyrian exhortation there was a sounding-board above, and I have seen pulpits in old Gothic churches that seemed, at a first glance, to have less method in their architecture. The last thing we reached was the most beautiful. From the cornice of a long gallery hung a thin, translucent sheet of spar, in the graceful and waving folds of a curtain; with a lamp behind, the hand could be seen through any part of it it was perhaps twenty feet in length, and hung five or six feet down from the roof of the cavern the most singular part of it was the fringe a ferruginous stain ran through it from one end to the other, with the exactness of a drawn line; and thence to the curving edge a most delicate rose-teint faded gradually down, like the last flush of sunset through a silken curtain had it been a work of art, done in alabaster and stained with the pencil, it would have been thought admirable.

"The guide wished us to proceed, but our feet were wet, and the air of the cavern was too chill we were at least *four miles*, they told us, from the entrance, having walked briskly for upwards of two hours the grotto is said to extend ten miles under the mountains, and has never been thoroughly explored parties have started with provisions, and passed forty-eight hours in it without finding the extremity. It seems to me that any city I ever saw might be concealed in its caverns I have often tried to conceive of the grottos of Antiparos, and the celebrated caverns of our own country; but I received here an entirely new idea of the possibility of space under ground there is no conceiving it unseen the river emerges on the other side of the mountain, seven or eight miles from its first entrance."

LESSON XVII

INTERROGATION-POINT.—EXCLAMATION-POINT.

§ 90 RULE I.—An interrogation-point must be placed after every interrogative sentence, member, and clause.

---

§ 90. Repeat Rule I., relating to the use of the interrogation-point.

EXAMPLES.

I. *After an interrogative sentence.*—" Are we not mortal?"
II. *After an interrogative member.*—" Our earthly pilgrimage is nearly finished; shall we not, then, think of eternity?"
III. *After an interrogative clause.*—" As we must soon die (who knows but this very night?), we should fix our thoughts on eternity."

§ 91. Some sentences which are declarative in form are really interrogative (see § 78, Remark IV.), and must of course be closed with interrogation-points. Thus the sentence, "You will remain all night," is declarative in form, and, followed by a period, indicates a positive announcement of the fact. If intended as an indirect question, however, ("You will remain all night, will you not?") it must be followed by an interrogation-point.

§ 92. After sentences which merely assert that a question has been asked, a period must be placed, unless the exact words of the question are given; in this case, an interrogation-point takes the place of a period, and must stand *before* the quotation-points enclosing the question. As, "They asked me whether I would return."—"They asked me, 'Will you return?'"

So, if a question is introduced into the middle of a sentence, in the exact words in which it was asked, an interrogation-point must be placed before the last quotation-points, the following word must commence with a small letter, and the remainder of the sentence must be punctuated as it would be if no quoted clause were introduced; as, "These frequent and lamentable catastrophes ask the question, 'Are you prepared to die?' with startling emphasis." The clauses of such sentences, however, are capable of a decidedly better arrangement; as will be seen by the following alteration: "These frequent and lamentable catastrophes ask, with startling emphasis, the question, 'Are you prepared to die?'"

§ 93. RULE II.—An exclamation-point must be placed after every exclamatory sentence, member, clause, and expression.

---

§ 91. What form have some interrogative sentences? How must they be closed? Illustrate this.
§ 92. State the principle relating to sentences which merely declare that a question has been asked. How must we punctuate questions introduced into the middle of a sentence? How is the rest of the sentence to be pointed? What is said respecting the arrangement of such sentences?
§ 93. Repeat Rule II., relating to the use of the exclamation-point.

EXAMPLES.

I. *After an exclamatory sentence.*—" How slow yon tiny vessel ploughs the main ! "
II. *After an exclamatory member.*—" The clock is striking midnight how suggestive and solemn is the sound ! "
III. *After an exclamatory clause.*—" We buried him (with what intense and heart-rending sorrow !) on the field which his life-blood had consecrated."
IV. *After exclamatory expressions.*—" Consummate horror ! guilt without a name ! "

§ 94. From the above examples it will be seen that the interrogation-point and exclamation-point do not always denote the same degree of separation, but are used when the connection is close as well as when it is remote. Thus in Examples I. and II. they are placed after propositions making complete sense, and indicate as entire separation from what follows as would be denoted by a period. In the last example, on the contrary, the exclamation-points are by no means equivalent, in this respect, to periods. The two points under consideration, therefore, not only separate complete and independent sentences with the force of periods; but are also placed between members like colons and semicolons, and even between clauses, like commas. In the first case, the words following these points must commence with capitals; in the last three cases, with small letters, as may be seen above. The sole criterion is the degree of connection subsisting between the parts thus separated.

§ 95. Sometimes the connection is so close that the different parts are dependent on each other in construction, or do not make sense when taken separately. In this case, if each division is of itself distinctly interrogative, varying the question each time by applying it to some new object; or, in other words, if it contains a repetition of the auxiliary that asks the question, or an interrogative adverb, or adverbial clause,—use an interrogation-point after each, and let the following word commence with a small letter; as, " How shall a man obtain the kingdom of God ! by impiety ? by murder ? by falsehood ? by theft ? "

If, however, such divisions do not apply the question to any new object, but merely state additional circumstances respecting that which

---

§ 94. What is said respecting the degree of separation denoted by the interrogation point and exclamation-point ? When they separate complete and independent sentences, how must the next word commence ? When they stand between members and clauses, how must the following word commence ?

§ 95. State the mode of punctuating, when the parts are dependent on each other in construction, and each varies the question by applying it to some new object. How are these parts separated if they do not thus vary the question ?

formed the original subject of the enquiry, they must not be separated by interrogation-points, but by commas, semicolons, or colons, as thereafter directed; as, "Where are now the great cities of antiquity, those vast and mighty cities, the pride of kings, the ornament of empires?" Here but one question is asked, and but one interrogation-point must be employed.

§ 96. Observe, moreover, that when a succession of interrogative adverbs or adverbial clauses commence a sentence, the incompleteness of the sense prevents us from placing an interrogation-point after each of them, as we would do if they stood at its close. The two following sentences illustrate this difference: "Under what circumstances, for what purpose, at whose instigation, did he come?"—"Under what circumstances did he come? for what purpose? at whose instigation?"

§ 97. The principles laid down in § 95, 96, apply to the exclamation-point with the same force as to the interrogation-point. The following examples will illustrate their application:—

UNDER § 95. What cold-blooded cruelty did Nero manifest! what disgusting sensuality! what black ingratitude! what concentrated selfishness! what utter disregard of his duties, as a monarch and as a man!—How quickly fled that happy season; those days of dreamy love, those nights of innocent festivity!

UNDER § 96. How extensive, how varied, how beautiful, how sublime, is the landscape!—How extensive is the landscape! how varied! how beautiful! how sublime!

§ 98. RULE III.—An exclamation-point must be placed after every interjection except *O*; as, *ah! alas! hold!*

For an explanation of the difference between *O* and *oh!*, see § 68.

§ 99. In some cases, when an interjection is very closely connected with other words, the exclamation-point is not placed between them, but reserved for the close of the expression; as, "Fie upon thee!"

§ 100. Two interrogative interjections, *eh* and *hey*, are usually followed by the interrogation-point; as, "You think it suits my complexion, hey?"

§ 101. RULE IV.—An exclamation-point may be placed

---

§ 96. In what case is an interrogation-point inadmissible after interrogative adverbs or adverbial clauses, following each other in a series?

§ 97. To what besides the interrogation-point do the principles just stated apply?

§ 98. Repeat Rule III. What is the difference in signification and punctuation between *O* and *oh?*

§ 99. When an interjection is very closely connected with other words, where is the exclamation-point placed?

§ 100. What interjections are usually followed by the interrogation-point?

after a vocative clause, containing an earnest or solemn invocation; as, "O Father Supreme! protect us from the dangers of this night."

The comma may, without impropriety, be substituted, in such a case, for the exclamation-point; as, "O Father Supreme, protect us from the dangers of this night."

§ 102. RULE V.—More than one exclamation-point may be placed after a sentence or expression denoting an extraordinary degree of emotion; as, "Political honesty!! Where can such a thing be found?'

As a general thing, this repetition of the exclamation-point is confined to humorous and satirical compositions.

EXERCISE.

Insert, in the following sentences, periods, interrogation-points, and exclamation-points, wherever required by the rules that have been given:—

UNDER § 90. There is no precedent applicable to the question; for when has such a case been presented in our past history When may we look for another such in the future. Who hath heard such a thing? Who hath seen such a thing? Shall the earth be made to bring forth in one day? Shall a nation be born at once?

UNDER § 91. I have not seen him in a year? He has grown I suppose—You intend starting in Saturday's steamer?—" You have quite recovered from your injury"? "Quite recovered? Oh no; I am still unable to walk"

UNDER § 92. They asked me why I wept—They asked me, "Why do you weep?"—This is the question: whether it is expedient to purchase temporal pleasure at the expense of eternal happiness—This is the question: "Is it expedient to purchase temporal pleasure at the expense of eternal happiness"—The question for debate was whether virtue is always a source of happiness—Pilate's question, "What is truth?", has been asked by many a candid enquirer—"Who is there," demanded the sentinel.

UNDER § 93. How heavily we drag the load of life How sweetly the bee winds her small but mellow horn —O, thoughts ineffable O, visions blest —O, the times, O the morals of the day —Such is the uncertainty of life; yet oh how seldom do we realize it —While in this part of the country, I once more revisited (and alas with what melancholy presentiments) the home of my youth.

---

§ 101. Repeat Rule IV. In such cases, what may be substituted for the exclamation point?

§ 102. Repeat Rule V. To what kinds of composition is this repetition of the exclamation-point confined?

UNDER § 95, 96. Who shall separate us from the love of Christ, shall tribulation, shall distress, shall persecution shall famine, shall peril, shall sword?—I am charged with being an emissary of France?. An emissary of France And for what end? It is alleged that I wished to sell the independence of my country. And for what end. Was this the object of my ambition and is this the mode by which a tribunal of justice reconciles contradictions !—When, where, under what circumstances, did it happen. —When did it happen where under what circumstances.

UNDER § 97. How calm was the ocean how gentle its swell —How wide was the sweep of the rainbow's wings how boundless its circle how radiant its rings —O virtue, how disinterested, how noble, how lovely, thou art —O virtue, how disinterested thou art how noble how lovely —O the depth of the riches both of the wisdom and knowledge of God how unsearchable are His judgments, and His ways past finding out

UNDER § 98. Hark daughter of Almon!—Hist he comes!—Hail sacred day!—Lo I am with you alway!—Zounds the man's in earnest!—Indeed then I am wrong. —O dear, what can the matter be.—Humph! this looks suspicious.—Pshaw! what can we do.

UNDER § 99. Woe to the tempter!—Woe is me!—Shame upon thy insolence —Ah me!—Away with him!—Hurrah for the right!—Henceforth, adieu to happiness.

UNDER § 101. King of kings and Lord of lords, in humility we approach Thy altar.

O Rome, my country, city of the soul,
The orphans of the heart must turn to thee,
Lone mother of dead empires

Men of Athens listen to my defence.—Ye shades of the mighty dead! listen to my invocation.

UNDER § 102. An honest lawyer! 'An anomaly in nature. Cage him when you find him, and let the world gaze upon the wonder —A discerning lover that is a new animal, just born into the universe — And this miserable performance, in which it is debatable whether there is more ignorance or pretension, comes before the world with the high-sounding title, "Dictionary of Dictionaries"!

MISCELLANEOUS.—Canst thou draw out leviathan with a hook, or his tongue with a cord which thou lettest down?—When saw we thee an hungered, or athirst, or a stranger, or naked, or sick, or in prison, and did not minister unto thee?—When saw we thee an hungered, and did not minister unto thee, or athirst, or a stranger or naked, or sick, or in prison?—The question, "What is man"? has occupied the attention of the wisest philosophers; yet how few have given a satisfactory answer.—An ancient sage, being asked what was the greatest good in the smallest compass, replied, "The human mind, in the human body." — "Am I dying?" he eagerly asked. "Dying! Oh no not dying," was the faint but hopeful response.—It rains still, hey!—Where have you been, eh!—Aroynt thee, witch.—"Ha, ha, ha"! roared the squire, who enjoyed the story amazingly. "Ha, ha, ha"! echoed the whole company.

LESSON XVIII.

THE COLON.

§ 103. The word COLON comes from the Greek language, and means *limb* or *member*. Its use appears to have originated with the early printers of Latin books. Formerly it was much used, and seems to have been preferred to the semicolon, which, with writers of the present day, too generally usurps its place. The Colon, however, has a distinct office of its own to perform; and there are many cases in which no point can with propriety be substituted for it. It indicates the next greatest degree of separation to that denoted by the period.

§ 104. RULE I.—A colon must be placed between the great divisions of sentences, when minor subdivisions occur that are separated by semicolons; as, "We perceive the shadow to have moved along the dial, but did not see it moving; we observe that the grass has grown, though it was impossible to see it grow: so the advances we make in knowledge, consisting of minute and gradual steps, are perceivable only after intervals of time."

The example just given is composed of three members, of which it is evident that the first two are more closely connected with each other than with the last. The former requiring a semicolon between them, as will appear hereafter, the latter must be cut off by a point indicating a greater degree of separation, that is, a colon.

§ 105. RULE II.—A colon must be placed before a formal enumeration of particulars, and a direct quotation, when referred to by the words *thus, following, as follows, this, these,* &c.; as, "Man consists of three parts: first, the body, with

---

§ 103. From what language is the word *colon* derived? What does it mean? With whom did this point originate? What is said of its use formerly and at the present day? What degree of separation does it denote?
§ 104 Repeat Rule I.
§ 105 Repeat Rule II. What is meant by a formal enumeration of particulars?

5

its sensual appetites; second, the mind, with its thirst fo knowledge and other noble aspirations; third, the soul, with its undying principle."—" Mohammed died with these words on his lips: 'O God, pardon my sins! Yes, I come among my fellow-citizens on high.'"

By "a formal enumeration" is meant one in which the particulars are introduced by the words *first, secondly*, &c., or similar terms. In this case, the objects enumerated are separated from each other by semicolons; and before the first a colon must be placed, as in the example given above. If the names of the particulars merely are given, without any formal introductory words or accompanying description, commas are placed between them, and a semicolon, instead of a colon, is used before the first; as, "Grammar is divided into four parts; Orthography, Etymology, Syntax, and Prosody."

§ 106. If the quoted passage consists of several sentences or begins a new paragraph, it is usual to place a colon followed by a dash (:—) at the end of the preceding sentence; as, "The cloth having been removed, the president rose and said:—
'Ladies and gentlemen, we have assembled,'" &c.

§ 107. If the quoted passage is introduced by *that*, or if it is short and incorporated in the middle of a sentence, a colon is not admissible before it; as, "Remember that 'one to-day is worth two to-morrows.'" "Bion's favorite maxim, 'Know thyself,' is worth whole pages of good advice."

§ 108. When the quoted passage is brought in without any introductory word, if short, it is generally preceded by a comma; if long, by a colon; as, "A simpleton, meeting a philosopher, asked him, 'What affords wise men the greatest pleasure?' Turning on his heel, the sage promptly replied, 'To get rid of fools.'" The use of the colon in this case is illustrated in § 105.

§ 109. RULE III.—A colon was formerly, and may be, placed between the members of a compound sentence,

---

When thus formally enumerated, how are the particulars separated from each other? What marks must precede the first? When the names merely are given, how are they separated, and by what preceded?

§ 106. If the quoted passage consists of several sentences or a paragraph, how is the preceding sentence generally closed?

§ 107. In what case is a colon inadmissible before a quoted passage?

§ 108. State the principle that applies to a quoted passage brought in without any introductory word.

§ 109. Repeat Rule III. What is said of usage in these cases? What is the highest point that can be used between members connected by a conjunction?

when there is no conjunction between them and the connection is slight; as, "Never flatter the people: leave that to such as mean to betray them."

With regard to the cases falling under this rule, usage is divided. Many good authorities prefer a semicolon; while others substitute a period, and commence a new sentence with what follows. It appears to be settled, however, that, if the members are connected by a conjunction, a semicolon is the highest point that can be placed between them; as, "Never flatter the people; but leave that to such as mean to betray them."

EXERCISE.

Insert, wherever required in the following sentences, periods, interrogation-points, exclamation-points, and colons:—

UNDER § 104. No monumental marble emblazons the deeds and fame of Marco Bozarris; a few round stones piled over his head are all that marks his grave: yet his name is conspicuous among the greatest heroes and purest patriots of history.—"Most fashionable ladies," says a plain-spoken writer, "have two faces; one face to sleep in and another to show in company: the first is generally reserved for the husband and family at home; the other is put on to please strangers abroad: the family face is often indifferent enough, but the out-door one looks something better".—You have called yourself an atom in the universe; you have said that you were, but an insect in the solar blaze: is your present pride consistent with these professions,

UNDER § 105. The object of this book is twofold: first, to teach the inexperienced how to express their thoughts correctly and elegantly; secondly, to enable them to appreciate the productions of others.—The human family is composed of five races, differing from each other in feature and color; first, the Caucasian, or white; second, &c.—Lord Bacon has summed up the whole matter in the following words: "A little philosophy inclineth men's minds to atheism; but depth in philosophy bringeth men's minds to religion".—Where can you find anything simpler yet more sublime than this sentiment of Richter's, "I love God, and little children?—He answered my argument thus: "The man who lives by hope will die by despair".

UNDER § 106. Cato, being next called on by the consul for his opinion, delivered the following forcible speech.—

Conscript fathers, I perceive that those who have spoken before me, &c

UNDER § 107. Socrates used to say that other men lived in order that they might eat, but that he ate in order that he might live.—The proposition that, "whatever is, is right", admits of question.—It is a fact on which we may congratulate ourselves, that "honor and shame from no condition rise".—The Spanish proverb, "he is my friend that grinds at my mill," exposes the false pretensions of persons who will not go out of their way to serve those for whom they profess friendship.

UNDER § 108. Solomon says: "Go to the ant, thou sluggard?"—Diogenes, the eccentric Cynic philosopher, was constantly finding fault with his pupils and acquaintances. To excuse himself, he was accustomed to say: "Other dogs bite their enemies; but I bite my friends, that I may save them."—A Spanish proverb says, "Four persons are indispensable to the production of a good salad first, a spendthrift for oil; second, a miser for vinegar; third, a counsellor for salt; fourth, a madman, to stir it all up."

UNDER § 109. Love hath wings beware lest he fly:—I entered at the first window that I could reach a cloud of smoke filled the apartment.— Life in Sweden is, for the most part, patriarchal almost primeval simplicity reigns over this northern land, almost primeval solitude and stillness;—Discretion is the perfection of reason, and a guide in all the duties of life cunning is a kind of instinct, that looks out only after its own immediate interest and welfare.

MISCELLANEOUS.—What a truthful lesson is taught in these words of Sterne: "So quickly, sometimes, has the wheel turned round that many a man has lived to enjoy the benefit of that charity which his own piety projected."—Colton has truly said that "kings and their subjects, masters and servants, find a common level in two places; at the foot of the cross, and in the grave."—We have in use two kinds of language, the spoken and the written, the one, the gift of God; the other, the invention of man.—How far silence is prudence, depends upon circumstances. I waive that question;—You have friends to cheer you on; you have books and teachers to aid you; but after all the proper education of your mind must be your own work;—Death is like thunder in two particulars, we are alarmed at the sound of it; and it is formidable only from what has preceded it.

LESSON XIX.

THE SEMICOLON

§ 110. THE word SEMICOLON means *half a limb* or *member*; and the point is used to indicate the next greatest degree of separation to that denoted by the colon. It was first employed in Italy, and seems to have found its way into England about the commencement of the seventeenth century.

§ 111. RULE I.—A semicolon must be placed between the

---

§ 110. What does the word *semicolon* mean? What degree of separation does it indicate? Where was it first employed? When did it find its way into England?

members of compound sentences (see § 41), unless the connection is exceedingly close; as, "Lying lips are an abomination to the Lord; but they that deal truly are His delight."

We have already seen, in § 109, that, wnen there is no conjunction between the members, a colon may be used, if the connection is slight; a semicolon, however, is generally preferred. On the other hand, when the members are very short and the connection is intimate, a comma ma without impropriety be employed; as, "Simple men admire the learned, ignorant men despise them." Usage on this point is much divided, the choice between semicolon and comma depending entirely on the degree of connection between the members, respecting which different minds cannot be expected to agree. In the example last given, either a semicolon or a comma may be placed after *learned*.

§ 112. RULE II.—A semicolon must be placed between the great divisions of sentences, when minor subdivisions occur that are separated by commas; as, "Mirth should be the embroidery of conversation, not the web; and wit the ornament of the mind, not the furniture."

§ 113. RULE III.—When a colon is placed before an enumeration of particulars, the objects enumerated must be separated by semicolons; as, "The value of a maxim depends on four things: the correctness of the principle it embodies; the subject to which it relates; the extent of its application; and the ease with which it may be practically carried out."

§ 114. RULE IV.—A semicolon must be placed before an enumeration of particulars, when the names of the objects merely are given without any formal introductory words or accompanying description; as, "There are three genders; the masculine, the feminine, and the neuter."

§ 115. RULE V.—A semicolon must be placed before the conjunction AS, when it introduces an example. For an illustration, see the preceding Rule.

---

§ 111. Repeat Rule I. What other point may be used, when there is no conjunction? When the connection is very close, what point may be employed?
§ 112. Repeat Rule II.
§ 113. Repeat Rule III.
§ 114. Repeat Rule IV.
§ 115. Repeat Rule V.

§ 116. RULE VI.—When several long clauses occur in succession, all having common dependence on some other clause or word, they must be separated by semicolons; as, "If we neglected no opportunity of doing good; if we fed the hungry and ministered to the sick; if we gave up our own luxuries, to secure necessary comforts for the destitute; though no man might be aware of our generosity, yet in the applause of our own conscience we would have an ample reward."

§ 117. If the clauses are short, they may be separated by commas; as, "If I succeed, if I reach the pinnacle of my ambition, you shall share my triumph."

EXERCISE.

Insert in the following sentences, wherever required by the rules, all the points thus far considered:—

UNDER § 111. Air was regarded as a simple substance by ancient philosophers; but the experiments of Cavendish prove it to be composed of oxygen and nitrogen.— The gem has lost its sparkle; scarce a vestige of its former brilliancy remains.— The porcupine is fond of climbing trees; and for this purpose, he is furnished with very long claws.— The Laplanders have little idea of religion or a Supreme Being; the greater part of them are idolaters, and their superstition is as profound as their worship is contemptible.

UNDER § 112. The Jews ruin themselves at their Passover; the Moors, at their marriages; and the Christians, in their law-suits.— The poisoned valley of Java is twenty miles in extent, and of considerable width; it presents a most desolate appearance, being entirely destitute of vegetation. — The poet uses words, indeed; but they are merely the instruments of his art, not its objects.— Weeds and thistles, ever enemies of the husbandman, must be rooted out from the garden of the mind; good seed must be sown, and the growing crop must be carefully attended to, if we would have a plenteous harvest.

UNDER § 113. The true order of learning should be as follows; first, what is necessary; second, what is useful; and third, what is ornamental. — God hath set some in the church; first, apostles; secondarily, prophets; thirdly, teachers after that, miracles then, gifts of healings, helps, governments, diversities of tongues.— The duties of man are twofold; first, those that be owes to his Creator; secondly, those due to his fellow-men.— Two paths open before every youth; on the one hand, that of vice, with its unreal and short-lived pleasures; on the other, that of virtue, with the genuine and permanent happiness it ensures.

UNDER § 114. We have three great bulwarks of liberty; viz., schools,

---

§ 116. Repeat Rule VI.
§ 117. If the dependent clauses are short, how may they be separated?

colleges, and universities;—There are three cases; the nominative, the possessive, and the objective;—According to a late writer, London surpasses all other great cities in four particulars; size, commerce, fogs, and pickpockets.

UNDER § 115. After interjections, pronouns of the first person are generally used in the objective case; as, "Ah me". Those of the second person, on the other hand, follow interjections in the nominative; as, "O! thou".

UNDER § 116. The greatest man is he who chooses the right, with invincible resolution; who resists the sorest temptations from within, and without; who bears the heaviest burdens cheerfully; who is calmest in storms, and most fearless under menace and frowns; and whose reliance on truth, on virtue, and on God, is most unfaltering.—The delightful freedom of Cowper's manner, so acceptable to those long accustomed to a poetical school, of which the radical fault was constraint; his noble and tender morality; his fervent piety; his glowing and well-expressed patriotism; his descriptions, unparalleled in vividness and accuracy; his playful humor and powerful satire,—all conspired to render him one of the most popular poets of his day.

UNDER § 117. Read not for the purpose of contradicting and confuting, nor of believing and taking for granted, nor of finding material for argument and conversation; but in order to weigh and consider the thoughts of others.—When I have gone from earth, when my place is vacant, when my pilgrimage is over, will thy faithful heart still keep my memory green.

MISCELLANEOUS. This wide-spread republic is the future monument to Washington. Maintain its independence; uphold its constitution; preserve its union; defend its liberty.—The ancients feared death; we, thanks to Christianity, fear only dying.—The study of mathematics, cultivates the reason; that of the languages, at the same time, the reason, and the taste. The former gives power to the mind; the latter, both power and flexibility. The former, by itself, would prepare us for a state of certainties which nowhere exists; the latter, for a state of probabilities, which is that of common life.—Woman in Italy; is trained to shrink from the open air, and the public gaze; she is no rider; is never in at the death in a fox-hunt; is no hand at a whip, if her life depended on it she never keeps a stall at a fancy fair; never takes the lead at a debating club; she never addresses a stranger, except, perhaps, behind a mask in carnival-season; her politics are limited to wearing tri-color ribbons, and refusing an Austrian as a partner for the waltz; she is a dunce, and makes no mystery of it; a coward, and glories in it.—Lord Chatham, made an administration so checkered and speckled; he put together a piece of joinery so crossly indented, and whimsically dovetailed; he constructed a cabinet so variously inlaid with whigs, and tories, patriots, and courtiers;—that it was utterly unsafe to touch, and unsure to stand on.—Helmets are cleft on high; blood bursts and smokes around.

LESSON XX.

THE COMMA.

§ 118. The word COMMA means *that which is cut off* and the mark so called denotes the least degree of separation that requires a point. In its present form, the comma is not found in manuscripts anterior to the ninth century; a straight line drawn vertically between the words was formerly used in its place.

§ 119. GENERAL RULE.—The comma is used to separate words, phrases, clauses, and short members, closely connected with the rest of the sentence, but requiring separation by some point in consequence of the construction or arrangement.

PARENTHETICAL EXPRESSIONS.

§ 120. Words, phrases, adjuncts, and clauses, are said to be PARENTHETICAL when they are not essential to the meaning of a sentence *and are introduced in such a way as to break the connection between its component parts*. They are generally introduced near the commencement of a sentence, between a subject and its verb; but they may occupy other positions. Every such parenthetical expression must be separated from the leading proposition by a comma before and after it.

As these expressions are of constant occurrence, and are always punctuated in the same manner, with a comma on each side of them, it is important that the pupil should be able to recognize them without difficulty. The following examples contain respectively a parenthetical word, phrase, adjunct, and clause, printed in italics; which, it will be

---

§ 118. What does the word *comma* mean? What degree of separation does the mark so called denote? In its present form, when was the comma first used? Before that time, what was employed in its stead?

§ 119. Repeat the General Rule.

§ 120. When are words, phrases, adjuncts, and clauses, said to be parenthetical? Where are they generally introduced? How must every parenthetical expression be

seen, may be omitted without injury to the sense, and stand, in every case, between the subject and its verb:—

EXAMPLES OF PARENTHETICAL EXPRESSIONS.

1. Napoleon, *unquestionably*, was a man of genius.
2. There is, *as it were*, an atmospheric maelstrom all about us.
3. History, *in a word*, is replete with moral lessons.
4. Thomson, *who was blessed with a strong and copious fancy*, drew his images from nature itself.

RESTRICTIVE EXPRESSIONS.

§ 121. The mere introduction of adjuncts and clauses between a subject and its verb, does not make them parenthetical. Sometimes they form an essential part of the logical subject, and cannot be omitted without rendering the sense incomplete. In that case, they are not parenthetical, but RESTRICTIVE; and there must be no comma between them and that which they restrict. Whether a comma is to be placed after such restrictive expressions, depends on principles hereafter explained.

Examples of restrictive adjuncts and clauses are furnished below. The pupil is requested to compare them carefully with the examples of parenthetical expressions just given, and to make himself so familiar with their distinguishing features that he can at once determine to which of the two classes any given adjunct or clause belongs. Few sentences occur without expressions of this kind; and, as they must have a comma on each side of them if parenthetical, but none before them if restrictive, constant mistakes will be made unless the distinction is thoroughly understood. The criterion is, will the meaning of the sentence be preserved if the expression is omitted? If so, it is parenthetical; if not, restrictive.

EXAMPLES OF RESTRICTIVE EXPRESSIONS.

1. The love *of money* is the root of all evil.
A bird *in the hand* is worth two in the bush.
2. A man *tormented by a guilty conscience* can not be happy.
Those *who sleep late* lose the best part of the day.

---

cut off from the rest of the sentence? Give examples, and show in each case how you know the expression to be parenthetical.

§ 121. Besides its position, what is necessary to make an expression parenthetical? When are adjuncts and clauses called restrictive? From what must restrictive adjuncts and clauses not be cut off by the comma? What is the criterion for determining whether a sentence is parenthetical or restrictive? Give examples, and show in each case how you know the expression to be restrictive.

THE COMMA.

RULE I.—PARENTHETICAL EXPRESSIONS.

§ 122. A comma must be placed before and after every parenthetical word, phrase, adjunct, clause, and expression, see the examples in § 120.

The words referred to in this rule are chiefly conjunctions and adverbs. Those of most frequent occurrence are as follows:—

too,	moreover,	apparently,
also,	likewise,	meanwhile,
then,	however,	consequently,
surely,	finally,	unquestionably,
indeed,	namely,	accordingly,
perhaps,	therefore,	notwithstanding.

The phrases most frequently introduced parenthetically are as follows:—

in truth,	in reality,	as a matter of course,
in fact,	no doubt,	at all events,
in fine,	of course,	to be brief,
in short,	above all,	to be sure,
in general,	generally speaking,	on the contrary,
in particular,	as it were,	now and then.

The most common parenthetical adjuncts are these:—

without doubt,	in the first place,	by chance,
without question,	in the mean time,	in that case,
beyond a doubt,	in a word,	for the most part,
beyond question,	in a measure,	on the other hand.

Any of the clauses enumerated in § 43 may be used parenthetically.

§ 123. A comma must be placed before and after parenthetical subjects introduced by *as well as;* as, "Industry, as well as genius, is essential to the production of great works."—"Printing, as well as every other important invention, has wrought great changes in the world."

§ 124. A comma must be placed on each side of negative adjuncts and clauses, when introduced parenthetically by way of contrast or opposition; as, "Prosperity is secured to a state, not by the acquisition of territory or riches, but by the encouragement of industry and the dissemination of virtuous principles."

If, however, the word expressing negation is removed from the ad-

---

§ 122. Repeat Rule I. What parts of speech, for the most part, are the words here referred to? Enumerate some of the principal. Mention the phrases most frequently introduced parenthetically. Give some of the commonest parenthetical adjuncts. What clauses may be used parenthetically?

§ 123. What subjects are introduced parenthetically, and fall under this rule?

§ 124. State the principle that applies to negative adjuncts and clauses. What change in the punctuation must be made, if the word expressing negation is removed

junct or clause in question and joined to the leading verb, one comma only must be used, and that before the conjunction which introduces the last of the contrasted expressions; as, "Prosperity is not secured to a state by the acquisition of territory or riches, but by the encouragement of industry and the dissemination of virtuous principles."

If the parts of the sentence are inverted, so that the clauses or adjuncts are brought before the leading verb with the introductory words, *it is*, then the clause or adjunct introduced by the conjunction receives the commas, one on each side; as, "It is not by the acquisition of territory or riches, but by the encouragement of industry and the dissemination of virtuous principles, that prosperity is secured to a state."

§ 125. Some are in the habit of omitting the comma before a parenthetical expression when it follows a conjunction. This is wrong; there, as in every other position, it must be cut off by a comma on each side: as, "Your manners are affable, and, for the most part, pleasing."

§ 126. Observe, with regard to the *words* referred to in Rule L, that it is only when they belong to the whole proposition, and not to individual words, that they are thus cut off by commas. A few examples, which the pupil is requested to compare, will illustrate this difference.

EXAMPLES.—The passions of mankind, *however*, frequently blind them. —*However* fairly a bad man may appear to act, we distrust him.—Is it, *then*, to be supposed that vice will ultimately triumph !—We *then* proceeded on our way.—I would, *too*, present the subject in another point of view.—It rains *too* hard to venture out.

EXERCISE.

Supply the commas omitted in the following sentences, remembering that none must be introduced unless required by a positive rule:—

UNDER § 122. Nothing on earth I tell you can persuade me to such a step.—There is it must be admitted something attractive in such dreamy speculations.—Nothing in my opinion is more prejudicial to the interests of a nation than unsettled and varying policy.—The fundamental principles of science at least those that were abstract rather than practical were deposited during the Middle Ages in the dead languages.—A whiff of tobacco smoke strange as it may appear gives among these barbarous tribes not merely a binding force but an inviola-

---

from the adjunct or clause and joined to the leading verb? What is the proper mode of pointing, when the parts of the sentence are inverted, and the introductory words *it is* are employed?

§ 125. In what case are some in the habit of omitting the comma before a parenthetical expression? Is this right?

126. In what case only are the *words* referred to in Rule L cut off by commas?

ble sanctity to treaties.—This added to other considerations will prevent me from coming.

UNDER § 123. Nations, as well as men, fail in nothing, which they boldly attempt.—The unprincipled politician like the chameleon is constantly changing his color.—Marie Antoinette, unlike most regal personages, was extremely affable in her manners.—The insect, as well as the man that treads upon it, has an office to perform.—Dangerous, as well as degrading, are the promptings of pride.—Printing, like every other important invention, has wrought great changes in the world.

UNDER § 124. This principle has been fully settled, not by any single act, but the repeated and deliberate declarations of government.—Songs, not of merriment and revelry, but of praise and thanksgiving were heard ascending.—A great political crisis is the time, not for tardy consultation, but for prompt and vigorous action.—A great political crisis is not the time for tardy consultation, but for prompt and vigorous action.—It is not tardy consultation, but prompt and vigorous action, that a great political crisis requires.—Juries, not judges, are responsible for these evils.—Not for his own glory, but for his country's preservation, did Washington take the field.—It was not in the hope of personal aggrandizement, that our forefathers embarked in the revolutionary struggle, but to secure for themselves and their posterity, that, without which they felt life was valueless.

UNDER § 125. Milton was like Dante, a statesman and a lover; and, like Dante, he had been unfortunate in ambition, and in love.—We may perhaps find it difficult to admire Queen Elizabeth, as a woman; but, without doubt, as a sovereign, she deserves our highest respect. She soon, if we may believe contemporáneous historians, gained incredible influence with her people; and while she merited all their esteem by her real virtues, she also engaged their affections by her pretended ones.

UNDER § 126. There were, besides, several other considerations, which led Columbus to believe that the earth was round.—There are others besides its soldiers, to whom a state should show its gratitude.—Now, from this, I would argue that all violent measures are at the present time, impolitic.—Who, now, believes in the divine right of kings?—Morning will come, at last, however, dark the night may be.—Galileo, however, was convinced of the truth of his theory, and therefore persisted in maintaining it, even at the risk of imprisonment and death. [In the last sentence, *therefore* does not break the connection sufficiently to be set off by commas.]

———•••———

LESSON XXI.

THE COMMA (CONTINUED).

RULE II.—CLAUSES, WORDS, PHRASES, AND ADJUNCTS.

§ 127. When clauses, and when words, phrases, and adjuncts, that may be used parenthetically, are introduced in such a way as not to break the connection between dependent parts, they are cut off by but one comma, which comes after them if they commence the sentence, but before them if they end it; as, "Unquestionably, Napoleon was a man of genius." —"Generally speaking, an indolent person is unhappy."—"This is the case, beyond a doubt."—"See the hollowness of thy pretensions, O worshipper of reason."

Observe, however, that such expressions as are restrictive do not fall under this rule.

§ 128. A comma must also be placed after the following and similar words, which are rarely, and some of them never, used parenthetically, when they stand at the commencement of sentences, and refer, not to any particular word, but to the proposition as a whole:—

again,	yes,	now,	first,
further,	no,	why,	secondly,
howbeit,	nay,	well,	thirdly, &c.

As, "Yes, the appointed time has come."—"Why, this is rank injustice."—"Well, follow the dictates of your inclination."

§ 129. A comma must be placed after *here* and *there*, *now* and *then*, when they introduce contrasted clauses or members; as, "Here, every citizen enjoys the blessings of personal freedom; there, despotism forges fetters for thought, word, and action."

§ 130. The comma may be omitted in the case of *too*, *also*, *therefore*, and *perhaps*, when introduced so as not to interfere with the harmonious flow of the period, and, particularly, when the sentence is short; as, "Industry gains respect and riches too."—"He delivered a lecture on Monday evening also."—"Perhaps they are safe."

§ 131. In the case of adjuncts immediately following a verb, the connection is often so close that a comma is inadmissible; as, "I did it with my own hand."

§ 132. Adverbial, adjective, and hypothetical clauses, if very short, closely connected, and introduced so as not to interfere with the harmo-

---

§ 127. Repeat Rule II. What expressions do not fall under this rule? -
§ 128. What other words, rarely used parenthetically, take a comma after them when they stand at the commencement of sentences?
§ 129. State the rule relating to *here* and *there*, *now* and *then*.
§ 130. In the case of what words may the comma be omitted?
§ 131. What is said of the connection in the case of adjuncts immediately following a verb?
§ 132. When may adverbial, adjective, and hypothetical clauses be used without the comma?

nious flow of the sentence, need not be cut off by the comma; as, "I began this work two years ago at Rome."

§ 133. A participial clause that relates to, and immediately follows the object of a verb, must not be separated from it; as, "We see our companions borne daily to the grave."

§ 134. Clauses that would otherwise be set off by the comma, if subdivided into parts which require the use of this point, must be separated by the semicolon, according to the rule in § 112, where an example given.

RULE III.—RESTRICTIVE ADJUNCTS AND CLAUSES.

§ 135. No comma must be placed between restrictive adjuncts or clauses (see § 121) and that which they restrict; as, "The eye of Providence is constantly upon us."—"Who can respect a man that is not governed by virtuous principles?"

Vocative and causal clauses (*see* § 43) are never restrictive, and must therefore be set off by the comma.

§ 136. Relative clauses introduced by the pronoun *that*, as well as those in which the relative is not expressed, are restrictive, and must have no comma before them; as, "Suspect the man that cannot look you in the eye."—"The day *we celebrate* is one of the proudest in our national history."

§ 137. A restrictive clause, however, must be set off by a comma, when it refers to several antecedents which are themselves separated by that point; as, "There are many painters, poets, and statesmen, whom chance has rendered famous rather than merit."

§ 138. A rule of syntax requires that a restrictive clause should stand immediately after its logical antecedent; if, however, a sentence is so loosely constructed as to have other words intervene between the antecedent and the restrictive clause, a comma should be placed before the latter; as, "He can have no genuine sympathy for the unfortunate,

---

§ 183. In what case may the comma be omitted before a participial clause?
§ 184. In what case does the semicolon take the place of the comma between clauses?
§ 135. Repeat Rule III., respecting restrictive adjuncts and clauses. What clauses are never restrictive? How must they, therefore, be set off?
§ 136. What relative clauses are restrictive, and must therefore have no comma before them?
§ 137. In what case must a restrictive clause be set off by a comma?
§ 188. What is the proper position for a restrictive clause? If other words are introduced between the clause and its antecedent, what change must be made in the punctuation?

that has never been unfortunate himself." With its parts correctly arranged, this sentence requires no point; as, "He that has never been unfortunate himself can have no genuine sympathy for the unfortunate."

§ 139. When there is a succession of restrictive clauses relating to the same antecedent, they are separated from each other by commas, and the first must be set off from the antecedent by the same point:— as, " Countries, whose rules are prompt and decisive, whose people are united, and whose course is just, have little to fear, even from more powerful nations."

§ 140. A comma is also generally placed before a restrictive clause containing *of which*, *to which*, or *for which*, preceded by a noun; as, "We have no sense or faculty, the use of which is not obvious to the reflecting mind."

§ 141. A participial clause is restrictive when the participle it contains can be exchanged for the relative *that* and a finite verb without injury to the sense. "A man discharging his duty under trying circumstances is worthy of our confidence"; here, *discharging* is equivalent to *that discharges*, and the clause is restrictive. In such a case, no comma must separate the clause from the antecedent, unless the principle embodied in § 137 applies.

EXERCISE.

In the following sentences, insert commas wherever required by rule:—

Under § 127. But for this event the future liberator of Rome might have been a dreamer. — Thou sayest right barbarian. — Great poet as Petrarch is he has often mistaken pedantry for passion. — When a people suffer in vain it is their own fault. — Happier had it been for many had they never looked out from their own heart upon the world. — What are good laws if we have not good men to execute them? — Low though the voice the boast was heard by all around. — Amazed at what had taken place the barons mechanically bent the knee. — Impatient to finish what he had begun Cæsar allowing his army no rest pushed forward to the capital. — Though neither honest nor eloquent the demagogue often controls the people. — To say the truth it was a goodly company. — From this time forth no sound of merriment

---

§ 139. State the principle that applies to a succession of restrictive relative clauses relating to the same antecedent.

§ 140. What is said of restrictive clauses containing *of which*, &c., preceded by a noun?

§ 141. When is a participial clause restrictive? In such a case, must it be separated from its antecedent?

was ever heard in tnose lordly halls; on the contrary silence and gloom hung over them like a pall. — Nevertheless, though you have wronged me thus, I inflict no vengeance. — When I became a man, I laid aside childish things. — Are ye bewildered still, O Romans!

UNDER § 128. Well, honor is the subject of my story — Yes, it often happens that when we get out of the reach of want we are just within the reach of avarice. — Again, one man's loss is sometimes another man's gain. — Verily, this is a troublous world. — Furthermore, we are always suspicious of a deceitful man's motives. — Nay, though the whole world should do wrong, this is no excuse for our offences. — First, let us look at the facts.

UNDER § 129. Then, the world listened with pleasure to the rude strains of the troubadour; now, the divine thoughts of the most gifted geniuses, can hardly command its attention. — Here, we have troubles, pains, and partings; there, we are allowed to look for an unbroken rest, the elevated pleasures of which (see § 140) no heart can conceive.

UNDER § 130. Perhaps there is no man so utterly unhappy, as the useless drone. — I have seen this, and can therefore describe it, with accuracy. — Pythagoras made many discoveries in geometry and astronomy, also. — I can give you some information on the subject, being a farmer and a practical one, too. — I was, also, there; you are, therefore, mistaken.

UNDER § 131. The love of life, is deeply implanted in the human heart. — To sum the matter up in a few words, his hand is against every man's. — A tree is known by its fruits. — Banished from his native country, Æschines retired to Rhodes, where he opened a school of oratory, that became famous throughout all Greece. —

The golden wain, rolls round the silent North,
And earth is slumbering, 'neath the smiles of heaven.

UNDER § 132. You may go, if you wish. — We frequently meet enemies, where we expect friends. — Columbus maintained his theory, with a confidence which went far towards convincing his hearers. — All these things will have passed away, a hundred years hence. — Satan goes about like a roaring lion, seeking whom he may devour.

UNDER § 133. How many have seen their affection slighted, and even betrayed by the ungrateful! — We hear the good slandered every day. — Alexander the Great, had a large city built, in honor of his favorite horse.

UNDER § 134. During the fourteenth century, Italy, was the India of a vast number of well-born, but penniless adventurers, who had inflamed their imaginations, by the ballads and legends of chivalry, who from youth had trained, themselves to manage the barb, and bear alike through summer's heat, and winter's cold, the weight of arms, and who passing into an effeminate and distracted land, had only to exhibit bravery in order to command wealth.

UNDER § 135. The quality of mercy is not strained. — How soft tne music of those village bells! — Good nature is a sun which sheds light on all around. — He, who is a traitor to his country, is a serpent, which turns to bite the bosom that warms it. — Mahomet always observed the forms of that grave and seremonious politeness, so common in his country.

UNDER § 136. Is there a heart that music cannot melt? — Anger is a fire that consumes the heart. — The evil that men do, lives after them. — The land we live in is on many accounts bound to our hearts by the strongest ties. — Men are willing for the most part to overlook the faults of those they love.

UNDER § 137. There was no man, woman, or child that the tyrant Nero did not heartily hate. — The profligate man is a stranger to the innocent social enjoyments, the gushing affections, and sacred domestic pleasures, which to the virtuous constitute a never-failing source of satisfaction and contentment. — The Lydians, the Persians, and the Arabians, that wish to leave the army, are at liberty to do so.

UNDER § 138. An author cannot be readily understood who is unacquainted with the art of punctuation. — All is not gold that glitters. — Clauses must be set off by commas which are introduced parenthetically. — That man is not fit to be the head of a nation who prides himself on being the head of a party. (*Punctuate the sentences in this paragraph as they stand; then arrange them in their proper order, and point them accordingly.*)

UNDER § 139. We should have respect for the theories of a philosopher whose judgment is clear, whose learning is extensive, and whose reasonings are founded on facts, even though his deductions may conflict with generally received opinions.

UNDER § 140. Have no desire for a reputation, the acquisition of which involves dishonesty or deceit. — The barometer is an instrument, the usefulness of which to the navigator can hardly be overestimated. — All physicians tell us that dyspepsia is a disease the remedy for which it is hard to find. — Napoleon had from youth fixed his eyes on a pinnacle of greatness the path to which he knew was filled with tremendous obstacles.

UNDER § 141. Those distinguished for honesty and activity rarely, if ever, in this land of business energy lack employment — This was to be expected in a country overrun with disbanded soldiers, whose only means of subsistence were theft and violence. — No person found guilty of felony, is allowed to hold office. — We cannot too much pity the lot of a child thrown at a tender age on the charities of the world.

LESSON XXII.

THE COMMA (CONTINUED).

RULE IV.—APPOSITION.

§ 142. Single words in apposition and appositional clauses must be set off by the comma; as, " The fate of Rienzi, the

---

§ 142. Repeat Rule IV., respecting words in apposition and appositional clauses.

last of the Roman tribunes, shows the fickleness of an ignorant populace."—" Darius, the king of the Persians."

§ 143. To this rule there are four exceptions. The comma must be omitted,

I. Between a proper name and a common noun placed immediately before or after it without an adjunct; as, "Darius the king"; "the Altai Mountains"; "the River Rhine".

II. When a pronoun other than *I* is in apposition with a substantive which it immediately precedes or follows; as, "Cicero himself"; "Ye mighty men of war".

III. When the word in apposition or the clause in question is necessary to the idea predicated, so that it cannot be left out without rendering the sense incomplete; as, "The people elected him *president*."—" He was chosen *umpire*."—" I regard him *as a traitor*."—" Whom his friends considered *an honest man*." In these examples, italics are used to indicate the words and clauses in question; and, as they cannot be omitted without injury to the sense, they are necessary to the idea predicated, and must not be set off by the comma.

IV. The comma is omitted between the parts of a compound proper name, when in their proper order; as, "The Rev. Samuel T. Wollaston"; "Marcus Tullius Cicero".

When, however, the order is inverted, as in alphabetical lists of names, directories, &c., a comma must be inserted; as, "Hone, James G."; "Lyle, Rev. S. Phillips".

When a title, either abbreviated or written in full, is annexed to a proper name, it must be set off by a comma; as, "Robert Horton, M. D., F. R. S."; "W. C. Doubleday, Esquire".

RULE V.—TRANSPOSED ADJUNCTS AND CLAUSES.

§ 144. When a transposition occurs, so that an adjunct or a clause which would naturally follow a verb is introduced before it, a comma is generally required to develop the sense

---

§ 143. How many exceptions are there to this rule? What is the first, relating to a proper name and common noun? What is the second, relating to pronouns? What is the third, relating to words and clauses necessary to the idea predicated? What is the fourth, relating to compound proper names? If the parts of the name are transposed, what stop must be inserted? When a title is annexed to a proper name, how must it be set off?

§ 144. Repeat Rule V., relating to transposed adjuncts and clauses. When the natural order is restored, what change is necessary in the punctuation?

EXAMPLES.

1. To those who labor, sleep is doubly pleasant.
2. Of the five races, the Caucasian is the most enlightened.
3. To all such, objections may be made.
4. Whom he loveth, he chasteneth

In the above examples, we have a rhetorical arrangement, the common order would be as follows:—"Sleep is doubly pleasant to those who labor"; "The Caucasian is the most enlightened of the five races"; &c. As just written, it will be seen that these sentences require no comma.

§ 145. The comma must be omitted in the following cases:—

I. When the transposed adjunct is short and closely connected with the verb; as, "With this I am satisfied." If, however, there is danger of a reader's mistaking the sense as in the third example under § 144, a comma must be placed after the adjunct.

II. When the transposed adjunct or clause is introduced by *It is*; as, "It is chiefly through books that we hold intercourse with superior minds."

III. When a verb preceding its nominative comes immediately after the transposed adjunct or clause; as, "Down from this towering peak poured a roaring torrent."

IV. When the transposition consists in placing an objective case with or without limiting words immediately before the verb that governs it: as, "Silver and gold have I none."

RULE VI.—LOGICAL SUBJECT.

§ 146. A comma must be placed after the logical subject of a sentence (*see* § 40) when it ends with a verb, or when it consists of several parts which are themselves separated by commas; as, "*Those who persevere*, succeed."—"*The world of gayety, of temptation, and of pleasure*, allures thee."

The object of this rule is to enable the eye readily to perceive what the logical subject is. In the last example, if the comma after *pleasure* were omitted, a false impression would be conveyed, as it would seem that the words *and of pleasure* were more closely connected with the verb *allures* than the rest of the subject,—which is not the case.

---

§ 145. In what four cases may the comma be omitted in the case of transposed adjuncts and clauses?

§ 146. What is meant by the logical subject of a sentence? Repeat Rule VI., relating to logical subjects. What is the object of this rule?

§ 147. A comma after the logical subject is, also, sometimes necessary to prevent ambiguity. Thus, in the sentence, "He who pursues pleasure only defeats the object of his creation," it is impossible to tell whether *only* modifies *pleasure* or *defeats*. If the meaning is that "he who pursues nothing but pleasure defeats, &c.," a comma should be inserted after *only;* if not, we should have one after *pleasure.* The reader should not be left in doubt.

§ 148. A comma, followed by a dash, is generally placed after a logical subject when it consists of several particulars separated by semicolons, or by commas, when, for the sake of greater definiteness, the words *all, these, all these, such,* or the like, referring to the particulars before enumerated, are introduced as the immediate subject of the verb; as, "To be overlooked, slighted, and neglected; to be misunderstood, misrepresented, and slandered; to be trampled under foot by the envious, the ignorant, and the vile; to be crushed by foes, and to be distrusted and betrayed even by friends,—such is too often the fate of genius."

RULE VII.—ABSOLUTE WORDS AND CLAUSES.

§ 149. Absolute participial clauses, and substantives in the nominative absolute with their adjuncts and limiting words, must be set off by the comma; as, "*Rome having fallen,* the world relapsed into barbarism."—"*His conduct on this occasion,* how disgraceful it was!"—"Yes, *sir.*"—"And thou too, *Brutus!*"

Some absolute participial clauses have the participle understood, but must, notwithstanding, be punctuated according to the above rule. Thus, in the following lines, though *being* is left out after *steeds* and *foe,* the clauses must be set off by the comma:—

"Winged with his fears, on foot he strove to fly,
His steeds too distant, and the foe too nigh."

§ 150. The second example under Rule VII. illustrates a construction admissible in poetry, but not to be imitated in prose. It should read, "How disgraceful was his conduct on this occasion!" As originally given, it may be punctuated with either a comma or a dash after *occasion.*

---

§ 147. On what other account is a comma sometimes necessary after the logical subject? Illustrate this, and show how a comma prevents ambiguity.

§ 148. In what case is a comma followed by a dash placed after a logical subject?

§ 149. Repeat Rule VII., relating to absolute words and clauses. What is sometimes omitted from a participial clause? Does this change the mode of punctuating?

§ 150. What is the second example in § 149? What is said respecting such constructions?

EXERCISE.

Insert in the following sentences whatever points are required by the rules that have been given:—

UNDER § 142. Mahomet left Mecca a wretched fugitive he returned a merciless conqueror. A professed Catholic he imprisoned the Pope a pretended patriot he impoverished the country. The Scriptures those lively oracles of God contain the only authentic records of primeval ages. I Nebuchadnezzar king of the Jews make this decree Aristides the just Athenian is one of the noblest characters in Grecian history. Richard the Lion-hearted. Charles the Bald king of France. We saw him tyrant of the East.

UNDER § 143. The River Volga and the Ural Mountains form according to some geographers the boundary between Asia and Europe. We humble men may admire the great if we can not equal them. John Howard Payne the author of "Home, sweet home," and Samuel Woodworth who composed "The old oaken bucket," occupy a prominent place among American poets. It has been said that if all the learned and scientific men of every age could meet in a deliberative assembly they would choose Sir Isaac Newton for their president. With modesty your guide, reason your adviser, and truth your controlling principle, you will rarely have reason to be ashamed of your conduct. Herodotus is called the father of profane history. These grumblers would not have considered Cæsar himself a good general. Henry F. Witherspoon junior LL.D.

UNDER § 144. At the talents and virtues of all who hold different views from their own certain partisan writers are accustomed to sneer. Of all the passions vanity is the most unsocial. To love many a soldier on the point of realizing his dreams of glory sacrifices the opportunity of so doing. Whether such a person as Homer ever existed we can not say. How the old magicians performed their miracles it is difficult to explain. That riches are to be preferred to wisdom no one will openly assert.

UNDER § 145. With a crash fell the severed gates. On me devolves the unpleasant task. In memory's twilight bowers the mind loves to dwell. It is only by constant effort that men succeed in great undertakings. To the poor we should be charitable. To the poor men should be charitable. History we read daily. At the bottom of the hill ran a little stream. In Plato's garden congregated a crowd of admiring pupils. Respecting the early history of Egypt little is known. Equivocation I despise truth and honor I respect. It is chiefly by constant practice and close attention to correct models that one learns to compose with ease and elegance. This he denied.

UNDER § 146. The miracles that Moses performed may have convinced Pharaoh but at first they humbled not his pride. Every impure, angry, revengeful, and envious thought is a violation of duty. The evil that men do lives after them. Whatever breathes lives. The boldness of these predictions, the apparent proximity of their fulfillment, and the imposing oratory of the preacher struck awe into the hearts of his

audience. Spring, Summer, Autumn, and Winter have each its office to perform.

UNDER § 147. He who stands on etiquette, merely shows his own littleness. To become conversant with a single department of literature, only has a tendency to make our views narrow, and our impressions incorrect. To remain in one spot always, prevents the mind from taking comprehensive views of things.

UNDER § 148. The solemn circle round the death-bed, the stifled grief of heart-broken friends, their watchful assiduities, and touching tenderness, the last testimonies of expiring love, the feeble, fluttering, pressure of the hand, the last fond look of the glazing eye, turning upon us even from the threshold of existence, the faltering accents, struggling in death, to give one more assurance of affection, all these recollections rush into our mind as we stand by the grave of those we loved.

UNDER § 149. Whose gray top shall tremble, he descending — The baptism of John, was it from Heaven, or of men. This point admitted, we proceed to the next division of our subject. The boy, oh! where was he. This said He formed thee Adam, thee O man. Man to man, steel to steel, they met their enemy. Shame being lost, all virtue is lost — Their countenances expressive of deep humiliation, they entered the palace. O wretched, we devoid of hope and comfort. That man of sorrow, oh how changed he was to those who now beheld him. The conquest of Spain, their object they left no means untried for effecting a landing on the Peninsula. Honor once lost, life is worthless. I, whither can I go. The summing up, having been completed on both sides, the judge next proceeded to charge the jury.

UNDER § 150. Our time, how swiftly it passes away. Her dimples, and pleasant smile, how beautiful, they are. My banks they are covered with bees. The companion of my infancy, and friend of my riper years, she has gone to her rest, and left me to deplore my bereavement. Earthly happiness, what is it, where can it be found. The bride, she smiled; and the bride she blushed. (*After punctuating the sentences in this paragraph, as they stand, give them the usual prose construction and punctuate accordingly.*)

LESSON XXIII.

THE COMMA (CONTINUED).

RULE VIII.—SHORT MEMBERS.

§ 151. A comma must be placed between short members of compound sentences, connected by *and, but, or, nor, for, because, whereas, that* expressing purpose, *so that, in order that,* and other conjunctions.

---

§ 151. Repeat Rule VIII., relating to short members. If the members are long, or contain subdivisions set off by commas, how must they be separated?

EXAMPLES.

1. Educate men, and you keep them from crime.
2. Man proposes, but God disposes.
3. Be temperate in youth, or you will have to be abstinent in old age.
4. Be virtuous, that you may be respected.
5. Travelling is beneficial, because it enlarges our ideas.
6. The ship of state is soon wrecked, unless honesty is at the helm.
7. Love not sleep, lest thou come to poverty.
8. The record is lost, so that we cannot now decide the point.

If the members are long, or contain subdivisions set off by commas, they must be separated, according to principles already laid down, by the semicolon.

§ 152. Observe that a comma must not be placed before *that*, when not equivalent to *in order that;* nor before *than* or *whether*: as, "He said that he would come."—"Honest poverty is better than fraudulent wealth."

§ 153. No comma must be placed before *lest* when it immediately follows a word with which it is closely connected; as, "Let those who stand, take heed lest they fall."

RULE IX.—COMPOUND PREDICATES

§ 154. A comma must be placed before *and*, *but*, *or*, and *nor*, when they connect parts of a compound predicate, unless these parts are very short and so closely connected that no point is admissible; as, "I love not the woman that is vain of her beauty, or the man that prides himself on his wisdom."—"We can neither esteem a mean man, nor honor a deceitful one."

§ 155. If the parts of a predicate consist of but two or three words each, construed alike, a comma is not necessary; as, "Pleasure beckons us and tempts us to crime."

§ 156. A comma must not be placed before *and* and *or*, when they connect two words that are the same part of speech, either unlimited, or both limited by adjuncts of similar construction; as, "Here I

---

§ 152. Before what conjunctions is it improper to place a comma?
§ 153. Before what conjunction is the comma generally omitted?
§ 154. Repeat Rule IX., relating to compound predicates.
§ 155. In what case is a comma unnecessary between the parts of a predicate?
§ 156. State the principle that applies to *and* and *or* connecting two words that are the same part of speech.

and Sorrow sit."—"Trust not an ungrateful son or a disobedient daughter."

§ 157. The words, however, referred to in the preceding paragraph must be separated by the comma, if one is limited by a word or words which might be erroneously applied to both; as, "I have seven brave sons, and daughters."

§ 158. A comma must be used before conjunctions, when they connect two words contrasted, or emphatically distinguished from each other; also, before the adverb *not*, used without a conjunction between contrasted terms; as, "Charity both gives, and forgives."—"Liberal, not lavish, is kind Nature's hand."

RULE X.—EQUIVALENTS.

§ 159. A comma must be placed before *or*, when it introduces an equivalent, an explanatory word, or a clause defining the writer's meaning; as, "Autography, or the art of determining a person's character from his handwriting, is coming into vogue."—"Herodotus was the father of history, or rather of profane history."

§ 160. In double titles of books, a semicolon is generally placed before *or*, and a comma after it; as, "Fascination; or, The Art of Charming".

RULE XI.—OMISSION OF WORDS.

§ 161. When, to avoid repetition, *and*, *or*, *nor*, or a verb previously used, is omitted, a comma takes its place.

EXAMPLES.

1. In what school did the Washingtons, Henrys, Hancocks, Franklins, and Rutledges, of America, learn the principles of civil liberty? (AND is here omitted after the first three proper names respectively.)

2. The merciful man will not maim an insect, trample on a worm, or cause an unnecessary pang to the humblest of created things. (OR is omitted after *insect*.)

3. In the well-trained heart, neither envy, jealousy, hatred, nor revenge, finds a resting-place. (NOR is omitted after *envy* and *jealousy*.)

---

§ 157. In what case must the words just referred to have a comma between them?
§ 158. State the principle that applies to conjunctions connecting contrasted words.
§ 159. Repeat Rule X., relating to equivalents.
§ 160. How are double titles of books to be punctuated?
§ 161. Repeat Rule XI, relating to the omission of words. Give examples, show the omissions, and state what point must be inserted.

4. Conversation makes a ready man; writing, an exact man. (In the last member *makes* is omitted, and a comma takes its place.)

§ 162. When this rule is followed, the clauses or members in which the omission occurs, must be separated by semicolons. When, however, the clauses are very short, the style is lively, and the connection close, the comma may be employed to set off the clauses or members, and no point need be used in the place of the omitted comma; as, "When the sot sings the praises of sobriety, the miser of generosity, the coward of valor, and the atheist of religion, we may easily judge what is the sincerity of their professions."

RULE XII.—LAST OF A SERIES.

§ 163. A comma must be placed before *and*, *or*, and *nor*, when they connect the last of a series of clauses, or of a succession of words that are the same part of speech and in the same construction. See Examples 1, 2, 3, under Rule XI.

EXERCISE.

Insert in the following sentences whatever points are required:—

UNDER § 151. Anger glances into the breast of a wise man, but it rests only in the bosom of fools.— The island on which the city of New York stands was originally bought from the Indians for twenty-four dollars whereas it is now valued at three hundred million.— Week followed week until at last Columbus and his followers were thousands of miles from their native shore.— Bad men are constantly in search of some new excitement that their minds may be diverted from the reproaches of conscience.— Science is constantly making new discoveries, while ignorance and prejudice refuse to receive those already made.— Love flies out at the window, when poverty comes in at the door.— The lives of men should be filled with beauty just as the earth and heavens are clothed with it.

UNDER § 152. Honorable peace is better than uncertain war.— It is easier to excite the passions of a mob than to calm them.— What injustice that the new world was not called after Columbus!— We know not whether to-morrow's sun will find us alive.— Shall we forget that truth is mighty.— It is a strange fact that man alone of living things delights in causing pain to his species.

UNDER § 153. Take care lest the spoiler come.— The falling leaves bid us beware lest we fix our affections too firmly on the things of earth.

---

§ 162. When this rule is followed, by what point must the clauses be separated? What exception is there?

§ 163. Repeat Rule XII., relating to the last of a series of clauses.

— We should have a care lest sinful pleasures seduce us with their manifold temptations.— Beware lest they suddenly fall upon thee.

UNDER § 154. The great astronomical clock of Strasburg is twenty-four feet higher than the tallest of the Egyptian pyramids, and one hundred and forty feet higher than St. Paul's in London.— Cicero was superior to Demosthenes in the finish of his periods, but inferior to him in energy and fire.— The fool neither knows whether he is right, nor cares whether he is wrong.— The world has gained wisdom from its years, and is quick to penetrate disguises.— The brave man will conquer, or perish in the attempt.

UNDER § 155. Study disciplines the mind and matures the judgment.— Virtue should be the aim of our youth and the solace of our declining years.— Years come and go.— Galileo read or wrote the greater part of the night.— Here sit we down and rest.— How sweetly and solemnly sound the evening chimes.

UNDER § 156. The bold man does not hesitate to take a position and maintain it.— Adams and Jefferson died by a singular coincidence, July 4, 1826.— The magnitude of the heavenly bodies, and their almost infinite distance from us, fill our minds with views at once magnificent and sublime.

UNDER § 157. I woke and thought upon my dream.— With the aid of the telescope we discern in the moon vast yawning pits, and huge volcanoes sending forth their awful fires.— In the bazaar may be seen tons of ice and vast quantities of ivory from Africa.— The relative pronoun *who*, is applied to persons and things personified.

UNDER § 158. Bear, and forbear.— Brave, not rash, is the true hero.— He is not a fool, but only foolish.— Remember the favors you receive, not those you confer.— The credulous may believe this wonderful story, not I — It is as great a sin to murder one's self as to murder another.

UNDER § 159. The period, or full stop denotes the end of a complete sentence.— Republics show little gratitude to their great men, or rather none at all.— Hence originated philosophy, or the love of wisdom — At this point the lake is ten fathoms, or sixty feet deep — The Marquis of Anglesea, or as he was then called Lord Paget, lost a leg at the battle of Waterloo.

UNDER §·160. (*Besides punctuating the following sentences, use capitals wherever required by* § 65.) We have just finished reading "six months in the gold-diggings, or a miner's experience in Eldorado." — A new book of travels, has just made its appearance entitled "The City of the doges, or Venice, and the Venetians in the nineteenth century."

UNDER § 161. Study makes a learned man, experience a wise one.— Rapid, exhaustless, deep his numbers flowed.— Let your pleasure be moderate, seasonable, innocent, and becoming (*comma after* INNOCENT *according to* § 163).— Mahomet's Paradise consisted of pure waters, shady groves, luscious fruits, and exquisite houris.— The author dreads the critic, the miser the thief, the criminal the magistrate, and every body public opinion.— My head is filled with dew, my locks with the drops of the night.— Benevolence is allied to few vices, selfishness to fewer virtues.

UNDER § 162 Without books justice is dormant, philosophy lame, literature dumb, and all things are involved in darkness.— Without modesty, beauty is ungraceful, learning unattractive, and wit disgusting.— Pride goeth before destruction, and a haughty spirit before a fall.— Talent is surrounded with dangers, and beauty with temptations.

UNDER § 163. Mahomet the founder of Islamism, did not hesitate to work with his own hands, he kindled the fire, swept his room, made his bed, milked his ewes and camels, mended his stockings, and scoured his sword.— So eagerly the Fiend o'er bog, or steep, through strait, rough, dense or rare, with head, hands, wings, or feet pursues his way.

> Suns, moons, and stars, and clouds, his sisters were.
> Rocks, mountains, meteors, seas, and winds and storms,
> His brothers.

LESSON XXIV.

THE COMMA (CONTINUED).

RULE XIII.—COMMON CONNECTION.

§ 164. When two or more antecedent portions of a sentence have a common connection with some succeeding clause or word, a comma must be placed after each; as, "She is as tall, though not so handsome, as her sister."

Commas are frequently required, under this rule, after different prepositions governing the same substantive; as, "They are fitted for, and accustomed to, very different modes of life."

In the case of a series of adjectives preceding their noun, a comma is placed after each but the last; and there general usage, by an unphilosophical anomaly, requires us to omit the point; as, "A quick, brilliant, studious, learned man". This usage violates one of the fundamental principles of punctuation; it indicates, very improperly, that the noun *man* is more closely connected with *learned* than with the other adjectives. Analogy and perspicuity require a comma after *learned*.

---

§ 164. Repeat Rule XIII., relating to common connection. After what part of speech are commas frequently required under this rule? What usage prevails in the case of a series of adjectives preceding their noun? What is said of this usage?

RULE XIV.—WORDS IN PAIRS.

§ 165. Words used in pairs take a comma after each pair; as, "The dying man cares not for pomp or luxury, palace or estate, silver or gold."—"Ignorant and superstitious, cunning and vicious, deceitful and treacherous, the natives of this island are among the most degraded of mankind.'

RULE XV.—WORDS REPEATED.

§ 166. Words repeated for the sake of emphasis must be set off, with their adjuncts if they have any, by the comma; as, "Verily, verily, I say unto you."

§ 167. If, however, the repetition is abrupt, proceeds from hesitation, or is accompanied with a break in the sentiment, a dash may be used; as, "He has gone to his rest—gone, to return no more."

RULE XVI.—THE INFINITIVE MOOD.

§ 168. A comma must be placed before *to*, the sign of the infinitive mood, when equivalent to *in order to;* as, "Cicero sent his son to Athens, to complete his education."

RULE XVII.—QUOTATIONS AND OBSERVATIONS.

§ 169. The comma must set off quotations, passages resembling them in form, and observations in general, when short and not formally introduced; as, "It was Bion that first said, 'Know thyself.'"—"I would here call attention to the fact, that nature has endowed the body with recuperative faculties, which often enable it to rally and recover from prostration when science has exhausted all its remedies in vain"

When formally introduced by the words *these, following,* or *as follows,* a colon must precede the quotation.

§ 170. When a quotation is divided, a comma must be placed on

---

§ 165. Repeat Rule XIV., relating to words used in pairs.
§ 166. Repeat Rule XV, relating to words repeated.
§ 167. In what case may a dash be used instead of a comma?
§ 168. Repeat Rule XVI., relating to the infinitive mood.
§ 169. Repeat Rule XVII., relating to quotations. When formally introduced, by what point is the quotation preceded?

each side of the words introduced between its parts; as, "One to-day," says Franklin, "is worth two to-morrows."

RULE XVIII.—CORRELATIVE TERMS.

§ 171. Members of sentences, containing correlative adverbs and conjunctions, are separated by the comma; as, "The harder we study, the better we like to study."—"As a cloud darkens the sky, so sorrow casts a gloom over the soul."

§ 172. The comma, however, is generally omitted in the case of *so—that, so—as, rather—than,* and *more—than,* especially when the parts they connect are clauses and not members; unless the related parts contain subdivisions separated by the comma, in which case the same point must be placed before the last correlative term.

EXAMPLES.

1. He is so exhausted that he cannot work.
2. So act as to gain the respect of men.
3. The Laplander would rather live in his own land than any other.
4. Marie Antoinette was more amiable in her life than fortunate in her death.

1. He is so unwell, weak, and exhausted, that he cannot work.
2. So think, speak, and act, as to gain the respect of men.
3. The Laplander, however, would rather live in his own land, than any other.
4. Marie Antoinette, queen of France, was more amiable in her life, than fortunate in her death.

RULE XIX.—AMBIGUOUS CONSTRUCTIONS.

§ 173. A comma must be used, even when not required by the grammatical construction, wherever it serves to develop the sense or prevent ambiguity.

Thus, after a long logical subject, a comma is of service; as, "That a man thoroughly educated in youth and who has ever since been in the habit of composing could make so gross a mistake through ignorance, is almost incredible."

Cases in which the comma prevents ambiguity have been noticed under several of the foregoing rules.

---

§ 170. What is the mode of punctuating, when a quotation is divided?
§ 171. Repeat Rule XVIII., relating to correlative terms.
§ 172. In the case of what correlatives is the comma generally omitted? What however, do they take it?
§ 173. Repeat Rule XIX., relating to ambiguous constructions. According to the rule, where is a comma of service?

RULE XX.—NUMBERS EXPRESSED BY FIGURES.

§ 174. Except in the case of dates, numbers written in Arabic characters take a comma after each period of three figures, beginning at the right; as, "In 1846, the planet Neptune was discovered, and found to be at a distance of 2,900,584,000 miles from the sun."

Dates must always be expressed by figures. So must large numbers, when many words would be required to denote them. Otherwise, as in the case of round numbers, and always for small ones, words are to be employed. Thus: "Venus is, in round numbers, sixty-five million miles from the sun; its exact distance is 65,392,000 miles."—"We leave the ninety-nine sheep that are safe, to look after the one that is lost."

EXERCISE.

Supply the points omitted in the following sentences:—

UNDER § 164. The spirit of liberty must change it is fast changing the face of the earth.—The world at this moment is regarding us with a willing but something of a fearful admiration.—The literature of a nation is one of its highest and certainly one of its most refined elements of greatness.—He who lacks decision of character may win the love but he certainly cannot gain the respect of his fellow men.—This doctrine is founded upon and consistent with the truth.

UNDER § 165. These shores rough and cold barbarous and barren devoid of comforts and even necessaries peopled with fierce beasts and fiercer savages became their home.—Sink or swim survive or perish I am for the Declaration.—Vicissitudes of good and evil of trials and consolations of joy and sorrow of cloud and sunshine fill up the life of man.—I M take thee N to my wedded wife to have and to hold from this day forward for better for worse for richer for poorer in sickness and in health to love and to cherish till death us do part.

UNDER § 166. Lend lend your wings I mount I fly.—Quit oh quit this mortal frame.—Speak not harshly speak not harshly to the orphan's tender heart.—Charge charge on the cravens.—Some shriek shriek madly in the whirling gulf.—He swam the Tiber unhurt unhurt alike by his fall and the weapons of the enemy.

UNDER § 167. Dust dust thou art vile and dishonored dust.—The tyrant slept slept but rested not.—We have promised we have promised but recollect under certain restrictions.—I fear I fear that he will play you false.—You think him happily situated happily situated with a conscience that allows him no rest a conscience which keeps his evil deeds constantly before his eyes.

---

§ 174. Repeat Rule XX., relating to numbers expressed by figures. How must dates always be expressed? How, large numbers? Round numbers? Small numbers?

UNDER § 168. The people of Mayence to show their gratitude to Gutenberg the inventor of printing have erected in his honor a magnificent statue wrought by the sculptor Thorwaldsen.—Tyrants when reason and argument make against them have recourse to violence to silence their opponents.—He comes to heal the sick and set the captive free.—Oh! that I had the wings of the morning to flee to the uttermost parts of the earth.

UNDER § 169. A poet aptly asks "What will not men attempt for sacred praise?"—Let the thought be deeply engraved upon your heart that every moment which flies is irrecoverably lost.—The schoolmen of the Middle Ages occupied themselves with discussing the important question whether spirits can move from one place to another without passing through the intervening space.—Let our fixed resolve be liberty or death.—The truth of Swift's assertion that no man ever wished himself younger, may well be questioned.

UNDER § 170. "Liars," says Aristotle "are not believed even when they speak the truth."—An angel's arm," says the poet Young "can't snatch me from the grave; legions of angels," he adds with equal truth, "can't confine me there."—With what motive it may be asked, did Chatterton commence his course of imposture? For pecuniary profit I answer, or perhaps for the pleasure of deceiving the world.

UNDER § 171. Neither can wealth make a bad man respectable nor can poverty sink a worthy person below the station his virtues deserve. —As thy day is so shall thy strength be.—Whether Jansen is entitled to the undivided honor of inventing the telescope, or Metius had previously discovered the principle involved in that instrument is a subject of discussion among the learned.—Though he slay me yet will I trust in him.

UNDER § 172. They now live more happily than ever.—They now live more respectably, comfortably, and happily, than ever.—Catiline was so overcome with shame that he could not speak.—Catiline was so overcome with shame, disappointment and anger that he could not speak. —The history of the United States shows a more rapid advance in power and importance than has ever been made by any other nation— Cicero was as vain as he was eloquent.

UNDER § 173. To assume that a person is guilty of an offence because appearances happen to be against him, is manifestly unjust.—The author of these profound and philosophical essays on the abstract questions of Moral Philosophy, was a poor blacksmith.—Men who have no desire to participate in the factious quarrels and personal animosities which now unhappily distract the land, are rudely dragged into the arena of politics. —Books and study only teach the proper use of books.

UNDER § 174. In 1800 the population of the city of New York was 60,489, in 1850 it was 515,597, showing an increase during this lapse of fifty years of 455,108 souls.—In 1850 the debt of the state of New York, amounted to $22,859,053, we may call it in round numbers twenty-three millions of dollars.—The comet of 1811 had a diameter of at least 560,000 geographical miles and a tail eighty-eight millions of miles in length.

LESSON XXV.

THE COMMA (CONTINUED).

§ 175. As the rules for the comma are numerous and more difficult of application than those relating to the other points, it has been thought best to illustrate them with a miscellaneous exercise, which will bring before the student's mind, in connection, all the cases in which this point is required. Cautions are first presented, for the purpose of warning the student against errors which the author has found that the inexperienced are most likely to make.

CAUTION I. Do not suppose that a sentence, simply because it is long, must contain a comma. Unbroken connection between the parts of a sentence, no matter how long it may be, precludes the use of this point. Thus: " It is hard for those who pride themselves on the greatness of man to believe that those mighty cities which were once the wonder and admiration of the ancient world could so entirely have disappeared that their position is now a subject of discussion among scholars and antiquaries."

CAUTION II. Do not insert a comma between a grammatical subject and its verb, when the one immediately follows the other. A rhetorical pause is, in this case, sometimes required before the verb; but a comma, never.

CAUTION III. There must be no comma before *and*, when it connects two words only; as, " A prosperous and happy country".

CAUTION IV. Observe the difference of punctuation in sentences like the following:—

> The Romans, having conquered the world, were unable to conquer themselves.
> The Romans having conquered the world, freedom of thought and action became extinct.

---

§ 175. What is said of the rules for the comma? What is the substance of Caution I.? of Caution II.? of Caution III.? of Caution IV.? of Caution V.?

In the first sentence, *Romans* is the grammatical subject of *were*, and the parenthetical participial clause between these words must be set off by a comma on each side. In the second, *Romans*, being used absolutely with the participle *having conquered*, must not be separated from it by a comma, but this point must be reserved for the termination of the entire absolute clause.

CAUTION V. When you are in doubt as to the propriety of inserting commas, omit them; it is better to have too few than too many.

MISCELLANEOUS EXERCISE.

Supply such points as are necessary in the following sentences:—

UNDER RULE I. Education, if it cannot accomplish every thing, can nevertheless accomplish much.— Achilles, unquestionably, was a puissant warrior, but had not the poetry of Homer immortalized his name, he would now, in all likelihood, have been as little known as the meanest soldier in the Grecian host.

UNDER RULE II. By all that you hold dear on earth, listen to my prayer.— To accomplish these ends, he left no means, however insignificant, untried.— If I were not Alexander, I would be Diogenes.— If fortune has played thee false to-day, do thou play true for thyself to-morrow.— Never be discouraged however gloomy the prospect.

UNDER RULE III. In every line of Dante's "Divine Comedy," we discern the asperity, which is produced by pride, struggling with misery. — We designate as the mind that part of us which feels, knows, and thinks. — A man renowned for repartee, often sacrifices the feelings of his friends, to his attempts at wit.— The means, by which men acquire glory, are various.

UNDER RULE IV. Hail Patience, blest source of peace, blest cure for every pain.— Sisters, and brothers, how many may you be.— Were I even declared king, or elected president of such a nation, I should esteem it no honor.— The genealogy of princes, the field-book of conquerors history, is well worthy of our attention.

UNDER RULE V. Among the noblest attributes of a virtuous man, is justice.— Over the matchless talents of Washington, probity threw her brightest lustre.— Of infancy, childhood, boyhood, and youth, we have been discoursing.— Than pleasure's exaggerated promises, nothing can be more alluring to youth.

UNDER RULE VI. All that live, must die.— Apostles, prophets, and martyrs have proved the truth of the Christian faith.— All the rules of eloquence, the precepts of philosophy, and the refined conversation of Athens, to which place he was sent by his father for the completion of his education, failed to make Cicero's son, an orator, or a man of talent.— Worlds above, around, beneath, and on all sides, arch thee about as a centre.

UNDER RULE VII. The ship having left her wharf a salute was fired from the shore — A habit of indolence once formed, it is extremely difficult to shake it off — The campaign thus fairly opened, both parties prosecuted the war with unprecedented vigor — Ye men of Rome shake off your sloth.

UNDER RULE VIII. The sun sets, but he will rise again — We obey the laws of society because it is expedient to do so — Art is long but time is fleeting — Great poets are rare while empty rhymesters can be counted by thousands — Must we submit to such indignities in order that we may have enough to eat.

UNDER RULE IX. Man wants but little here below nor wants that little long — Sincerity is as valuable as knowledge and on some accounts more so — Cunning and avarice may gain an estate but cannot gain friends — We are naturally inclined to praise those who praise us, and to flatter those who flatter us

UNDER RULE X. English Grammar, or the art of speaking and writing the English language correctly, cannot in this country be too much studied — The Persians or rather the survivors of them retreated from the field of battle with all possible despatch — Young ladies' seminaries or as they were formerly called girls' schools abound in this part of the country

UNDER RULE XI, XII. Modern times with all their boasted progress, have never produced as strong a man as Samson, as meek a man as Moses, or as wise a man as Solomon — Life is short, unsatisfactory, and uncertain — Men, women and children stare, cry out, and run — Cæsar came, saw, and conquered.

UNDER RULE XIII. Deeds not words are the proper tests by which to try a man's character — Who is so beautiful, who so graceful as the maid of Lodore — I beg of you, beware of, and avoid the evil-doer — How sweet the voice, how blessed the words of him who offers consolation to the mourner.

UNDER RULE XIV. Poverty and distress, desolation and ruin, are the consequences of civil war — Virtue, without industry, and idleness without vice, are impossibilities — Generous but not prodigal frugal but not parsimonious brave but not rash, learned but not pedantic, this prince maintained a happy medium between all objectionable extremes

UNDER RULE XV. Onward! onward! strong, and steady — Blessed, thrice blessed, is the peace-maker — There we hope to enjoy rest never-ending rest, rest in which are concentrated all conceivable pleasures — Suddenly there came a tapping, as of some one gently rapping, rapping at my chamber door — Lochiel! Lochiel! beware of the day.

UNDER RULE XVI. We must respect ourselves to have others respect us — A man must be a genius indeed to say anything new about Niagara — Eat to live, do not live to eat — He is going to Europe, to see whether travelling will benefit his health.

UNDER RULE XVII. It was a principle of O'Connell's that no political advantage is worth a crime — When Xerxes sent a haughty message to Leonidas that he should deliver up his arms, the Spartan warrior answered in true Laconic style "Let him come and take them" — "Language", says Talleyrand " was given us to conceal our thoughts

UNDER RULE XVIII.—Though Tycho de Brahe, who lived near the close of the sixteenth century, certainly recognized the correctness of the Copernican system, at an early period, yet his ambitious vanity and religious prejudices urged him to oppose it,—Either you must confess your crime, or I shall have to suffer unjustly

UNDER RULE XIX. To contemplate abstract subjects only, disciplines the mind, rarely, if ever interesting it.— A long course of conduct so entirely opposed to what honest men consider required by the great principles of truth and justice, cannot be passed over without the strongest reprobation

UNDER RULE XX. The loftiest mountain in the moon is said by astronomers to be 17138 feet high,—The surface of the sun contains 1865312000000 square miles, that of the moon 10350400 that of the earth 148512000

LESSON XXVI.

THE DASH.

§ 176. The dash, a character of comparatively recent introduction, has of late, both by writers and printers, been very wrongly endowed with the functions of parentheses, comma, semicolon, colon, and even period; and is now extensively used by many, who find it a convenient substitute when ignorance prevents them from employing the proper point. Against this prevailing abuse the student can not be too impressively warned. The dash has its legitimate uses, and performs a part in which no other point can properly take its place ; but it must not be allowed to overstep its proper limits. Use this point, therefore, only where it is strictly required by the following rules :—

RULE I.—BREAKS, SUSPENSIONS, TRANSITIONS, &c.

§ 177. The dash is used to denote a break in the construction, a suspension of the sense, an unexpected transition in

---

§ 176. When was the dash first introduced? What is said of its use at the present day?

§ 177. Repeat Rule I., relating to breaks, suspensions, &c.

the sentiment, a sudden interruption, and hesitation in the speaker.

EXAMPLES.

1. Nero, Domitian, Caligula, Heliogabalus—one and the same character belongs to them all.
2. Politicians are brilliant, versatile, profound, far-seeing—everything but honest.

He had no malice in his mind—
No ruffles on his shirt.

4. "No one is aware of your imprisonment but Sir William, and he is——"
 "Here!" interrupted a deep voice, as the door flew open.
5. "I would do it, but—but— to say the truth—I——"
 "To say the truth, you are afraid," broke in the earl.

RULE II.—AFTER OTHER POINTS.

§ 178. A dash may be used after other points, when a greater pause than they usually denote is required.

Hence it appears that the dash is a rhetorical as well as a grammatical point.

Under this rule, a dash is used in the following cases:—

I. After a period, interrogation-point, and exclamation-point.

1. When a writer passes to a new branch of his subject without commencing a new paragraph; as, "From this it is evident that friendship had its origin in the social feelings which nature has implanted in the breast of man.—Let us now look at its effects."

2. In dialogues, when in the same paragraph one person ceases speaking and another begins; as, "' Art thou not—'—' What?'— 'A traitor!'—'Yes.'—'A villain!'—'Granted.'"

3. A dash is generally placed after the three points above mentioned, between a passage quoted and the name of the author or book it is taken from; also, between a side-head and the subject-matter to which it belongs; also, between sentences that have no connection when brought together in the same paragraph.

---

§ 178. Repeat Rule II., relating to the use of the dash after other points. What kind of a point does this show the dash sometimes to be? After what points is a dash sometimes required by a change of subject? In what case? When is a dash required after the period, interrogation-point, and exclamation-point, in dialogues? State the principle that applies to the use of the dash after these three points, in the case of quoted passages, side-heads, and unconnected sentences. When must a dash follow

EXAMPLES.

a. Men of humor are always, in some degree, men of genius.—COLE-
RIDGE's *Table-Talk.*

b. FORM OF THE EARTH.—Heraclitus supposed that the earth had the
form of a canoe ; Aristotle, that it was shaped like a timbrel
Anaximander, that it was a vast cylinder.

c. For dashes between unconnected sentences, see Exercise on p. 130.

II. After a colon, when reference is made by *this, these, following,* or
as follows, to several succeeding sentences or a new paragraph ; as,
" The cloth having been removed, the president rose and made the
following address :—

 ' Ladies and gentlemen, we have assembled, &c. "

III. After a semicolon a dash is sometimes used, though not absolutely
necessary, when the last member is placed in lively contrast with
the first, or implies strong opposition to it ; as, " He chastens ;—but
he chastens to save."

IV After a comma,

 1. When it follows a logical subject consisting of several particulars
separated by semicolons, or by commas, when, for the sake of
greater definiteness, the words *all, these, all these, such,* or the
like, referring to the particulars before enumerated, are introduced as the immediate subject of a verb; as, " To be overlooked.
slighted, and neglected ; to be misunderstood, misrepresented and
slandered ; to be trampled under foot by the envious, the ignorant, and the vile ; to be crushed by foes, and to be distrusted
and betrayed even by friends,—such is too often the fate of
genius."

 2. When, in consequence of the omission of *namely,* or a similar
word, a longer pause is required than that usually denoted by
the comma, though the connection is so close as not to admit a
higher point ; as, " There is one feeling, and only one, that seems
to pervade the breasts of all men alike,—the love of life."

RULE III.—REPETITIONS.

§ 179. The dash is used before a repeated word or expression, when the repetition is abrupt or exclamatory, proceeds

---

colon ? When is this point sometimes used after a semicolon ? In what two cases is a
dash required after a comma ?

§ 179. Repeat Rule III , relating to repetitions.

from hesitation, or is accompanied with a change in the sentiment.

EXAMPLES.

1. Here sleeps the dust of Cicero — Cicero! who once thrilled a world with his eloquence.
2. He is a—a—a—excuse me, but I must say it—a cold-blooded villain.
3. Such is your affected, sentimental lover—a lover of nothing but himself.

RULE IV.—OMISSIONS.

§ 180. The dash is used to denote an omission of letters, figures, and words; as, "On a bright summer day in the year 18—, the stirring little village of —— was thrown into unusual excitement by the arrival of the E—— family from London."

EXERCISE.

In the following sentences supply the omitted points:—

UNDER § 177. I am your lordship's most obsequious zounds what a peer of the realm And bid her you mark me on Wednesday next but soft what day is this Rich honesty often dwells in a poor house like your pearl in a spoiled oyster If it should rain I request the poor thing may have a—a what's this coat coat no coach I'm off Sir Charles I'll do your errands A double-barrelled gun two scruples of jalap my lady's poodle your lordship's wig a sticking-plaster they shall be here within the hour "My friend the counsellor." "Say learned friend if you please sir." "There is a business Mr. Alderman fallen out which you may oblige me infinitely by I am very sorry that I am forced to be troublesome but necessity Mr. Alderman" "Ay sir as you say necessity; But upon my word dear sir I am very short of money at present still" "That's not the matter sir." They poisoned my very soul hot burning poisons. Away ungrateful wretch A father's curse rest Alas what am I doing I cannot curse my son It was a sight that child in the agony of death that would have moved a heart of stone.

A crimson handkerchief adorned his head,
His face was cheerful and his nose was red.

UNDER § 178. They were about laying violent hands upon me in the senate-house. What must this empire then be unavoidably overturned. "Inform me friend is Alonzo the Peruvian confined in this dungeon?" "He is" "I must speak with him" "You must not" "He is my friend" "Not if he were your brother" "What is to be his fate? He dies at sunrise" "Ha then I am come in time" I find it profitable sometimes to indulge in such reflections as these All men are mortal Since the creation only two men have escaped death Therefore

---

§ 180. Repeat Rule IV., relating to omissions.

however likely it may appear that I shall hold a perpetual lease of life the time comes when like my fathers I must close my eyes on this pleasant world — I go but when I come 'twill be the burst of ocean in the earthquake I go but not to leap the gulf alone — The ambition of man constantly making him dissatisfied with what he has and inspiring him with desires for what is beyond his reach his envy which renders a neighbor's prosperity odious in his eyes his selfishness which robs him of the purest enjoyment God has ever vouchsafed that of doing good to his species these ignoble passions entail on him a succession of miseries and make life one scene of trial — I pause for a reply None Then none have I offended — The bounding of Satan over the walls of Paradise his sitting in the shape of a cormorant on the tree of life his alighting among the herd of animals which are so beautifully represented as playing about Adam and Eve his transforming himself into different shapes in order to hear their conversation all these circumstances give an agreeable surprise to the reader — Copernicus was instructed in that school where it is fortunate when one can be well taught the family circle

ANGER. As the whirlwind in its fury teareth up trees and deformeth the face of nature or as an earthquake in its convulsions overturneth cities so the rage of an angry man throweth mischief around him danger and destruction wait on his hand *Dodsley*

UNDER § 179. Merciful yes merciful as the hawk is to the dove — Prominent among the philosophers of antiquity is Socrates Socrates who looked beyond the absurd fables of his country's mythology Socrates who lifted his voice in behalf of truth and died a martyr in its cause Socrates who advanced as far in moral enlightenment as it was possible for the human intellect to do unaided by a revelation from on high — " I would not return if if " " If you thought I would allow you to remain " interrupted the earl harshly — Shall I who have spent my life in the camp I who have shed my blood in defence of my country I who am a soldier by experience as well as profession shall I compare myself with this flaunting captain — He has a weakness a weakness of the head as well as the stomach — " I will inquire into the matter and if if " · " Well if " broke in my father impatient of delay — He is full of love love for himself — Our friend is afflicted with a grievous consumption a consumption of victuals

UNDER § 180. A series of observations made in 18 showed that of one hundred shooting stars four had an elevation from the earth of 1—3 miles fifteen of 3 6 miles twenty-two of 6 10 miles thirty-five of 10 15 miles thirteen of 15 20 miles three of about 30 miles one of 45 46 miles one of about 60 miles and one of over 100 miles — In the year I visited L— In the winter of 1849 50 I studied this subject attentively and obtained much useful information respecting it from Grld smith's " History of the Earth and Animated Nature " chaps 4 9

LESSON XXVII

PARENTHESES.—BRACKETS.

§ 181. The word PARENTHESIS means *a putting in beside*; and the term is applied to a word or words introduced into a sentence for the purpose of explaining, modifying, or adding to, the leading proposition, but inserted abruptly, in such a way as to break the connection between dependent parts and interfere with their harmonious flow. Such an expression is placed between curves, known as *parentheses* or *marks of parenthesis*. It is indicated in reading by using a lower tone of voice and more rapid delivery than are employed for the rest of the passage. An example is presented in the following sentence: "Shall we continue (alas that I should be constrained to ask the question!) in a course so dangerous to health, so enfeebling to mind, so destructive to character?"

§ 182. Old writers, with whom intricate constructions and violations of unity were common, made frequent use of parentheses. The obvious disadvantage, however, of introducing propositions within propositions, a practice which draws off the reader's attention from the main point, and too often involves the sacrifice of perspicuity, harmony, and strength, has led late critics to advise the use of less intricate sentences, and to proscribe parentheses as incompatible with nervousness of style.

"On some occasions," says Blair, "these [parentheses] may have a spirited appearance; as prompted by a certain vivacity of thought, which can glance happily aside as it is going along. But, for the most part, their effect is extremely bad; being a sort of wheels within wheels; sentences in the midst of sentences; the perplexed method of disposing of some thought, which a writer wants art to introduce in its proper

---

§ 181. What does the word parenthesis mean? To what is the term applied? What marks are used to enclose such expressions? How are they indicated in reading?

§ 182. By whom were parentheses often employed? What is the advice of later critics, and on what is it based? What is the substance of Blair's remark on the sub-

place." Watts, also, remarks on this subject, "Do not suffer every occasional thought to carry you away into a long parenthesis." The propriety of such observations is so evident that good writers at the present day avoid formal parentheses as much as possible. The marks by which they are denoted have now, therefore, become comparatively rare; but in the cases covered by the following rule they cannot well be dispensed with.

§ 183. RULE I.—Marks of parenthesis are used to enclose words which explain, modify, or add to, the leading proposition of a sentence, when introduced in such a way as to break the connection between dependent parts and interfere with their harmonious flow.

EXAMPLES.

1. Matilda (such was the lady's name) smiled sweetly at this address.
2. The doctrine of the immortality of the soul and a system of future rewards and punishments was taught explicitly (at least as explicitly as could be expected of an ancient philosopher) by Socrates.
3. Are you still (I fear from the tone of your letter you must be) troubled with these apprehensions?

§ 184. Doubts may sometimes arise as to whether it is better to use parentheses, or commas, as prescribed in § 122 for parenthetical clauses. The latter point is preferable when the words in question coalesce readily with the rest of the sentence, but is inadmissible when a complete or independent member is inserted; particularly if it is brought in abruptly or its construction differs from that of the parts between which it stands. The following examples will illustrate these cases.

1. Every star, as we infer from indisputable facts, is the centre of a planetary system.
2. Every star (and this great truth is inferred from indisputable facts) is the centre of a planetary system.

§ 185. The proper place for parentheses is the middle of a sentence; yet loose writers sometimes place them at the end; as, "Such is the wonderful account given by travellers of the natives of Patagonia (travellers, you know, are sometimes fond of the marvellous)."

---

ject? What does Watts advise? What is said of the use of parentheses at the present day?

§ 183. Repeat Rule I., relating to the purpose for which marks of parentheses are used.

§ 184. What is sometimes a matter of question? When is the comma preferable? When is it inadmissible?

§ 185. What is the proper place for parentheses? Where do loose writers sometimes place them?

§ 186. Expressions of approbation or disapprobation introduced into reports of speeches as having been made by the audience, as well as remarks by the person reporting or publishing them, must be enclosed in parentheses; as,

This doctrine, as long as I have breath, I shall oppose. (Hear hear!) I shall oppose it in this hall; I shall oppose it on the hustings. (Cheers, mingled with hisses.) Nor shall I hesitate to publish to the world on whom rests the responsibility of advocating so arbitrary, unjust, and in all respects infamous, a measure. (Cries of "Order! Order!" from all parts of the hall.)

§ 187. In dramatic compositions, directions to the performers and all other parts not strictly belonging to the dialogue are enclosed in parentheses; except the names of the speakers, as they successively take up the discourse, which, constituting side-heads, are set off by a period and dash, or by a period alone; thus:—

CICERO.—Expel him, lictors. Clear the senate-house.
    (*They surround him.*)
CATILINE (*struggling through them*).—I go,—but not to leap the gulf alone.
You build my funeral-pile, but your best blood
Shall quench its flame.—(*To the lictors*) Back, slaves!—I will return.
    (*He rushes out. The scene closes.*)

§ 188. RULE II.—Matter within parentheses must be punctuated just as it would be in any other position, except before the last parenthetical mark. There, if the matter introduced is complete in itself as regards both construction and *sense*, an interrogation-point, an exclamation-point, or (in the case of the remarks and directions alluded to in § 186, 187) a period, may be used, according to the character of the sentence. If the parenthesis is incomplete in sense, however, there must be no point before the last mark. See the examples under § 186, 187, as well as the following:—

1. Men are born equal (here I see you frowning, biting your lip, and shaking your head); it is circumstances only that cast their lots in different stations.

---

§ 186. In reports of speeches, what are parentheses used for enclosing?
§ 187. In dramatic compositions, what are enclosed within parentheses? What points follow the names of the speakers, used as side-heads?
§ 188. Repeat Rule II., relating to matter within parentheses.

2. Robert is wasting his time (was it for this his family made such sacrifices?) in idle amusements.

3. The poets (tender-hearted swains!) have portrayed love as no prose-writer has ever been able to paint it.

§ 189. RULE III.—Marks of parenthesis are not necessarily accompanied with other points; neither, on the other hand, do they supersede the latter. Whatever point would be needed between the parts if the parenthesis were left out, must be retained. If a colon or semicolon is required, it must stand after the last parenthetical mark; if a comma, it must occupy the same position unless a parenthetical clause immediately precedes, in which case it must stand before the first mark of parenthesis.

"Matilda (such was the lady's name) smiled sweetly at this address." Here we have no comma, because none would be needed if the parenthesis were left out;—"Matilda smiled sweetly at this address."

"If a tree is known by its fruits (and who that believes Scripture can doubt it?), what must we think of these men?" Here the comma required after the hypothetical clause is inserted after the last mark of parenthesis.

"Are you still, my friend, (I fear from the tone of your letter you must be) troubled with these apprehensions?" Here the required comma is placed before the parenthesis because the parenthetical clause, *my friend*, immediately precedes.

§ 190. RULE IV.—An interrogation-point within parentheses is often placed after an assertion or supposition, to throw doubt on it; and an exclamation-point similarly enclosed is used to denote wonder, irony, or contempt; as, "When I get the office (?), I shall spend my leisure time in reading."— "This accurate scholar (!), who went to Eton and graduated at Cambridge has actually made a dozen grammatical mistakes within the compass of one short paragraph."

BRACKETS.

§ 191. BRACKETS are used principally in quoted passages,

---

189. What does Rule III. say respecting the use of other marks when parentheses are employed? Where must a colon or semicolon, if required, stand? Where, a comma? Give the examples, and show why they are so punctuated.

190. Repeat Rule IV., relating to the enclosing of interrogation-points and exclamation-points within parentheses.

to enclose words improperly omitted by the author or, introduced to correct a mistake. Sometimes, like parentheses, they enclose an observation, an explanatory word, or a critical remark, that does not belong to the quotation. They are also employed in dictionaries and similar works to enclose the figured pronunciation of a word, the primitive from which it is derived, or a reference to some other term.

EXAMPLES.

1. He might have been happy, and now [he] is convinced of it.
2. A variety of pleasing objects meet [meets] the eye.
3. Mrs. Hemans was born to be a great poet. [She may have been born to be a great poet; but, if so, we cannot help thinking that she woefully missed her mark.]
4. PETIT-MAITRE [pet'te-mā'tr] n. A coxcomb.

As regards the points to be used in connection with brackets, and the proper method of punctuating the matter contained within them, the same principles apply as those laid down for parentheses v. § 188, 189.

When an independent sentence is enclosed, as in Example 3 given above, a period, an interrogation-point, or an exclamation-point must be used before the last bracket, according to the character of the sentence.

EXERCISE.

In the following sentences, supply the points required :—

UNDER § 183, 185. Is it I must take the liberty of asking because no law touches the case that you thus violate justice — For I know that in me that is in my flesh dwelleth no good thing — He had not been there so I was informed by those who lived in the neighborhood since the year 1840 — He Mr. Brown had never before found himself in so embarrassing a position He was overcome and he begged the company would not think he was exaggerating his feelings with this unexpected mark of esteem — I expected to find every thing that great wealth for my friend is a man of property and taste for his taste is admitted to be unexceptionable could bestow — Here we took dinner though conscience will hardly allow me to dignify sour bread and musty eggs by so high-sounding a name

UNDER § 186, 187. I agree with the honorable gentleman Mr Allen that it is pleasing to every generous mind to obey the dictates of sympathy but sir truth and justice impose on us higher obligations Lengthened applause and confusion in the galleries during which several sen-

---

§ 191. For what are brackets used? What use is made of them in dictionaries? What points may be used in connection with brackets? How must the matter they enclose be punctuated? When an independent sentence is enclosed, what point must precede the last bracket?

tences were lost Mr Chairman I cannot vote for this resolution Cheers I owe it not only to my country but to the rights of man of which so much is said to preserve the wise and long-established policy of the former and to stand by the principle of non-intervention as a high moral defence and security for the latter The speaker took his seat amid loud applause

SENTINEL Go in *Exit Sentinel*
ROLLA *calls* Alonzo Alonzo
 Enter Alonzo speaking as he comes in
ALONZO How Is my hour elapsed Well I am ready

UNDER § 188. The honorable gentleman on the right Mr Doubleday of Louisiana has overlooked one important point — I wish and why should I deny it that this compliment had been paid to any one rather than myself — She had managed this matter so well oh she was the most artful of women that my father's heart was gone before I suspected it was in danger — Consider and oh may the consideration sink deep into your heart that one crime inevitably leads the way to others

UNDER § 189. While we earnestly desire the approbation of our fellow-men and this desire the better feelings of our nature cannot fail to awaken we should shrink from gaining it by dishonorable means — Such was the creed of the Stoics see Tenneman's Manual Vol II p 230 and their principles were for the most part strictly carried out in life — The baron left to himself malice itself could not wish him a worse adviser resolved on a desperate course — Could he possibly have committed this crime I am sure he could not which as all will acknowledge is at variance with the whole tenor of his life

UNDER § 190. This would-be scholar once declared that the Iliad was the noblest poem in the Latin language — Her intellectual beauty is certainly surpassed only by her physical charms — Entering into conversation with his most Christian Majesty I was shocked to hear views advanced which would almost have disgraced a heathen.

UNDER § 191. A man had four sons and he divided his property between among them — Be more anxious to acquire knowledge than about showing to show it — He has little more of the scholar besides than the name — Some alas too few for the well-being of society place their bliss in action some in ease — ELUDE Latin *cludo* v. t. to escape — ENNUI ong-we weariness dullness of spirit — PETER-WORT n. A plant. *See* SAINT PETER'S WORT

LESSON XXVIII.

APOSTROPHE.—HYPHEN.—QUOTATION-POINTS.

Besides the grammatical points, various other marks are employed in written and printed matter; the principal of these are the Apostrophe ('), the Hyphen (-), and Quotation-points (" ").

Besides the grammatical points, what other marks are employed?

THE APOSTROPHE.

§ 192. The word *apostrophe* means *a turning from* or *away*. The mark so called has the same form as the comma, and differs from it only in being placed above the line.

RULE I.—OMISSION OF LETTERS.

§ 193. The apostrophe is used to denote the omission of a letter or letters; as, *'tis, I'll, o'er, tho'*.

The period and the dash are also employed, as we have already seen, for this purpose. The following distinction, however, is to be observed:—

1. The period is employed mainly in abbreviations of titles, proper names, technical and tabular terms, and foreign words; as, *P. M. G.*, for *Post-master General;—Jas. K. Polk*, for *James Knox Polk;—D. V.*, for *Deo volente, God willing;—bu.*, for *bushel*.
2. The dash is used when it is desired to allude to an object without making known what it is; as, "In the year 18—, the usually quiet village of L—— was thrown into a state of excitement," &c.
3. In most other cases, that is, when the object is merely to abbreviate common English words which do not fall under the above classes, or to contract two words into one, the apostrophe is employed.

RULE II.—POSSESSIVE CASE.

§ 194. The apostrophe is used to denote the possessive case of nouns; as, *India's treasures;—kings' daughters*.

To form the possessive case, singular nouns take *'s*; as, *fancy's flight;—Thomas's unbelief*. Plural nouns ending in *s* take the apostrophe alone; as, *the cities' gates:* other plural nouns take *'s*; as, *men's sorrows*. But if, by reason of a succession of *s* sounds, or from any other cause, euphony would be violated by the introduction of an *s*, the apostrophe alone is used in forming the possessive; as, *Moses' staff;—for conscience' sake;—Felix' speech*.

§ 192. What does the word apostrophe mean? How does the mark so called differ from the comma?

§ 193. Repeat Rule I., relating to the omission of letters. What other points are employed for this purpose? In what case is the period used? In what, the dash? In what, the apostrophe?

§ 194. For what other purpose is the apostrophe used, according to Rule II.? How do singular nouns form their possessive case? How, plural nouns? When is the apostrophe alone used in forming the possessive?

§ 195. Observe that this rule applies only to nouns. The possessive case of the personal pronouns, whether ending in *s* or not, must have no apostrophe; as, *mine, her, hers, ours, yours, theirs.*

§ 196. The apostrophe followed by *s* is also used to form the plural of the names of letters, figures, and signs; as, "Dot your *i's*, cross your *t's*, make your 6*'s* better, and insert two +*'s.*"

THE HYPHEN.

§ 197. The word *hyphen* is derived from two Greek words meaning *under one;* and the mark so called is used to denote that the parts between which it stands belong to one and the same word.

RULE I.—COMPOUND EPITHETS AND SUBSTANTIVES.

§ 198. The hyphen must be placed between words that unite to form a single epithet, and also between the parts of a compound substantive when each receives the stress of the voice; as, *laughter-loving, good-natured, twenty-one, never-to-be-forgotten, glass-house, self-conceit, one's-self.*

§ 199. Compound words, however, whose parts have so completely coalesced that they have but one accent, are written without the hyphen; as, *watchman, lapdog, broadsword, himself.*

RULE II.—DISTINCTION OF WORDS.

§ 200. The hyphen is used to distinguish words of similar spelling, but different pronunciation and meaning; also, to form one compound term of words which, if not thus united, would have a different signification.

Thus *re-creation* means *the act of creating again;* and, when the word so written, the first *e* is long, as in *me.* If we omit the hyphen, we

---

§ 195. What is said of the possessive case of pronouns?
§ 196. How is the plural of the names of letters, figures, and signs, formed?
§ 197. What is the meaning of the word *hyphen?* What does the mark so called denote?
§ 198. Repeat Rule I., relating to compound epithets and substantives.
§ 199. What compounds are written without the hyphen?
§ 200. For what other purposes is the hyphen used, according to Rule II.? Illustrate

have *recreation*,—quite a different word, equivalent to *relaxation, amusement;* and we must give the first vowel the sound of *e* in *met.*

The words *monk's-hood* and *dog's-ear* will serve as examples of the second case mentioned in the rule. Leave out the hyphen, and we no longer have the familiar plant known as *monk's-hood,* but a *monk's hood,* that is the head-covering of a monk. *Dog's-ear* means the corner of a leaf turned or twisted over; but remove the connecting mark, and we have the ear of a dog.

§ 201. The hyphen may also be used instead of the diæresis, to denote that two adjacent vowels do not unite to form a diphthong, when these vowels respectively terminate a prefix and commence the radical with which it is joined; as, *pre-existent, co-operate.*

RULE III.—BETWEEN SYLLABLES.

§ 202. When, from want of space, a portion of a word has to be carried to a new line, the division must be made after a complete syllable, and the hyphen is used at the end of the line, to connect the separated parts; as, 'Virtue cannot be bought."

§ 203. With regard to SYLLABICATION, or the division of words into syllables, it is proper to remark that two systems prevail. The English method divides on the vowels, that is, without reference to pronunciation, throws consonants as much as possible into the beginning of syllables; as, *me-lon, wi-dow, di-li-gent, a-stro-no-my.* This method, as Webster justly remarks, contradicts the very definition of a syllable. "A syllable in pronunciation", says this author, "is an *indivisible* thing; and, strange as it may appear, what is *indivisible* in utterance is *divided* in writing; when the very purpose of dividing words into syllables in writing, is to lead the learner to a just pronunciation." Some English writers, however, and among them Lowth, advocate the method generally adopted in this country, of making such divisions as most nearly exhibit the true pronunciation. According to this system, the examples

---

the first case with the word *recreation.* Illustrate the second with the words *monks-hood* and *dog's-ear.*

§ 201. For what purpose is the hyphen, like the diæresis, sometimes used? In what case?

§ 202. Repeat Rule III., relating to the use of the hyphen at the end of a line.

§ 203. What is syllabication? How many systems prevail? Describe the English system. What does Webster say of it? Describe the system pursued in this country.

given above would be divided thus: *mel-on, wid-ow, dil-i-gent, as-tron-o-my.* A few rules covering most cases may be of service.

RULE I.—Join consonants to the vowels whose sounds they modify; as, *ep-i-dem-ic, an-i-mos-i-ty.*

RULE II.—Let prefixes and suffixes form distinct syllables when this can be done without the pronunciation's being misrepresented: as, *re-print, out-run; re-ject-ed,* not *re-jec-ted; form-er,* not *for-mer,* when the meaning is *one that forms.*

RULE III.—In the case of compounds, syllabic divisions should fall between the simple words that compose them; as, *horse-man, more-over, gentle-woman.*

RULE IV.—The terminations *cial, tial, sion, tion, cious, tious,* and others that are pronounced as one syllable, must not be divided.

§ 204. After the numerous instances in which it has just been so employed, it is hardly necessary to add that the hyphen is used by lexicographers and others, not only at the end of a line, but wherever they desire to show the syllables of which a word is composed.

QUOTATION-POINTS.

§ 205. QUOTATION-POINTS, called in French and sometimes in English, from the name of the person who first used them, GUILLEMETS, consist of two inverted commas and two apostrophes [" "]. They are used to enclose words quoted from an author or speaker, or represented in narratives as employed in dialogue; as, "By doing nothing," says an old writer, "men learn to do evil."—"Quick! quick! or I perish," shrieked the exhausted hunter. "One moment longer! The rope has come!" shouted a hundred voices from the top of the crag.

When the substance merely is given, and not the exact words, quotation-points are unnecessary; as, *Diogenes used to say that other dogs*

In dividing into syllables, with what must consonants be joined? What is said about prefixes and suffixes' forming distinct syllables? How are compounds divided? What terminations must not be divided?

§ 204. What use is made of the hyphen by lexicographers?

§ 205. What are quotation-points called in French? Why are they so called? Of what do they consist? What are they used to enclose? When the substance merely

bit their enemies, but that he bit his friends that he might save them. Had the exact words used by the philosopher been given, quotation points would have been required. Thus: Diogenes used to say, "Other dogs bite their enemies; but I bite my friends, that I may save them."

In the case of passages cited in a foreign language, titles of books, names of newspapers, &c., some writers prefer italics to quotation-points; as, "Virgil's *Labor omnia vincit* has passed into a proverb."—"The *Athenæum* has a well written review of Pearson's *History of the Puritans*."

§ 206. Matter within quotation-points is to be punctuated just as if it stood in any other position. If at the close of a quoted passage any grammatical point is required, it may be placed before the two apostrophes if it is applicable to the extract alone, but after them if it belongs to the sentence or member as a whole; as, *He answered briefly*, "Am I a knave that you should suspect me of this?"—Are our lots indeed cast in "the brazen age"?

§ 207. Single Points [' '] are used to enclose a quotation within a passage which is itself quoted; as, "The great rule," says Lavater, "of moral conduct, or 'ethics', as it is styled by philosophers, is to make the best use of one's time."

If within a passage thus enclosed between single quotation-points, there is occasion to introduce another extract, double points are used for the sake of distinction; as, "King Louis asked Joinville, 'Would you rather be a leper, or commit what the church calls "a deadly sin"?'"

§ 208. When an extract consists of several successive paragraphs, inverted commas must stand at the commencement of each, but the apostrophes are not used till the quotation ends; as,

---

is given, are quotation-points necessary? For what do some writers prefer italics to quotation-points?

§ 206. How is matter within quotation-points punctuated? If a grammatical point is required at the close of a passage, how must it be placed as regards the two apostrophes?

§ 207. What are single quotation-points used to enclose? If within a passage thus enclosed another extract is introduced, how must it be denoted?

§ 208. How are the inverted commas and apostrophes used in an extract consisting of several paragraphs?

"No man can be happy, if self is the sole object of his thoughts and wishes.

"No man can be happy, if conscience tells him that he has left a single duty unperformed.

"No man can be happy who is destitute of good principles and generous feelings."

LESSON XXIX.

EXERCISE ON THE APOSTROPHE, THE HYPHEN, AND QUOTATION POINTS.

In the following sentences, supply the omitted points and marks :—

UNDER § 193. He whos virtuous and pious in this life will be happy i the next — Tis one who ll neer forget you — Tho the heavens and the earth pass away truth shall live forever — Oer hill through vale mid snow een tho gainst his own will he steadily pursues his way — I ll take a milder medcine than revenge for Ive lovd her as few have lovd

UNDER § 194, 195. Swans down ; — a ladys fan ; — ladies dresses ; — childrens hats ; — Misses shoes ;—eagles wings ; — All Saints Church.— Peters wifes mother lay sick of a fever — Much depends on this principles being understood and these rules being strictly observed — Racines and Corneilles tragedies hold the same rank in French literature as Shakspeares enjoy in English — "Mens virtues" says a splenetic writer "like angels visits are few and far between" — This volume of Grays poems is neither his hers yours nor theirs it is either mine or my brothers — A few moments conversation convinced me of my friends sincerity — Xerxes soldiers ; — for goodness sake ; — Crœsus son ; —Musæus songs ; — Hercules sword

UNDER § 196. Make your *f*s better give your *g*s the same slant and let your — *s* be of the same length — A supply of *es hs qs .s* and *;s* must be procured from the foundry — Three 5*s* — five 3*s*

UNDER § 198. At twenty one my sister in law was a laughter loving bright eyed pure hearted single minded girl — The market women are bringing in an abundance of water melons musk melons and a new variety of apple called seek no furthers — My fellow traveller had a dare devil look that made me regard his double barrelled pistols with some apprehension and wish myself safe back in my old farm house — Such bottle of small beer comparisons ought to be avoided — The ladies hats the present season give their faces a bewitching kiss me if you dare expression

UNDER § 199. These boatmen are allowed to sleep in the daytime — She makes a good housewife — Gunpowder for sale

UNDER § 200, 201. The stolen articles were restored — The goods were taken from one warehouse and restored in another — Ripe fruits recreate the nostrils with their aromatic scent — Instead of reinforcing it was found necessary to recreate the army — To reform public abuses is one of the aims of every true patriot — The troops were reformed into a hollow square — My health is reestablished — Articles are sometimes reexported — These two bodies were thus reunited — What mortal knows his preexistent state — We have been gathering wolfs bane and bears foot

UNDER § 203 (*Divide the following words into syllables by means of hyphens:*) Helen, never, every, abomination, apostolical, trinitarian, heretic, ejecting, reflected, lioness, poetaster, preexistent, transacted, obvious, nevertheless, notwithstanding, official, courageous, officious, palatial, paleaceous, occasion, termination, adhesion, meandered, anathematizing.

UNDER § 205. All things rare and brilliant says Goldsmith in his History of Man and Quadrupeds will ever continue to be fashionable while men derive greater advantage from opulence than virtue — After Phocion was condemned to death one of his friends asked him if he had any message to leave his son Tell him said the magnanimous patriot to serve his country as faithfully as I have done and to forget that she rewarded my services with an unjust death — Every day thousands are going to that bourne from which no traveller returns — This morning's courier contains a full description of the Great Eastern the largest vessel in the world — The British Critic has an able article on Bonners Inquiry into the Origin of Language and a lengthy review of the same authors Hints on the Subject of Reform

UNDER § 206. Then said he Lo I come — The prose of Tasso is placed by Corniani almost on a level with his poetry for beauty of diction We find in it he says dignity of rhythm and elegance purity without affectation and perspicuity without vulgarity — We naturally ask How can these things be — Can any one help admiring the great genius of him whom all Europe designates as the man of destiny — We can only weep and cry with the poet Alas poor Yorick

UNDER § 207, 208. "Hallam justly remarks There is more of the conventional tone of amorous song than of real emotion in Surreys poetry The

Easy sighs such as men draw in love

are not like the deep sorrows of Petrarch or the fiery transports of the Castilians" — "The tale made every ear which heard it tingle and every heart thrill with horror It was in the language of Ossian the song of death"

"The history of the present king of Great Britain is a history of repeated injuries and usurpations all having in direct object the establishment of an absolute tyranny over these States To prove this let facts be submitted to a candid world

He has refused his assent to laws the most wholesome and necessary for the public good

He has dissolved Representative Houses repeatedly for opposing with manly firmness his invasions on the rights of the people

He has made judges dependent on his will alone for the tenure of their offices and the amount and payment of their salaries

He has erected a multitude of new offices and sent hither swarms of officers to harass our people and eat out their substance

---

LESSON XXX

OTHER MARKS USED IN WRITING AND PRINTING.

§ 209. Besides the marks already described, there are others occasionally used for different purposes, as follows:—

I. ACCENTS, or marks placed over vowels to indicate their pronunciation. They are three in number:—

1. The ACUTE ACCENT [´] is placed over the vowel *e* in some words from the French language, to indicate that it is not silent, but has the sound of *a* in *cane;* as, *condé, bal paré.*

    It is used by elocutionists to denote the rising inflection, as, "Are they *hére?*"

    Placed after a syllable, it shows that the accent or stress of the voice falls thereon; as, *el'ement, philos'opher.*

2. The GRAVE ACCENT [`] is sometimes placed over the vowel *e* in poetry, to denote that it must not be suppressed in pronunciation; as,

    "The *bruisèd* sea-weed wastes away;
    Its atoms on the breezes ride."

    By elocutionists it is used in contradistinction to the acute, to denote the falling inflection; as, "They are *hère.*"

3. The CIRCUMFLEX ACCENT [ˆ] is placed by lexicographers over certain vowels, to indicate a peculiar sound; as, *hâll, marîne, bûll.*

    Writers on oratory use it to denote a wave, or combination of the rising and the falling inflection in the pronunciation of the same syllable; as, "It is not he; it is *shê.*"

---

§ 209. What are accents? How many are there? What are they called? Over what vowel is the acute accent sometimes placed? In words derived from what language? So placed, what does it indicate? For what is it used by elocutionists? Placed after a syllable, what does it show? Over what vowel is the grave accent sometimes placed in poetry? For what purpose? How do elocutionists use it? For what is the circumflex accent used by lexicographers? For what, by elocutionists?

II. QUANTITY-MARKS. These are two in number :—

1. The MACRON [¯], placed over a vowel to denote its long sound; as fāte, mēte, nōte, Hēliōgabālus.
2. The BREVE [˘], placed over a vowel to denote its short sound; as, făt, mĕt, nŏt, Heliŏgăbalŭs.

III. EMPHASIS-MARKS, used generally at the beginning of paragraphs, to attract the special attention of the reader They are found in newspapers, cards, hand-bills, &c., but rarely in books. They are,

1. The INDEX, or HAND [☞].
2. The ASTERISM [⁂].

IV. DIVISION-MARKS, which denote the commencement of a new branch of the subject. The marks generally used for this purpose are,

1. The PARAGRAPH [¶], rarely found in modern books, but common in the Bible and other old publications. The beginning of a new subject is now indicated simply by a break; that is, by commencing on a new line, a little to the right. The word *paragraph* is derived from the Greek; and literally means *a marginal note, something written near or alongside.*
2. The SECTION [§], the mark for which seems to be a combination of two *s*'s, standing for *signum sectionis, the sign of the section.* This mark is placed before subdivisions of books in connection with numbers, to facilitate reference; it is so used throughout this volume.

V. REFERENCE-MARKS, used to connect a word or words in the text with remarks in the margin, or at the bottom, of the page on which they occur. Their names are given below, in the order, in which, by the common consent of printers, they are introduced.

How many quantity-marks are there? What are they called? What does the macron denote? What, the breve?

Where do emphasis-marks generally stand? For what are they used? Name and describe them.

What do division-marks denote? Name them. Where is the paragraph found? Is it used in modern publications? How is the beginning of a new subject now indicated? From what language is the word *paragraph* derived? What does it mean? From what is the section formed? How is this mark used?

For what are reference-marks employed? Give their names in the order in

1. The ASTERISK . . . . . . *
2. The OBELISK, or DAGGER . . †
3. The DOUBLE DAGGER . . . ‡
4. The SECTION . . . . §
5. PARALLELS . . . . ‖
6. The PARAGRAPH . . . . ¶

When more than six reference-marks are required, some printers double and treble those just enumerated. The better way, however, is to use small figures or letters, technically called *superiors*.

VI. MARKS OF ELLIPSIS, [———], [.....], or [* * * *], are used to show that letters are omitted from a word, words from a sentence, sentences from a paragraph, or entire paragraphs and chapters from a work; as,

1. "The k—g, (k..g, *or* k**g) promenades the city at night in disguise."
2. "If an Artist love his Art for its own sake, he will delight in excellence wherever he meets it, as well in the work of another as in his own. * * * * Nor is this genuine love compatible with a craving for distinction."

In Example 1, *k—g, k..g*, or *k**g*, is used for *king*. It will be observed that, when periods or stars are thus introduced into words, there must be one for each letter omitted. When they are used, as in Ex. 2, to denote the omission of one or more sentences, any number may be employed; but too many mar the beauty of a printed page.

VII. The BRACE [⌒] is used to connect several terms or expressions with one to which all have a common relation; as,

Bagatelle, ⎫
Cortége,   ⎬ may be translated ⎧ trifle;
Ennui,   ⎭   ⎨ escort;
                               ⎩ weariness.

The brace is, also, sometimes employed to connect a triplet, or three lines of poetry rhyming together, when introduced into a poem, most of whose lines rhyme in pairs or couplets; as,

So slowly, by degrees, unwilling fame ⎫
Did matchless Eleonora's fate proclaim, ⎬
Till public as the loss the news became. ⎭

VIII. The DIÆRESIS (¨), placed over either (generally the

---

which they are used by printers? When more than six are required, what is it best to employ?

Describe the different marks of ellipsis. For what are they used? When periods or stars are used to denote the omission of letters, how many must there be? When they denote the omission of a sentence, how many must there be?

For what is the brace used? For what is it sometimes employed in poetry?

latter) of two contiguous vowels, shows that they do not form a diphthong, but must be pronounced separately; as, *zoölogy, aëronaut, phaëton.* The word is of Greek origin, and signifies *a division.*

IX. The CEDILLA is a mark sometimes placed under the letter *c* (ç) standing before *a* and *o*, to show that, contrary to analogy, it has the sound of *s*. This mark seldom occurs except in certain French words not yet fully naturalized in English; as, *façade, garçon.*

X. The DOUBLE COMMA („) is used to denote that a word is to be supplied from a line above in the space immediately beneath it. Names of persons, however, are generally repeated; as,

      Harvey Johnson, jr., Steubenville, Ohio.
      Jacob J. Johnson, jr.,   „   „

Sometimes inverted commas (") are preferred for this purpose.

XI. LEADERS (.....) are dots placed at short intervals, to carry the eye from words at the commencement of a line to matter at its end with which they are connected. It is chiefly in tables of contents and indexes of books that leaders are required. Thus:—

      Media of Communication .... page 13.
      Spoken Language ....:............. „   17.
      Written   „   .... „   20.

XII. The CARET (‸), used only in manuscript, shows where interlined words are to be introduced; as, "No man is exempted from ‸ ills of life." The name of this mark is a Latin word, meaning *it is wanting.*

Where is the diæresis placed? What does it show? From what language is the word derived, and what does it signify?
Under what letter is the cedilla placed? Before what vowels? In what words?
Where and for what is the double comma employed? What other mark is preferred by some for this purpose?
What are leaders? Where, principally, are they required?
Where is the caret used? What does it show? What is the origin, and what the meaning, of the word?

XIII. There are, also, certain characters which may with propriety be here enumerated.

In Prices Current, Book-keepings, &c., we meet with ℔ for *per*, *a*, *each*, and @, *at*, *to*. In almanacs, treatises on Astronomy, and the like, the following marks constantly occur:—

☿	. . .	Mercury.	⚳	. .	Ceres.	○	. .	New Moon.
♀	. . .	Venus.	⚴	. .	Pallas.	☽	. .	First Quarter.
⊕	. . .	Earth. .	♃	. .	Jupiter.	●	. .	Full Moon.
♂	. . .	Mars.	♄	. .	Saturn.	☾	. .	Last Quarter.
⚶	. . .	Vesta.	♅	. .	Uranus.	☌	. .	Conjunction.
⚵	. . .	Juno.	⚴, ☉	.	Sun.	☍	. .	Opposition.

TECHNICAL TERMS PERTAINING TO BOOKS.

§ 210. NAMES OF BOOKS.—A book is said to be in folio, or as abbreviated fol., when the sheets of which it is composed are folded once, each making two leaves, or four pages. The size of a folio volume, and indeed of all the others enumerated below, depends on that of the sheet; but, with the same sheet, a book of folio form is twice as large as one in quarto, and four times the size of an octavo, as will be presently seen. Formerly, almost all books were printed in folio; but the weight of such volumes, and the difficulty of handling them, rendering them decidedly objectionable, they have gradually gone out of fashion; and now no book is published in folio, unless a large page is required for exhibiting illustrations, or some similar purpose.

A quarto, or 4to volume is one whose sheets are folded into four leaves or eight pages. An octavo, or 8vo, consists of sheets divided into eight leaves or sixteen pages each; and so a duodecimo, or 12mo, a 16mo, 18mo, 24mo, 32mo, 48mo, and 64mo, denote volumes composed respectively of sheets folded into twelve, sixteen, eighteen, twenty-four, thirty-two, forty-eight, and sixty-four leaves.

What does the character ℔ denote? What, the character @? Learn the astronomical marks.

§ 210. When is a book said to be in folio? On what does the size of a folio volume depend? Were folio volumes formerly more or less in vogue than at present? Why have they gone out of fashion? What is meant by a quarto volume? an octavo? a 12mo? a 16mo? a 24mo? a 32mo? a 48mo? a 64mo?

§ 211. KINDS OF TYPE.—There are different sizes of type of which the following are most used:—

English, abcdefghijklmnopqrstuvwxyz.
Pica, abcdefghijklmnopqrstuvwxyz.
Small Pica, abcdefghijklmnopqrstuvwxyz.
Long Primer, abcdefghijklmnopqrstuvwxyz.
Bourgeois, abcdefghijklmnopqrstuvwxyz.
Brevier, abcdefghijklmnopqrstuvwxyz.
Minion, abcdefghijklmnopqrstuvwxyz.
Nonpareil, abcdefghijklmnopqrstuvwxyz.
Agate, abcdefghijklmnopqrstuvwxyz.
Pearl, abcdefghijklmnopqrstuvwxyz.
Diamond, abcdefghijklmnopqrstuvwxyz.

Putting matter in type is technically called *composing*, or *setting up*. The amount of matter composed is estimated in *ems*, or spaces of the length of the letter *m*; which differ, of course, according to the size of the type employed.

By Leads are meant thin plates of type-metal, with which the lines are sometimes separated. When these plates are employed, the matter is said to be leaded; when not, solid.

§ 212. ITALICS, so called from their having been first used by Italian printers, are letters inclined to the right, *like those in which this clause is printed;* and are indicated in manuscript by a line drawn under the words to be italicized. They are used for emphatic, important, and contrasted terms; for words and sentences introduced to illustrate rules; for names of newspapers, vessels, &c.; and for words and quotations from foreign languages.

As no more definite rule for their use can be given, the composer must exercise his judgment in deciding when they may with propriety be employed. It is necessary only to caution him against using them too freely. Like every thing else, when made familiar, they lose their effect; and, besides offending the eye, tend rather to perplex the reader than to aid him in determining what is really emphatic.

In the English Bible, italics are not used for emphatic words; but

§ 211. Mention the different sizes of type, in order. What is meant by composing, or setting up, type? How is the amount of composed matter estimated? What is an *em*? What are leads? What is meant by leaded matter? What, by solid?

§ 212. Describe italics. Why are they so called? How are they indicated in manuscript? For what are they used? What is the effect of employing them too freely? In the Bible, what do italics denote?

for such as are wanting in the original Hebrew or Greek, and were introduced by the translators to complete or explain the meaning.

§ 213. RUNNING TITLES, or HEAD-LINES, consist of a word or words placed at the top of a page to show the subject of which it treats. They are usually printed in capitals or small capitals. Such headings, when placed over chapters and paragraphs, are known as CAPTIONS and SUB-HEADS; and as SIDE-HEADS, when commencing the first line of the paragraph to which they refer.

§ 214. The first page of a book contains the title, and is therefore styled the TITLE-PAGE. A plate facing it is known as the FRONTISPIECE. A small ornamental engraving sometimes found on the title-page, and often at the commencement of chapters, is called a VIGNETTE. This term means *a little vine;* and the engraving in question was so designated from the fact that originally a vine, or a wreath of vine-leaves, was the favorite form for such ornaments.

In old books, printers were in the habit of placing under the last line of each page the word with which the following page was to commence, either as a guide in the arrangement of the pages, or to prevent hesitation on the part of the reader while turning from one to another. These are called CATCH-WORDS; they are now no longer used.

LESSON XXXI.

GRAMMATICAL INACCURACIES.

§ 215. WHATEVER merits of style or thought an author may possess, or whatever applause he may temporarily receive, he cannot expect permanently to hold an honorable position in

---

§ 213. Of what do running titles, or head-lines, consist? How are they usually printed? When placed over chapters and paragraphs, what are such headings called? What is meant by side-heads?

§ 214. What is meant by the title-page of a book? What, by the frontispiece? What is a vignette? What is the meaning of this term, and why was the engraving in question so called?

In old books, what was placed at the bottom of each page? What were these words called?

literature, unless he is thoroughly acquainted with the rules of grammar, and observes them in composition. Without a preparatory knowledge of this art, but little benefit can be derived from exercises in rhetoric. Before entering on the latter study, therefore, it is expected that the student will not only have made himself familiar with the principles of language in general, but will also have devoted particular attention to the grammar of his own tongue : it is presupposed that he is well versed in its etymology; that he can analyze or parse its sentences ; and that he has intelligently applied its rules in the correction of false syntax. Yet, even after such preparation, when he comes to the construction of original sentences, he will inevitably find that in guarding against the violation of one principle he often overlooks another ; and that, notwithstanding his utmost care, he is occasionally betrayed into inaccuracies, and even solecisms. If this is the case with one who is conversant with grammar (and that it is, the pages of many well-educated writers conclusively show), how liable to error must those be whose acquaintance with the art is imperfect or superficial! While the latter are advised to pursue a complete course of syntax with the aid of some standard textbook, the author has deemed it proper to insert here for their benefit, as well as that of all whose memory may need refreshing on these essential points, a few rules covering those cases in which he has found that beginners are most liable to err.

§ 216. When two or more adjectives belong to a noun with which there is occasion to use the article also, the latter is placed before the first adjective alone if reference is made to a single object, but before each if several objects are referred to. Thus: " A white and red flag" signifies one flag, partly red and partly white ; " a white and a red flag" means two flags, one red and the other white. Do not, therefore, omit the article before the last adjective, unless it is clear that but one thing is intended.

§ 217. The possessive case and the word that governs it must not be

---

§ 215. What is essential to an honorable position in literature? What is expected of the student before he enters on the study of rhetoric?

§ 216. State the principle relating to the use of the article before a noun with which several adjectives are connected. (Give examples in each case.)

separated by an intervening clause; thus, "The knave thereupon commenced rifling his friend's, as he facetiously called him, pocket," must be changed to "The knave thereupon commenced rifling the pocket of his friend, as he facetiously called him."

§ 218. In addressing the same person, do not, in the progress of a sentence, use pronouns of different number; but preserve either the singular or the plural throughout. Thus, it is wrong to say, "I owe thee a heavy debt of gratitude, and will you not allow me to repay it?" We should have either "I owe *you* a heavy debt," or, "and *wilt thou* not," &c.

§ 219. *Each* is singular; and a pronoun or verb agreeing with it must also be singular; as, "Let them depend each on *his* own exertions," not *their* own.

So, several nouns preceded respectively by *each*, *every*, or *no*, whether connected by *and* or not, require a singular verb and pronoun; as, "Every lancer and every rifleman *was* at *his* post."

§ 220. Recollect that, under all circumstances, a verb must agree with its subject in person and number. When a plural substantive is introduced between a singular subject and its verb, be careful not to put the verb in the plural. "Too great a variety of studies perplex and weaken the judgment." *Variety*, the subject, being in the singular, *perplex* and *weaken* should be *perplexes* and *weakens*.

§ 221. When in two connected clauses the leading verb is in the present or the future tense, the dependent one must not be in the past. Thus, in the sentence, "Ye will not come unto me that ye might have life," *might* is wrong, because it is connected in the past tense with the leading verb *will come*, which is future. *Might have* should be changed to *may have*, which is present.

On the other hand, if the leading verb is in the past tense, the dependent verb must be past also. Thus, in the example last given, if *will come* were changed to *would come*, *might have* would be correct; as, "Ye *would not come* unto me that ye *might have* life."

§ 222. Two verbs connected by a conjunction without separate

---

§ 217. State the principle that relates to the position of the possessive case and the word that governs it.

§ 218. What is to be observed respecting the use of pronouns in the progress of a sentence?

§ 219. What number is *each*? What number must a pronoun or verb agreeing with be? State the other rule laid down in this section.

§ 220. Give the rule for the agreement of the verb? What common error must be avoided?

§ 221. What is the rule for the tenses of the leading and the dependent-verb in connected clauses?

nominatives, must be in the same mood. This rule is violated in the following sentence; *would go* being in the potential mood, and *suffered* in the indicative: "The Pharisees would neither go into the kingdom of Heaven themselves, nor suffered others to enter." Either a new nominative must be introduced for *suffered* to agree with, or one of the verbs must be altered to the same mood as the other. The sentence is best corrected by changing the second verb. "The Pharisees would neither go into the kingdom of Heaven themselves, nor *suffer* others to enter."

§ 223. The transitive verbs *lay, raise,* and *set,* must not be confounded with the intransitive, *lie, rise,* and *sit*. This common error must be carefully avoided. Compare these verbs, as conjugated below.

TRANSITIVE.			INTRANSITIVE.		
Lay,	laid,	laid.	Lie,	lay,	lain.
Raise,	raised,	raised.	Rise,	rose,	risen.
Set,	set,	set.	Sit,	sat,	sat.

We *lay* a thing down, *raise* it up, and *set* it in its place. We *lie* abed when we are sick, but *rise* as soon as we are able to *sit* up.

§ 224. When several auxiliaries belonging to different tenses are used with the same participle or verbal form, care must be taken to have them consistent. "I can make as much money as he has." As he has what? Evidently *has make*, which would be bad grammar. The sentence should read, "I can make as much money as he has *made*."

§ 225. *Whom*, and not *who*, must be used as the object of a verb. "He is a man *whom* I honor next to the king himself;" not *who*, for the verb *honor* governs the relative in the objective case, although the latter stands before it.

§ 226. A preposition must not be introduced after a transitive verb, to govern a substantive which is really the object of the latter. "Covet earnestly *for* the best gifts;" *covet* being a transitive verb, *for* should be omitted.

§ 227. Never use *to*, the sign of the infinitive, for the infinitive itself; as in the sentence, "I have not seen him, and I am not likely *to*." It should be, "I am not likely to see him."

---

§ 222. What is said of the mood of two verbs connected by a conjunction? How may sentences in which this rule is violated be corrected?

§ 223. What verbs must not be confounded? Conjugate the transitive verbs *lay, raise, set*. Conjugate the intransitives *lie, rise, sit*.

§ 224. Give the rule relating to auxiliaries.

§ 225. What is the objective of the relative *who*, and when must it be used?

§ 226. What part of speech must not be introduced to govern the object of a transitive verb?

§ 227. What must not be used for the infinitive?

§ 228. Appropriate prepositions must follow certain words. In the following sentence, *to* should be changed to *from*, after the adjective *different*. "This account is very different *to* what I told you."

As this rule is constantly violated, a list of a few common adjectives and verbs is here presented, together with the prepositions properly used in connection with them.

Abhorrence *of*.
Accompanied *with* an inanimate object; *by* any thing that has life.
Accuse *of*.
Acquaint *with*.
Adapted *to*.
Agree *with* a person; *to* a proposition from another; *upon* a thing among ourselves.
Analogy *between* (when two objects follow the preposition); *to*, *with* (when one of the substantives precedes the verb).
Arrive *at*, *in*.
Attended *with* an inanimate object; *by* anything that has life.
Averse *to*, *from*.
Capacity *for*.
Charge *on* a person; *with* a thing.
Compare *with* (in respect of quality); *to* (for the sake of illustration).

Congenial *to*.
Conversant *with* men; *with* or *in* things: *about* and *among* are sometimes used.
Copy *after* a person; *from* a thing.
Correspond *with*.
Die *of* a disease; *by* an instrument or violence.
Disappointed *of* what we fail to obtain; *in* what does not answer our expectations, when obtained.
Entrance *into*.
Expert *in*, *at*.
Followed *by*.
Militate *against*.
Profit *by*.
Reconcile (in friendship) *to*; (to make consistent) *with*.
Reduce (subdue) *under*; (in other cases) *to*.

Between is applicable to two objects only; *among*, to three or more. "A father divided a portion of his property *between* his two sons; the rest he distributed *among* the poor."

In must not be used for *into*, after verbs denoting entrance. "'Come *into* (not *in*) my parlor,' said the spider to the fly."

§ 229. It is inelegant to connect a transitive verb and a preposition, or two different prepositions, with the same object; as, "We confide in and respect the good;"—"I called on, and had a conversation with, him." It is better, in such cases, either to supply an object for each of the governing words, or to omit one of the latter if it can be done without injury to the sense: thus, "We confide in the good, and respect them;"—"I called, and had a conversation with him."

---

228. By what must certain words be followed? To how many objects is *between* applicable? To how many, *among*? By what must verbs denoting entrance be followed?

§ 229. What must not be connected with the same object?

LESSON XXXII.

EXERCISE IN FALSE SYNTAX.

CORRECT the grammatical errors in the following sentences :—

UNDER § 216. Between the old and new mansion is a fine grove of trees.—A gold and silver medal were presented to the inventor.—The educated and uneducated man are very different personages.—A white, red, and blue flag, was displayed from the castle.—A white, red, and blue flag, were displayed from the castle.—This veil of flesh parts the visible and invisible world.—The past and present we know, but who can guess the future?—Sing the first and second stanza.—A red and white rose is a great rarity.—Here are a red and white rose, growing together on the same bush.

UNDER § 217. This politician's (for statesman we can hardly call him) dishonorable course has alienated most of his friends.—Richard the Lion-hearted's, as he is styled in history, glorious career, made him the idol of his subjects.—She began to extol the farmer's, as she called him, excellent understanding.—Critics find fault with the poets' of the Middle Ages numerous metrical inaccuracies.

UNDER § 218. Thou hast protected us, and shall we not honor you?—To thee I owe many favors, and you may therefore rely on my executing thy command.—'Tis thine to command, mine to obey; let me, therefore, know your pleasure.

UNDER § 219. The king of Israel and the king of Judah sat each on their throne.—Let each esteem other better than themselves.—Every passenger must hold their own ticket.—Each of the sexes should keep within its proper bounds, and content themselves with the advantages of their particular spheres.—Some of our principal schools have each a grammar of their own.—Every bone, every muscle, every fibre, of man, are known to his Creator.—Every leaf, every twig, every drop of water, teem with life.—Each day, each hour, each moment, bring their own temptations.—No pain, no parting, no trial, no temptation, are to be encountered there.—Every man is entitled to freedom of speech, if they do not pervert it to the injury of others.—Every body trembled for themselves or their friends.—Every one has passed through scenes which are indelibly impressed on their memory.

UNDER § 220. Perfect submission to the rules of the school are required.—The column of murders, robberies, fires, and accidents, are more attractive to many readers than any other department of a newspaper.—Glad tidings of great joy is brought to the poor.—The train of our ideas are often interrupted.—Three months' notice are required before a pupil is allowed to leave.—Seven men's assertion are better than one man's oath.—Six months' sojourn among these mountains have restored me to perfect health.

UNDER § 221. If he dislikes you, why did you associate with him?—

If he was a good man, why do you accuse him?—I would be obliged to you if you will lend me that book.—I should like it if you will go.—We informed him of the difficulty, that he may be prepared for it.—They will study, if they could be sure of taking the first prize.—Let me feel that I can succeed, and I would work hard to accomplish it.—Cultivate the acquaintance of the learned; for they might be of service to you.

UNDER § 222. He writes and can read.—Many persons can command their passions, but will not do so.—He would neither go himself nor sent his servant.—I am engaged in a great work, and would not leave it for one of less importance.—They might have been happy, and now are convinced of it.

UNDER § 223. By laying abed late in the morning, you lose a tenth part of your life.—Take not up what you have not lain down.—The price of new-lain eggs has raised.—He lay himself out to please us.—The wicked man lays in wait for his adversary.—The ship sat sail at eight o'clock, and we set on the deck till midnight.—Ye have sat at nought all my counsel.—He sits a horse well. (In this sentence *sits* is correct, the preposition *on* being understood, to govern *horse*.)

UNDER § 224. Some dedications may serve for any book that has, is, or shall, be published.—He neither has, nor will, gain anything by this course.—He may have, and I think did, esteem her.—He doth leave the ninety and nine, goes into the mountains, and seeks that which is gone astray.—I did go, and answered my accusers.—No man in this world has, or will be, perfectly happy.—I have labored as much as a person in my situation can.

UNDER § 225. Few men have friends, who, under all circumstances, they can trust. They slew Varus, who in a former chapter I have mentioned.—Who should I meet the other day, but my old friend?—Be careful who you trust.—Do you know who you are speaking to?—There are some who, though we do not like them, we cannot help respecting.— Who have we here?

UNDER § 226. Let me consider of the matter.—Great benefit may be reaped from reading of history.—His servants ye are to whom ye obey.— I shall commence by premising with a few observations.—We cannot allow of any interference.—The peasants do not seem to want for any thing.—The prisoner declined answering to the judge's questions.—Of this we have considered.—She was afraid to enter in the room.

UNDER § 227. The good man tries to live as God designed him to.—I will attend the meeting myself, and induce all my friends to.—Explain this point, or ask your friend to.—The book is so uninteresting, that I have not read it through, and never expect to.

UNDER § 228. Your affairs have been managed in a different manner than what I advised.—Let us profit from the misfortunes of others.—We are often disappointed in things which we seemed sure to obtain.—We are often disappointed of things which before possession promised much enjoyment.—Socrates was accused for having introduced innovations in religion.—Confide on the virtuous, and rely in those who have not deceived you.—Such a course is attended by many dangers.—Catiline fled from Rome, attended with a few followers.—Bestow favors to the deserving only.—Many die annually from the plague.—How can this fact be reconciled to his statements?—How many ridiculous customs have been brought in use during the last hundred years.—Let your actions correspond to your professions.—The Anglo-Saxons soon quarrelled between themselves.—Virgil has often been compared to Homer.—Good humor may be compared with the sun, which sheds light on all around.

UNDER § 229. It is well when pupils love, and entertain respect for, their teachers.—Music naturally has a great charm for, and power over, the young.—No one ought to injure, or wound the feelings of, his neighbor.—Poetry has a natural alliance with, and often strongly excites, our noblest emotions.—Endeavor to alter, or rather prevent the introduction of, so pernicious a fashion.—Good men are not always found, as regards their views and conduct, consistent with, but, on the other hand, are often opposed to, each other.

PART III.

RHETORIC.

LESSON XXXIII.

PROVINCE AND OBJECTS OF RHETORIC.

§ 230. The word RHETORIC is derived from the Greek verb ῥέω, to speak, and in its primary signification had reference solely to the art of oratory; in this sense, moreover, we find it generally used by ancient writers. As, however, most of the rules relating to the composition of matter intended for delivery are equally applicable to other kinds of writing, in the course of time the meaning of the term was naturally extended; so that even as early as in the age of Aristotle it was used with reference to productions not designed for public recitation.

At the present day, Rhetoric, in its widest acceptation, comprehends all prose composition; and it is with this signification we here use the term: in its narrowest sense it is limited to persuasive speaking.

---

§ 230. What is the derivation of the word *rhetoric?* What did it originally signify? To what has it since been extended? In its widest acceptation, what does it comprehend?

§ 231. The ancients thought it necessary for one who would master this subject to study with care everything connected with the great object proposed, the conviction of the hearer or reader; and with this view some rhetoricians introduced into their system Treatises on Law, Morals, Politics &c., on the ground that no one could write or speak well on these subjects without properly understanding them. Quintilian even insists on virtue as essential to the perfect orator because an audience is necessarily influenced by the consideration that candor, truth, and uprightness, distinguish the person addressing them. This, however, is assuming too much. As the art of architecture has nothing to do with the collection of materials, though without materials it is impossible to build; so a knowledge of the subject of which the orator or essayist is to treat, constitutes no part of the art of Rhetoric, though essential to its successful employment: nor does virtue, whatever unction it may impart to the words of a writer or speaker, fall within the province of this art any more than wealth or rank, which are also likely to produce a prejudice in his favor.

Some modern writers, in imitation of the ancients, and with a greater show of justice, have introduced Invention as a division of Rhetoric; insisting that even perfection in the art of expressing, arranging, and beautifying, is valueless, unless the thoughts to be so treated are judicious and appropriate. But the same objection here applies. Rhetoric, properly speaking, has no reference to the creation of thoughts, but merely to the manner of expressing them. The rules and principles of Invention, however, though independent of the art under consideration, must be carefully studied in connection with it, by all who would give effect to their compositions. This subject will hereafter receive attention; we shall first proceed to consider Rhetoric proper.

§ 232. Rhetoric may be regarded as either a science or an

---

§ 231. What did the ancients regard as essential to the mastery of this art? What did some rhetoricians introduce into their systems? What does Quintilian consider essential to the perfect orator? Is this just? Illustrate the case by a comparison with the art of architecture. What have some modern writers introduced as a division of rhetoric? What objection is there to this? What is said of the rules and principles of invention?

art. As a science, it investigates, analyzes, and defines, the principles of good writing; as an art, it enables us to apply these principles, or in other words teaches us the best method of communicating our thoughts.

All art is founded on science. The relation between the two is that of offspring and parent. Valuable knowledge always leads to some practical result; and practical skill is rarely of general utility or extended application, unless it originates in knowledge. On the most sublime of sciences, for instance, theology and ethics, is founded the most important of arts, the art of living. So, from abstract mathematical science are derived the arts of the surveyor, the architect, the navigator, and the civil engineer. Nor can it be denied that their practical application in these arts constitutes the chief value of mathematical studies; and that, were they not so applied, they would be as much neglected as they are now cultivated. In like manner, it is on account of its practical utility that Rhetoric is deemed worthy of a prominent place among the branches of a polite education.

§ 233. As an art, Rhetoric has been classed by some among the useful arts, the object of which is to aid or benefit mankind; by others, among the elegant arts, which aim simply to please. It seems, however, to partake of the nature of both; and may therefore with propriety be denominated a mixed art.

Both the elegant and the useful arts are founded on experience, but differ in their origin and growth. The latter, being the offspring of necessity, are cultivated even in the ruder stages of society; whereas the former have their origin in leisure, and are disregarded until provision has been made for the bodily wants. The useful arts, however, although first to originate in a community, are slower than the fine arts in their progress towards perfection. Thus, modern workmen immeasurably excel the ancients in the art of ship-building; and how far

---

§ 232. How may rhetoric be regarded? As a science, what is its province? What, as an art? What is the relation of art to science? On what sciences is the art of living founded? From abstract mathematical science what arts are derived? What constitutes the chief value of mathematics? In like manner, why is rhetoric deemed an important branch of education?

§ 233. What is the object of the useful arts? What, of the elegant arts? To which does rhetoric belong? On what are both the useful and the elegant arts founded? In what do they differ? At what period of a nation's history do they respectively originate?

Show the difference in their development and progress towards perfection. Illus-

this superiority may be carried by means of future discoveries and improvements, no one can say. In literature, however, we find the reverse to be the case; while naval architecture was yet comparatively in its infancy, the art of composition reached so high a degree of perfection among the Greeks, that modern times, with all their genius and learning, have produced nothing superior to the master-pieces of antiquity. In the rapidity of its development, as well as the zeal with which it endeavors to please by elaborate embellishment, Rhetoric partakes of the nature of the elegant arts; it resembles the useful arts in its utility, we may almost say its absolute necessity to mankind, as facilitating the means of communication.

§ 234. From the study of Rhetoric, two great advantages result: first, it enables us to discern faults and beauties in the compositions of others; and, secondly, it teaches us how to express and embellish our own thoughts, so as to produce the most forcible impression.

The first of these results, were there no other, would be sufficient recompense for the labor involved in pursuing a rhetorical course. Nor, it must be remembered, is this labor great. The questions that arise exercise our reason without fatiguing it. They lead to inquiries, acute but not painful; profound, but neither dry nor difficult. They keep the mind active, but do not require from it the effort necessary for the investigation of purely abstract truth.

By a trifling expenditure of time and attention, we are thus enabled to judge of literary productions for ourselves, to weigh in the balance of taste and criticism, and form our opinions independently of others. We are not obliged to give or withhold our admiration as the world or the critic may decide.

Nor is this independence the only advantage gained. The study of belles-lettres* furnishes a never-failing means of entertainment for our

---

* BELLES-LETTRES, the general term used in the French language to denote the art of which we are treating and kindred subjects, is exceedingly indefinite in its signification, being by some writers limited to rhetoric and poetry, and by others made to embrace natural philosophy

---

trate this by a comparison of naval architecture with literature. In what respect does rhetoric resemble the elegant arts ? In what, the useful arts ?

§ 234. What advantages result from the study of rhetoric ? What is said of the first of these? Is much labor involved in pursuing a rhetorical course? What does a trifling expenditure of time enable us to do ? What other advantage is gained ? How is the pleasure received from the creations of art greatly increased ?

What term do the French apply to rhetoric and kindred branches? What subjects

leisure hours. Thorough acquaintance with the principles of an art doubles the pleasure we receive from it; and one whose taste has been cultivated by assiduous study of the philosophy of criticism will find, on almost every page, beauties which the common reader overlooks, is incapable of appreciating, and consequently entirely loses. A love for the standard master-pieces of literature is thus awakened; and he who has once acquired such a relish is in no danger of being a burden to himself, or of yielding to the seductions of false and destructive pleasures.

These studies, however, do more than entertain and please; they improve the understanding. To apply the principles of sound criticism to composition, to examine what is beautiful and why it is so, to distinguish between affected and real ornaments, can hardly fail to improve us in the most valuable department of philosophy, the philosophy of human nature. Such examinations teach us self-knowledge. They necessarily lead us to reflect on the operations of the judgment, the imagination, and the heart; and familiarize us with the most refined feelings that ennoble our race. Beauty, harmony, grandeur, and elegance; all that can soothe the mind, gratify the fancy, or move the affections,—belong to the province of these studies. They bring to light various springs of action, which, without their aid, might have passed unobserved; and which, though delicate, often exercise an important influence in life.

Lastly, the cultivation of taste by the study of belles-lettres has in all ages been regarded as an important aid in the enforcement of morality. Let the records of the world be canvassed, and we shall find that trespasses, robberies, and murders, are not the work of refined men; that though, in some instances, the latter have proved unequal to temptation, and are betrayed into gross crimes, yet they constitute the exception and not the rule. Nor does the study of rhetoric operate as

---

and geometry; one author even goes so far as to introduce in a treatise on the subject a discourse on the seven sacraments of the Roman Catholic Church. At the Lyceum of Arts in Paris, the department of belles-lettres comprehends general grammar, languages, rhetoric, geography, history, antiquities, and numismatics. In this country, the term is generally used in a more limited sense, to denote polite literature, including criticism, taste, the pleasures of the imagination, &c.

---

are by some embraced under this head? At the Lyceum of Arts in Paris, what does the department of belles-lettres comprehend? As used in this country, what does the term signify?

Besides entertainment, what may we gain from the study of belles-lettres? What do critical examinations teach us?

What else results from the cultivation of taste by the study of belles-lettres? What

a preventive to the more heinous offences only; it elevates the tone of the mind, increases its sensibility, enlarges the sphere of its sympathies, and thus enables it to repress its selfishness and restrain its more violent emotions. To a man of acute and cultivated taste, every wrong action, whether committed by himself or another, is a source of pain; and, if he is the transgressor, his lively sensibility brings him back to duty, with renewed resolutions for the future. Even the highest degree of cultivation may, to be sure, prove insufficient to eradicate the evil passions; yet its tendency will certainly be to mitigate their violence. The poet has truly said:—

"These polished arts have humanized mankind; Softened the rude, and calmed the boisterous mind."

Noble sentiments and high examples, constantly brought before the mind, cannot fail to beget in it a love of glory, and an admiration of what is truly great. Though these impressions may not always be durable, they are at least to be ranked among the means of disposing the heart to virtue.

§ 235. As an aid in enabling us to communicate our thoughts in the best manner, it would seem as if the value of rhetoric would be obvious to all; yet there are some who venture to call it in question. Rules, they say, hamper the mind, fetter genius, and make stiff and artificial composers. They prefer leaving the writer, untrammelled, to chance or the inspiration of the moment; ridiculing the idea of his inquiring, while in the act of giving utterance to a thought, what is required, or what prohibited, by rule. This principle, if true of Rhetoric, obviously applies to logic, grammar, and even the elementary branches of education; and it follows that, through fear of cramping the natural powers, we should do away with training of all kinds. The absurdity of this conclusion is manifest.

Such reasoning can come only from a shallow mind, which would thus excuse its own ignorance. A writer can not hope to attain perfection in his art, without paying due attention to its rules and principles. Men are not born great composers, any more than they are born skilful

---

feeling does a wrong action generally awaken in a man of cultivated taste? What do noble sentiments and high examples produce in the mind?

§ 235. What objection is made by some to the study of rhetoric? To what do they prefer leaving the writer? Expose the fallacy of this objection. What is the ad-

carpenters or expert shoemakers. Proficiency in either vocation is the result of study and practice. It is not necessary that, while composing, the writer should keep rules constantly before him, and thus make his style mechanical and lifeless. But the principles of his art should be so familiar to his mind, as, without consciousness on his part, to control its action. He thus intuitively avoids what is wrong, while there is nothing to prevent his sentences from being as easy, natural, and unconstrained, as those of the loosest and most ignorant scribbler.

LESSON XXXIV.

TASTE.—ITS UNIVERSALITY AND CULTIVATION.

§ 236. The rules of Rhetoric and Criticism are not arbitrary, but have been deduced from examinations and comparisons of those great productions which in all ages have elicited the admiration of men. Striking passages have been analyzed; the peculiarities which render them pathetic, sublime, or beautiful, have been investigated; and thus rules have been formed, by which the critic is enabled to judge of other literary performances, and the writer is shown how to express his thoughts in such a way as to reproduce similar impressions.

Thus, Aristotle, who was the first to lay down rules for unity of action in dramatic and epic poetry, did not arrive at them by a train of inductive reasoning, but by close observation of Sophocles and Homer. Perceiving that these writers, by confining themselves in each of their respective works to one action complete in itself, awakened deeper interest in their readers than those who combined unconnected facts, he generalized the important principle that in the drama and the epic poem

---

vantage of studying principles and rules? Is a constrained style likely to be the result?

§ 236. What is said of the rules of rhetoric and criticism? Whence have they been deduced? Describe the process. How did Aristotle arrive at his rules for unity of action?

unity of design is essential to success. All the rules of the rhetorician have been deduced in a similar manner, and are thus based at once on experience and nature.

§ 237. The works from which the principles of Rhetoric are deduced, have, as already remarked, elicited the universal admiration of men. This implies the existence in the human mind of a faculty capable of forming opinions respecting them. Such a faculty does, indeed, exist; nor is its action limited to the works of literature. It extends alike to all the creations of nature and art; and is known by the name of TASTE.

§ 238. TASTE may be defined as that faculty of the mind which enables it to perceive, with the aid of reason to judge of, and with the help of imagination to enjoy, whatever is beautiful or sublime in the works of nature and art.

The word *taste* is thus used metaphorically. It literally signifies the sense residing in the tongue by which we distinguish different flavors, and is hence appropriately applied to the analogous faculty of the mind which recognizes alike the most delicate beauties and the most minute imperfections.

So contradictory are the definitions of Taste given by different authors, so obscure is their language, and so inconsistent are many of them with themselves, that it is difficult to ascertain their real views on the subject. Hume calls Taste "a natural sensibility". Hutcheson makes it distinct faculty, perfect in itself: he maintains that it is entirely independent of both judgment and imagination, not only receiving impressions, but also passing judgment on them, and producing the pleasures arising therefrom; or, in other words, that it perceives and at the same time judges and enjoys. With this view Blair for the most part agrees; nor are Addison's views, as set forth in No. 409 of the Spectator, materially different. An opposite theory is advocated by Burke and Akenside. The former unhesitatingly attributes the perception and the enjoyment arising therefrom to entirely different faculties, confining Taste to the perception. Akenside distinctly teaches that all the pleasures connected with the sublime and beautiful have their source in the

---

§ 237. What does the general admiration of the master-pieces of literature imply in the human mind? To what does this faculty extend? What is it called?

§ 238. What is Taste? What does this term literally signify? What is said of the definitions of Taste given by different authors? What does Hume call Taste? State Hutcheson's view. What writers agree with him in the main? What is Burke's theory? Akenside's? Alison's? Cousin's?

imagination. Alison, also, in parts of his Essay ably advocates this theory; yet, with strange inconsistency, in his very definition makes Taste "to be that faculty of the human mind by which we perceive and *enjoy* whatever is beautiful or sublime in the works of nature or art." The French philosopher Cousin says, "Three faculties enter into that complex faculty that is called taste,—imagination, sentiment, reason." Sentiment, according to this author, receives the impression; reason passes judgment on it; while imagination produces the sensation of pleasure experienced by the mind.

Amid these conflicting theories, the author has adopted that which seems to him least liable to objection.

§ 239. Taste is common, in some degree, to all men. Even in children it manifests itself at an early age, in a fondness for regular bodies, an admiration of statues and pictures, and a love of whatever is new or marvellous. In like manner, the most ignorant are delighted with ballads and tales; the simplest intellects are struck with the beauties of earth and sky; and savages, by their ornaments, their songs, and the rude eloquence of their harangues, show that along with reason and speech they have received the faculty of appreciating beauty. We may therefore conclude that the principles of Taste are deeply and universally implanted in the minds of men.

§ 240. Though Taste is common to all men, yet they by no means possess it in the same degree. There are some endowed with feelings so blunt, and tempers so cold and phlegmatic, that they hardly receive any sensible impressions even from the most striking objects; others are capable of appreciating only the coarsest kind of beauties, and for these have no strong or decided relish; while in a third class pleasurable emotions are excited by the most delicate graces. There seems, indeed, to be a greater difference between men as respects Taste than in point of common sense, reason, or judgment. In this Nature discovers her beneficence. In facul-

---

§ 239. What is said of the universality of Taste? How does it manifest itself in children? How, in the ignorant? How, in savages? What is the natural inference?

§ 240. Is Taste possessed by all men in the same degree? What is said of the difference between individuals in this respect? How does nature show her beneficence?

ties necessary to man's well-being, she makes little distinction between her children; whereas those that have reference rather to the ornamental part of life she bestows sparingly and capriciously, and requires a higher culture for bringing them to perfection.

This difference in the degrees of Taste possessed by men is owing, in a great measure, as we have seen, to nature; which has endowed some with more sensitive organs than others, and thus made them capable of greater intellectual enjoyment. Yet education has even more to do than nature with the formation of Taste; a fact which becomes obvious when we compare barbarous with enlightened nations in this respect, or contrast such individuals of the latter as have paid attention to liberal studies with the uncultivated and vulgar. We shall at once perceive an almost incredible difference in the degrees of Taste which they respectively possess,—a difference attributable to nothing but the education of the faculty in the one case and its neglect in the other.

Hence it follows that Taste is eminently an improvable faculty; and in the case of this, as well as all the mental and bodily powers, exercise is to be regarded as the great source of health and strength.

Even the senses are rendered peculiarly acute by constant use. The blind, for instance, who can make themselves acquainted with the forms of bodies only by their touch, and are therefore constantly employing it, acquire exquisite sensibility; so that they can even read fluently by passing their fingers over raised letters. In like manner, watchmakers, engravers, proof-readers, and all who are accustomed to use the eye on minute objects, acquire surprising accuracy of sight in discerning with ease what to others is almost invisible. Every one, moreover, has seen the result of cultivating an ear for music. He who at first relishes only the simplest compositions gradually appreciates finer melodies, and is at last enabled to enjoy all the intricate combinations of harmony. So, an eye for painting can not be acquired at once, but is formed by close study of the works of the best masters.

It is thus that diligent study, and close attention to models of style, are necessary to a full appreciation of the great works of literature. One slightly acquainted with the productions of genius sees no more in them than in common-place compositions; their merits are lost upon him; he

---

In the distribution of Taste and common sense? What besides nature operates in the formation of Taste? How is this shown? How may Taste be improved?

What effect has exercise on the senses? Give examples. What is the result of cultivating an ear for music? How is an eye for painting acquired? What is necessary to an appreciation of the great works of literature?

is equally blind to their excellencies and defects. His Taste, however, becomes cultivated in proportion as his acquaintance with works of this character is extended. He is gradually enabled, not only to form judgments, but to give satisfactory reasons for them. His Taste is developed and improved by exercise; just as the musician's ear and the painter's eye are cultivated by a similar process.

LESSON XXXV.

ELEMENTS AND CHARACTERISTICS OF TASTE.

§ 241. TASTE, we have seen, is founded on sensibility; not, however, the sensibility of mere instinct, but that of reason. The judgment has so much to do with the operations and decisions of this faculty, that we must regard it as one of the essential elements of the latter. The mind may or may not be conscious of the train of reasoning by which it arrives at its conclusions; but in most cases there must be such reasoning before taste can perform its functions. We are pleased through our natural sensibility to impressions of the beautiful, aided, as we shall presently see, by the imagination; but an exertion of reason is first required, to inform us whether the objects successively presented to the eye are beautiful or not.

Thus, in reading such a poem as the Æneid, much of our gratification arises from the story's being well conducted, and having a proper connection between its parts; from the fidelity of the characters to nature, the spirit with which they are maintained, and the appropriateness of the style to the sentiments expressed. A poem thus conducted is enjoyed by the mind, through the joint operation of the Taste and the imagination; but the former faculty, without the guidance of reason, could form no opinion of the story, would be at a loss to know whether it was properly conducted, and would therefore fail to receive

---

§ 241. On what is Taste founded? What faculty, nevertheless, has much to do with its decisions? Before Taste can perform its functions, what must take place? In reading such a poem as the Æneid, from what does much of our pleasure arise? Show

pleasure from its perusal. In like manner, whenever in works of Taste an imitation of nature is attempted, whenever it becomes necessary to consider the adaptation of means to an end, or the connection and consistency of parts uniting to form a whole, the judgment must always play an important part.

In the operations of Taste, then, two different elements seem to have a share; first, a natural susceptibility or sensitiveness to pleasurable emotions arising from the contemplation of beauty and sublimity; and, secondly, a sound judgment, to enable this faculty, with or without consciousness of such assistance, to appreciate what is beautiful and sublime, and admire it intelligently. To the exercise of this faculty, however, in its perfection, a good heart is no less essential than a sound head. Not only are the moral beauties superior to all others, but their influence is exerted, in a greater or less degree, on many objects of Taste with which they are connected. The affections, characters, and actions of men, certainly afford genius the noblest subjects; and of these there can be no due appreciation by minds whose motives and principles conflict with those which they respectively contemplate or describe. On the selfish and hard-hearted man the highest beauties of poetry are necessarily lost.

§ 242. The characteristics of Taste, in its most improved state, are reducible to two, Delicacy and Correctness.

Delicacy of Taste implies the possession of those finer organs and powers which enable us to discover beauties that lie hid from the vulgar eye. It may be tested by the same process that enables us to estimate the delicacy of an external sense. As the acuteness of the palate is tried, not by strong flavors, but by a mixture of different ones, each of which, notwithstanding it is blended with others, is detected and recognized; so the Delicacy of internal Taste appears by a lively sensibility

---

where the exercise of judgment is necessary. In what cases does this faculty always play an important part?

What two elements have a share in the operations of Taste? To the exercise of Taste in its perfection, what is essential? Show how this is the case. What effect have the highest beauties of poetry on selfish men?

§ 242. What are the characteristics of an improved Taste? What does delicacy of Taste imply? How may it be tested? Show some of the peculiarities of a delicate

to the finest, minutest, and most latent objects, even when most intimately blended and compounded together. Many have strong sensibility, yet are deficient in Delicacy. They may be deeply impressed by such beauties as they perceive, but can perceive only what is coarse, bold, or palpable; chaster and simpler graces escape their notice. The man of delicate Taste, on the other hand, has not only strength, but also nicety, of feeling. He sees distinctions and differences which are lost on others; neither the most concealed beauties nor the minutest blemishes escape him.

Addison, in his Spectator, No. 409, gives a striking illustration of delicacy of taste. "We find," says he, "there are as many degrees of refinement in the intellectual faculty as in the sense which is marked out by this common denomination. I knew a person who possessed the one in so great a perfection, that, after having tasted ten different kinds of tea, he would distinguish, without seeing the color of it, the particular sort which was offered him; and not only so, but any two sorts of them that were mixed together in an equal proportion; nay, he has carried the experiment so far, as, upon tasting the composition of three different sorts, to name the parcels from whence the three several ingredients were taken. A man of fine taste in writing will discern, after the same manner, not only the general beauties and imperfections of an author, but discover the several ways of thinking and expressing himself which diversify him from all other authors, with the several foreign infusions of thought and language, and the particular authors from whom they were borrowed."

Correctness of Taste implies soundness of understanding. It judges of every thing by the standard of good sense; is never imposed on by counterfeit ornaments; duly estimates the several beauties it meets with in works of genius; refers them to their proper classes; analyzes the principles from which their power of pleasing proceeds; and enjoys them according to their respective merits.

These two qualities, Delicacy and Correctness, though quite distinct, to a certain extent imply each other. No Taste can be exquisitely delicate without being correct, or thoroughly correct without being delicate. Still one or the other characteristic predominates.

Taste. What striking illustration does Addison give of delicacy of Taste? What does correctness of Taste imply? By what standard does it judge of things? Show how a correct Taste deals with works of genius. What relation subsists between delicacy and correctness? What critics among the ancients are respectively distinguished for delicacy and correctness of Taste? Who, among modern critics?

Among ancient critics, Longinus possessed most Delicacy; Aristotle, most Correctness. Of moderns, none exceed Addison in Delicacy; and few in Correctness equal Johnson and Kames.

§ 243. We have thus far contemplated Taste in its sound or healthy state; we find, however, from our own experience, as well as from the history of the past, that it is liable to change, and may in both individuals and nations become weakened and even vitiated. There is, indeed, nothing more fluctuating or capricious. The inconsistencies of this faculty, and the wrong conclusions at which it often arrives, have even created in some a suspicion that it is merely arbitrary; that it is not grounded on invariable principles, is ascertainable by no standard, and is dependent exclusively on the changing fancy of the hour; and that therefore all labored enquiries concerning its operations are useless.

One or two examples of the opposite Tastes which have prevailed in different parts of the world, and the revolutions that have taken place from time to time in the same country, may here be cited with propriety. In eloquence and poetry, nothing has ever pleased the Asiatics except the tumid, the ornamental, the artificial, and the gaudy; whereas the ancient Greeks, despising Oriental ostentation, admired only what was chaste and simple. In architecture, the models of Greece for centuries met with general preference; subsequently, however, the Gothic style prevailed to the exclusion of all others; and this in turn was afterwards laid aside, while the Grecian was again received into popular favor. Again, in literature, how completely opposite is the taste of the present day to that which prevailed during the reign of Charles II.! Nothing was then in vogue but an affected brilliancy of wit; the simple majesty of Milton was overlooked; labored and unnatural conclusions were mistaken for scintillations of genius, sprightliness for tenderness, and bombast for eloquence. Examples of vitiated Taste, whether we apply this term, literally, to the external sense, or, figuratively, to the internal faculty, meet us on all sides. The Hottentot smears his body with putrid oil; the Greenlander delights in rancid fat; the Al-

---

§ 243. How have we thus far contemplated Taste? To what do we find it liable? What character does it sometimes assume in both individuals and nations? What suspicion have the inconsistencies of this faculty produced in some? What example is cited of opposite Tastes in eloquence and poetry? in architecture? Compare the literary taste of Charles Second's era with that of the present day. Give examples of vitiated Taste?

pine hunter takes pride in the swollen neck peculiar to his people; the woman of fashion prefers rouge to the roses which nature has planted in her cheeks; and some intellects admire Jack the Giant-killer more than the sublimest strains of the Epic Muse.

§ 244. In view of such facts as these, it is natural to fall back on the trite proverb *de gustibus non disputandum*, "there is no disputing about tastes;" and to conclude that, as long as there is so great a diversity, all standards and tests must be arbitrary, and consequently worthless. But let us see to what this doctrine leads. If the proverb is true of Taste in its literal signification, it must be equally true of the other senses. If the pleasures of the palate are superior to criticism, those of sight, smell, sound, and touch, must be equally privileged. At this rate, we have no right to condemn one who prefers the rude head on a sign to Raphael's glorious creations, the odor of a decaying carcass to that of the most fragrant flower, or hideous discord to exquisite harmony. This principle, applied to Taste in its figurative acceptation, is equivalent to the general proposition that, as regards the perceptions of sense, by which some things appear agreeable and others disagreeable, there is no such thing as *good* or *bad*, *right* or *wrong*; that every man's Taste is to him a standard without appeal; and that we cannot, therefore, properly censure even those who prefer the empty rhymester to Milton. The absurdity of such a position, when applied to extremes, is manifest. No one will venture to maintain that the Taste of a Hottentot or an Esquimaux is as delicate as that of a Longinus or an Addison; and, as long as this is the case, it must be admitted that there is some foundation for the preference of one man's Taste to another's, some standard by which all may be judged.

It must be observed that the diversity of men's Tastes does not

---

§ 244. What conclusion may naturally be drawn from this variety in Tastes? Where does this doctrine lead us? Applied to the faculty of Taste, to what is this principle equivalent? Show the absurdity of such a position. If one man's Taste is to be preferred to another's, what must exist? In what case is diversity of Tastes not only admissible but to be expected? Show in what Tastes may differ and yet be correct.

necessarily imply incorrectness in any Where the objects considered are different, such diversity is not only admissible but to be expected. One man relishes poetry most; another takes pleasure in history alone. One prefers comedy; another, tragedy. One admires the simple; another, the ornamental. Gay and sprightly compositions please the young; those of a graver cast afford more entertainment to the old. Some nations delight in bold delineations of character and strong representations of passion; others find superior charms in delicacy of thought and elegance of description. Though all differ, yet all select some one beauty which suits their peculiar tone of mind; and therefore no one has a right to condemn the rest. It is not in matters of Taste as in questions of mere reason, that but one conclusion is true, and all the rest are erroneous. Truth, which is the object of reason, is one; beauty, which is the leading object of Taste, is manifold.

LESSON XXXVI.

STANDARD OF TASTE.

§ 245 Tastes, we have seen, admit of variety; but only when exercised on different things. When on the same object men disagree, when one condemns as ugly what another admires as beautiful, then we have no longer diversity, but direct opposition; and one must be right and the other wrong, unless we allow the absurd position that all Tastes are equally good.

Suppose a certain critic prefers Virgil to Homer; I, on the contrary, give the preference to the latter. The other party is struck with the elegance and tenderness which characterize the Roman bard; I, with the simplicity, sublimity, and fire, of the Greek. As long as neither of us denies that both these poets have great beauties, our difference merely exemplifies that diversity which, as we have seen, is natural and allowable. But, if the other party asserts that Homer has no beauties whatever, that he is dull and spiritless, that his Iliad is in no

---

§ 245. In what case may Tastes differ without being directly opposite? Illustrate this point by a comparison of Virgil with Homer. In case of an opposition of Tastes,

respect superior to any old legend of knight-errantry,—then I have a right to charge my antagonist with having either no Taste at all, or one in a high degree corrupted; and I appeal to whatever I regard as the standard of Taste, to show him his error.

It remains to enquire what this standard is, to which, in such opposition of Tastes, we must have recourse. The term properly denotes something established as a rule or model, of such undoubted authority as to be the test of other things of the same kind. Thus, when we say a standard weight or measure, we mean one appointed by law to regulate all other weights and measures.

§ 246. Whenever an imitation of any natural object is aimed at, as for instance when a description of a landscape or a portraiture of human character is attempted, fidelity to nature is the proper criterion of the truly beautiful, and we may lay down the proposition that *Nature is our standard*. In such cases reason can readily compare the copy with the original; and approve or condemn, as it finds the peculiarities of the object imitated more or less truthfully represented.

§ 247. In many cases, however, this principle is inapplicable; and for these we are obliged to seek some other standard. Were any person possessed of all the mental powers in full perfection, of senses always exquisite and true, and particularly of sound and unerring judgment, his opinions in matters of Taste would beyond doubt constitute an unexceptionable standard for all others. But as long as human nature is liable to imperfection and error, there can be no such living criterion; no one individual who will be acknowledged by his fellow-men to possess a judgment superior to that of all the rest. Where, then, can we find the required standard? Manifestly, in *the concurrent Tastes of the majority of mankind*. What most men agree in admiring must be considered

---

to what does it become necessary to appeal? What does the term *standard* denote? What do we mean by a standard weight or measure?

§ 246. When an imitation of any natural object is aimed at, what is the criterion of the beautiful? What faculty is called on to approve or condemn? On what is its decision based?

§ 247. In what cases is this principle inapplicable? Why can not the Taste of a person of sound judgment be taken as a standard? What is the only safe standard that can be adopted? Show how we appeal to this standard in cases of literal taste.

beautiful; and his Taste alone can be esteemed true who coincides with the general sentiment of his species.

If any one should maintain that sugar is bitter and tobacco sweet, no reasoning could avail to prove it, because it contradicts the general voice of mankind. The taste of such a person would inevitably be regarded as diseased. In like manner, with regard to the objects of internal Taste, the common opinion of mankind carries the same authority, and constitutes the only test by which the impressions of individuals can be tried.

§ 248. When we speak of the concurrent Tastes of men as the universal standard, it must be understood that we mean men placed in situations favorable to the proper development of this faculty. Such loose notions as may be entertained during ages of ignorance and darkness, or among rude and uncivilized nations, carry with them no authority. In such states of society, Taste is either totally suppressed or appears in its worst form. By the common sentiments of men, therefore, we mean the concurrent opinions of refined men in civilized nations, by whom the arts are cultivated, works of genius are freely discussed, and Taste is improved by science and philosophy.

Even among such nations, accidental causes occasionally pervert the Taste; superstition, bigotry, or despotism, may bias its decisions; or habits of gaiety and licentiousness of morals may bring false ornaments and dissolute writings into vogue. Admiration of a great genius may protect his faults from criticism, and even render them fashionable. Sometimes envy obscures for a season productions of great merit; while personal influence or party-spirit may, on the contrary, exalt to a high though short-lived reputation what is totally undeserving. Such inconsistencies may lead us to doubt the correctness of our standard; but it will be found that these vagaries in the course of time invariably correct themselves; that the genuine Taste of mankind in general ultimately triumphs over the fantastic notions which may have attained temporary currency with superficial judges. The latter soon pass away; whereas

---

§ 248. What do we mean by the concurrent Tastes of men, which we make the universal standard? Even among cultivated nations, what may pervert the Taste? how how its decisions are sometimes influenced. What feeling is likely to be produced by these inconsistencies? Ultimately, however, what will we find?

the principles of true philosophic Taste are unchangeable, being the same now that they were five thousand years ago.

The universality of Taste and the consistency of its decisions, except when temporarily perverted by external causes, prove that it is far from being arbitrary, is independent of individual fancies, and employs a practical criterion for determining their truth or falsehood. In every composition, what captivates the imagination, convinces the reason, or touches the heart, pleases all ages and all nations. Hence the unanimous testimony which successive generations have borne to the merit of some few works of genius. Hence the authority which such works have acquired as standards of composition; since from them we learn what beauties give the highest pleasure, and elicit the general admiration of mankind.

§ 249. The terms Taste and Genius being frequently confounded, though signifying quite different things, it is of importance clearly to define the distinction subsisting between them. Taste consists in the power of judging; Genius, in that of creating. Genius includes Taste; whereas the latter not only may, but generally does, exist without the former. Many are capable of appreciating poetry, eloquence, and the productions of art, who have themselves no abilities for composing or executing. Delicate and correct Taste forms a good critic; but Genius is further necessary to form a poet, an orator, or an artist. Genius, therefore, is a higher power than Taste. It implies a creative or inventive faculty, which not only perceives beauties already existing, but calls new ones into being, and so exhibits them as strongly to impress the minds of others.

The term *Genius*, as commonly used, extends further than to the objects of Taste. Thus we speak of a genius for mathematics, for war, for politics, and even for mechanical employments. In this acceptation, it signifies a natural talent or aptitude for excelling in any particular vocation.

How is it proved that the principles of Taste are not arbitrary? How have the great works of genius been regarded in all ages?

§ 249. What terms are often confounded? Show the difference between Taste and genius. Which forms the critic, and which the poet? Which is the higher power? What is the common acceptation of the term *genius*? As possessed by individual minds, which extends to the wider range of objects, genius or Taste? What is said of

Genius, the creative faculty, as possessed by individual minds, does not extend to so wide a range of objects as Taste. It is not uncommon to meet persons possessed of good Taste in several of the elegant arts, in painting, sculpture, music, and poetry; but to find one who is an excellent performer in all these is much more rare, or rather not to be expected at all. A universal genius is not likely to excel in any thing; only when the creative powers of the mind are directed exclusively to one object, is there a prospect of attaining eminence. With Taste the reverse is the case; exercising it on one class of objects is likely to improve it as regards all.

§ 250. Genius, as remarked above, implies the existence of Taste; and the more the latter is cultivated and improved, the nobler will be the achievements of the former. Genius, however, may exist in a higher degree than Taste; that is, a person's Genius may be bold and strong, while his Taste is remarkable for neither delicacy nor correctness. This is often the case in the infancy of a literature or an art: for Genius, which is the gift of nature, attains its growth at once; while Taste, being in a great degree the result of assiduous study and cultivation, requires long and careful training to attain perfection. Shakspeare is a case in point. Full of vigor and fire, and remarkable for the originality of his thoughts, he still lacks much of that delicacy, both of conception and expression, which has been attained by later writers of far inferior Genius. Indeed, those who dazzle the minds of their readers with great and brilliant thoughts are too apt to disregard the lesser graces of composition.

---

a universal genius? What is the result of exercising Taste on any particular class of objects?

§ 250. What is implied in genius? May it exist without a high degree of Taste? When is this often the case? What author is a case in point?

LESSON XXXVII.

PLEASURES OF THE IMAGINATION.

§ 251. THE pleasures of Taste, since they arise from impressions made on the imagination, are generally known as the Pleasures of the Imagination.

§ 252. The Imagination is that faculty of the mind by which it conceives ideas of things communicated to it by the organs of sense, and, selecting parts of different conceptions, combines them into new wholes of its own creation.

Imagination, like every other faculty of mind, is of course confined to man. Opening to him, as it does, an enlarged sphere of manifold and multiform pleasures, it affords a striking proof of Divine benevolence. The necessary purposes of life might have been answered, though our senses had served only to distinguish external objects, without conveying to us any of those delightful emotions of which they are now the source. The Creator, however, has seen fit to vouchsafe to man these pure and innocent enjoyments for the purpose of elevating his aspirations, ennobling his emotions, banishing unworthy thoughts from his breast, freeing him from the control of passion and sense, and leading him to look beyond the earth, and

"Before the transient and minute
To prize the vast, the stable, the sublime."

The mind that has once feasted on the pleasures which imagination affords, will never be satisfied to leave them for meaner enjoyments; any more than one who from some height views a majestic river rolling its waves through spacious plains and past splendid cities, will withdraw his gaze from the inviting prospect, to contemplate the stagnant pool at his feet.

§ 253. The process by which the emotions alluded to affect the imagination next requires attention. Whenever an object

---

§ 251. From what do the pleasures of Taste arise? What are they generally called?

§ 252. What is meant by the imagination? To whom is it confined? Show how its bestowal is a proof of divine beneficence. How do the pleasures of the imagination compare with other enjoyments?

§ 253. Describe the process by which the sensations in question affect the imagination

calculated to produce them is presented to the mind, unless its attention is previously engrossed, a train of thought is immediately awakened, analogous in character to the object exciting it. It must be observed, however, that the simple perception of the object is insufficient of itself to excite the emotion. No pleasurable impression will be produced, unless the mind operates in connection with the sensation; unless he imagination busies itself with the pursuit of such trains of thought as are awakened.

We find that the same thing is true of the creations of art. A fine landscape, a beautiful poem, a thrilling strain of harmony, excite feeble emotions in our minds, as long as our attention is confined to the qualities they present to our senses. We fully appreciate them only when our imaginations are kindled by their power, when we lose ourselves amid the images summoned before us, and wake at last from the play of fancy as from the charm of a romantic dream.

§ 254. That pleasurable emotions are not produced by mere impressions on the external senses, but remain unfelt unless these impressions are transferred to the imagination, is susceptible of conclusive proof. If, for instance, the mind is in such a state as to prevent the play of imagination, the sensation of pleasure is entirely lost, although of course the effect on the outward sense is the same. A man in pain or affliction will contemplate without the slightest admiration scenes and objects, which, were his imagination at liberty, would afford him the liveliest pleasure. The sublimity and beauty of external nature are almost constantly before us, and not a day passes without presenting us objects calculated to charm and elevate the mind; yet it is in general with a heedless eye that we regard them, and only at particular moments that we are sensible of their power. There are few that have not contemplated with delight the beauties of a glowing sunset; yet every one knows that, at times, all the gorgeous magnificence

---

What, beside the sensation, is essential to the production of a pleasurable emotion in the mind? What is said of the emotions produced by the creations of art?

§ 254. Prove that pleasurable emotions are not produced by mere impressions on the external senses. To what is the difference in the impressions produced by the same

with which Nature paints the heavens at the close of day falls powerless on the eye.

This difference of effect is clearly not attributable to the objects themselves, nor to the external senses on which the impression is primarily produced: it arises from a difference in the state of our imaginations; from our disposition at one time to follow out the train of thought awakened, and our incapacity to do this, at another, in consequence of the pre-occupation of our minds by some engrossing idea. The pleasures of Taste are enjoyed in their perfection only when the imagination is free, and the attention is so little occupied as to leave us open to all the impressions created by the objects before us. It is, therefore, always in leisure hours that we turn to music and poetry for amusement. The seasons of care, of grief, of business, have other occupations; and destroy, for the time at least, our sensibility to the beautiful or the sublime, in proportion as the state of mind produced by them is unfavorable to the exercise of the imagination.

Another proof that imagination is the source of the pleasures of Taste may be derived from what is observed in the process of criticising. When, in considering a poem or painting, we attend minutely to the language and structure of the one, or the coloring and design of the other, we cease to feel the delight which they otherwise produce. The reason of this is that by so doing we restrain our imagination, and, instead of yielding to its suggestions, resist them by fixing our attention on minute and unconnected parts. On the contrary, if the imagination is ardent and is left to its free exercise, the mind receives pleasure from the performance as a whole, and takes no note of the minor details of criticism.

It is this chiefly that makes it difficult for young persons with lively imaginations to form correct judgments of the productions of literature and art, and which so often induces them to approve of mediocre performances. It is not that they are incapable of learning in what merit of composition consists; for the principles which direct us in the forma-

---

object at different times attributable? When are the pleasures of taste enjoyed in their perfection? When do we turn to music or poetry for amusement?

What do facts observable in the process of criticising prove with regard to the pleasures of Taste? State the arguments thus derived. What kind of critics are persons with ardent imaginations likely to become? What renders it difficult for the young to form correct judgments of literary performances? What effect has the labor

tion of critical opinions are neither numerous nor abstruse. It is not that sensibility increases with age; for this all experience contradicts. But it is because at this period of life the imagination is fresh, and is excited by the slightest causes; because the young decide on the merits of a composition according to the impression it makes on this faculty; because their estimate of its value is formed, not by comparing it with other works or with any abstract or ideal standard, but from the facility with which it leads them into those enchanting regions of fancy where youth loves to wander. It is their own imagination that in reality possesses the charms which they attribute to the work that excites it; and the simplest tale is as capable of exciting this faculty in the young, and is therefore advanced to as high a rank in their estimation, as the most meritorious performances would be at a later period.

All this flow of imagination, however, in which youth and men of sensibility are apt to indulge, and which so often yields them pleasure while it involves them in incorrect judgments, the labor of criticism destroys. Thus employed, the mind, instead of being free to follow the trains of imagery successively awakened, is either fettered to the consideration of minute and isolated parts, or pauses to weigh the various ideas received. Thus distracted, it loses the emotion, whether of beauty or sublimity; and, since the impression on the outward sense is evidently the same as before, it must be the restraint of imagination alone that makes the difference, and consequently this faculty is the sole source whence the pleasures of Taste flow. Accordingly, the mathematician who investigates the demonstrations of the Newtonian philosophy, the painter who studies the designs of Raphael, the poet who reasons on the measure of Milton,—all in such occupations lose the delight which these several productions give; and, when they wish to recover the emotion of pleasure, must withdraw their attention from minute considerations, and leave their fancy to revel amid the great and pleasing conceptions with which it is inspired.

§ 255. The pleasures received from objects of Taste depending, as we have seen, on the action of the imagination, it follows that whatever facilitates the lively exercise of this faculty heightens the pleasurable emotions experienced. This is obviously the effect of those interesting associations with

---

*criticism on the flow of imagination? What is said of the mathematician, th painter, and the poet, when studying the great masters of their respective arts?

§ 255. On what do the pleasures received from objects of Taste depend? What, therefore, heightens the pleasurable emotions experienced? Of what is this obviously the effect? In how many classes are associations comprised? What is the first class?

particular objects which exist in every mind. These associations are comprised in three classes :—

I. *Personal.* No man is indifferent to a view of the house where he was born; the school where he was educated, or the scenes amid which his infancy was spent. So many images of past affections and past happiness do they recall, that, common-place as they may seem to others, to him they are a source of indescribable rapture. There are melodies, also, that were learned in infancy, or were sung perhaps by beloved voices now silent, which awake strong feeling within us whenever they are heard, and are through life preferred to all others.

II. *National.* Next to personal associations, those connected with our country are most calculated to heighten our emotions of pleasure. What American can visit the localities consecrated by the blood of his struggling ancestors, can behold Bunker Hill, Bennington, Valley Forge, Cowpens, or Yorktown, and not feel his heart touched with a far higher and stronger enthusiasm than would be kindled by the mere beauty of the respective scenes? To others, they may be objects of indifference; to us, they are hallowed by their connection with our country's history. In like manner, the fine lines which Virgil, in his Georgics, has dedicated to the praises of his native land, beautiful as they are to us, were undoubtedly read with far greater pleasure by the ancient Roman.

The influence of such associations in increasing the beauty or sublimity of musical compositions must have been generally observed. Swiss soldiers in foreign lands have been so overwhelmed with melancholy on hearing their celebrated national air, that it has been found necessary to forbid its performance in the armies in which they serve. This effect is not attributable to the composition itself, but to the recollections with which it is accompanied; to the images it awakens of peace and domestic pleasures, from which they have been torn, and to which they may never return. So the tune called Bellisle March is said to have owed its popularity in England to the supposition that it was the air played when the British army marched into Bellisle, and to its consequent association with images of conquest and military glory.

III. *Historical.* Powerful, though in a less degree than the asso-

---

Describe personal associations. Show how they impart additional intensity to the pleasure received from certain melodies. What associations, next to personal ones, are most calculated to heighten our pleasurable emotions? What scenes are likely to kindle enthusiasm in an American's heart? Why? In whom is it likely that the lines dedicated by Virgil to his country awakened the liveliest pleasure? What compositions have their effect greatly increased by such associations? What illustration is sited, touching the Swiss soldiers? To what is the effect of this national air attributable? In like manner to what does the air called Bellisle March owe its popularity?

siations connected with our own land, are those founded on general history or the lives of distinguished persons. The valley of Vaucluse is celebrated for its beauty; yet how little would it have been esteemed, had it not been the residence of Petrarch! In like manner, there are many landscapes, no doubt, more beautiful than Runnymede; yet those who remember that this place witnessed the granting of the great charter which has guaranteed the rights and liberties of millions, will find few scenes affect their imaginations so strongly.

LESSON XXXVIII.

SOURCES OF THE PLEASURES OF THE IMAGINATION.

THE NOVEL.—THE WONDERFUL.—THE PICTURESQUE.

§ 256. Of the five senses that have been given to man, three,—taste, smell, and touch,—are incapable by themselves of awakening the imagination to pleasure. Coöperating with the other two, they may contribute to the effect produced on this faculty; or, by the associations connected with their sensations, they may occasionally produce pleasing trains of thought: but, independently exercised, they cannot be regarded as sources of the pleasures of Taste. Hence the intensity of the affliction with which the blind and deaf man is visited. Cut off from the manifold enjoyments ensured by sight and hearing, and by these alone, he finds but little solace in the possession of the three inferior senses.

Taste (in its literal signification) has to do with the body; it flatters and serves the grossest of all masters, the stomach. No sense has less

---

What is the third class of associations? How do they rank as regards effect? What Illustrations are given to prove their power?

§ 256. Which of the five senses are incapable of affecting the imagination? When do they contribute to the effect produced on this faculty? How are they sometimes instrumental in producing pleasing trains of thought? Independently exercised, are they sources of the pleasure of Taste? What follows with respect to the blind and deaf man?

To what does the sense of Taste appeal? What kind of pleasures is it incapable of

connection with the mind, or is so utterly incapable of yielding it pleasure.

Smell may sometimes seem to yield perceptions of the beautiful; but it is because the odor is exhaled from an object that we already know to be beautiful, and that is so independently of its fragrance. Thus the rose charms us with its symmetrical proportions and the richness and variety of its shades; its odor is agreeable, not beautiful, and suggests the idea of beauty only because we know it to proceed from a beautiful object.

Touch may in a measure judge of smoothness, regularity, and symmetry; but not with sufficient promptness and accuracy to make it a source of pleasure to the imagination, unless sight comes to its aid.

Agreeable trains of thought may, indeed, occasionally be awakened by the taste, smell, and perhaps touch, of particular objects with which striking recollections of the past are connected; yet we cannot on that account say that the sensations produced through these media are a source of mental pleasure.

§ 257. The only senses capable of kindling the imagination and exciting its pleasures are SIGHT and HEARING. The impressions of the former are the more striking, and the enjoyment they yield is both more lasting and more intense. The blind, therefore, apart from the greater helplessness to which they are reduced, lose incomparably more of the pleasures of the imagination, whether awakened by nature or art, than the deaf.

These senses seem to be particularly in the service of the soul. The sensations they produce are pure, not gross; intellectual, not corporeal. They contribute to the refining rather than the sustaining of life. They procure us pleasures which are not selfish and sensual, but noble and elevating.

§ 258. To these two senses, then, through the operation of which natural objects excite a flow of imagination and con-

---

producing? Of what may smell sometimes seem to yield perceptions? Explain how this is, and illustrate it in the case of the rose. Of what qualities may touch, in a measure, judge? Why is it not, then, a source of pleasure to the imagination? To what are the agreeable trains of thought sometimes awakened by these senses attributable?

§ 257. What senses alone are capable of kindling the imagination? Which produces the more striking impressions? How, then, does the affliction of the blind compare with that of the deaf? What is said of the sensations and pleasures produced by sight and hearing?

sequent pleasure, art must be addressed, in order to make an impression on the mind. The eye being, as we have seen, the medium of the most vivid and abundant sensations, to it most of the fine arts,—painting, sculpture, architecture, and landscape-gardening,—are exclusively addressed. Music, poetry, and rhetoric (which we have seen is a mixed art), address themselves to the ear.

§ 259. We may divide those objects of sight and hearing which constitute the source of pleasure to the imagination, into two great classes, the productions of nature and those of art. Strictly speaking, our subject leads us to treat only of the latter, or rather of that class of the latter which pertains exclusively to the art of composition. Yet, as the relation subsisting between the two is intimate and they often afford striking illustrations of each other, we shall briefly extend our notice to both.

§ 260. The different characteristics which an object must possess to excite the imagination are known as the novel, the wonderful, the picturesque, the sublime, and the beautiful. Of these the last two are by far the most fruitful sources of pleasure.

These five qualities belong alike to natural and artificial objects. Two others must here be mentioned, more limited in extent, because applicable only to the creations of art.

I. Fidelity of imitation. Art in many cases aims at nothing more than a reproduction of nature. In these cases, the closer resemblance the copy bears to the original, the greater pleasure does it afford. Nor is this less true, though the object copied be destitute of beauty, or even repulsive. In a picture we can endure the filthy lazzaroni and disgusting dwarf, from whom in life we would turn away with uncontrol-

---

§ 258. To what must art be addressed? Which arts are addressed to the eye? Which, to the ear?

§ 259. Into what two great classes are the objects of sight and hearing divided? What is said of the relation subsisting between them?

§ 260. Enumerate the characteristics which an object must possess, to excite the imagination. Which of these are the most fruitful sources of pleasure? To what objects do these qualities belong? What two others are more limited in extent? In what cases is fidelity of imitation a source of pleasure? Illustrate the fact that a faith-

iable aversion. The mind is pleased with the fidelity of the representation, because in the triumphs of art the whole species may be said to have a common concern and pride.

II. Wit, humor, and ridicule, in literary compositions, are the source of various pleasures. These are of such importance as to require future consideration at some length.

§ 261. THE NOVEL is an important source of the pleasures of Taste, producing, as it does, a lively and instantaneous effect on the imagination. An object which has no merit to recommend it, except its being uncommon or new, by means of this quality gives a quick and pleasing impulse to the mind. A degree of novelty, indeed, though not essential to the production of impressions by the beautiful or the sublime, considerably heightens them; for objects long familiar, however attractive, are apt to be passed over with indifference.

The emotion produced by novelty is of a livelier and more pungent nature than that excited by beauty; but is proportionally shorter in its continuance. If there is no other charm to rivet our attention, the shining gloss thus communicated soon wears off.

The desire to see and hear what is new is universal, and is known as *curiosity*. No emotion of the mind is stronger or more general. Conversation is never more interesting than when it turns on strange objects and extraordinary events. Men tear themselves from their families in search of things rare and new, and novelty converts into pleasures the fatigues and even the perils of travelling. By children, also, this feeling is constantly manifested. We see them perpetually running from place to place, to hunt out something new; they catch, with eagerness and often with very little choice, at whatever comes before them. Now, by reason of its nature, novelty cannot for any length of time engross our attention; and hence curiosity is the most versatile of all our

---

ful representation pleases, though the object copied may be absolutely repulsive. Explain the reason. What source of pleasure to the imagination belongs exclusively to literary compositions?

§ 261. What is the effect of *the novel* on the imagination? What, on the impressions produced by the beautiful and the sublime? How does the emotion produced by novelty compare with that excited by beauty? What is the desire to see and hear new things called? How do men show that they are under its control? How is it manifested by children? What is the leading characteristic of curiosity?

affections. It is constantly changing its object, and always presents an appearance of anxiety and restlessness.

§ 262. Novelty is possessed by objects in different degrees, to which its effects are proportioned.

I. The lowest degree is found in objects surveyed a second time after a long interval.

Experience teaches us that, without any decay of remembrance, absence always gives an air of novelty to a once familiar object. Thus, a person with whom we have been intimate, returning from abroad after a long interval, appears almost like a new acquaintance. Distance of place contributes to this effect no less than lapse of time; a friend, for example, after a short absence in a remote country, has the same air of novelty as if he had returned after a longer interval from a place nearer home. The mind unconsciously institutes a connection between him and the distant region he has visited, and invests him with the singularity of the objects he has seen.

II. The next degree of novelty belongs to objects respecting which we have had some previous information.

Description, though it contributes to familiarity, cannot altogether remove the appearance of novelty when the object itself is presented. The first sight of a lion, for instance, is novel, and therefore a source of pleasure, although the beholder may have previously obtained from pictures, statues, and natural history, a thorough acquaintance with all his peculiarities of appearance.

III. A new object that bears some distant resemblance to one already known is an instance of the third degree of novelty.

We are familiar, for example, with the features of the Caucasian race of men, having seen them from infancy; the first sight of a Chinese, however, is novel and pleasing, because, although he bears a resemblance to those we already know, the points of difference are sufficient to excite our curiosity.

IV. The highest degree of novelty is that which character-

---

§ 262. To what are the effects of novelty proportioned? In what objects is novelty found in the lowest degree? What is always the effect of absence? What besides lapse of time contributes to this effect? Illustrate this. What connection is unconsciously instituted by the mind? What objects are characterized by novelty in the second degree? What is the effect of description? Illustrate this. What is the next highest degree of novelty? Give an illustration. To what objects does the highest degree of novelty belong?

izes objects entirely unknown and bearing no analogy to any with which we are acquainted.

§ 263. THE WONDERFUL is analogous in character to the novel, and is by some confounded with it. It is equally a source of pleasure, its charm consisting principally in the production of unexpected trains of thought.

The difference between the novel and the wonderful is readily illustrated. A traveller who has never seen an elephant, goes to a jungle in India for the purpose of meeting with one; if he succeeds, the sight is novel and pleasing, but not wonderful, for it was fully expected. A Hindoo, wandering in America, suddenly sees an elephant feeding at large in a field: the sight is not novel, for he is accustomed to the animal; it is wonderful, however, because totally unexpected,—and is pleasing in proportion.

The Chinese appreciate the fact that the wonderful pleasurably excites the imagination in a high degree, and take advantage of it in the embellishment of their gardens, which, we may add, are among the finest in the world. A torrent, for example, is conveyed under the ground, that the visitor may be at a loss to divine whence the unusual sound proceeds; and, to multiply still stranger noises, subterranean cavities are devised in every variety. Sometimes one is unexpectedly led into a dark cave, which still more unexpectedly terminates in a landscape enriched with all the beauties that nature can afford. In another quarter, enchanting paths lead to a rough field, where bushes, briers, and stones, interrupt the passage; and, while means of egress are being sought, a magnificent vista opens on the view.

§ 264. THE PICTURESQUE is by some regarded simply as a variation of the beautiful, and treated under that head. The term seems, however, to be applied to objects which have a rugged appearance, in contradistinction to such as are sublime or beautiful, particularly when introduced among the latter by way of contrast. Affecting the mind at first with an emotion of surprise, such objects soon give birth to an additional train

---

§ 263. To what is *the wonderful* analogous? In what does its charm consist? Illustrate the difference between the novel and the wonderful. What use do the Chinese make of the fact that the wonderful pleasurably excites the imagination? Show how they apply this principle in their gardens.

§ 264. To what do some regard *the picturesque* as belonging? To what objects does this term seem rather to be applied? With what emotion do picturesque objects first affect the mind? To what do they soon give birth? Mention some picturesque ob-

of images which the scene itself would not have suggested. A ruined tower in the midst of a deep wood, an old bridge flung across a chasm between rocks, a moss-covered cottage on a precipice, are instances of the picturesque. We have other examples in a stream with a broken surface and an irregular motion; and, among trees, not in the smooth young beech or the fresh and tender ash, but in the gnarled oak and knotty elm.

It is not necessary that picturesque objects should be of great size; it is enough if they are rough and scraggy, if they indicate age by their appearance and have forms characterized by sudden variations. Among animals, the ass is generally regarded as more picturesque than the horse; and, among horses, it is to the wild and rough forester or the worn-out cart-horse, that this epithet is applied. In our own species, objects merely picturesque are to be found among the wandering tribes of gypsies and beggars; who, in all their characteristics, bear a close analogy to the wild forester and worn-out cart-horse, as well as to old mills, hovels, and similar inanimate objects.

LESSON XXXIX.

THE SUBLIME.

§ 265. THE term SUBLIMITY, for which GRANDEUR is by some used as an equivalent, is applied to great and noble objects which produce a sort of internal elevation and expansion. The emotion, though pleasing, is of a serious character, and, when awakened in the highest degree, may be designated even a severe, solemn, and awful; being thus readily distinguishable from the livelier feelings produced by the beautiful.

---

jects. What is the leading characteristic of such objects? Is the ass or the horse the more picturesque? To what kind of horses is this epithet applicable? What members of our own species present a picturesque appearance? To what are they analagous in character?

§ 265. What word is used as an equivalent for *sublimity*? To what are these terms applied? Describe the emotion produced by sublimity.

The principal source of the sublime is might, or power in a state of active exertion. Hence the grandeur of earthquakes and volcanoes; of great conflagrations; of the stormy ocean and mighty torrent; of lightning, tempests, and all violent commotions of the elements.

A stream that confines itself to its banks is a beautiful object; but, when it rushes with the impetuosity of a torrent, it becomes sublime. "The sight of a small fire," says Longinus, "produces no emotion; but we are struck with the boiling furnace of Etna, pouring out whole rivers of liquid flame." The engagement of two great armies, being the highest exertion of human might, constitutes one of the noblest and most magnificent spectacles that can be presented to the eye, or exhibited to the imagination in description. Lions and other animals of strength are subjects of some of the grandest passages. In what sublime terms is the war-horse described in Job!

"Hast thou given the horse strength? hast thou clothed his neck with thunder? Canst thou make him afraid as a grasshopper? The glory of his nostrils is terrible. He paweth in the valley, and rejoiceth in his strength; he goeth on to meet the armed men. He mocketh at fear, and is not affrighted; neither turneth he back from the sword. The quiver rattleth against him, the glittering spear and the shield. He swalloweth the ground with fierceness and rage; neither believeth he that it is the sound of the trumpet. He saith among the trumpets, Ha, ha! and he smelleth the battle afar off."

The description of the leviathan is worked up in the same book with fine effect.

"Canst thou draw out leviathan with an hook? or his tongue with a cord which thou lettest down? Canst thou put an hook into his nose? or bore his jaw through with a thorn? Wilt thou play with him as with a bird? or wilt thou bind him for thy maidens? By his neesings a light doth shine, and his eyes are like the eyelids of the morning. Out of his mouth go burning lamps, and sparks of fire leap out. Out of his nostrils goeth smoke, as out of a seething pot or cauldron. His breath kindleth coals, and a flame goeth out of his mouth. In his neck remaineth strength, and sorrow is turned into joy before him."

§ 266. The simplest form in which sublimity develops it-

What is the principal source of the sublime? From this source what derive their grandeur? How is a stream that confines itself to its banks characterized? When does the same stream become sublime? Repeat the remark of Longinus. What is the highest exertion of human might? What kind of a spectacle does a battle, therefore, constitute? What animals form the subject of some of the grandest passages? Where are the war-horse and the leviathan described in sublime terms? Repeat these descriptions.

§ 266. What is the simplest form in which sublimity develops itself? Give some

self is vastness. Wide-extended plains, to which the eye discerns no limit; the firmament of heaven; the boundless expanse of ocean,—furnish us with familiar examples.

To connect greatness of size with greatness of character is natural, particularly with unenlightened minds. The Scythians, for example, were so impressed with the fame of Alexander the Great that they thought he must be a giant, and were astonished when they found him to be rather under than above their own size.

The mind is inadequate to the conception of infinity, and intuitively invests whatever approaches it with a character of grandeur. Hence, infinite space, endless numbers, and eternal duration, possess this quality in an eminent degree. It must be observed, however, that where there is such variety in the parts of any object that one cannot be inferred from another, unless they are of such size that all can be taken in at one view, a portion of the sublimity is lost. When there is such immensity that the whole cannot be comprehended at once, the mind is distracted rather than satisfied, and is excited only to an inferior degree of pleasure. With the sky and the ocean this is not the case; because what is invisible is the counterpart of what we see, and from such portions as meet the eye imagination can readily draw the picture of such as are concealed from it. When, however, every part must be seen that an idea of the whole may be formed, any degree of magnitude inconsistent with distinctness diminishes the effect. Addison's observation is therefore just, that there would have been more true sublimity in one of Lysippus' statues of Alexander, though no larger than life, than in the vast Mount Athos, had it been cut into the figure of the hero, according to the proposition of Phidias, with a river in one hand, and a city in the other.

§ 267. All vastness produces the impression of sublimity. This impression, however, is less vivid in objects extended in length or breadth than in such as are vast by reason of their height or depth. Though a boundless plain is a grand object, yet a high mountain to which we look up or an awful preci-

---

familiar examples. With what is it natural to connect greatness of character? What did the Scythians think respecting Alexander the Great? To what is the mind inadequate? What objects, therefore, are eminently grand? When there is variety in the parts of an object, what degree of magnitude is inconsistent with the highest sublimity? Why does not this principle operate in the case of the sky and the ocean? What remark does Addison make in illustration of this point?

§ 267. With the same size, in what directions must bodies be extended, to be most sublime? How does a boundless plain compare with a high mountain or an awful

pice or tower from which we contemplate objects beneath, is still grander. The sublimity of the firmament arises as well from its height as from its vast extent.

Our every-day actions show that we are aware of the effect produced on the mind by elevation. We raise lofty monuments, and on their tops place the statues of our heroes, at as great a height as is compatible with distinctness of view. So thrones are erected for kings, and elevated seats for judges and magistrates. Among all nations, Heaven is placed far above, Hell far below. Why are these directions preferred to all others, if the mind does not instinctively connect an idea of grandeur with great height and depth?

§ 268. The solemn and the terrible are important elements of the sublime; hence, darkness, solitude, and silence, which have a tendency to fill the mind with awe, contribute much to sublimity. It is not the gay landscape, the flowery field, or the flourishing city, that produces the emotion of grandeur: but the hoary mountain, and the solitary lake; the aged forest, and the torrent falling down the precipice.

Hence, too, night scenes are generally the most sublime. The firmament, when filled with stars in magnificent profusion, strikes the imagination with a more awful grandeur than when we view it enlightened by the brightest noon-day sun. The sound of a bell and the striking of a large clock are at any time grand; but they become doubly so, when heard amid the stillness of night. In descriptions of the Deity, darkness is often introduced, and with great effect, as a means of imparting additional sublimity to the subject. "He maketh darkness his pavilion," saith the inspired writer; "He dwelleth in the thick cloud." So, Milton:—

> "How oft, amidst
> Thick clouds and dark, does Heaven's all-ruling Sire
> Choose to reside, his glory unobscured,
> And with the majesty of darkness round
> Circles his throne!"

§ 269. Obscurity is another source of the sublime. We

---

precipice? To what is the sublimity of the firmament owing? How, in every-day life, do we avail ourselves of the effects produced by elevation? Why do all nations locate Heaven above them, and Hell below?

§ 268. What other elements contribute largely to the sublime? Give instances of their effect. As regards sublimity, what is the effect of darkness on the heavens, the sound of bells, &c.? What is often introduced into descriptions of the Deity, and with what effect? Give an example from Scripture; from Milton.

have seen that in natural and visible objects, when a portion of the form is seen, it is essential that the whole be within reach of the eye, unless there is such uniformity that its appearance can be readily inferred. When no part, however, is visible or material, but the whole is left to imagination, the obscurity and uncertainty fill the mind with indescribable awe. Thus we find that descriptions of supernatural beings are characterized by sublimity, though the ideas they yield are confused and indistinct. The superior power we attribute to such beings, the obscurity with which they are veiled, and the awe they awaken in our minds, necessarily render them sublime. The grand effect of obscurity is obvious in the following passage from the book of Job :—

"In thoughts from the visions of the night, when deep sleep falleth on men, fear came upon me, and trembling, which made all my bones to shake. Then a spirit passed before my face; the hair of my flesh stood up. It stood still, but I could not discern the form thereof: an image was before mine eyes, there was silence, and I heard a voice, saying, 'Shall mortal man be more just than God? shall a man be more pure than his Maker?'"

As a general principle, all objects greatly elevated, or far removed as regards either space or time, are apt to strike us as grand. Whatever is viewed through the mist of distance or antiquity looms larger than its natural size. Hence epic poets find it expedient to select as heroes the great personages of bygone times, rather than those of their own day, though equally distinguished.

It follows that no ideas are so sublime as those connected with the Supreme Being, the least known but incomparably the greatest of all things; the infinity of whose nature and the eternity of whose duration, joined to the immensity of His power, though they transcend our conceptions, yet exalt them in the highest degree.

§ 270. Sublimity is also frequently heightened by disor-

---

§ 269. What is another source of the sublime? Show the difference in this respect between material and immaterial things. What is said of supernatural objects? Quote from Job a sublime passage descriptive of a spirit. As a general principle, what objects strike us as grand? Why do epic poets select as heroes personages of bygone times? With whom are our sublimest ideas connected?

§ 270. By what is sublimity frequently heightened? What feeling does strict regu-

der. When we gaze at things strictly regular in their outline and methodical in the arrangement of their parts, we feel a sense of confinement incompatible with mental expansion.

Exact proportion of parts, though it often contributes additional effect to the beautiful, seldom enters into the sublime. A great mass of rocks thrown wildly and confusedly together by the hand of nature produces a greater impression of grandeur in the mind than if they had been adjusted to each other with the utmost taste and care.

§ 271. We have thus far considered sublimity as belonging to visible things merely; it may, however, characterize objects of hearing, as well as those of sight. Among the arts which please the imagination through the ear, poetry and rhetoric have already been enumerated. Though, with the aid of conventional characters which represent words and thereby ideas, they address the eye, and may therefore be understood by the deaf, yet they are to be regarded as primarily appealing to the ear, and governed by principles laid down with the direct view of producing the liveliest effect on that organ. Accordingly, under the head of sublimity, as pertaining to objects of hearing, we must treat of the sublime in writing; and this, by reason of its importance, will constitute a separate lesson. It remains for us here to enumerate the sounds characterized by sublimity. These are included in five classes, as follows:—

I. Those associated with ideas of danger; such as, the howling of a storm, the rumbling of an earthquake, the groaning of a volcano, the roaring of thunder, the report of artillery.

II. Those associated with great power actively exerted; as, the noise of a torrent, the fall of a cataract, the uproar of a tempest, the dash of waves, the crackling of a conflagration.

III. Those associated with ideas of majesty, solemnity, deep melancholy or profound grief; as, the sound of the trumpet and other warlike instruments, the notes of the organ, the tolling of the bell, &c.

---

larity produce? To what does exact proportion of parts contribute? In what position do massive rocks produce the greatest impression of grandeur?

§ 271. To what, besides objects of sight, does sublimity belong? To what sense are the arts of poetry and rhetoric addressed? With what three classes of ideas must

IV. Of the notes of animals, those awaken the emotion of grandeur which are known to proceed from strong or ferocious creatures. As examples of this class, the roar of the lion, the growling of bears, the howling of wolves, and the scream of the eagle, may be mentioned.

V. Those sounds of the human voice may be accounted sublime which indicate that the more serious emotions,—sorrow, terror, and the like,—are strongly excited. The tones which, in general, denote a high degree of emotion, will be found to be loud, grave, lengthened, and swelling.

§ 272. It will be seen that the sublimity of sound arises, not from any inherent quality or independent fitness to produce the emotion, but exclusively from the association of ideas.

This is evident from the fact that, as soon as the sound is separated from the idea, it ceases to be sublime. Thus, persons who are afraid of thunder frequently mistake some common sound for it, such as the rolling of a cart or carriage. While the mistake continues, they feel an emotion of sublimity; but, the moment they are undeceived, they are the first to laugh at their error and ridicule the noise that occasioned it. Similar mistakes are often made, in those countries where earthquakes are common, between inconsiderable sounds and the low rumbling noise which is said to precede such an event; there can be no doubt that, the moment the truth is discovered, the emotion of sublimity is at an end. So, children are at first as much impressed with the thunder of the theatre as with that of the genuine tempest; but, when they understand the delusion, regard it as no more than the insignificant noises they hear every day. Again, to the Highlander the sound of the bag-pipe is sublime, because it is the martial instrument of his country, and is constantly associated with splendid and magnificent images; to the rest of the world, the instrument is at best barely tolerable. Finally, that sublimity in the tones of animals arises from associations with their character seems obvious from several considerations. The howl of the wolf differs little from that of the dog either in tone or strength;

---

sounds be associated, in order to be sublime? Give examples of each. Of the notes of animals, which awaken the emotion of grandeur? What sounds of the human voice are accounted sublime? What tones denote a high degree of emotion?

§ 272. From what does the sublimity of sound arise? What evidence is there of this? Illustrate the point by stating what takes place when some insignificant sound is mistaken for thunder or the rumbling of an earthquake. How is the sound of the bag-pipe regarded by the Highlander? How, by the rest of the world? What occa

but there is no comparison between them in point of sublimity, because we know the one to be a savage, and the other a domestic, animal. There are few animal sounds so loud as the lowing of a cow; yet it will be admitted that it is far from being characterized by sublimity. We may therefore infer that sounds possess this quality, not by reason of any inherent character, but only through the associations connected with them.

LESSON XL.

THE SUBLIME IN WRITING.

§ 273. For a literary composition to possess sublimity, it is necessary that the subject be sublime; that, if a scene or natural object, it be one which, exhibited to us in reality, would inspire us with thoughts of the elevated, awful, and magnificent character that has been described. This excludes what is merely beautiful, gay, or elegant. If it be attempted, with the aid of rhetoric, to make any such object the theme of a sublime composition, the effort will prove a failure, and bombast or frigidity of style will result.

§ 274. We shall find, then, that the passages generally accounted sublime are, for the most part, descriptions of the natural objects mentioned in the last lesson as capable of producing the emotion of grandeur; or, in other words, of what is vast, mighty, magnificent, obscure, dark, solemn, loud, pathetic, or terrible.

Shakspeare, in the following lines, furnishes us with a fine example of sublimity, arising from the vastness of the objects successively pre-

---

sions the difference? From what does sublimity in the tones of animals arise? Illustrate this.

§ 273. What is essential to sublimity in a literary composition? If a scene or natural object is treated of, what must be its character? What is excluded? What will result, if it be attempted to write sublimely on a trivial subject?

§ 274. Of what, then, for the most part, are sublime passages descriptions? Repeat the quotation from Shakspeare, and show wherein its sublimity consists.

sented, and the pathetic thought that all this magnificence and greatness is destined to destruction.

> "The cloud-capt towers, the gorgeous palaces,
> The solemn temples, the great globe itself,
> Yea, all which it inherit, shall dissolve;
> And, like an insubstantial pageant faded,
> Leave not a rack behind."

As observed in § 265, battles are among the sublimest spectacles on which the eye can gaze, by reason of their displaying immense power in the act of violent exertion. We may, therefore, look for the same element of grandeur in descriptions of such scenes. Homer furnishes one of the sublimest, as well as earliest, in the whole range of poetry.

"When now gathered on either side, the hosts plunged together in fight; shield is harshly laid to shield; spears crash on the brazen corselets; bossy buckler with buckler meets; loud tumult rages over all; groans are mixed with the exulting shouts of men; the slain and the slayer join their cries; the earth is floating round with blood. As when two rushing streams from two mountains come roaring down, and throw together their rapid waters below, they roar along the gulfy vale. The startled shepherd hears the sound, as he stalks o'er the distant hills; so, as they mixed in fight, from both armies clamor with loud terror arose."

From Ossian we take another description of a battle-scene, which bears, it will be observed, a decided resemblance to the one last quoted, both in the enumeration of circumstances, and in the comparison of the contending hosts to two mountain torrents. Both are eminently sublime, presenting to us in a few words a succession of striking images.

"Like Autumn's dark storms pouring from two echoing hills, towards each other approached the heroes; as two dark streams from high rocks meet and roar on the plain, loud, rough, and dark in battle, meet Lochlin and Inisfail. Chief mixes his strokes with chief, and man with man! Steel sounds on steel, and helmets are cleft on high: blood bursts and smokes around: strings murmur on the polished yews: darts rush along the sky: spears fall like circles of light which gild the stormy face of night.

"As the noise of the troubled ocean when roll the waves on high, as the last peal of thundering heaven, such is the noise of battle. Though Cormac's hundred bards were there, feeble were the voice of a hundred bards to send the deaths to future times; for many were the deaths of the heroes, and wide poured the blood of the valiant."

What are among the sublimest spectacles, and why? What follows with respect to descriptions of battle-scenes? From what two authors are general descriptions of battles quoted? How do they compare in point of sublimity? In what respects do they resemble each other? What other poet's description of a similar scene is presented? Repeat it. How, in your opinion, does it compare in point of grandeur with the two extracts just given?

Compare with these the fine passage in the sixth book of Paradise Lost, than which nothing could be more lofty or forcible.

> "Now storming fury rose,
> And clamor such as heard in Heaven till now
> Was never; arms on armor clashing brayed
> Horrible discord, and the madding wheels
> Of brazen chariots raged; dire was the noise
> Of conflict; over-head the dismal hiss
> Of fiery darts in flaming volleys flow,
> And flying vaulted either host with fire.
> So under fiery cope together rushed
> Both battles main, with ruinous assault
> And inextinguishable rage; all Heaven
> Resounded; and, had earth been then, all earth
> Had to her centre shook."

Darkness, obscurity, and difficulty, are introduced with fine effect into the following passage from Milton, which describes the travelling of the fallen angels through their dismal habitation:—

> "O'er many a dark and dreary vale
> They passed, and many a region dolorous;
> O'er many a frozen, many a fiery Alp;
> Rocks, caves, lakes, fens, bogs, dens and shades, of death—
> A universe of death."

Seldom has a supernatural being been represented with such genuine sublimity as in the following fine extract from Ossian, descriptive of Fingal's interview with the spirit of Loda. The ghost is invested with obscurity, might, and terror; the king of Morven, with fearless heroism; the darkness of night is around: all things contribute to intensify the sublimity, with which, it may be added, the simple sententiousness of the style is eminently in keeping.

> "A blast came from the mountain: on its wings was the spirit of Loda. He came to his place in his terrors, and shook his dusky spear. His eyes appear like flames in his dark face: his voice is like distant thunder. Fingal advanced his spear in night, and raised his voice on high. 'Son of night, retire: call thy winds, and fly! Why dost thou come to my presence with thy shadowy arms? Do I fear thy gloomy form, spirit of dismal Loda? Weak is thy shield of clouds; feeble is that meteor thy sword! The blast rolls them together: and thou thyself art lost. Fly from my presence, son of night! call thy winds and fly!'

What other passage is presented from Milton? What points are introduced with fine effect? What specimen is given of descriptions of supernatural objects? With what is the ghost invested? With what, the king? What contributes to intensify the sublimity?

How is the spirit of Loda described? What does it command Fingal to do? What is the result of the interview?

" 'Dost thou force me from my place!' replied the hollow voice. 'I turn the battle in the field of the brave. I look on the nations, and they vanish: my nostrils pour the blast of death. I come abroad on the winds: the tempests are before my face. But my dwelling is calm above the clouds; pleasant are the fields of my rest.'

" 'Dwell in thy pleasant fields,' said the king. 'Let Comhal's son be forgotten. Do my steps ascend from my hills into thy peaceful plains? Do I meet thee with a spear on thy cloud, spirit of dismal Loda? Why then dost thou frown on me. Why shake thine airy spear? Thou frownest in vain: I never fled from the mighty in war; and shall the sons of the wind frighten the king of Morven? No—he knows the weakness of their arms.'

" 'Fly to thy land,' replied the form; 'take to the wind, and fly! The blasts are in the hollow of my hand: the course of the storm is mine. Fly to thy land, son of Comhal, or feel my flaming wrath!'

" He lifted high his shadowy spear! he bent forward his dreadful height. Fingal, advancing, drew his sword, the blade of dark-brown Luno. The gleaming path of the steel winds through the gloomy ghost. The form fell shapeless into air."

§ 275. Besides the objects enumerated in the last lesson, there is another class from which the subjects of the sublimest passages are often taken. They consist of the great and heroic feelings and acts of men; and the elevation which distinguishes them is generally known as *the moral or sentimental sublime*. When, in an extremely critical position, a person forgets all selfish interests and is controlled by high inflexible principles, we have an instance of the moral sublime.

The most fruitful sources of moral sublimity are these:—

I. Firmness in the cause of truth and justice.

Of this species of heroism, ancient Roman history furnishes many distinguished examples. Brutus, with unyielding sternness, sentencing his sons to death, for having conspired against their country; and Titus Manlius, ordering his son to the stake, for engaging with an enemy contrary to his command;—excite in our minds the most elevated ideas. Socrates is another instance, who chose to die by hemlock, though means of escape were in his power, because their employment might have been construed into an admission of guilt. Above all, among never-to-

---

§ 275. What is meant by the moral or sentimental sublime? When have we instances of the moral sublime? What is the first source of moral sublimity? What history furnishes us examples of this species of heroism? Mention two. What illustration is afforded by Socrates' career? What other memorable examples are cited? What is the second source of the moral sublime? Show how the story of Damon and Pythias furnishes two examples of moral sublimity. What instance is cited from Roman his

be-forgotten instances of the moral sublime, are to be mentioned the heroic deaths of the Christian martyrs, who, amid tortures inconceivable, in flames and on the rack, testified to the reality of their faith.

II. Generous self-sacrifice in behalf of another.

The story of Damon and Pythias, the former of whom, having incurred the enmity of the tyrant Dionysius, was by him sentenced to death, furnishes us with two remarkable examples: first, that of Pythias, who remains as hostage during his friend's farewell visit to his family, on condition of suffering in his stead if he does not return at the appointed time; and, secondly, that of Damon, who, refusing to profit by the self-devotion of Pythias, comes back in season to redeem his pledge. We find another forcible illustration in the career of Coriolanus; when, after having been besought in vain by the leading men of Rome, he yields to his mother's tears and prayers, though aware that the consequences will be fatal to himself, and consents to withdraw his army with the sad words, "Mother, thou hast saved Rome,—but lost thy son!" Equally sublime is the self-devotion of Codrus, the last Athenian king. Informed by the oracle, that, in a battle which was about to take place, Athens or her king must perish, he rushed into the thickest of the fight, and by the sacrifice of himself saved, as he thought, his country.

III. Self-possession and fearlessness in circumstances of danger.

Of such elevated emotion, an incident in the career of Cæsar affords a striking illustration. Crossing, on one occasion, a branch of the sea, he was overtaken by a tempest of such violence that the pilot declared himself unable to proceed, and was in the act of turning back. "*Quid times? Cæsarem vehis!*" "What do you fear! You carry Cæsar!" was the sublime reply. We have another example of heroism in Mucius Scævola, thrusting his arm into Porsenna's camp-fire, to show how he scorned his threatened tortures, and keeping it there with unmoved countenance till it was entirely consumed. More than this, we see the effect produced by the act; for Porsenna was so struck with it that he gave the youth, who had come to murder him, his life, and subsequently negotiated a peace with Rome.

IV. Exalted patriotism.

Wolfe's death-scene embodies the height of the moral sublime.

---

tory? What, from the early history of Athens? What is the third source of moral sublimity? Exemplify it with incidents drawn from the career of Cæsar and that of Mucius Scævola. What is the fourth source of moral sublimity? Illustrate this with an ac-

Wounded on the Plains of Abraham, in the very death-agony, he heard the distant shout, "They fly! they fly!"—"Who fly?" eagerly asked the dying hero.—"The enemy," replied one of his officers.—"Then," said he, "I die happy!" and expired. Another notable instance, quoted by all French critics, occurs in one of Corneille's tragedies. In the famous combat between the Horatii and the Curiatii, the old Horatius, being informed that two of his sons are slain, and that the third has betaken himself to flight, at first will not believe the report; but, being thoroughly assured of the fact, he is filled with grief and indignation at this supposed unworthy behavior of his surviving son. He is reminded that his son stood alone against three, and is asked what he wished that he had done. "That he had died!" (*Qu'il mourut!*) is the reply.

LESSON XLI.

THE SUBLIME IN WRITING (CONTINUED).

§ 276. To give effect to the description of a sublime object, a clear, strong, concise, and simple, style, must be employed.

These different qualities of style will be treated of hereafter; their general character is sufficiently understood for our present purpose. Every thing must be painted in such terms as to leave no room for misapprehension. To ensure strength, such circumstances must be selected for the description as exhibit the object in a striking point of view. It is plain that things present different appearances to us according to the side we look upon; and that, when there are a variety of circumstances, our descriptions will vary in character according to those we select. In this selection lies the great art of the composer, and the difficulty of sublime writing. If the description is too general, and barren of circumstances, we can not present a forcible picture; while, if any trivial or common-place circumstance is introduced, the whole is degraded.

---

count of Wolfe's death-scene. What notable instance of exalted patriotism occurs in one of Corneille's tragedies?

§ 276. To give effect to the description of a sublime object, what kind of a style must be employed? How must every thing be painted? To ensure strength, what circumstances must be selected for the description? In what lies the great art of sublime writing? If the description is too general, what follows? What, if a trivial cir-

Thus, if a storm is the subject, something else is necessary than to say that torrents of rain pour down, and trees and houses are overthrown. We must seize on the more striking phenomena with which it is attended, and dwell only on its grander effects.

§ 277. Conciseness is one of the most important essentials of sublimity in writing. The greatest thoughts must be presented in the fewest words. If the specimens in the last lesson, particularly those from Homer and Ossian, are examined, it will be seen that this is their leading feature; no words are introduced unless essential to the idea.

"I love God and little children," says the German philosopher Richter. In what more elevated terms could he have expressed his love for sinlessness and innocence! The sentence is grand, because so strikingly condensed. The same conciseness constitutes the sublimity of Cæsar's famous VENI, VIDI, VICI, in which he announced to the Senate the result of one of his battles; a saying which loses just half its terse energy, when translated into English, "I came, I saw, I conquered."

In the sentence before quoted, "*Quid times? Cæsarem vehis,*" the effect is also due, in a measure, to the sententiousness of the style. It is readily seen how much is gained by conciseness, when we compare with these brief and eloquent words of the fearless conqueror, Lucan's account of the scene, in which, by attempting to amplify and adorn the thought, he has diluted it into insignificance.

> "But Cæsar, still superior to distress,
> Fearless and confident of sure success,
> Thus to the pilot loud :—'The seas despise,
> And the vain threatening of the noisy skies;
> Though gods deny thee yon Ausonian strand,
> Yet go, I charge you; go, at my command.
> Thy ignorance alone can cause thy fears,
> Thou know'st not what a freight thy vessel bears;
> Thou know'st not I am he to whom 'tis given
> Never to want the care of watchful Heaven.
> Obedient fortune waits my humble thrall,
> And, always ready, comes before I call.
> Let winds and seas loud wars at freedom wage,
> And waste upon themselves their empty rage!

cumstance is introduced? If a storm is the subject, what must be seized on, and what left untouched?

§ 277. What quality of style is particularly conducive to sublimity? What must be the character of the thoughts, and what of the words? What will be found, on examining the specimens in the last lesson? Give a sentence from Richter, which is sublime by reason of its conciseness. Give one from Cæsar. When translated into English how does this sentence compare in sublimity with the original? What other

> A stronger, mightier, demon is thy friend;
> Thou and thy bark on Cæsar's fate depend.
> Thou stand'st amazed to view this dreadful scene,
> And wonder'st what the gods and fortune mean:
> But artfully their bounties thus they raise,
> And from my danger arrogate new praise;
> Amidst the fears of death they bid me live,
> And still enhance what they are sure to give."—Rowe.

§ 278. Simplicity is no less essential to sublimity than conciseness. The words employed must be, not only few, but plain. High-flown and turgid expressions must be avoided no less carefully than mean, low, and trivial ones. Ornament, however conducive to beauty of style, is here out of place. Nothing is more mistaken than to suppose that magnificent words, accumulated epithets, and swelling expressions, constitute real elevation.

This will be apparent from an illustration. Longinus and all critics from his time to the present have concurred in attributing the highest sublimity to the verse in Genesis which describes the creation of light: "And God said, Let there be light: and there was light." But exchange its simplicity for misplaced ornament,—" The sovereign arbiter of nature, by the potent energy of a single word, commanded light to exist and immediately it sprang into being,"—and the sound is indeed magnified, but the sentiment is degraded, and the grandeur is gone.

The reason why a deficiency of conciseness or simplicity is fatal to the sublime appears to be this. The emotion in question raises the mind considerably above its ordinary tone. A temporary enthusiasm is produced, extremely agreeable while it lasts, but from which the mind is every moment in danger of sinking to its usual level. Now when an author has brought us, or is attempting to bring us, into this state of elevated rapture, if he indulges in unnecessary words, if he stops to introduce glittering ornaments, if he even throws in a single decoration that is inferior to the leading image, he loses the critical moment; the tension of the mind is relaxed; the emotion is dissipated. The beautiful may survive; the sublime is sacrificed.

---

sentence of Cæsar's owes a portion of its sublimity to conciseness? How is this shown?

§ 278. What besides conciseness is essential to sublimity? What kind of expressions must be avoided? Illustrate the different effects produced by simple and by high-flown language. Explain why a deficiency of conciseness or simplicity is fatal to the sublime.

§ 279. The writer must not only be concise and simple; he must also have a lively impression of his subject. If his own enthusiasm is not awakened, he cannot hope to excite emotion in others.

All forced attempts by which a writer endeavors to excite himself and his readers, when his imagination begins to flag, have just the opposite effect from what is intended. A poet gains nothing by labored appeals, invocations of the muses, or general exclamations concerning the greatness, terribleness, or majesty, of what he is about to describe. We find an example of such forced introductions in Addison's description of the Battle of Blenheim.

> "But, O my muse! what numbers wilt thou find,
> To sing the furious troops in battle joined?
> Methinks I hear the drum's tumultuous sound,
> The victor's shouts, and dying groans confound;" &c.

§ 280. When, therefore, an awe-inspiring object is presented in nature, a grand creation in art, an exalted feeling in the human mind, or a heroic deed in human action; then, if our own impression is vivid, and we exhibit it in brief, plain, and simple terms, without rhetorical aids, but trusting mainly to the dignity which the thought naturally assumes, we may hope to attain to the sublime.

Sublimity, by its very nature, awakens but a short-lived emotion. By no force of genius can the mind for any considerable time be kept so far raised above its common tone. Neither are the abilities of any human writer sufficient to furnish a long continuation of uninterruptedly sublime ideas. The utmost we can expect is that the fire of imagination should sometimes flash upon us, like lightning from heaven, and then disappear. No author is sublime throughout, in the true sense of the word. Yet there are some, who, by the strength and dignity of their conceptions, and the current of high ideas that runs throughout their compositions, keep their readers' minds in a state of comparative

---

§ 279. What else must a writer have, to write sublimely? What is said of forced attempts to excite one's self and one's readers? From what does a writer gain nothing? Illustrate this from Addison.

§ 280. How, then, may we hope to attain to the sublime? What kind of an emotion does sublimity awaken? Why can not the emotion continue for any length of time? What is the utmost we can expect? Can any author hope to be sublime throughout? What is the nearest approach to it? What writers among the ancients, and who among moderns, are distinguished for the elevated tone which runs throughout their compositions?

elevation. In this class Pindar, Demosthenes, and Plato, among the ancients, and Ossian and Milton, among moderns, are worthy of being ranked.

§ 281. An unimproved state of society is peculiarly favorable to the production of sublime compositions. When the mind is unaccustomed to the ornamental, it is more apt to appreciate and admire the grand. In the infancy of nations, men are constantly meeting with objects to them new and striking; the imagination is kept glowing; and the passions are often vehemently excited. They think boldly, and express their thoughts without restraint. Advances towards refinement are conducive to the development of beauty in style, but signally limit the sphere of the sublime.

We find this theory borne out by fact. As a general thing, the sublimest writers have flourished either in the early ages of the world or in the infancy of their respective nations. Thus, the grandest of all passages are found in the earliest of books, the Bible. The style of the inspired writers is characterized by a sublimity commensurate with the majesty and solemnity of their subjects. What can transcend in grandeur the following descriptions of the Almighty? The student is requested to observe how they combine the various elements mentioned above as calculated to elevate the mind and affect the imagination.

"In my distress I called upon the Lord, and cried unto my God: He heard my voice out of His temple, and my cry came before Him, even into His ears. Then the earth shook and trembled; the foundations also of the hills moved and were shaken, because He was wroth. There went up a smoke out of His nostrils, and fire out of His mouth devoured: coals were kindled by it. He bowed the heavens also, and came down: and darkness was under His feet. And He rode upon a cherub and did fly: yea, He did fly upon the wings of the wind. He made darkness His secret place; His pavilion round about Him were dark waters and thick clouds of the skies."—PSALM XVIII, 6-11.

"Before Him went the pestilence, and burning coals went forth at His feet. He stood, and measured the earth: He beheld, and drove asunder the nations; and the everlasting mountains were scattered, the perpetual hills did bow: His ways are everlasting. The mountains saw Thee, and they trembled: the overflowing of the waters passed by:

---

§ 281. What state of society is favorable to the sublime? Explain the reason. To what are advances towards refinement conducive? At what period do we find that the sublimest writers have flourished? What book contains the grandest of all passages? What descriptions are peculiarly sublime? Repeat the description of the Almighty from Psalm xviii. Repeat that from Habakkuk. Wherein consists the sub

the deep uttered his voice, and lifted up his hands on high."—HABAK-KUK, III., 5, 6, 10.

The same remark holds true in Greek literature. Homer, who was the earliest, is also the most sublime, poet that has written in that language, his ideas being grand and his diction unaffected. We have already seen how magnificently he describes a battle. A similar passage, worthy of special mention, occurs in the 20th book of the Iliad. It represents the gods as taking part in an engagement between the Greeks and Trojans. All heaven and earth are in commotion. Jupiter thunders from on high. Minerva and Mars gird themselves for the terrible conflict. Neptune strikes the earth with his trident; the ships, the cities, and the mountains, shake; the earth trembles to its centre. Pluto starts from his throne, in dread lest the secrets of the infernal regions be laid open to the view of mortals.

After the magnificent passages quoted from Ossian, it is hardly necessary to say that he is one of the most sublime of writers. He possesses the plain and venerable manner of antiquity. He deals in no superfluous or gaudy ornaments, but throws forth his images with a rapid conciseness which appeals powerfully to the mind. Among poets of more polished times we must look for elaborate graces, exact proportion of parts, and skilfully conducted narratives. In the midst of smiling landscapes, the gay and beautiful have their home; the sublime dwells among the rude scenes of nature and society which Ossian describes; amid rocks and torrents, whirlpools and battles.

LESSON XLII

THE SUBLIME IN WRITING (CONTINUED).

§ 282. Rhyme, which generally forms a feature of English verse, is unfavorable to sublimity in writing, by reason of its constrained elegance, its studied smoothness, and the super-

---

limity of these passages? Who is the sublimest of Greek poets? Give the substance of a fine passage in the 20th book of the Iliad. What is said of Ossian? Describe his style. Where must we look for the elaborate graces of writing? Where, for the sublime?

§ 282. What is the effect of rhyme as regards sublimity? How does it produce this

fluous words often brought in to produce a recurrence of the same sound.

Homer's description of the nod of Jupiter has been admired in all ages as a model of elevated thought:—" He spoke, and, bending his sable brows, gave the awful nod ; while he shook the celestial locks of his immortal head, all Olympus was shaken." Pope translates this passage into English verse, with a decided loss of sublime effect. It will be seen that he enlarges on the thought and attempts to beautify it; but the result is that he only weakens it. The third line is entirely expletive, being introduced for no other reason than to furnish a rhyme for the preceding one.

> "He spoke: and awful bends his sable brows,
> Shakes his ambrosial curls, and gives the nod,
> The stamp of fate, and sanction of a god.
> High heaven with trembling the dread signal took,
> And all Olympus to its centre shook."

§ 283. The freedom and variety of our blank verse render it a decidedly better medium than rhyme for the expression of sublime ideas. Hence it is much to be preferred for epic poetry. Milton has availed himself of this fact. The images he successively presents in Paradise Lost are unsurpassed for grandeur. Take, for instance, the description of Satan after his fall, at the head of the infernal hosts :—

> "He, above the rest,
> In shape and gesture proudly eminent,
> Stood like a tower; his form had not yet lost
> All her original brightness, nor appeared
> Less than archangel ruined; and the excess
> Of glory obscured: as when the sun, new risen,
> Looks through the horizontal misty air,
> Shorn of his beams; or, from behind the moon,
> In dim eclipse, disastrous twilight sheds
> On half the nations, and with fear of change
> Perplexes monarchs. Darkened so, yet shone
> Above them all the archangel."

This passage is justly eulogized by Blair. "Here," he says, "concur

---

effect? Repeat Homer's description of the nod of Jupiter, as literally translated. Repeat Pope's translation of the same. How does it compare with the literal version? Explain the reason.

§ 283. What kind of verse is preferable to rhyme for the expression of sublime ideas? Hence, for what should it be employed? Who has thus used it with great success? What is said of the images successively presented in Paradise Lost? Repeat Milton's description of Satan after his fall. What does Blair say about this passage?

variety of sources of the sublime: the principal object eminently great; a high superior nature, fallen indeed, but erecting itself against distress the grandeur of the principal object heightened, by associating it with so noble an idea as that of the sun suffering an eclipse; this picture, shaded with all those images of change and trouble, of darkness and terror, which coincide so finely with the sublime emotion; and the whole expressed in a style and versification, easy, natural, and simple, but magnificent."

§ 284. Those who aim at the sublime are liable to fall into two faults,—frigidity and bombast.

§ 285. Frigidity consists in degrading an object or sentiment which is sublime in itself, by our mean conception of it, or by a weak, low, and childish description. No fault is more to be avoided.

As a forcible example of frigidity, we quote a passage from a poem of Sir Richard Blackmoor's, descriptive of an eruption of Etna; in which, as humorously observed by Dr. Arbuthnot, he represents the mountain in a fit of colic.

> Etna, and all the burning mountains, find
> Their kindled stores with inbred storms of wind
> Blown up to rage, and roaring out complain,
> As torn with inward gripes, and torturing pain;
> Laboring, they cast their dreadful vomit round,
> And with their melted bowels spread the ground."

So Ben Jonson, in a battle-scene, rather injudiciously caps the climax of his would-be sublimity by representing the sun in a perspiration.

> "The sun stood still, and was, behind the cloud
> The battle made, seen sweating to drive up
> His frighted horse, whom still the noise drove backward."
> *Catiline*, Act V

§ 286. Bombast consists in attempting to raise an ordinary or trivial object above its level, and to endow it with a sublimity it does not possess. Such attempts illustrate the old saying that there is but a step from the sublime to the ridic-

---

§ 284. Into what faults are those who aim at the sublime liable to fall?

§ 285. In what does frigidity consist? Quote a passage from Blackmoor, illustrative of this fault. Point out wherein the frigidity lies. What has been humorously observed respecting these lines? How does Ben Jonson represent the sun in a battle-scene? Of what fault is he therein guilty?

§ 286. In what does bombast consist? What is the mind prone to do? Into what

ulous. When under the control of violent passions, the mind, it is true, is prone to magnify the objects of its conceptions beyond their natural bounds; but such hyperbolical description has its limits, and, when carried too far, degenerates into the burlesque. Ben Jonson, Blackmoor, and Dryden, have fallen into this fault.

> "Great and high
> The world knows only two, that's Rome and I.
> My roof receives me not; 'tis air I tread,—
> And at each step I feel my advanced head
> Knock out a star in heaven."
>
> BEN JONSON. *Sejanus*, Act V.

> Give way, and let the gushing torrent come;
> Behold the tears we bring to swell the deluge,
> Till the flood rise upon the guilty world,
> And make the ruin common."
>
> BEN JONSON. *Lady Jane Gray*, Act IV.

> "To see this fleet upon the ocean move,
> Angels drew wide the curtains of the skies;
> And heaven, as if there wanted lights above,
> For tapers made two glaring comets rise."
>
> DRYDEN.

LESSON XLIII.

THE BEAUTIFUL.

§ 287 BEAUTY does not afford the imagination so high a degree of pleasure as sublimity; but, characterizing a greater variety of objects than the latter quality, it is a more fruitful source of gratification to that faculty. The emotion it awakens is easily distinguishable from that of grandeur. It is calmer and more gentle, and is calculated, not so much to elevate the mind, as to produce in it an agreeable serenity. Sublimity raises a feeling too violent to be lasting; the pleasure arising from beauty admits of longer continuance.

---

does hyperbolical description degenerate? What writers have fallen into this fault? Give examples, and show wherein the bombast lies.

§ 287. Which affords the higher degree of pleasure, beauty or sublimity? Which is

Few words in the language are applicable to as wide a range of objects as beauty. It is used in connection with whatever pleases the eye or ear; with many of the graces of writing; and even with the abstract terms of science. We speak of a beautiful tree or flower; a beautiful poem; a beautiful character; and a beautiful theorem in mathematics.

§ 288. Frequent attempts have been made to discover in what the beautiful consists; what quality it is, which all beautiful objects possess, and which is the foundation of the agreeable sensations they produce. Yet no theory has been advanced on this subject which is not open to objection; and it would, therefore, seem as if the various objects so denominated are beautiful, by virtue, not of any one principle common to them all, but of several different qualities. The same agreeable emotion is produced by them all, and they are therefore designated by the common appellation *beautiful*; but this emotion seems to spring from sources radically different.

Of the theories here alluded to, several are worthy of mention. The principle of the beautiful has been made to consist in,

I. *Agreeableness.* Experience, however, which is the great test of theory, proves this hypothesis false. All agreeable things are not beautiful; nor do those which have the one quality in the highest degree possess the other in proportion. We never speak of a beautiful taste or a beautiful smell; but would certainly do so if the beautiful and the agreeable were synonymous. As long as they can be separated and are not commensurate with each other, they cannot be identical.

II. *Utility.* Here again, applying the test of experience, we find the theory does not hold good. A three-legged stool may be very useful, yet is far from being generally regarded as beautiful.

III. *Unity and variety.* This has been a favorite theory, and makes beauty to consist in a variety of contrasting features so combined that

---

the more fruitful source of gratification? Why? Show the difference in the emotions they respectively produce. To what is the term *beauty* applicable?

§ 288. What attempts have been made by different writers? What is said of the various theories advanced? What would seem to follow, with respect to the source of the beautiful?

In what does the first theory mentioned make the beautiful to consist? What is the great test of theory? What does experience prove with respect to this hypothesis? Show how this is proved. According to the second theory, in what does beauty consist? Show how this hypothesis does not always hold good. What has been a favorite

unity of design characterizes the whole. Thus, in a beautiful flower, there is a unity of proportion and symmetry, and at the same time a diversity in the size and tints of the leaves. Even in mathematics, what is beautiful is not merely an abstract principle; it is a great truth, carrying with it a long train of consequences. Yet it is objected, and with justice, that many things please us as beautiful in which we are unable to detect any variety at all; and others, again, in which variety is carried to such a degree of intricacy as to preclude the idea of unity.

As, therefore, we can discover no common and universal source of beauty, we shall next consider the different qualities from which it proceeds in individual cases.

§ 289. COLOR is one of the chief elements of beauty; though why it is so we can explain no further than by saying, that the structure of the eye is such as to receive more pleasure from some modifications of the rays of light than others. This organ, moreover, is so variously constituted, that a color which is agreeable to one may excite no special admiration in another. Still, we find there are some peculiarities belonging to colors, which, in the estimation of all, enhance their beauty.

I. They must not be dusky or muddy, but clear and fair.

II. They must be delicate rather than strong. Light straw-color and mellow pink are generally considered more beautiful than deep and dazzling yellow and red.

III. If the colors are strong and vivid, they must be mingled and contrasted with each other, the strength and glare of each being thus abated. This constitutes the charm of variegated flowers.

These various traits are found to characterize the beautiful colors which nature everywhere employs to render her works attractive, and which art finds it extremely difficult to imitate. They will be recognized in the blending shades with which she paints the feathers of birds,

---

theory with many? Exemplify it. What objection is justly made to it? What, therefore, are we unable to discover?

§ 289. What is one of the chief elements of beauty? How far are we able to explain this? What three peculiarities, in the general estimation, enhance the beauty of colors? In what natural objects do these peculiarities characterize color? As in the

the complexion of blooming youth, the floral creation, and the sunset sky As in sounds, so in the case of colors, there is little doubt that the association of ideas often contributes to the pleasure received. Green, for instance, may appear more beautiful from being connected in our minds with rural scenes; white, from its being the type of innocence; and blue, from its association with the serenity of the sky.

§ 290. FIGURE.—Regular figures, or such as we perceive to be formed according to fixed principles, are, as a general rule, beautiful. Such is the character of circles, squares, triangles, and ellipses. The mind unconsciously connects with well-proportioned forms the idea of practical adaptation to some useful end. Regularity, however, does not involve the idea of sameness, which would tire and disgust the eye; on the contrary, variety is generally united with it in the most attractive works of nature.

Gradual variation in the parts uniting to form a whole seems to be one of the commonest sources of natural beauty. There is generally a constant change of direction in the outline; but it is so gradual that we find it difficult to determine its beginning or end. Thus, in the form of a dove, the head increases insensibly to the middle, whence it lessens gradually until it becomes blended with the neck. The neck loses itself in a larger swell, which continues to the middle of the body, whence there is a corresponding diminution towards the tail. The tail takes a new direction; but, soon varying its course, blends with the parts below: and thus the outline is constantly changing.

Curves change their direction at every point, and hence afford the commonest instances of gradual variation. Circular figures, therefore, are generally more beautiful than those bounded by straight lines. This is a theory of Hogarth's, who makes beauty of figure consist chiefly in the preponderance of two curves, which he calls the line of beauty and the line of grace. The former is a waving line, inclining alternately backwards and forwards, something like the letter ∞. It is con-

---

case of sounds, what often contributes to the pleasure received from colors? Exemplify this in the case of green, white, and blue.

§ 290. What figures, as a general rule, are beautiful? What idea does the mind connect with well-proportioned forms? What does regularity not involve? On the contrary, in the works of nature, what is generally united with it? What is said of the outline of the most attractive natural objects? Illustrate this in the case of the dove What figures are the most beautiful? Why? In what does Hogarth make beauty consist? Describe his line of beauty. In what does it constantly occur? Describe Hogarth's line of grace. In what is it exhibited?

stantly occurring in shells, flowers, and other ornamental works of nature, and enters largely into the decorations employed by painters and sculptors. This curve twisted round a solid body, or having the same appearance as if it had been so twisted, constitutes the line of grace. The latter is exhibited familiarly in the cork-screw; also, in a winding stair-case, and a lady's ringlet loosely curled.

§ 291. SMOOTHNESS.—Smoothness is another quality essential to beauty. We receive pleasure from contemplating the smooth leaves of flowers, smooth slopes of earth, smooth streams in a landscape, smooth coats in birds and beasts, smooth skins in our own species, and smooth and polished surfaces in furniture. Give any beautiful object a broken and rugged surface; and, however well it may be formed in other respects, it pleases no longer.

Smoothness appeals, not only to the sight, but also to the touch. The slightness of the resistance made to that part of the body with which a smooth surface comes in contact, produces a pleasing emotion, though one of inferior degree.

§ 292. MOTION.—Other things being equal, bodies in motion are more attractive than those at rest; and such as move in undulating lines please us in a higher degree than those that undeviatingly pursue the same direction. This fact is readily accounted for by Hogarth's principle. Upward motion, moreover, affords greater pleasure than that in the opposite direction. This, together with its waving character, constitutes the beauty of curling smoke; a feature which painters are fond of introducing into their landscapes.

Motion is an element of beauty, only when gentle in its character. When very swift or forcible, it becomes sublime. The motion of a bird gliding through the air, or of a placid brook, is beautiful; that of the lightning as it darts from heaven, or a mighty river chafing against its banks, partakes rather of sublimity.

§ 291. What other quality is essential to beauty? In what natural objects is it found? What results from giving any beautiful object a rugged surface? To what sense besides sight does smoothness appeal? Show how it produces a pleasing emotion through the touch.

§ 292. What imparts an additional attraction to bodies? What kind of motion is the most beautiful? What feature are painters fond of introducing into landscapes? In what does its beauty consist? In what case does motion contribute to sublimity rather than beauty?

THE BEAUTIFUL.

§ 293. SMALLNESS AND DELICACY.—As vastness and strength are elements of the sublime, so smallness and delicacy belong to the beautiful. The former qualities excite our astonishment and admiration; the latter, our sympathy and love. Whatever we are fond of is associated in our minds with the idea of smallness. Hence the diminutives used in every language to express affection and tenderness. So, an air of robustness and strength, however conducive to the sublime, is incompatible with the beautiful. To the latter an appearance of delicacy is essential, which may even be carried to the borders of fragility.

It is not the immense and mighty oak of the forest that we consider beautiful; but the delicate myrtle, the fragile violet, the modest forget-me-not. For the same reason we are more pleased with the slender grey-hound than the burly mastiff, and with the slight Arabian courser than the stout carriage-horse. To these qualities, too, much of woman's beauty is attributable.

§ 294. DESIGN.—Another source of beauty is found in design, as evidenced in the skilful combination of parts in a whole, or the adaptation of means to an end. So largely does this enter into the beautiful, that some have considered it the leading principle of the latter. This causes our pleasure when we contemplate the wonderful structure of the hand, and see with what nicety its many parts are adjusted, to form a member unequalled in strength, flexibility, and usefulness.

The pleasure arising from the sense of design is entirely distinct from that produced by the various qualities described above. Thus, in a watch, we recognize beauty in the exterior, by reason either of the color, polish, smoothness, or regularity of shape; but the pleasure pro-

---

§ 293. As regards size, what is essential to the beautiful? What feelings are excited by vastness and strength? What, by smallness and delicacy? What idea do we associate with beloved objects? What are diminutives in every language used to express? What effect has an air of robustness and strength? Illustrate this. To what is much of woman's beauty attributable?

§ 294. In what is another source of beauty found? What causes our pleasure when we contemplate the wonderful structure of the hand? In the case of a watch, show how distinct emotions of pleasure are produced by the before-mentioned qualities and

duced by an examination of the internal machinery arises entirely from our consciousness of design, our appreciation of the admirable skill with which so many complicated pieces are united for one useful purpose.

This element has an influence in the formation of many of our opinions. It is the foundation of the beauty which we discern in the proportions of doors, arches, pillars, and the like. However fine the ornaments of a building may be, they lose most of their attractions, unless, either in appearance or reality, they conduce to some useful end.

This principle should be constantly borne in mind by the composer. In a poem, a history, an oration, or any other literary work, unity of design and an adjustment of the parts in one symmetrical whole, are as essential to effect as in architecture and other arts. The finest descriptions and most elegant figures lose all their beauty, or rather become actual deformities, unless connected with the subject, and consistent with the leading design of the writer. Let the object proposed be constantly kept in view, and nothing foreign to it, however beautiful in itself, be introduced to distract the attention.

§ 295. Such are some of the leading elements of beauty, possessed, in different measures, by the various creations of nature and art. Some objects combine them all, and thereby become attractive in the highest degree. Thus, in flowers and birds, we are entertained at once with color, regularity of form, unity in variety, smoothness, delicacy, and, at times, motion. Different sensations are produced by each of these qualities; yet they blend in one general perception of beauty.

The most beautiful object that nature presents is a landscape, which combines, in rich variety, luxuriant fields, picturesque trees, running water, birds skimming the air, animals moving in the pasture, and human figures as the climax of the whole. The charms of the picture are enhanced by the judicious introduction of the creations of art,—an arching bridge, a moss-covered cottage with graceful smoke ascending from the chimney, a busy mill, an unpretending house of worship. A taste capable of appreciating such scenes is essential to success in poetical description.

---

by the sense of design. How does this element influence us in the formation of our opinions? How does this principle apply to literary compositions? What must be constantly kept in view?

§ 295. What objects are attractive in the highest degree? With what are we entertained in the case of flowers and birds? What is the most beautiful object that nature presents? What is essential to success in poetical description?

§ 296. There is a moral beauty, as well as a moral sublimity. The latter, we have seen, characterizes great and heroic acts, self-devotion, fearlessness, and patriotism. The moral beautiful belongs to the gentler virtues, affability, generosity, compassion, and the like. The emotion they excite resembles that produced by beautiful external objects.

LESSON XLIV.

GRACEFULNESS.—THE BEAUTIFUL IN THE HUMAN COUNTENANCE, IN SOUND, AND IN WRITING.

§ 297. GRACEFULNESS.—In the effect it produces on the mind, gracefulness is analogous to beauty. This quality belongs chiefly to posture and motion. Grace requires that there should be no appearance of difficulty; that the body should not be kept rigidly erect, but slightly bent, and that its parts should be so disposed as neither to embarrass each other, nor to be divided by sharp and sudden angles. In this roundness of shape and delicacy of attitude, resides a charm which must be obvious to all who consider attentively the Venus de Medici, the Antinous, or any other great statue.

§ 298. THE BEAUTIFUL IN THE HUMAN COUNTENANCE.—The beauty of the human countenance is more complicated than that belonging to most natural objects. It depends at once on color, or complexion; on figure, or outline; and on unity of design, that is, the adaptation of its various parts to the purposes for which they were formed. The chief

---

§ 296. What is meant by moral beauty? Wherein consists the difference between it and moral sublimity? What does the emotion produced by the moral beautiful resemble?

§ 297. What, in its effect, is analogous to beauty. To what, chiefly, does gracefulness belong? What does it require? In what statues is it exhibited?

§ 298. How does the beauty of the human countenance compare with that of most natural objects? On what does it depend In what does its chief beauty lie? What

beauty of the countenance, however, lies in what is called its expression, or the idea which it conveys respecting the qualities of the mind. If good-humor, intelligence, frankness, benevolence, or any other amiable quality, is indicated, the beauty of the face is heightened even more than by faultlessness of feature.

It is difficult to explain how certain conformations of feature give us the impression of certain peculiarities of mind and disposition. Perhaps both instinct and experience have a share in producing this connection. Some regard the relations subsisting between the two as exceedingly intimate. The celebrated physiognomist Campanella, who made extensive observations on human faces and was wonderfully expert in imitating such as were in any way remarkable, held that it was impossible for one even temporarily assuming a particular expression, to avoid, for the time his countenanance was so changed, the mental disposition connected therewith. When desirous of becoming acquainted with a person's feelings, he imitated his expression, his carriage, and all his other peculiarities of face and body, as nearly as possible, and then carefully observed what turn of mind he seemed to acquire by the change, thus, he claimed, he could enter into any one's thoughts as effectually as if he were converted into the man himself.

§ 299. THE BEAUTIFUL IN SOUND.—Beauty, as well as sublimity, extends to the objects of hearing equally with those of sight. It belongs, in a high degree, to that composition of different sounds which we call MUSIC, the principles of which are so various and complex as to constitute an independent science.

Musical compositions that combine grand and magnificent sounds, that are remarkable for loudness, strength, and quick transitions, properly belong to the sublime. Most music, however, is distinguished by sweetness, and is, therefore, simply beautiful. Milton, in his L'Allegro, happily describes airs of this character. It will be observed how perfectly the passage is in keeping with the subject, how easy and flowing

---

heightens the beauty of the countenance even more than faultlessness of feature? What, perhaps, combine to give us pleasure from certain conformations of feature? What was Campanella? What did he hold with regard to the countenance? By what process did he claim that he could enter into a person's thoughts?

§ 299. To what besides objects of sight does beauty extend? To what does it belong in a high degree? What musical compositions properly belong to the sublime? By what, however, is most music distinguished? Repeat the lines in which Milton describes airs of this character. By what are these lines themselves characterized?

the measure, and how pleasing the harmony of the words, both as taken individually and as combined together. We should vainly seek for a more striking example of the beautiful in writing.

> "And ever, against eating cares,
> Lap me in soft Lydian airs;
> In notes with many a winding bout
> Of linkèd sweetness long drawn out;
> With wanton head and giddy cunning,
> The melting voice through mazes running;
> Untwisting all the chains that tie
> The hidden soul of harmony."

Of simple sounds, those fall under the head of the beautiful that are characterized by sweetness, softness, and delicacy. Much here, also, is due to association. The notes of beautiful animals are, by reason of a connection of ideas, themselves beautiful. This is the chief reason why we find so much to admire in the warbling of birds. The minuteness and delicacy of their forms, their modes of life, and the domestic attachments subsisting between them, render them objects of special interest and tenderness on the part of the human family; and hence, their notes, intuitively connected in our minds with the objects from which they proceed, awaken a strong emotion of beauty.

Superstitious feelings sometimes impart effect to sounds which would otherwise be far from awaking any special admiration. To most persons the cry of the stork is hardly tolerable; but, for the Hollander, with whom this bird is the object of a popular and pleasing superstition, it possesses a singular charm.

Those sounds of the human voice are generally accounted most beautiful which are low and grave, and gradually increase in volume.

§ 300. THE BEAUTIFUL IN WRITING.—The term *beauty*, as applied to writing, is often used with but little definite meaning. When we speak of a beautiful sonnet, letter, or oration, we mean simply one that is well composed; that is agreeable,

---

What simple sounds fall under the head of the beautiful? To what is much of the pleasure received from them due? Why do we admire the warbling of birds? What feelings sometimes impart effect to sounds? How does the cry of the stork affect most persons? How, the Hollander? Why? What sounds of the human voice are accounted most beautiful?

§ 300. As generally applied to writing, what does the term *beauty* signify? Properly speaking, to what is it applied? Show how it differs from sublimity of style. How

either by reason of the sentiment it embodies, or the style in which it is expressed. But, properly speaking, this term has a more limited signification; being applied, not to what is impassioned, sparkling, vehement, or elevated, but to all that raises in the reader a gentle, placid emotion, similar to that produced by the contemplation of beauty in natural objects.

The beautiful in writing is not confined to descriptions of attractive external objects, but extends to all subjects except those of an abstract or elevated character. It does not, like sublimity, exclude ornament, or require plainness of words; nor is it necessarily confined to occasional passages. It may characterize an author's style throughout. Among the ancients, Virgil is as much distinguished for the beauty of his periods as Homer is for the sublimity of his conceptions. So, Cicero's orations have more of the beautiful than the sublime; in this latter quality they are surpassed by those of Demosthenes. Among moderns, Fénélon and Lamartine in French, Addison in English, and Irving in American, literature, possess those various graces of composition which constitute the beautiful.

EXERCISE.

As an example of the beautiful in writing, Eve's account of her first consciousness of existence and her introduction to Adam is quoted from Milton. Let the student point out its successive beauties, and, as an exercise in punctuation, supply the omitted points.

> "That day I oft remember when from sleep
> I first awaked and found myself reposed
> Under a shade on flowers much wondering where
> And what I was whence thither brought and how.
> Not distant far from thence a murmuring sound
> Of waters issued from a cave and sprend
> Into a liquid plain then stood unmoved
> Pure as the expanse of heaven I thither went
> With unexperienced thought and laid me down
> On the green bank to look into the clear
> Smooth lake that to me seemed another sky.
> As I bent down to look just opposite
> A shape within the watery gleam appeared
> Bending to look on me. I started back

Do Virgil and Homer compare, as regards beauty and sublimity? How, Cicero and Demosthenes? What modern writers possess those graces of composition which constitute the beautiful?

It started back but pleased I soon returned
Pleased it returned as soon with answering looks
Of sympathy and love. There I had fixed
Mine eyes till now and pined with vain desire
Had not a voice thus warned me What thou seest
What there thou seest fair creature is thyself
With thee it came and goes but follow me
And I will bring thee where no shadow stays
Thy coming and thy soft embraces he
Whose image thou art. *　　*
　*　　*　　* What could I do
But follow straight invisibly thus led ?
Till I espied thee fair indeed and tall
Under a platane yet methought less fair
Less winning soft less amiably mild
Than that smooth watery image. Back I turned
Thou following criedst aloud Return fair Eve
Whom fliest thou ? Whom thou fliest of him thou art
His flesh his bone to give thee being I lent
Out of my side to thee nearest my heart
Substantial life to have thee by my side
Henceforth an individual solace dear.
Part of my soul I seek thee and thee claim
My other half. With that thy gentle hand
Seized mine I yielded."

LESSON XLV.

WIT.

§ 301. SUBLIMITY and beauty are not the only sources of the pleasure derived from literary compositions. Wit, humor, and ridicule, when introduced judiciously, have an agreeable effect, and must next be considered.

§ 302. WIT is that quality of thoughts and expressions which excites in the mind an agreeable surprise, not by means of any thing marvellous in the subject, but merely by employ-

---

§ 301. What besides sublimity and beauty are sources of pleasure in literary compositions?
§ 302. What is wit?

ing a peculiar imagery, or presenting in a novel and singular relation ideas remotely connected.

§ 303. This agreeable surprise is excited in four ways :—

I. By degrading elevated things.

II. By aggrandizing insignificant things.

III. By representing objects in an unusual light by means of singular imagery.

IV. By paronomasia, or play upon words.

§ 304. Of wit consisting in the degrading of elevated subjects, Butler furnishes many specimens in Hudibras. From these we select the following lines, descriptive of early dawn; in which the low metaphorical style of the first couplet and the singular simile used in the second, constitute the witty points :—

> "And now had Phœbus in the lap
> Of Thetis taken out his nap:
> And, like a lobster boiled, the morn
> From black to red began to turn."

Another example follows, in which the comparison of the sublime blast and the angry thunder to trivial objects produces the effect in question.

> "I love to hear the shrieking wind,
> Magnificently wild!—
> Like the melodious music of
> A bastinadoed child.

> "I love to hear the thunder burst,
> O'er woodland, plain, and hill;—
> Like the loud note of angry swine,
> Petitioning for swill."

The object being to surprise the mind with an unexpected depreciation of what is by nature serious or grand, homely expressions, vulgar idioms, and cant phrases, are often the source of this species of wit.

To this division of the subject belong parodies and travesties, or writings in which serious productions by occasional alterations of words are made applicable to other subjects, particularly those of a ludicrous

---

§ 303. In what four ways is this agreeable surprise excited?

§ 304. Who furnishes many specimens of the first species of wit? Repeat the lines in which he describes the early dawn. What constitute the witty points? In the second example quoted, what produces the effect in question? What are often the source of this species of wit? What belong to this division of the subject? What is meant

character. Of a similar nature are compositions which maintain a serious tone throughout, until at the close some unexpected allusion, sentiment, or image, is introduced, which entirely changes the tenor of the piece. The following will serve as a specimen:—

> "'Old man! old man! for whom digg'st thou this grave?'
>   I asked, as I walked along;
> For I saw, in the heart of London streets,
>   A dark and busy throng.
>
> "'Twas a strange wild deed! but a wilder wish
>   Of the parted soul, to lie
> 'Midst the troubled numbers of living men,
>   Who would pass him idly by!
>
> "So I said, 'Old man, for whom digg'st thou this grave,
>   In the heart of London town?'
> And the deep-toned voice of the digger replied:—
>   'We're laying a gas-pipe down!'"

§ 305. The second species of wit is the converse of that just illustrated, and is often denominated *burlesque*. Its object being to give a mock importance to trivial things, it affects pompous and sonorous language, just as the first species admits of the lowest and most vulgar.

Pope's writings abound in this kind of pleasantry. In the following extract from the "Rape of the Lock," he represents a lady's toilet under the allegory of a solemn religious ceremony. The belle herself figures as priestess of the mysteries, assisted in her sacred office by the dressing-maid, while her mirrored image is the divinity whose rites are thus celebrated.

> "And now unveiled, the toilet stands displayed,
> Each silver vase in mystic order laid.
> First, robed in white, the nymph intent adores,
> With head uncovered, the cosmetic powers.
> A heavenly image in the glass appears,
> To that she bends, to that her eyes she rears.
> The inferior priestess at her altar's side,
> Trembling, begins the sacred rites of pride;
> Unnumbered treasures ope at once, and here
> The various offerings of the world appear;
> From each she nicely culls with curious toil,
> And decks the goddess with the glitter'ng spoil."

---

by *parodies?* What other compositions are of a similar nature? Give the substance of the piece quoted, and show wherein the wit consists.

§ 305. What is the second species of wit often denominated? What is its object, and what does it affect? Whose writings abound in this kind of pleasantry? What is the subject of the passage quoted? How does the author represent it? Wherein consists the wit?

Under this head fall the applications of grave reflections to frivolous subjects, as in the following lines from Phillips:—

> "My galligaskins, that have long withstood
> The winter's fury and encroaching frosts,
> By time subdued (what will not time subdue!),
> An horrid chasm disclose."

Analogous to this is the connection of small things with great, whereby they are represented as of equal importance. Pope furnishes many passages in point.

> "Then flashed the livid lightning from her eyes,
> And screams of horror rend the affrighted skies.
> Not louder shrieks to pitying heaven are cast,
> When husbands, or when lap-dogs, breathe their last!
> Or when rich china vessels, fallen from high,
> In glittering dust and painted fragments lie!"

> "Not youthful kings in battle seized alive,
> Not scornful virgins who their charms survive,
> Not ardent lovers robbed of all their bliss,
> Not ancient ladies when refused a kiss,
> Not tyrants fierce that unrepenting die,
> Not Cynthia when her manteau's pinned awry,—
> E'er felt such rage, resentment, and despair,
> As thou, sad virgin! for thy ravished hair."

§ 306. Of the third species of wit, which surprises the mind with the singularity of the images it employs, there are many varieties, of which a few specimens may be presented.

The first consists in connecting things between which there is an apparent contrariety. Thus, Roger de Coverley, in the Spectator, says that he would have given his widow 'a coal-pit to have kept her in clean linen; and that her fingers should have sparkled with one hundred of his richest acres.' So, Garth, in the following lines, compares the dropsy to a miser, and produces an agreeable surprise in the mind by representing it as poor in the midst of opulence, and thirsty though drenched with water:—

> "Then Hydrops next appears among the throng;
> Bloated and big, she slowly sails along:
> But like a miser in excess she's poor,
> And pines for thirst amid her watery store."

What else fall under this head? Give an example, and show where the wit lies. In what other way is a similar effect produced? In the passages quoted from Pope, show what constitutes the wit.

§ 306. With what does the third species of wit surprise the mind? In what does the first variety consist? How is this exemplified in the Spectator? To what does Garth compare the dropsy? How does he produce an agreeable surprise in the mind?

A second variety consists in artfully confounding the literal and figurative sense of an expression. In this way, what at first sight presents a specious appearance is presently seen to be absurd; as in the following lines from Hudibras:—

> "While thus they talked, the knight
> Turned the outside of his eyes to white,
> As men of inward light are wont
> To turn their optics in upon 't."

The eye is naturally turned to light, and hence the closing line at first seems reasonable; but when we reflect that it is the metaphorical light of knowledge to which reference is here made, the absurdity becomes manifest.

A third variety attributes corporeal or personal attributes to what is incapable, by its very nature, of possessing them. Thus, in the following passage, grace, or piety, and virtue, are represented as so nearly related to each other that a marriage between them (that is, their union in the same person) would be unlawful:—

> "What makes morality a crime
> The most notorious of the time;
> Morality, which both the saints
> And wicked too cry out against?
> 'Cause grace and virtue are within
> Prohibited degrees of kin:
> And therefore no true saint allows
> They shall be suffered to espouse."

A fourth variety consists in attributing to a person as a virtue what is merely a necessity; as in the following:—

"The advantage of the medical profession is that the dead are distinguished by wonderful charity and discretion; we never hear them complain of the physic that has killed them."

There are many other phases in which this species of wit is displayed. We shall content ourselves with mentioning but one more; that in which premises are introduced that promise much but perform nothing; as in the following:—

Beatrice. —— With a good leg and a good foot, uncle, and money enough in his purse, such a man would win any woman in the world, if he could get her good-will.
Much Ado about Nothing, Act II., Sc. I.

Beatrice. I have a good eye, uncle, I can see a church by day light.—*Ibid.*

In what does the second variety of this kind of wit consist? Illustrate it from Hudibras, and show the point. Describe the third variety. Give the substance of the quotation from Hudibras which illustrates it. In what does the fourth variety consist? Illustrate it. Describe the fifth variety. Illustrate it.

§ 307. The last species of wit is what the French call *jeu de mots*, and what we recognize in English as the pun, or a play upon words. Though regarded as the lowest kind of wit, yet there are few to whom it is not, at times, a source of amusement. In tracing its history, we find that it has been a favorite entertainment with all nations in a certain stage of their progress towards refinement of taste and manners, and has afterwards gradually, though invariably, fallen into disrepute. Thus, in England, during the reigns of Elizabeth and James I., it was regarded as one of the chief graces of writing, and as such entered, not only into the works of Shakspeare and other great dramatists, but also into the sermons and moral essays of grave divines.

As soon as a language is formed into a system, and the meaning of words is ascertained with tolerable accuracy, opportunity is afforded for expressions, which, by the double meaning of certain words, in reality have an entirely different meaning from what at first sight they seem to have; and the penetration of the reader or hearer is gratified by detecting the true sense in spite of its disguise. But, in process of time, the language becomes matured; the meaning of its words is more strictly defined; those capable of a double application, having been once used in this way, lose their effect for the future, inasmuch as without novelty they can excite no surprise or pleasure in the mind: and thus the pun falls in the estimation of the tasteful and judicious.

Novelty, as just remarked, is essential to the effect of a pun; as, indeed, it is to all kinds of wit. Nothing is more tasteless, we may almost say disgusting, than a joke that has become stale through frequent repetition. Any appearance of study or premeditation also detracts from the effect of a pun; and hence, what appears excellent when thrown out extemporaneously in conversation, may be intolerable when put in print.

Examples of paronomasia, or a play upon words, are so common that only a few specimens are here necessary for the illustration of the subject. The word in whose double meaning the point lies, is in italics.

---

§ 307. What is the last species of wit here presented, called by the French? What do we call it in English? How is it regarded? In tracing its history, what do we find? At what time was it much esteemed in England? Into whose writings did it largely enter? At what period of the history of a language is an opportunity afforded for effective puns? What takes place in process of time? What is essential to the effect of a pun? Explain how a pun may appear excellent when extemporaneously thrown

HUMOR AND RIDICULE. 231

We may add that conundrums, rebuses, and riddles in general are embraced in this class of witticisms.

"They say thine eyes, like sunny skies,
Thy chief attraction form;
I see no sunshine in those eyes,—
They take one all *by storm.*"

"Here thou, great Anna! Whom three realms obey,
Dost sometimes counsel *take*——and sometimes tea."

"Prince Eugene is a great *taker* of snuff as well as of towns"

EPITAPH ON A SCOLDING WIFE.

"Beneath this stone my wife doth lie;
She's now *at rest*, and so am I."

EPIGRAM ON A SHREW.

"They tell me that your brow is fair,
And is surpassed by none;
To me the cause is very clear—
You *brow-beat* every one."

Sometimes the wit of the pun consists, not in the double meaning of a word, but in its having the same sound as some other word, with which it is brought into juxta-position for the purpose of temporarily misleading the hearer. This is illustrated at the beginning and close of the following Baker's Advertisement:—"The subscriber, knowing that all men *need* bread, wishes the public to know that he also *kneads* it. He is desirous of feeding all who are hungry, and hopes his *good works* may be *in the mouth* of every one. He is well-disposed towards all men; and the *best bred* people among us will find him, he hopes, one of the *best bread*-men in the city."

LESSON XLVI.

HUMOR AND RIDICULE

§ 308. HUMOR consists, for the most part, in a representation of imaginary, short-lived, or over-strained emotions,

---

off, yet very poor when subsequently related. What is the technical name of the pun? What else are embraced in this class of witticisms?
In what does the wit of the pun sometimes consist? Give an example.
§ 308. In what does humor consist? Under what head do representations of rea

which display themselves preposterously, or so as to excite derision rather than sympathy.

Representations of real emotion, in the display of which there is no violation of taste or good sense, fall under the head of the pathetic, to which, consequently, the humorous is opposed. These two kinds of writing are much heightened in effect by being presented in contrast; a fact of which writers of fiction often avail themselves. This constitutes he chief charm of Dickens' novels,

§ 309. The subject of humor is character: not everything in character; not its graver faults or vices; but its peculiarities, its foibles, caprices, extravagances, anxieties, jealousies, childish fondnesses, and weaknesses generally,—its affectation, vanity, and self-conceit.

One who possesses a talent for the humorous finds the greatest scope for its display in telling familiar stories, or acting a whimsical part in an assumed character. Even the mimicking of minute peculiarities of pronunciation, or grammatical faults in discourse, is admissible in the humorous production. The object is to expose the weak points of the individual under description; and these are often best set forth by entering into the minutest details. Even over-acting, if not immoderate, contributes to the entertainment of the picture.

§ 310. Humor is not, like wit, sudden and short-lived; a brilliant scintillation, which flashes forth, and is then lost in obscurity. It often extends through entire productions; and, indeed, forms the staple of comic writing in general. Buckingham justly says of comedy,

"Humor is all. Wit should be only brought
To turn agreeably some proper thought."

Novelty, moreover, is not essential to humor. Its truthfulness to nature prevents it from being tiresome; and it endures readings and re-readings, which would make mere wit absolutely disgusting.

---

emotion fall? Of what fact do writers of fiction often avail themselves? Of whose works does this constitute the chief charm?

§ 309. What is the subject of humor? In what does a talent for the humorous find the best field for its display? How are the weak points of an individual often best exposed? What is the effect of over-acting?

§ 310. How does humor compare with wit in duration? Of what does it form the staple? What does Buckingham say of its use in comedy? What prevents humor from being tiresome?

§ 311. In every literature, humor has been employed, to a greater or less extent, in the lighter departments of composition, as a means of pleasing. Cervantes, perhaps, in his Don Quixote, has carried it to a greater degree of perfection than any other writer. Into English literature, particularly its dramatic compositions, it enters largely. Shakspeare, Gay, Farquhar, and others, have used it with great effect.

It is to be regretted that English comedy has not confined itself to pure and legitimate humor. To the discredit of our stage, obscenity and ribaldry are too often allowed to take its place. This can hardly be attributed to a lack of natural refinement. The cause seems rather to be that the first great master-pieces in this department of literature, written in a licentious age, were stained with gross indelicacy, which subsequent authors, with this precedent before them, deemed it necessary to imitate. With obscenity, humor has nothing in common.

§ 312. The aim of humor is simply to raise a laugh. When there is an ulterior object,—that is, when it is sought by means of this laugh to influence the opinions and purposes of the hearer or reader,—then humor becomes RIDICULE. In this case, a keener contempt of the weakness under review must be awakened than in the case of humor.

Ridicule is to argumentative composition what the *reductio ad absurdum* is to a mathematical demonstration,—a negative, yet satisfactory, way of arriving at the object proposed. It may be effectively applied to whatever is absurd, and, in a measure, also, to what is false. When sober argument would be too dignified and formidable a weapon to employ, ridicule may with propriety take its place. To a certain extent, the same foibles feel its lash as are open to the more genial attacks of humor. It goes, however, a step further; adding to the former category, ignorance, cowardice, profligacy, and dishonesty. Great crimes are beyond its sphere. To raise a laugh at cruelty, perfidy, or murder, would be intolerable.

---

§ 311. In what departments of literature is humor extensively employed? Who has carried it to the greatest perfection? What is said of English comedy? What seems to be the cause of this?

§ 312. What is the aim of humor? When does humor become ridicule? What feeling is in this case awakened? To what is the relation between ridicule and argumentative composition compared? To what may ridicule be applied? When may it with propriety take the place of argument? What are beyond its sphere, and why?

§ 313. The attack of ridicule is, from its very nature, a covert one. What we profess to contemn, we scorn to confute. Hence, the reasoning of which ridicule is the medium must be carried on under a species of disguise. Sometimes the contempt itself is dissembled, and the railer assumes an air of arguing gravely in defence of what he is exposing as ridiculous. He affects to be in earnest; but takes care to employ so thin a veil that one can easily see through it and discern his real intent. Such a course of reasoning is known as *irony*, and it often constitutes the most effective way of dealing with folly and falsity.

We have a brief specimen of ironical ridicule in Elijah's address to the priests of Baal, who were endeavoring by sacrifices and prayers to draw a manifestation of power from their false god:—"Cry aloud: for he is a god: either he is talking, or he is pursuing, or he is in a journey, or peradventure he sleepeth, and must be awakened."

EXERCISE.

The first extract given below illustrates humor; the second, ridicule. Let the student point out their distinguishing features; and, as an exercise in punctuation, let him supply such points as are omitted.

THE LANGUID LADY.

"The languid lady next appears in state
Who was not born to carry her own weight
She lolls reels staggers till some foreign aid
To her own stature lifts the feeble maid.
Then if ordained to so severe a doom
She by just stages journeys round the room
But knowing her own weakness she despairs
To scale the Alps that is ascend the stairs
My fan let others say who laugh at toil
Fan hood glove scarf is her laconic style
And that is spoke with such a dying fall
That Betty rather sees than hears the call
The motion of her lips and meaning eye
Piece out the idea her faint words deny.

---

§ 313. What is the character of the attack of ridicule? How must the reasoning of which it s the medium be carried on? Sometimes, what does the railer seem to be doing? What does he take care, however, that the hearer or reader shall discover? What name is given to this species of ridicule? What is said of its effect? Repeat the quoted specimen of ironical ridicule.

Oh listen with attention most profound
Her voice is but the shadow of a sound.
And help oh help her spirits are so dead
One hand scarce lifts the other to her head.
If there a stubborn pin it triumphs o'er
She pants she sinks away and is no more.
Let the robust and the gigantic carve
Life is not worth so much she'd rather starve
But chew she must herself ah cruel fate
That Rosalinda can't by proxy eat.—YOUNG.

THE PROFOUND WRITER.

"By these methods in a few weeks there starts up many a writer capable of managing the profoundest and most universal subjects For what though his head be empty provided his common-place book be full And if you will bate him but the circumstances of method and style and grammar and invention allow him but the common privileges of transcribing from others and digressing from himself as often as he shall see occasion he will desire no more ingredients towards fitting up a treatise that shall make a very comely figure on a bookseller's shelf there to be preserved neat and clean for a long eternity adorned with the heraldry of its title fairly inscribed on a label never to be thumbed or greased by students nor bound to everlasting chains of darkness in a library but when the fullness of time is come shall happily undergo the trial of purgatory in order to ascend the sky.—SWIFT.

LESSON XLVII.

FIGURES OF ORTHOGRAPHY, ETYMOLOGY, AND SYNTAX.

§ 314. FIGURES are intentional deviations from the ordinary spelling, form, construction, or application of words. They are arranged in four classes; figures of orthography, figures of etymology, figures of syntax, and figures of rhetoric. Though admissible in both prose and poetry, they occur more frequently in the latter.

§ 315. Figures of orthography are intentional deviations from the ordinary spelling of words. They are two in number; Mi-me'-sis and Ar'-cha-ism.

---

§ 314. What are figures? Into what classes are they divided? In what do they most frequently occur?

Mimesis consists in imitating the mispronunciation of a word, by means of false spelling; as, "Well, *zur*, I'll *argify* the topic."

Archaism consists in spelling a word according to ancient usage; as, "The *gret Kyng hathe*, every day, fifty fair *Damyseles, alle Maydenes*, that *serven* him *everemore* at his *Mete.*"

§ 316. Figures of etymology are intentional deviations from the ordinary forms of words. Those most used are eight in number; A-phær′-e-sis, Pros′-the-sis, Syn′-co-pe, A-poc′-o-pe, Par-a-go′-ge, Di-ær′-e-sis, Syn-ær′-e-sis, and Tme′-sis.

Aphæresis is the elision of a letter or letters from the beginning of a word: as, '*bove*, for *above;* '*neath*, for *beneath*.

Prosthesis is the prefixing of a letter or letters to a word: as, a*down*, for *down;* be*decked*, for *decked*.

Syncope is the elision of a letter or letters from the middle of a word: as, *e'en*, for *even;* *ha'penny*, for *halfpenny*.

Apocope is the elision of a letter or letters at the end of a word: as, *th'*, for *the;* *tho'*, for *though*.

Paragoge is the annexing of a letter or letters to a word; as, *vasty*, for *vast;* *withouten*, for *without*.

Diæresis is the separation into different syllables of two contiguous vowels that might unite in a diphthong. This figure is usually indicated by placing two dots over the last of the separated vowels. Thus, *aëronaut*, instead of *æronaut;* *coöperate*, for *cooperate*.

Synæresis is the condensing of two syllables into one: as, *walk'st*, for *walkest;* *hallowed*, for *hallow-ed*.

It was formerly customary to make the participial termination *ed* a separate syllable; as, *lov-ed, drown-ed*. This practice is still adhered to by some in solemn discourse; but, in common pronunciation, Synæresis

---

§ 315. What are figures of orthography? Name them. In what does Mimesis consist? In what, Archaism?

§ 316. What are figures of etymology? Mention the principal ones, observing that an acute accent in each case denotes the syllable that receives the stress of the voice. Define them in turn, and give examples of each. In the case of Aphæresis and other figures that consist in elisions, what mark must be employed? How is Diæresis indicated? What termination was formerly made a separate syllable? What is the practice at the present day?

incorporates the final *ed* with the preceding syllable, whenever this is not impossible by reason of the nature of the letters.

Tmesis is the separating of the parts of a compound, by introducing a word or words between them: as, what *way* soever *he turned;* to *us* ward.

§ 317. Figures of syntax are intentional deviations from the ordinary construction of words. Those most in use are five in number; El-lip'-sis, Ple'-o-nasm, Syl-lep'-sis, En-al'-la-ge, and Hy-per'-ba-ton.

Ellipsis is the omission of a word or words, necessary to the construction of a sentence, but not essential to its meaning; as, "[He] who steals my purse, steals trash."—"To whom thus Eve [spoke]."

Words thus omitted are said to be *understood.* They are used in the syntactical parsing of sentences, to explain the agreement or government of the words expressed.

Pleonasm is the use of superfluous words; as, "The boy, oh! where was *he?*"—"I know thee, *who thou art.*" This figure often imparts force to expressions, and is generally employed when the feelings are strongly excited.

Syllepsis is the construing of words according to the meaning they convey, and not by the strict requirements of grammatical rules; as, "Philip went down to the city of Samaria, and preached Christ unto *them.*"—"The moon *her* silver beams dispenses."

In the first example, *city* is 3d person, singular number; and, according to strict grammatical rules, *them* should be *it.* By *the city*, however, the writer means *the people in the city;* and he is, therefore, at liberty to use a pronoun in the plural. In the last example, it will be seen, there is a species of inferior personification, by which sex is attributed to the moon, an inanimate object; we may therefore substitute a feminine pronoun for *its*, which, strictly speaking, it would be necessary to use. As in this last case, the deviation which constitutes Syllepsis often arises from the introduction of a rhetorical figure, such as personification or metaphor.

---

§ 317. What are figures of syntax? Name those most in use. What is Ellipsis? What is said of words omitted according to this figure? In what are they used? What is Pleonasm? What does this figure impart to expressions, and when is it generally employed? What is Syllepsis? Point out how this figure operates in the two

Enallage is the use of one part of speech, or one modification of a word, for another; as, "They fall *successive* and *successive rise*."—"Sure some disaster has *befell*."

In the first example, we should have the adverb *successively* to modify the verbs *fall* and *rise*, instead of the adjective *successive;* and, in the last, the participle *befallen*, in place of the imperfect *befell*. The truth is, that this figure has been found necessary, to excuse the grammatical errors that occur in distinguished writers. The young composer is warned against supposing that Enallage can justify a violation of the rules of Syntax. Perhaps the only case in which it may with propriety be used, is the substitution of *you* for *thou* and *we* for *I*, when reference is made to a single person.

Hyperbaton is the transposition of words; as, "He wanders earth around,"—for, "He wanders around earth."

This figure constitutes one of the chief features that distinguish poetry from prose. Judiciously used in either, it imparts variety, strength, and vivacity, to composition. Care must be taken, however, not to carry it to such an extent as to occasion ambiguity or obscurity

EXERCISE.

Point out the figures that occur in the following passages, and show, if they were not employed, what changes would have to be made in the words:—

1. There's but one pang in death,—leaving the loved. 2. Thro' me shine the pearly pebbles. 3. Maister, have you any wery good weal in your vallet? 4. E'en 'neath the earth I'll him pursue. 5. At her feet he bowed, he fell, he lay down: at her feet he bowed, he fell; where he bowed, there he fell down dead. 6. It's never a trouble, so plase your honor, for an Irishman to do his duty. 7. He touchethe no thing, he handlethe nought, but holdethe everemore his Hondes before him, upon the Table. 8. Adown the steepy hill they toil. 9. Th' aërial pencil forms the scene anew. 10. So little mercy shows who needs so much. 11. Pr'ythee, peace. 12. There lament they the live day long. 13. I lay in Sion a stumbling-stone, and rock of offence; and whosoever believeth on him shall not be ashamed. 14. Turn thou me, and I shall be turned. 15. He that hath charity, for him the prayers of many ascend. 16. First Evening draws her crimson curtain, then Night

---

given examples. From what does Syllepsis often arise? What is Enallage? Show how it operates in the given examples. For what has this figure been found necessary? Against what is the composer warned? In what case may Enallage be properly employed? What is Hyperbaton? In what is this figure most used? What does it contribute to produce? What may result from its immoderate use?

throws down her pall. 17. Consider the lilies of the field, how they grow.

 18. Dan Chaucer, Well of English undefyled,
   On Fame's eternall beadroll worthie to be fyled

 19.   *   *   Let us instant go,
   O'erturn his bowers, and lay his castle low.

 20. 'Tis Fancy, in her fiery car,
   Transports me to the thickest war.

 21. Who never fasts, no banquet e'er enjoys.

 22. Bliss is the same in subject as in king,
   In who obtain defence, or who defend.

LESSON XLVIII.

FIGURATIVE LANGUAGE.

§ 318. THE figures defined in the last lesson, though it is important that the student should be able to recognize them, and, if need be, use them, have but little to do with style, compared with those which we shall next consider, and which are known as figures of rhetoric. Before proceeding to treat of these separately, we may with propriety consider figurative language in general, its origin, its peculiarities, and the advantages gained by its use.

§ 319. DEFINITION.—Figurative language implies a departure from the simple or ordinary mode of expression; a clothing of ideas in words which not only convey the meaning, but, through a comparison or some other means of exciting the imagination, convey it in such a way as to make a lively and forcible impression on the mind.

Thus, if we say, "Saladin was shrewd in the council, brave in the field," we express the thought in the simplest manner. But if we vary

---

§ 318. How do the figures just defined compare in importance with figures of rhetoric? Before proceeding to treat of the latter, what is it proposed to consider?

§ 319. What does figurative language imply? Illustrate its use with the two examples given.

the expression thus, " Saladin was a fox in the council, a lion in the field," we clothe the same sentiment in figurative language. Instead of cunning and courage, we introduce the animals that possess these qualities in the highest degree, and thus present livelier images to the mind. So, we have a plain and simple proposition in the sentence, "It is impossible, even by the most careful search, fully to ascertain the divine nature." " But when we say, " Canst thou, by searching, find out God? Canst thou find out the Almighty to perfection? It is high as heaven, what canst thou do? deeper than hell, what canst thou know?" we unite with the same proposition questions expressive of admiration, and thus render it more forcible.

§ 320. ORIGIN.—To account for the origin of figures, we must go back to that of language itself, for they are coeval. At this early period, men would naturally begin with giving names to the different objects with which they came in contact. Their nomenclature was at first, of course, limited and imperfect; but, as knowledge increased and ideas multiplied, the store of words would naturally increase also. Nevertheless, to the infinite variety of objects and ideas, language was inadequate; or rather, to extend it so as to have a separate word for each, would have involved a vocabulary too cumbrous for even the best memories. This difficulty was to be avoided; and a natural expedient was adopted,—that of making a word already applied to one idea or object stand for another, between which and the primary one they found or fancied some resemblance to exist. Thus, *compassion* in the human breast, as well as *mildness* of speech, seemed to be a kindred idea to *softness* in material bodies. The latter term was therefore extended to the two former ideas; we speak with equal propriety of *a soft bed, a soft heart* and *soft words*.

Figures of this kind abound in all languages. The operations of the mind and affections, in particular, are designated by words originally applied to sensible objects. These words, being earliest introduced,

---

§ 320. To account for the origin of figures, to what must we go back? With what would men naturally begin? What was the character of their nomenclature at first? When did it begin to be extended? What was the objection to inventing a separate word for each idea and object? What natural expedient was adopted? Give an illustration. To what objects were names first given? To what, in particular, were these names afterwards extended? Cite some expressions which arose in this way. What

were naturally extended, by degrees, to those mental peculiarities of which men had more obscure ideas and to which they found greater difficulty in assigning distinct names. Hence arose such expressions as a *piercing* judgment, a *warm* and a *cold* heart, a *rough* temper. In some cases, these figurative words are the only ones that can well be applied to such ideas; as the student will be convinced, on attempting to find a synonymous expression for " a *cold* or *freezing* reception".

With the origin of figures, moreover, imagination has had much to do. Every object that makes an impression on the mind is accompanied with certain cognate ideas. Nothing presents itself in an isolated manner. There are relations which inseparably connect every material object with other things which either precede or follow it, produce it or are produced by it, resemble it or are opposed to it. Thus every idea carries others in its train, which may be regarded as its accessories; and the latter often strike the mind more forcibly than the principal idea itself. They are pleasanter, perhaps, or more familiar; or they recall to remembrance a greater variety of important circumstances. The imagination, thus disposed to rest on the accessory rather than on the principal object, often applies to the latter the name or epithet originally appropriated to the former. Hence, choice, as well as the necessity alluded to above, has given currency to a great number of figurative expressions, and men of lively imaginations are adding to them every day. Thus, instead of saying, " Under Augustus, Rome enjoyed greater power and glory than at any other period," we take an analogous idea, suggested by imagination from the growth of a plant or tree, and say, " Rome *flourished* most under Augustus;" or, remembering that, when a heavenly body is directly overhead, and therefore apparently at the highest point of its orbit, astronomers say it is *at its zenith*, we substitute this accessory and say, " Under Augustus, Rome was *at the zenith* of her power and glory",—and thus express the thought more tersely and pointedly than by the literal language above cited.

§ 321. HISTORY.—Such was the origin of figurative language. First introduced by necessity, it was found to yield such pleasure to the imagination and communicate so much life to composition, that men used it in preference to plain

---

culty of the mind, also, had much to do with the origin of figures? Describe the way in which it operated to produce them. Express, in plain language, the fact that under Augustus, Rome attained her greatest power and glory. Express the same sentiment figuratively in two different ways. Show, in each case, whence the figure is derived.

§ 321. What two causes, then, led to the use of figurative language? When did

language, even when they could express their meaning equally well by means of the latter. Both these causes operated with special force in the early stages of society. The barrenness of language made it necessary to use words in a figurative sense; while imagination, then more vivid than in subsequent ages, gave a decided preference to terms so employed. As it was in the infancy of society, so we find it generally to be with savage tribes. New objects strongly impress their minds. They are governed by imagination and passion, rather than reason; and this is shown in their language. The North American Indian tongues afford striking illustrations of this fact. Bold, picturesque, and metaphorical, they abound in allusions to material objects, particularly such as are most striking in a wild and solitary life. An Indian chief, in an ordinary harangue to his tribe, uses more metaphors than a European would employ in an epic poem.

As a language progresses in refinement, precision is more regarded, and there is a tendency to give every object a distinct name of its own. Still, figurative words continue to occupy a considerable place. We find, on examination, that, while there are some which, by reason of frequent use, have come to be regarded as purely literal expressions, such as *a clear head, a hard heart*, and the like; there are many others which, in a greater or less degree, retain their figurative character and impart to style the peculiar effect described above. As examples, we may point to such phrases as the following: "*to enter upon* a subject," "*to follow out* an argument," "*to stir up* strife," "*to move* the feelings," &c. In the use of such expressions, the correct writer will always carry out the figure; that is, will regard the allusion on which it is based, and introduce in the same connection nothing inconsistent therewith. One may, for instance, "be sheltered under the patronage of a great man"; but it would be wrong to say, "sheltered under the mask of dissimulation,"—for a mask does not shelter, but conceals.

§ 322. ADVANTAGES.—The advantages which accrue from the use of figures are as follows:—

---

these causes operate with special force? Why? In what languages do they also operate strongly? What tongues afford striking illustrations of this fact? What is the character of these Indian tongues? As a language progresses in refinement, what tendency prevails? What follows, as regards figurative expressions? What do we find, in process of time, with respect to them? In the use of figurative expressions, what must the writer be careful to do? Illustrate this.

I. They enrich language by increasing its facilities of expression. By their means, words and phrases are multiplied, so that all kinds of ideas, the minutest differences, and the nicest shades of thought, can be distinctly and accurately expressed.

II. They dignify style. Words and phrases to which the ear is accustomed are often too colloquial and familiar to be employed in connection with elevated subjects. When treating of the latter, we should be greatly at a loss were it not for figures. Properly used, they have the same effect on language that is produced by the rich and splendid dress of a person of rank; that is, by imparting a general air of magnificence, they exact admiration and respect. Assistance of this kind is often necessary in prose; in poetry, it is indispensable.

To say *the sun rises,* for instance, is trite, and fails to awaken any pleasure in the mind; but the same thought is pleasing in the highest degree as figuratively expressed by Thomson:

> "But yonder comes the powerful king of day,
> Rejoicing in the East."

So, what a contrast is presented by the plain proposition, "all men are subject alike to death," and the same sentiment as expressed by Horace:

> "With equal pace, impartial Fate
> Knocks at the palace and the cottage gate."

III. They bring before the mind two objects simultaneously yet without confusion. We see one thing in another, and this is always a source of pleasure. In nothing does the mind more gladly employ itself than in detecting and tracing resemblances.

When, for example, for *youth* we substitute *the morning of life,* the fancy is entertained with two ideas at once,—the early period of existence, and the opening of the day; each of which has its own associations, and awakens its peculiar train of images. The fancy is thus ex

---

§ 822. What is the first advantage resulting from the use of figures? What, the second? When we are treating of elevated subjects, what words must not be used? In such cases, to what must we have recourse? To what is the effect of figurative language compared? In what department of composition is assistance of this kind indispensable? Show, by means of two examples, the difference in effect between trite and figurative language? What is the third advantage gained by the use of figures? Ex-

cited in a two-fold degree; and this double pleasure is enhanced not a little by the evident resemblance between the objects compared.

IV. Again, as already seen, figures frequently convey the meaning more clearly and forcibly than plain language. This is particularly true in the case of abstract conceptions, which, in a greater or less degree, they represent as sensible objects, surrounding them with such circumstances as enable the mind fully to comprehend them. A well-chosen figure, indeed, not unfrequently, with the force of an argument, carries conviction to the mind of the hearer; as in the following illustration from Young: "When we dip too deep in pleasure, we always stir a sediment that renders it impure and noxious."

§ 323. RULES.—In the use of figures, rules are of service, as they are in every other department of composition. There is no force in the argument that they are unnecessary, because people who have never heard of a rule use figures properly every day.

We constantly meet with persons who sing agreeably and correctly without knowing a note of the gamut; is it, therefore, improper to reduce the notes to a scale, or unnecessary for a musician to study the principles of his art? The ornaments of composition are certainly as capable of improvement as the ear or the voice; and the only means of ensuring this improvement are careful study of the various rules founded on nature and experience, and constant practice with reference to the principles they establish.

§ 324. USE.—Though the advantages arising from the use of figurative language have been dwelt on at some length, it must not be supposed, either that its frequent use is absolutely essential to beauty of composition, or that figures alone, without other merits, can constitute such beauty. As the body is more important than the dress, so the thought is

---

plain and illustrate this point. Fourthly, how do figures frequently convey a writer's meaning? In the case of what is this particularly true? To what is a well-chosen figure often equivalent in force? Give an illustration from Young.

§ 323. What is said of rules for the use of figures? What argument is urged against them? Expose the fallacy of this argument.

§ 324. What must not be supposed with respect to figurative language? Which is more important,—the thought, or its dress?

of more moment than the mode of expressing it. No figure can render a cold or empty composition interesting; while, on the other hand, if a sentence is sublime or pathetic, it can support itself without borrowed assistance.

LESSON XLIX.

EXERCISES ON FIGURATIVE LANGUAGE.

EXERCISE I.

In the following passages, change the figurative to plain language:—

EXAMPLE. *Figurative.*—The king of terrors.
The waves are asleep on the bosom of ocean.
Plain.—Death.
The ocean is calm.

1. The *morning of life;*—the *veil* of night;—a *fiery* temper;—a *deep* thinker;—a *light* disposition;—a *cold* heart;—a *warm* friend:—an *attack* of sickness;—a *thin* audience;—*high* hopes;—a *hard* lot. 2. Athens was now at the *pinnacle* of glory. 3. The sea *swallows* many a vessel. 4. Beside the warrior *slept* his bow. 5. Guilt *is wedded* to misery. 6. Homer's genius *soars higher* than Virgil's. 7. Some great men are noted for the *roughness* of their behavior. 8. Time had left *his footprints* on her brow. 9. The *breath* of spring infuses new life into the vegetable world. 10. The sanguine man is sometimes rudely *wakened* from his *dreams.* 11. Even at imaginary woes the heart will sometimes *ache.* 12. Abstinence is the only *talisman* against disease. 13. This lamentation *touched* his heart. 14. We should not be *cast down* by *light* afflictions.

15. "Adversity's *cold frosts* will soon be o'er:
It *heralds brighter days:*—the *joyous* Spring
Is cradled on the Winter's *icy breast,*
And yet comes *flushed* in beauty."

16. "Vice is a *monster* of so *frightful mien,*
As to be hated needs but to be *seen;*
Yet *seen* too oft, familiar with *her face,*
We first endure, then *pity,* then *embrace.*"

EXERCISE II.

In each of the following passages, introduce figurative language without altering the sense. Punctuate the sentences so formed, and be careful to carry out the figure properly.

The student may form figures of his own, or may employ those suggested by the words in parentheses.

EXAMPLE. *Plain.*—The uncompassionate man has no sympathy for the unfortunate.

Figurative.—The *hard-hearted* man *turns a deaf ear to* the unfortunate.

1. The mind should be kept uncontaminated (*weeds, garden*). 2. Let us be virtuous, and not yield to the temptations of pleasure (*path, listen, voice*). 3. With the ancient Stoics it was a principle never to indulge their appetites unduly (*overstep*). 4. Suspicion is a source of great unhappiness (*poison*). 5. Providence has wisely ordained that we shall not know the future (*sealed*). 6. Calumnious reports are often circulated about those whose lives afford the least reason for them (*aim, arrows*). 7. He is dying (*tide*). 8. Fortune, though it may involve us in temporal difficulties, can not make us permanently unhappy, if we do no evil. 9. Time makes many changes. 10. The young man, on leaving college, should pause a moment for serious thought before engaging in active life (*launching*). 11. We should constantly have regard to the requirements of truth and justice. 12. We meet with few utterly stupid persons; with still fewer noble geniuses: the generality of mankind are between the two extremes. 13. Often, when apparently gay, the heart is sad. 14. Seldom do the old form very ardent friendships. 15. Our worst enemies are our own evil passions. 16 The rising sun shines on the tops of the mountains (*gilds*). 17. The lightning is seen first on one peak and then on another (*leaps*). 18. He is in love.

LESSON L.

FIGURES OF RHETORIC.

§ 325. FIGURES of rhetoric are intentional deviations from the ordinary application of words. They are constantly occurring in every department of composition, and are a source of life and beauty to style. Rhetoricians have devoted much attention to defining, analyzing, and classifying them; and, by making slight shades of difference sufficient ground for the formation of new classes, have succeeded in enumerating more than two hundred and fifty. Such minuteness is of no practical use; and we shall limit our consideration to

---

§ 825. What are figures of rhetoric? How many have been enumerated by rhetoricians? How have they succeeded in making so many? How many are here con-

the sixteen leading figures, which embrace many of the subdivisions above alluded to, are all that it is necessary to understand or of advantage to employ.

The sixteen principal figures are Sim′-i-le, Met′-a-phor, Al′-le-go-ry, Me-ton′-y-my, Sy-nec′-do-che, Hy-per′-bo-le, Vis′ion, A-pos′-tro-phe, Per-son-i-fi-ca′-tion, In-ter-ro-ga′-tion, Ex cla-ma′-tion, An-tith′-e-sis, Cli′-max, I′-ro-ny, A-poph′-a-sis and On-o-mat-o-pœ′-ia.

Several of these figures are called *tropes* (a term derived from the Greek, meaning *turns*), because the word is *turned*, as it were, from its ordinary application.

§ 326. *Simile* is the comparison of one object to another, and is generally denoted by *like*, *as*, or *so* ; as, " He shall be *like* a tree planted by the rivers of water."—" Thy smile is *as* the dawn of the vernal day."

Comparisons are sometimes made without any formal term to denote them; as, " Too much indulgence does not strengthen the mind of the young; plants raised with tenderness are seldom strong." Here a comparison is made just as much as if the word *as* were introduced before *plants*. So, Chaucer employs a simile in the following beautiful line without directly indicating it:—

"Up rose the sun, and up rose Emilie."

All comparisons may be divided, according to the purpose for which they are employed, into two classes, known as Explanatory Similes and Embellishing Similes. The former may be used without impropriety even in abstruse philosophical compositions, which, indeed, they often illustrate in the happiest manner. One of this class is successfully employed by Harris, to explain the distinction between the powers of sense and those of imagination. " As wax would not be adequate to the purpose of signature, if it had not the power to retain as well as to receive the impression; the same holds of the soul, with respect to sense and imagination. Sense is its receptive power; imagination its retentive. Had it sense without imagination, it would not be as wax, but as water, where, though all impressions be instantly made, yet as soon as

---

sidered? Name them. What are several of these figures called? What does the word *tropes* mean?

§ 326. What is Simile? By what words is it indicated? How are comparisons sometimes made? Give an example. Into what two classes are Similes divided? Define each, and give examples.

they are made, they are instantly lost." The Embellishing Simile, on the other hand, is introduced, not for the sake of explanation or instruction, but simply to beautify the style. Such, for instance, is the effect of the following from Ossian:—" Pleasant are the words of the song, said Cuchullin, and lovely are the tales of other times. They are like the calm dew of the morning on the hill of roes, when the sun is faint on its side, and the lake is settled and blue in the vale.

§ 327. *Metaphor* indicates the resemblance of two objects by applying the name, attribute, or act of one directly to the other; as, "He shall be a tree planted by the rivers of water."

Metaphor is the commonest of all the figures. It assumes a variety of forms, under some of which it is constantly appearing in composition. Sometimes there is no formal comparison; but, as was instanced in the last lesson, an act is assigned to an object, which, literally, it is incapable of performing, to represent in a lively manner some act which it can perform; as, "Wild fancies *gambolled unbridled* through his brain." We may properly apply the term *metaphorical* to words used in this figurative sense, like many of those in the last Exercise.

§ 328. *Allegory* is the narration of fictitious events, whereby it is sought to convey or illustrate important truths. Thus, in Psalm lxxx., the Jewish nation is represented under the symbol of a vine:—" Thou hast brought a vine out of Egypt. thou hast cast out the heathen, and planted it. Thou preparedst room before it, and didst cause it to take deep root, and it filled the land. The hills were covered with the shadow of it, and the boughs thereof were like the goodly cedars."

It will be seen that an Allegory is a combination of kindred metaphors so connected in sense as to form a kind of story. The parables of Scripture, as well as fables that point a moral, are varieties of this figure. Sometimes an Allegory is so extended as to fill a volume; as in the case of Bunyan's "Pilgrim's Progress".

§ 329. *Metonymy* is the exchange of names between things

---

§ 327. What does Metaphor indicate? What is said of the forms under which it appears? How is it sometimes used in connection with a single object? What term may be properly applied to words used figuratively?

§ 328. What is Allegory? Of what is it a combination? What are mentioned as varieties of this figure? How far is an Allegory sometimes extended?

§ 329. What is Metonymy? On what is this figure not founded? Mention the va-

related. It is founded, not on resemblance, but on the relation of, 1. Cause and effect: as, "They have *Moses* and *the prophets*", i. e., *their writings;* "*Gray hairs* should be respected", i. e., *old age*. 2. Progenitor and posterity; as, "Hear, O *Israel*", i. e., *descendants of Israel*. 3. Subject and attribute; as, "*Youth* and *beauty* shall be laid in dust", i. e., *the young* and *beautiful*. 4. Place and inhabitant; as, "What *land* is so barbarous as to allow this injustice?" i. e., *what people*. 5. Container and thing contained; as, "Our *ships* next opened a fire", i. e., our *sailors*. 6. Sign and thing signified; as, "The *sceptre* shall not depart from Judah", i. e., *kingly power*. 7. Material and thing made from it; as, "His *steel* gleamed on high", i. e., his *sword*.

§ 330. *Synecdoche* is using the name of a part for that of the whole, the name of the whole for that of a part, or a definite number for an indefinite: as, "The sea is covered with *sails*", i. e., *ships;* "Our *hero* was gray, but not from age", i. e., his *hair* was gray; "*Ten thousand* were on his right hand", i. e., *a great number*.

§ 331. *Hyperbole* is the exaggeration of attributes, or the assigning to a subject of a wonderful and impossible act as the result of ardent emotion; as, "They [Saul and Jonathan] were *swifter than eagles*, they were *stronger than lions*."— "And trembling Tiber *dived beneath his bed*."

Hyperbolical expressions are of frequent occurrence in common conversation; we often say, *as cold as ice, as hot as fire, as white as snow,* &c., in all which phrases the quality is exaggerated beyond the bounds of truth. Their frequency is to be attributed to the imagination, which always takes pleasure in magnifying the objects before it. Languages are, therefore, more or less hyperbolical, according to the liveliness of this faculty in those who speak them. Hence the Orientals indulge in

---

rious relations subsisting between objects whose names are exchanged, and illustrate each.

§ 330. What is Synecdoche?

§ 331. What is Hyperbole? Where does this figure frequently occur? Give some common colloquial hyperbolical expressions. To what is their frequency attributable? According to what is a language found to be more or less hyperbolical? By whom is Hyperbole most frequently used?

11*

Hyperbole more freely than Europeans, and the young use it to a much greater extent than those of maturer years.

§ 332. *Vision,* also called *Imagery,* is the representation of past events, or imaginary objects and scenes, as actually present to the senses; as, " Cæsar *leaves* Gaul, *crosses* the Rubicon, and *enters* Italy", i. e., *left* Gaul, *crossed* the Rubicon, &c. ; " They *rally,* they *bleed,* for their kingdom and crown." It will be seen from the examples that this figure often consists in substituting the present tense for the past.

§ 333. *Apostrophe* is a turning from the regular course of the subject, into an invocation or address; as, " Death is swallowed up in victory. O death, where is thy sting? O grave, where is thy victory?"

§ 334. *Personification,* or *Pros-o-po-pœ′-ia,* is the attributing of sex, life, or action to an inanimate object; or the ascribing of intelligence and personality to an inferior creature; as, " The sea *saw it* and *fled*."—" The Worm, *aware* of his intent, *harangued* him thus."

§ 335. *Interrogation* is the asking of questions, not for the purpose of expressing doubt or obtaining information, but in order to assert strongly the reverse of what is asked; as, " Doth God pervert judgment? or doth the Almighty pervert justice?" This figure imparts animation to style. It is constantly employed in the Book of Job.

§ 336. *Exclamation* is the expression of some strong emotion of the mind; as, "Oh! the depth of the riches both of the wisdom and the knowledge of God!" This figure employs exclamatory sentences and vocative clauses.

§ 337. *Antithesis* is the placing of opposites in juxta-position, for the purpose of heightening their effect by contrast;

---

§ 332. What is Vision sometimes called? Define this figure. What tense does it often require?
§ 333. What is Apostrophe?
§ 334. What is Personification?
§ 335. What is Interrogation? Where does it constantly occur?
§ 336. What is Exclamation? What does this figure employ?
§ 337. What is Antithesis? Where is it used with great effect?

as, "*A good man* obtaineth favor of the Lord; but *a man of wicked devices* will He condemn."—" Though *grave*, yet *trifling;* *zealous*, yet *untrue*." This figure is used with great effect in the Book of Proverbs, x.-xv. It is one of the most effective ornaments that can be employed in composition. "To extirpate antithesis from literature altogether," says the author of Lacon, "would be to destroy at one stroke about eight-tenths of all the wit, ancient and modern, now existing in the world."

§ 338. *Climax* is the arrangement of a succession of words, clauses, members, or sentences, in such a way that the weakest may stand first, and that each in turn, to the end of the sentence, may rise in importance, and make a deeper impression on the mind than that which preceded it; as, "Who shall separate us from the love of Christ? Shall *tribulation*, or *distress*, or *persecution*, or *famine*, or *nakedness*, or *peril*, or *sword?*"

This term is derived from the Greek word, *klimax*, "a ladder." The definition given above has reference to the Climax of sense. We have also a Climax of sound, which consists in arranging a series of words or clauses according to their length, that is, so that the shortest may come first: as, "He was a great, noble, disinterested man;" not, "He was a disinterested, noble, great man." A fine effect is produced by combining the Climax of sense with that of sound. Cicero understood this fact, and, in his orations, constantly availed himself of it, with the greatest success.

The faulty arrangement of words and clauses in the opposite order to that prescribed by this figure, that is, so that they successively decrease in importance, is known as Anti-climax. It is well illustrated in the following couplet:—

"And thou, Dalhousie, thou great god of war,
Lieutenant-colonel to the earl of Mar!"

The term *Climax* is also applied by some to sentences in which, for the sake of emphasis, an expression occurring in one member is re-

---

§ 388. What is Climax? From what is this term derived? What is meant by a Climax of sound? How is a fine effect produced? Who has availed himself of this fact? What is Anti-climax? Cite a couplet in point. To what sentences is the term Climax also applied? Repeat the illustration quoted from Pope. What other name is given to this variety of Climax?

peated in another; as, "When we have practised good actions a while they become easy; and, when they are easy, we begin to take pleasure in them; and, when they please us, we do them frequently; and, by frequency of acts, they grow into a habit." So, Pope, to heighten compassion for the fate of an unfortunate lady, repeats the idea that she lacked friendly sympathy in her distress:—

> "By foreign hands thy dying eyes were closed,
> By foreign hands thy decent limbs composed;
> By foreign hands thy humble grave adorned,
> By strangers honored and by strangers mourned."

Some make this an independent figure, and style it *Repetition*.

§ 339. *Irony* is a figure by which is expressed directly the opposite of what it is intended shall be understood; as when Elijah said to the priests of Baal, who were trying to induce their false god to manifest himself miraculously, "Cry aloud, for he is a god," &c. This figure has been already considered under the head of Ridicule.

§ 340. *Apophasis*, *Paralipsis*, or *Omission*, is the pretended suppression of what one is all the time actually mentioning; as, "I *say nothing* of the notorious profligacy of his character; *nothing* of the reckless extravagance with which he has wasted an ample fortune; *nothing* of the disgusting intemperance which has sometimes caused him to reel in our streets; —but I aver that he has exhibited neither probity nor ability in the important office which he holds."

§ 341. *Onomatopœia* is the use of a word or phrase formed to imitate the sound of the thing signified; as when we say, *rat tat tat*, to denote a knocking at the door; *bow wow*, to express the barking of a dog; or, *buzz, buzz*, to indicate the noise made by bees.

---

§ 339. What is Irony?
§ 340. What other names has Apophasis? Define this figure.
§ 341. What is Onomatopœia? Exemplify it.

LESSON LI.

EXERCISE ON FIGURES.

POINT out the figures that occur in the following passages, and state to which of the four classes they belong. There may be more than one in the same sentence.

1. They that are of a froward heart are abomination to the Lord: but such as are upright in their way are His delight. 2. As a jewel of gold in a swine's snout, so is a fair woman which is without discretion. 3. For I am persuaded, that neither death, nor life, nor angels, nor principalities, nor powers, nor things present, nor things to come, nor height, nor depth, nor any other creature, shall be able to separate us from the love of God, which is in Christ Jesus our Lord. 4. The depth saith, It is not in me: and the sea saith, It is not with me. 5. Weep on the rocks of roaring winds, O maid of Inistore! Bend thy fair head over the waves, thou lovelier than the ghost of the hills, when it moves on the sunbeam, at noon, over the silence of Morven. He is fallen: thy youth is low! 6. He smote the city. 7. There are a million truths that men are not concerned to know. 8. On this side, modesty is engaged; on that, impudence: on this, chastity; on that, lewdness: on this, integrity; on that, fraud: on this, piety; on that profaneness: on this, constancy; on that, fickleness: on this, honor; on that, baseness: on this, moderation; on that, unbridled passion. 9. For all the land which thou seest, to thee will I give it, and to thy seed forever. And I will make thy seed as the dust of the earth; so that, if a man can number the dust of the earth, then shall thy seed also be numbered. 10. Ignorance is a blank sheet, on which we may write; but error is a scribbled one, from which we must first erase. 11. Horatius was once a very promising young gentleman; but in process of time he became so addicted to gaming, not to mention his drunkenness and debauchery, that he soon exhausted his estate, and ruined his constitution. 12. Hast thou eyes of flesh? or seest thou as man seeth? Are thy days as the days of man? Are thy years as man's days? 13. Streaming grief his faded cheek bedewed. 14. My heart is turned to stone: I strike it, and it hurts my hand. 15. Friendship is no plant of hasty growth. 16. Cool age advances, venerably wise. 17. Oh! that ye would altogether hold your peace and it should be your wisdom. 18. Whoso loveth instruction loveth knowledge; but he that hateth reproof is brutish. 19. His arm soon cleared the field.

20. Some lead a life unblamable and just,
Their own dear virtue their unshaken trust.

21. The combat thickens. On, ye brave,
Who rush to glory or the grave!

22. Oh! unexpected stroke, worse than of death!
Must I thus leave thee, Paradise! thus leave
Thee, native soil, these happy walks, and shades,
Fit haunt of gods!

23. O books, ye monuments of mind, concrete wisdom of the wisest;
Sweet solaces of daily life; proofs and results of immortality;
Trees yielding all fruits, whose leaves are for the healing of the nations,
Groves of knowledge, where all may eat, nor fear a flaming sword.

24. Earth felt the wound; and Nature from her seat
Sighing, through all her works, gave signs of woe
That all was lost.

25. How slow yon tiny vessel ploughs the main!
Amid the heavy billows now she seems
A toiling atom; then from wave to wave
Leaps madly, by the tempest lashed; or reels,
Half wrecked, through gulfs profound.

26. Me miserable! which way shall I fly
Infinite wrath, and infinite despair?
Which way I fly is hell, myself am hell,—
And in the lowest depth, a lower deep,
Still threatening to devour me, opens wide,
To which the hell I suffer seems a heaven.

27.   The earth
Gave signs of gratulations, and each hill.
Joyous the birds; fresh gales and gentle airs .
Whispered it to the woods, and from their wings
Flung rose, flung odor from the spicy shrub,
Disporting.

28. Dash along! | On! on! with a jump,
    Slash along! | And a bump,
    Crash along! | And a roll,
    Flash along! | Hies the fire-fiend to his destined goal!

LESSON LII.

RULES FOR THE USE OF RHETORICAL FIGURES.

§ 342. For a practical view of the figures defined in Lesson L., and to learn under what circumstances they are most effectively introduced, the young writer is recommended to a careful and critical perusal of standard authors. A few remarks, however, on figures in general, and some brief rules respecting the use of the most important ones, will be found of service.

§ 343. In the first place, an observation already made must be remembered, that composition is by no means dependent on figures for all, or even the greater part, of its beauties and

---

§ 342. Where is the student referred for a practical view of figures?
§ 343. What observation is first made respecting the effect of figures on compo-

merits. Examples of the most sublime and pathetic writing abound, and many have been cited above, in which, powerful as is their effect, no assistance is derived from this source Figures, therefore, though valuable as auxiliaries, should not be the chief object had in view. If a composition is destitute of striking thoughts, or even if the style is objectionable, all the figures that can be employed will fail to render it agreeable. They may dazzle a vulgar eye, but can never please a judicious one.

In the second place, to be beautiful, figures must rise naturally from the subject. Dictated by imagination or passion, they must come from a mind warmed by the object it would describe. They must flow in the same train as the current of thought. If deliberately sought out, and fastened on where they seem to fit, with the express design of embellishing, their effect will be directly the opposite of what is intended.

Again, even when imagination prompts and the subject naturally gives rise to figures, they should not be used to excess. The reader may be surfeited with them; and, when they recur too often, they are apt to be regarded as evidence of a superficial mind that delights in show rather than in solid merit.

Lastly, without a genius for figurative language, no one should attempt it. Imagination is derived from nature; we may cultivate it, but must not force it. We may prune its redundancies, correct its errors, and enlarge its sphere; but the faculty itself we can not create. We should therefore avoid attempts which can result only in making our weakness apparent.

With these general principles in view, we proceed to certain rules and cautions relating to simile, metaphor, and hyperbole, the commonest ornaments of style.

§ 344. SIMILE.

---

ation? What is essential to the beauty of figures? When they are deliberately sought for, what is their effect? What is said of using them to excess, even when they arise naturally from the subject? What writers should avoid attempts at figurative language?

I. Objects must not be compared to things of the same kind, that closely resemble them. Much of the pleasure we receive from this figure arises from its discovering to us similitudes where at first glance we would not expect them. When Milton compares Satan's appearance, after his fall, to that of the sun suffering an eclipse and terrifying the nations with portentous darkness, we are struck with the point and dignity of the simile. But when he likens Eve's bower in Paradise to the arbor of Pomona, or Eve herself to a wood-nymph, we receive but little entertainment, as one bower and one beautiful woman must obviously, in many respects, resemble another.

II. Still less should similes be founded on faint resemblances. In this case they neither explain nor embellish, and instead of entertaining the mind distract and perplex it. Shakspeare, bold in his use of figures, rather than delicate or correct, frequently violates this rule. The following is a case in point:—

> "Give me the crown.—Here, Cousin, seize the crown:
> Here on this side, my hand; on that side, thine.
> Now is this golden crown like a deep well,
> That owes two buckets, filling one another;
> The emptier ever dancing in the air,
> The other down, unseen and full of water:
> That bucket down, and full of tears, am I,
> Drinking my griefs, whilst you mount up on high."

III. Trite similes are by all means to be avoided. Among these may be classed the comparison of a hero to a lion, that of a person in sorrow to a flower drooping its head, of a violent passion to a tempest, of a ruddy cheek to a rose, of a fair brow to alabaster,—which have been handed down from one generation to another, and are still in great favor with second-rate writers. As originally used by those who took them direct from nature, they were beautiful; but frequent use has divested them of all their charm. Indeed this is one criterion by which the true genius may be distinguished from the empty imitator. To the former, the treasures of nature are open; he discerns new shapes and forms, and points of resemblance before unobserved: the latter must humbly follow in the train of those more gifted than himself. Unable to originate any new comparison, he can only re-express the inventions of others.

---

§ 344. To what must objects not be compared? From what does much of the pleasure we receive from the use of simile arise? Illustrate this by a reference to two of Milton's similes. What is said of similes founded on faint resemblances? Who frequently violates this rule? To what does he make one of his characters compare a crown? What is the effect of this figure? What is the third class of similes that must be avoided? Instance some of these. Show the difference in this respect between the true genius and the imitator. In the fourth place, to what must objects not be com-

IV. Nothing is gained by comparing objects to things respecting which little is known, as in the following from Cowley:—

> "It gives a piteous groan, and so it broke;
> In vain it something would have spoke;
> The love within too strong for 'twas,
> Like *poison put into a Venice-glass.*"

Comparisons, therefore, founded on local allusions or traditions, on the career of obscure mythological personages, on matters strictly belonging to science or philosophy, or on any thing with which persons of a certain trade or profession only are conversant, must be avoided. To be effective, the object to which comparison is made must be familiar to the reader,—one of which, if not personally known to him, he has at least a well-defined conception.

V. Similes must not be drawn from resemblances to low or trivial objects. Figures so derived degrade style, instead of adorning it. Bear witness the following:—

> "As wasps, provoked by children in their play,
> Pour from their mansions by the broad highway,
> In swarms the guiltless traveller engage,
> Whet all their stings, and call forth all their rage;
> All rise in arms, and, with a general cry,
> Assert their waxen domes, and buzzing progeny:
> Thus from the tents the fervent legion swarms,
> So loud their clamors, and so keen their arms."—POPE's HOMER.

We certainly have no higher idea of the prowess of an army from its being said to resemble a swarm of wasps. In like manner, objects should be compared to things that possess the quality in which the resemblance lies in a greater degree than themselves. Thus, in the sentence, "The moon is like a jewel in the sky," the simile is bad, because the moon sheds more light than a jewel, and should not therefore be compared to the latter.

VI. So, to compare low or trivial objects to things far exceeding them in greatness is no beauty, but constitutes one of the varieties of burlesque. This is exemplified in a passage from the Odyssey, in which the click of a lock is compared to the roaring of a bull.

> "Loud as a bull makes hill and valley ring,
> So roared the lock when it released the spring."

---

pared? How does Cowley violate this rule? What comparisons are thus excluded? Fifthly, from what resemblances must similes not be drawn? What is the effect of figures thus derived? In the illustration cited from Homer, to what is the Grecian host likened? What is the fault in comparing the moon to a jewel? Describe and illustrate the sixth class of faulty similes. What emotions do not admit of comparisons Show how Shakspeare violates this principle.

VII. Similes are out of place, when anger, terror, remorse, or despair is the prevalent passion. Men under the influence of such emotions are not likely to indulge in comparisons. Shakspeare, in Henry VI., grossly violates this principle, when he makes the dying Warwick say:—

> "My mangled body shows,
> My blood, my want of strength, my sick heart shows,
> That I must yield my body to the earth,
> And, by my fall, the conquest to my foe.
> Thus yields the cedar to the axe's edge,
> Whose arms gave shelter to the princely eagle;
> Under whose shade the ramping lion slept;
> Whose top-branch overpeered Jove's spreading tree,
> And kept low shrubs from winter's powerful wind."

§ 345. METAPHOR.

I. Metaphors being in most cases similes with the term denoting the comparison omitted, the rules laid down in the last section for the latter figure are equally applicable to the former. In other words, we must avoid unmeaning, far-fetched, trite, obscure, degrading, bombastic, and unreasonable metaphors. These different faults having been illustrated under the simile, it is not thought necessary to give further examples.

II. Care must be taken that the metaphor be appropriate. Thus, the clergyman who prayed that God would be "*a rock* to them that are afar off upon the sea," used a very inappropriate figure; because, as *rocks* in the sea are a source of great danger to mariners, he was in reality asking for the destruction of those for whose safety he intended to pray.

III. The commonest error in the use of metaphors is the blending of figurative with plain language in the same sentence; that is, the construction of a period in such a way that a part must be interpreted metaphorically and the remainder literally. Thus Pope, in his translation of Homer's Odyssey (the error is not found in the original), makes Penelope say with reference to her son,

> "Now from my fond embrace by tempests torn,
> Our other column of the state is borne,
> Nor took a kind adieu, nor sought consent."

In the second line she calls her son a "*column* of the state," and in the third speaks of his *taking a kind adieu* and *seeking consent*. Now, as

---

§ 345. What is the difference between similes and metaphors? What is said of the rules relating to the former? Accordingly, what kind of metaphors must be avoided? In the second place, what quality is essential to the correct metaphor? Give an example of the inappropriate use of this figure. What is the commonest error in the use metaphors? Illustrate this from Pope's translation of the Odyssey, and show the

columns can not very well *take kind adieus* or *seek consent*, there is an inconsistency, and the metaphor is faulty. The poet should either have avoided likening Telemachus to a column, or else should not have attributed to him an act which it is impossible for a column to perform.

So Pope elsewhere says, addressing the king,

"To thee the world its present homage pays,
The harvest early, but mature the praise."

Here, had it not been for the rhyme, he would evidently have said, "The harvest early, but mature the *crop*." He would thus have carried out the figure.

IV. Mixed metaphors,—that is, the use of two different figures in the same period, with reference to the same object,—confound the imagination, and are to be strictly guarded against. Thus Addison, in his "Letter from Italy," says,

"I bridle in my struggling muse with pain,
That longs to launch into a bolder strain."

He first makes his muse a horse which may be *bridled*, then a ship which may be *launched*. How can it be both, at one and the same moment? How can being *bridled* prevent it from *launching*? With equal impropriety Shakspeare uses the expression, "*To take arms against a sea of troubles*," comparing the troubles in question, in the same breath, to an *enemy* and to a *sea*.

V. Lastly, metaphors should not be carried too far; if all the minor points of resemblance are sought out and dwelt upon, the reader will inevitably become wearied.

§ 346. HYPERBOLE.

I. Violent hyperboles are out of place in mere descriptions. A person in great affliction may indulge in wild exaggeration, but for a writer merely describing such a person to use language like the following is pure bombast:—

"I found her on the floor,
In all the storm of grief, yet beautiful;
Pouring forth tears at such a lavish rate,
That, were the world on fire, they might have drowned
The wrath of Heaven, and quenched the mighty ruin."—LEE.

II. Hyperboles may be so extravagant as to render the writer and his subject ridiculous. Lucan furnishes a case in point. The later

---

error. Give another couplet from Pope containing a violation of this principle. What are mixed metaphors? What is their effect? Show how Addison and Shakspeare violate this rule. What is said about carrying metaphors too far?

§ 346. In what are violent hyperboles out of place? Give an example of bombast

Roman poets, as a compliment to their emperors, were in the habit of asking them in their addresses what part of the heavens they would choose for their habitation after they had become gods. Lucan, however, resolving to outdo all his predecessors in an address to Nero, gravely beseeches him not to choose his place near either of the poles, lest his weight overturn the universe.

LESSON LIII.

EXERCISE ON FIGURES.

Point out the figures of orthography, etymology, syntax, and rhetoric, that occur in the following extracts. In each passage, there is a faulty figure, which violates one or more of the rules laid down in the last lesson. Show wherein the error lies, and suggest, in each case, a figure by which the difficulty in question may be avoided.

FAULTY SIMILES.

1. "The holy Book, like the eighth sphere, doth shine."—COWLEY.

2. "The sun, in figures such as these,
   Joys with the moon to play:
     To the sweet strains they advance,
     Which do result from their own spheres;
     As this nymph's dance
   Moves with the numbers which she hears."—WALLER.

3. In Shakspeare's Richard II., a gardener gives these directions to his servants:—

   "Go, bind thou up yon dangling apricots,
   Which, like unruly children, make their sire
   Stoop with oppression of their prodigal weight;
   Give some supportance to the bending twigs.
   Go thou; and, like an executioner,
   Cut off the heads of too fast-growing sprays,
   That look too lofty in our commonwealth;
   All must be even in our government."

---

produced by this figure. What is said of extravagant hyperboles? Cite one in which Lucan indulges.

4. In Addison's Cato, Portius, bidding his beloved Lucia an eternal farewell, uses the following language:—

"Thus o'er the dying lamp the unsteady flame
Hangs quivering on a point, leaps off by fits
And falls again, as loath to quit its hold.
——— Thou must not go ; my soul still hovers o'er thee,
And can't get loose."

5. "Nor could the Greeks repel the Lycian powers,
Nor the bold Lycians force the Grecian towers.
As, on the confines of adjoining grounds,
Two stubborn swains with blows dispute their bounds,
They tug, they sweat; but neither gain nor yield,
One foot, one inch, of the contended field."—POPE'S HOMER.

6. Speaking of the fallen angels, searching for mines of gold, Milton says:—

"A numerous brigade hastened : as when bands
Of pioneers, with spade and pick-axe armed,
Forerun the royal camp to trench a field
Or cast a rampart."

FAULTY METAPHORS.

7. "Trothal went forth with the stream of his people, but they met a rock : for Fingal stood unmoved ; broken, they rolled back from his side. Nor did they roll in safety ; the spear of the king pursued their flight."—OSSIAN.

8. A torrent of superstition consumed the land.

9. "Where is the monarch who dares resist us? Where is the potentate who doth not glory in being numbered among our attendants? As for thee, descended from a Turcoman sailor, since the vessel of thy unbounded ambition hath been wrecked in the gulf of thy self-love, it would be proper that thou should'st take in the sails of thy temerity, and cast the anchor of repentance in the port of sincerity and justice, which is the port of safety ; lest the tempest of our vengeance make thee perish in the sea of the punishment thou deservest."—TAMERLANE.

10. Dryden, in the following lines, describes the Supreme Being as extinguishing the fire of London in accordance with the supplications of His people:—

"A hollow crystal pyramid He takes,
In firmamental waters dipped above
Of this a broad extinguisher He makes,
And hoods the flames that to their quarry strove."

11. ——— "The Alps,
The palaces of Nature, whose vast walls
Have pinnacled in clouds their snowy scalps."—NEWSPAPER POET.

12. "There is a time when factions, by the vehemence of their own fermentation, stun and disable one another."—BOLINGBROKE.

13. "The tackle of my heart is cracked and burnt;
   And all the shrouds wherewith my life should sail
   Are turnèd to one thread, one little hair:
   My heart hath one poor string to stay it by,
   Which holds but till thy news be uttered."—SHAKSPEARE.

FAULTY HYPERBOLES.

14. "By every wind that comes this way,
    Send me at least a sigh or two;
    Such and so many I'll repay
    As shall themselves make winds to get to you."—COWLEY.

15. "All armed in brass, the richest dress of war,
    (A dismal, glorious sight) he shone afar.
    The sun himself started with sudden fright
    To see his beams return so dismal bright." – COWLEY.

16. "Aumerle, thou weep'st, my tender-hearted cousin!
    We'll make foul weather with despisèd tears:
    Our sighs, and they, shall lodge the summer-corn,
    And make a dearth in this revolting land."—SHAKSPEARE.

LESSON LIV.

STYLE AND ITS VARIETIES.

§ 347. IF we examine the compositions of any two individuals on the same subject, we shall generally find that, not only do their respective sentiments differ, but also their modes of expressing those sentiments. This is no more than natural. We must expect the thoughts and words of men to differ similarly with their actions and dispositions. Now, the peculiar manner in which a writer expresses his thoughts by means of words is called STYLE,—a word derived from the Latin *stylus*, the name of a pointed steel instrument employed by the Romans in writing on their waxen tablets. Yet, while the mental peculiarities of most writers are apparent in their diction, there are some general distinctive features which enable

---

§ 347. On examining the compositions of two different persons on the same subject, what will we generally find? What is style? From what is the word derived? Enu-

us to divide their various styles into different classes, as follows: the Dry, the Plain, the Neat, the Elegant the Florid, the Simple, the Labored, the Concise, the Diffuse, the Nervous, and the Feeble. These we shall now consider, premising that (with the exception of the Dry, the Labored, and the Feeble, which are always to be avoided) they are appropriate to different subjects, and must be selected by a writer with reference to the matter he proposes to treat. It is obvious that the swelling style of an oration would be altogether out of place in a philosophical essay or an unpretending letter. As we define each, we shall note to what compositions it is adapted.

§ 348. The difference between the first five of the styles enumerated above, consists chiefly in the amount of ornament employed.

A dry style excludes ornament of every kind. Aiming only to be understood, it takes no trouble to please either the fancy or the ear. Such a style is tolerable in didactic writing alone, and even there only solidity of matter and perspicuity of language enable us to endure it. This is so generally felt that we have but few specimens of a purely dry style. Aristotle's may be mentioned among the most striking; and, in modern times, Berkley has perhaps approached it as nearly as any other writer

A plain style rises one degree above that last described. While the plain writer is at no pains to please us with ornament, he carefully avoids disgusting us with harshness. In addition to perspicuity, which is the only aim of the dry writer, he studies precision, purity, and propriety. Such figures as are naturally suggested and tend to elucidate his meaning, he does not reject; while such as merely embellish he avoids as beneath his notice. To this class of writers Locke and Swift belong.

Next in order is *the neat style.* Here ornaments are employed, but

---

merate the principal varieties of style. By what must a writer be guided in making a selection between them?

§ 348. In what does the difference between the first five of these styles consist? escribe the dry style. In what kind of writing alone is it tolerable? What authors afford the most striking specimens of this style? Describe the plain style. Besides perspicuity, what does the plain writer study? What figures does he employ? What writers belong to this class? What style is next in order in point of ornament? De-

not those of the most elevated or sparkling kind; they are appropriate and correct, rather than bold and glowing. Beauty of composition is sought to be attained rather by a judicious selection and arrangement of words than by striking efforts of imagination. The sentences employed are of moderate length, and carefully freed from superfluities. This style is adapted to every species of writing; to the letter, the essay, the sermon, the law-paper, and even the most abstract treatise.

Advancing a step, we come to *the elegant style;* which possesses all the beauty that ornament can add, without any of the drawbacks arising from its improper or excessive use. It may be regarded as the perfection of style. "An elegant writer," says Blair, "is one who pleases the fancy and the ear, while he informs the understanding; and who gives us his ideas clothed with all the beauty of expression, but not overcharged with any of its misplaced finery." Such a one preëminently is Addison; and such, though in a less degree, are Pope, Temple, and Bolingbroke.

A florid style is one in which ornament is everywhere employed. The term is used with a two-fold signification:—for the ornaments may spring from a luxuriant imagination and have a solid basis of thought to rest upon: or, as is too often the case, the luxuriance may be in words alone and not in fancy; the brilliancy may be merely superficial, a glittering tinsel, which, however much it may please the shallow-minded, cannot fail to disgust the judicious. As first defined, this style has been employed by several distinguished writers with marked success; among these the most prominent is Ossian, whose poems consist almost entirely of bold and brilliant figures. But it is only writers of transcendent genius that can thus indulge in continued ornament with any hope of success. Inferior minds inevitably fall into the second kind of floridity alluded to above, than which nothing is more contemptible. Vividness of imagination in the young often betrays them into this fault; it is one, however, which time generally corrects, and which is therefore to be preferred to the opposite extreme. "Luxuriance," says Quintilian, "can easily be cured; but for barrenness there is no remedy."

Careful revision is the best means of correcting an over-florid style.

---

scribe it. To what varieties of composition is it adapted? What is the next style? Describe it. What does Blair say of the elegant writer? What authors have excelled in this style? What is meant by a florid style? State in what two senses this term is used. As first defined, by whom has it been employed? What writers alone can hope to use it with success? Into what are inferior minds that attempt it apt to fall? Who are often betrayed into this fault by vividness of imagination? What does Quintilian say respecting luxuriance and barrenness? What is the best means of correcting an over-florid style? What other means is suggested? Show how it operates.

Unnecessary words must be stricken out, and even the whole sentence must sometimes be remodelled. On the ornamental parts, in particular, the file must be freely used. Figures which are not in all respects chaste and appropriate to the subject, must be unceremoniously removed. To write frequently on familiar themes will be found another effective means of correcting excessive floridity. In such exercises, the inappropriateness of too much ornament will be obvious to the writer himself, and the effort made to repress it will have a beneficial effect on all his compositions.

§ 349. *The simple* and *the labored style* are directly opposed to each other, the difference between them lying principally in the structure of their respective sentences.

The simple writer expresses himself so easily that the reader, before making the attempt, imagines he can write as well himself. His diction bears no marks of art; it seems to be the very language of nature. The man of taste and good sense is unable to suggest any change whereby the author could have dealt more properly or efficiently with his subject. Simplicity does not imply plainness; when ornaments are suited to the subject, it adopts them, its chief aim being consistency with nature. The best specimens of simplicity are afforded by the writers of antiquity,—particularly Homer, Herodotus, Xenophon, and Cæsar and the reason is plain, because they wrote from the dictates of natural genius, and imitated neither the thoughts nor the style of others. Among moderns, Goldsmith's writings are characterized by this quality in the highest degree.

Simplicity having been thus defined at length, it is unnecessary to say much respecting the labored style, which is in all respects its reverse. The characteristics of the latter are affectation; misplaced ornament, a preponderance of swelling words, long and involved sentences, and a constrained tone, neither easy, graceful, nor natural.

§ 350. Styles are distinguished as *concise* and *diffuse*, according as few or many words are employed by the writer to express his thoughts.

The concise writer, aiming to express himself in the briefest possi-

---

§ 349. What is the opposite of a simple style? In what does the difference between them chiefly consist? Describe the diction of the simple writer. What ornaments does he employ? Who afford the best specimens of simplicity? Why? What modern writer possesses this quality in a high degree? What are the characteristics of the labored style?

§ 350. What constitutes the difference between the concise and the diffuse style? How does the concise writer express himself? How, the diffuse? When do both these

ble manner, rejects as redundant every thing not material to the sense. He presents a thought but once, and then in its most striking light. His sentences are compact and strong rather than harmonious, and suggest more than they directly express.

The diffuse writer, on the other hand, presents his thoughts in a variety of lights, and endeavors by repetition to make himself perfectly understood. Fond of amplification, he indulges in long sentences making up by copiousness what he lacks in strength.

Each of these styles has its beauties, and each becomes faulty when carried to excess. Too great conciseness produces abruptness and obscurity; while extreme diffuseness dilutes the thought, and makes but a feeble impression on the reader. In deciding to which of these qualities it is best to incline in any particular instance, we should be controlled by the nature of the subject. Discourses intended for delivery require a more copious style than matter which is to be printed and read at leisure. When, as in the case of the latter, there is an opportunity of pausing and reviewing what is not at first understood, greater brevity is allowable than when the meaning has to be caught from the words of a speaker, and is thus, if too tersely expressed, liable to be lost. As a general thing, in descriptions, essays, and sublime and impassioned writing, it is safer to incline to conciseness. The interest is thus kept alive, the attention is riveted, and the reader's mind finds agreeable exercise in following out the ideas suggested, without being fully presented, by the author.

The most concise, as well as the simplest, writers are found among the ancients. Aristotle and Tacitus, above all others, are characterized by terseness and brevity of expression; the former, indeed, in a greater degree than propriety allows. The genius of our language, as we have already seen, is opposed to the pointed brevity which constitutes the principal charm of the classics. We shall therefore find comparatively few specimens of concise composition in our literature; while, on the contrary, we can boast of many writers, who, in elegant diffuseness, will not compare unfavorably with Cicero, the great model of antiquity in this variety of style.

§ 351. *The nervous* and *the feeble style* produce re-

---

styles become faulty? What results from too great conciseness? What, from extreme diffuseness? In deciding, in any particular instance, to which it is best to incline, by what should we be controlled? Which of these styles is recommended for matter that is to be spoken, and on what grounds? Which is the better for sublime and impassioned writing, and why? Where must we look for the most concise writers? What two, in particular, are mentioned? Which of these styles does the genius of our language favor?

spectively a strong and a slight impression on the reader or hearer.

They are by some considered synonymous with the diffuse and the concise, but not properly; for, however much the latter qualities may contribute to produce the former, there are instances of a feeble brevity as well as a nervous copiousness. When considering the essential properties of style, we shall have occasion to treat of strength, and it will then appear in what that quality consists. Meanwhile, we may say that unmeaning epithets, vague expressions, and improper arrangements of words and clauses, are to be avoided, as inevitable sources of weakness.

LESSON LV.

EXERCISE ON THE VARIETIES OF STYLE.

BRIEF examples of the principal styles described in the last lesson are presented below. The judicious writer aims at variety in his compositions; and hence, though a work, as a whole, may have a prevailing tone or manner, it does not follow that successive sentences are so distinguished. We can therefore better exemplify the different styles by short passages than by lengthy extracts. Besides pointing out the peculiarities which lead us to characterize these extracts as dry, elegant, florid, &c., show what figures occur, and name them; also, supply the omitted points.

DRY STYLE.

The Sceptic.—Whether the principles of Christians or infidels are truest may be made a question but which are safest can be none. Certainly if you doubt of all opinions you must doubt of your own and then for aught you know th Christian may be true. The more doubt the more room there is for faith a sceptic of all men having the least right to demand evidence. But whatever uncertainty there may be in other points thus much is certain either there is or is not a God there is or is

---

§ 851. What styles remain to be considered? With what are they by some considered synonymous? Show why this is not a correct view. What are to be avoided as inevitable sources of weakness?

not a revelation man either is or is not an agent the soul is or is not immortal. If the negatives are not sure the affirmatives are possible. If the negatives are improbable the affirmatives are probable. In proportion as any of your ingenious men finds himself unable to prove any one of these negatives he hath grounds to suspect he may be mistaken. A minute philosopher therefore that would act a consistent part should have the diffidence the modesty and the timidity as well as the doubts of a sceptic.—BERKLEY.

ELEGANT STYLE.

Reflections in Westminster Abbey.—When I look upon the tombs of the great every emotion of envy dies in me when I read the epitaphs of the beautiful every inordinate desire goes out when I meet with the grief of parents upon a tombstone my heart melts with compassion when I see the tomb of the parents themselves I consider the vanity of grieving for those whom we must quickly follow. When I see kings lying by those who deposed them when I consider rival wits placed side by side or the holy men that divided the world with their contests and disputes I reflect with sorrow and astonishment on the little competitions factions and debates of mankind. When I read the several dates of the tombs of some that died yesterday and some six hundred years ago I consider that great day when we shall all of us be contemporaries and make our appearance together.—ADDISON.

FLORID STYLE.

The Flowery Creation.—The *snowdrop* foremost of the lovely train breaks her way through the frozen soil in order to present her early compliments to her lord dressed in the robe of innocency she steps forth fearless of danger long before the trees have ventured to unfold their leaves even while the icicles are pendent on our houses.—Next peeps out the *crocus* but cautiously and with an air of timidity. She hears the howling blasts and skulks close to her low situation. Afraid she seems to make large excursions from her root while so many ruffian winds are abroad and scouring along the æther.—Nor is the *violet* last in this shining embassy of the year which with all the embellishments that would grace a royal garden condescends to line our hedges and grow at the feet of briers. Freely and without any solicitations she distributes the bounty of her emissive sweets while herself with an exemplary humility retires from sight seeking rather to administer pleasure than to win admiration emblem expressive emblem of those modest virtues which delight to bloom in obscurity which extend a cheering influence to multitudes who are scarce acquainted with the source of their comforts motive engaging motive to that ever-active beneficence which stays not for the importunity of the distressed but anticipates their suit and prevents them with the blessings of its goodness!—HERVEY.

SIMPLE STYLE.

The Village Schoolmaster.

Beside yon straggling fence that skirts the way
With blossomed furze unprofitably gay
There in his noisy mansion skilled to rule
The village master taught his little school.

A man severe he was and stern to view
I knew him well and every truant knew.
Well had the boding tremblers learned to trace
The day's disasters in his morning's face
Full well they laughed with counterfeited glee
At all his jokes for many a joke had he
Full well the busy whisper circling round
Conveyed the dismal tidings when he frowned
Yet he was kind or if severe in aught
The love he bore to learning was a fault.
The village all declared how much he knew
'Twas certain he could write and cipher too
Lands he could measure terms and tides presage
And e'en the story ran that he could gauge
In arguing too the parson owned his skill
For e'en though vanquished he could argue still
While words of learned length and thundering sound
Amazed the gazing rustics ranged around
And still they gazed and still the wonder grew
That one small head could carry all he knew.
But past is all his fame the very spot
Where many a time he triumphed is forgot.— GOLDSMITH.

LABORED STYLE.

The Good Housewife.—Next unto her sanctity and holiness of life it is meet that our English housewife be a woman of great modesty and temperance as well inwardly as outwardly inwardly as in her behavior and carriage towards her husband wherein she shall shun all violence of rage passion and humor coveting less to direct than to be directed appearing ever unto him pleasant amiable and delightful and though occasion of mishaps or the misgovernment of his will may induce her to contrary thoughts yet virtuously to suppress them and with a mild sufferance rather to call him home from his error than with the strength of anger to abate the least spark of his evil calling into her mind that evil and uncomely language is deformed though uttered even to servants but most monstrous and ugly when it appears before the presence of a husband outwardly as in her apparel and diet both which she shall proportion according to the competency of her husband's estate and calling making her circle rather straight than large for it is a rule if we extend to the uttermost we take away increase if we go a hair's breadth beyond we enter into consumption but if we preserve any part we build strong forts against the adversaries of fortune provided that such preservation be honest and conscionable.—MARKHAM.

CONCISE STYLE.

Studies.—Some books are to be tasted others to be swallowed and some few to be chewed and digested that is some books are to be read only in parts others to be read but not curiously and some few to be read wholly and with diligence and attention. Some books also may be read by deputy and extracts made of them by others but that would be only in the less important arguments and the meaner sort of books else distilled books are like common distilled waters flashy things.

Reading maketh a full man conference a ready man and writing an exact man and therefore if a man write little he had need have a great memory if he confer little he had need have a present wit and if he read little he had need have much cunning to seem to know what he doth not.—BACON.

NERVOUS STYLE.

On the Impeachment of Warren Hastings.—In the course of all this proceeding your lordships will not fail to observe he is never corrupt but he is cruel he never dines with comfort but where he is sure to create a famine. He never robs from the loose superfluity of standing greatness he devours the fallen the indigent the necessitous. His extortion is not like the generous rapacity of the princely eagle who snatches away the living struggling prey he is a vulture who feeds upon the prostrate the dying and the dead. As his cruelty is more shocking than his corruption so his hypocrisy has something more frightful than his cruelty. For whilst his bloody and rapacious hand signs proscriptions and sweeps away the food of the widow and the orphan his eyes overflow with tears and he converts the healing balm that bleeds from wounded humanity into a rancorous and deadly poison to the race of man.—BURKE.

LESSON LVI.

ESSENTIAL PROPERTIES OF STYLE.—PURITY.—PROPRIETY.

§ 352. IT has been observed that the peculiarities of individual minds, appearing in their respective styles of composition, give rise to the varieties enumerated in the last lesson. In some, this peculiarity of manner is so decided that the author, even when he writes anonymously, is easily recognized. Such marked individuality of style, adhered to by an author throughout his compositions, is known as *mannerism*. While these peculiarities of diction are by no means forbidden by the rules of composition, there are certain properties which every style ought to possess. These are seven in number; Purity, Propriety, Precision, Clearness, Strength, Harmony, and Unity

---

§ 352. From what do the varieties of style take their rise? What is Mannerism? What is meant by the essential properties of style? Mention them.

§ 353. PURITY consists in the use of such words and constructions as properly belong to the genius of the language. It may be violated, therefore, in two ways: first, by the Barbarism, or use of an impure word; and, secondly, by the Solecism, or use of an impure construction. Of these faults there are several varieties.

§ 354. *Barbarisms.*—These consist of,

I. Obsolete words; that is, such as have gone out of use.

Among these we may mention the following, sometimes employed by affected writers:—

Behest, command.	*Quoth*, said.
Bewray, betray.	*Sith*, since.
Erst, formerly.	*Stroam*, roam.
Irks, wearies.	*Whilom*, of old.
Let, hinder.	*Wist*, knew.
Peradventure, perhaps.	*Wot*, know.

Whatever these and similar words may have been in the days of our forefathers, they cannot now be regarded as pure English. They are sometimes used in poetry, in burlesques, and in narratives of ancient times, to which, being in keeping with the characters and objects described, they are peculiarly appropriate; but in all other varieties of composition they should be carefully avoided. Analogous to this fault is that of employing a word in good use with an obsolete signification. Thus in the days of Shakspeare the verb *owe* often had the meaning of *own*:—

"Thou dost here usurp
The name thou *owest* [ownest] not."

The writer who should, at the present day, use *owe* in this sense would be guilty of a barbarism.

II. Newly-coined words; or such as find their way into conversation and newspapers, but are not authorized by good usage; as *obligate*, for *oblige; deputize*, for *commission*, &c.

What we are to regard as good usage will be explained hereafter.

---

§ 353. In what does purity consist? In how many ways may it be violated? What is the barbarism? What, the solecism?

§ 354. What is the first variety of barbarism? Mention some of the obsolete words occasionally used by affected writers, and give their modern equivalents. In what varieties of writing are they sometimes used with propriety? What fault is analogous to this? Illustrate this with the verb *owe*, as used in Shakspeare. What is the second species of barbarism? What writers are at liberty to coin words? How must the

A writer who is unfolding the principles of a new science, and who is thus destitute of words with which to express his meaning, is at liberty to coin such terms as he needs. He must do it, however, with caution, and must first satisfy himself that there is no suitable word already in the language. In such cases, recourse is generally had to Latin and Greek, particularly the latter; and etymological analogies must be regarded in the process of formation.

With this exception, the coining of words is strictly prohibited; and the judicious writer will avoid, not only such terms as have been thus recently formed, but also those which, though invented years ago by authors of note, have not been received into general use. It had been better for our language, perhaps, had this principle in later times been more carefully followed. We should thus have avoided such cumbrous words as *numerosity, cognition, irrefragability*, and hundreds like them, whose meaning can be as accurately, and far more intelligibly, conveyed by words in existence long before they were invented. With some writers, the coining of these Latin derivatives seems to have been a passion. Saxon they reserved for conversation; their compositions they deemed it necessary to adorn with ponderous Latin. The former was their natural idiom; the latter, their labored after-thought. Dr. Johnson was their great leader, respecting whom an anecdote is related which strikingly illustrates this propensity. Speaking, on one occasion, of "The Rehearsal," he said, "it has not wit enough to keep it sweet;" then, after a pause which he had employed in translating this thought into his latinized dialect, he added, "it has not sufficient virtue to preserve it from putrefaction."

As our language now stands, it is abundantly copious for all purposes; and not only is the coining of new words inadmissible, but we should also, as we have seen, avoid the frivolous and unnecessary innovations of others. The only latitude allowed is in the formation of compound words by the union of two or more simple ones with the hyphen, whereby lengthy circumlocutions are sometimes avoided; but even here care must be taken to combine only such as naturally coalesce, are clearly understood, and convey an idea which no word already existing bears. Thus, *stand-point* is an unobjectionable compound; but *side-hill* is not to be tolerated as long as *hill-side* continues in good standing.

---

privilege be exercised? In such cases, to what languages is recourse generally had? What must be regarded in the process of formation? With this exception, what is said of the coining of words? Had this principle been generally followed, what cumbrous words would we have avoided? What is said of the passion of some writers for Latin derivatives? Illustrate this with an anecdote of Dr. Johnson. In what may some latitude be allowed? Even here, what must be observed? Illustrate this. What is

III. Foreign words. These are to be rejected, when there are pure English words which express the thought equally well.

As in former years there was a passion for Latin, so at the present time there is a great fondness for French; and Gallicisms, or words and idioms from this language, are abundantly interlarded in the current compositions of the day. Some of these expressions, such as *ennui*, *hor de combat*, &c., express the idea intended more accurately than it can be conveyed by any pure native word or phrase; and we can not, therefore, prohibit their use. In the case of the following, however, and many others, there are corresponding English words equally expressive; and, by using their foreign substitutes, we only incur the imputation of pedantry.

Amende honorable, apology.
A propos, appropriate.
Bagatelle, trifle.
Beau monde, fashionable world.
Canaille, rabble.
Coup d'état, stroke of state policy.
Delicatesse, delicacy.
Dernier resort, last resort.
Émeute, disturbance.
Fougue, turbulence.
Fraîcheur, coolness.
Hauteur, haughtiness.
Haut ton, people of fashion.
Naïveté, simplicity.
N'importe, no matter.
Nous verrons, we shall see.
Par excellence, pre-eminently
Politesse, politeness.

IV. Provincial words; that is, such as are employed in particular districts, but are not in general use. Thus, *chuck-hole* in some localities denotes a steep hole in a wagon rut; and *chuffy* in Sussex and Kent means *surly*: but such words cannot properly be introduced into composition.

§ 355. *Solecisms.*—As above defined, a solecism is a deviation from the proper construction of words. It appears in many different forms, as follows:—

I. Syntactical errors. All violations of the rules of Syntax fall under this head. Some of the principal of these we have already considered in § 216-229.

II. Phrases which, when looked at grammatically, convey

---

the third variety of barbarism? For what is a fondness manifested by many writers at the present day? What are gallicisms? What is said of some of them, such as *ennui* and *hors de combat*? When there are corresponding English expressions, what effect has the use of French words? Repeat the list of French words often used, and give their English equivalents. What is the fourth species of barbarism? Give examples.

§ 355. What is a solecism? What is the first form in which it appears? What, the second? Exemplify it. What, the third? Give illustrations.

a different meaning from that intended as, "He sings a good song," for "He sings well." A good song may be ill sung, and therefore the grammatical meaning of the sentence is different from that which it is made to bear. Similar solecisms are involved in the expressions, "He tells a good story," "He plays a good fiddle," &c.

III. Foreign idioms: such as, "He knows to sing," for "He knows how to sing;"—"It repents me," for "I repent," &c.

§ 356. In § 354 we spoke of words not authorized by good usage; it becomes necessary to inquire into the meaning of this expression. It is evident that usage is the only standard both of speaking and writing; that it is the highest tribunal to which, in cases of grammatical controversy, we can appeal. This, however, can not be the case with all usage; if it were, we might with propriety defend the grossest violations of orthography and syntax, for which abundant precedents can be found. That usage alone must be regarded as a standard, which is,

I. *Reputable*, that is, authorized by the majority of writers in good repute: not such as are most meritorious, because on this point individual views may disagree; but those whose merit is generally acknowledged by the world, respecting which there can be little diversity of opinion.

II. *National*, as opposed to provincial and foreign.

The ignorant naturally regard the limited district in which they live as the world at large, and all that it authorizes as correct. The learned are apt to conceive a fondness for foreign tongues, and to transplant thence peculiarities of diction into their own vernacular. Thus originate provincial and foreign usage, neither of which carries with it any weight of authority.

III. *Present*, as opposed to obsolete. The authority of

---

§ 356. What is the only standard of speaking and writing? Why may we not regard all usage as a standard? To be so regarded, what three essential qualities must usage possess? What is meant by reputable usage? Why are not meritorious, rather than reputable, authors selected as standards? What is meant by national usage? Show how provincial and foreign usage originate. To what is present usage opposed? How far may the authority of old writers be admitted?

old writers, however great their fame, can not be admitted in support of a term or expression not used by reputable authors of later date.

§ 357. We sometimes find, however, that good usage is not uniform; that is, that respectable authors can be produced on both sides of a question, in support of two different forms of expression, respecting which there is controversy. In this case, we can not characterize either as barbarous; yet between them we have to select: and it is the province of criticism to establish principles by which our choice may be directed. Reference is here made to controverted points; not to those differences in words and constructions which are not questions of right and wrong, but allowable variations of expression.

In doubtful cases, the following rules will be found of service:—

I. When usage is divided as to any two words or phrases, if either is ever used in a different sense from the one in question while the other is not, employ the latter. Thus, to express *consequently*, the two phrases *by consequence* and *of consequence* are employed. The former is preferable, because the expression *of consequence* may also mean *of moment, of importance*.

II. In the forms of words, consult the analogies of the language. Thus, *contemporary* is preferable to *cotemporary;* because, in words compounded with *con*, the final *n*, though expunged before a vowel or *h* mute, is generally retained before a consonant: as, *coincide, coheir, concomitant*. We have, indeed, an exception in *copartner;* in which, though the radical commences with the consonant *p*, the final *n* of *con* is omitted: but in doubtful cases we must be guided by the rule, and not the exception.

III. When there are several different forms in other respects equal, that ought to be preferred which is most agreeable to the ear. Thus *amiableness* and *amiability* are both correct and authorized words, formed according to the analogies of the language; but, under this rule, the latter, being the more harmonious, should have preference.

IV. When there is doubt, if either of the words or expressions in

---

§ 357. What do we sometimes find with respect to good usage? In this case, to what must we have recourse? Give the substance of the first rule, and illustrate it. As regards the forms of words, what must we consult? Exemplify this with the word *contemporary*. Other things being equal, which form of a word, according to the

question would seem, from its etymological form, to have a signification different from that which it commonly bears, we should reject it. Thus, *loose* and *unloose* are both used to denote the same idea. Since, however, the prefix *un* negatives the meaning of the radical, *to unloose* would etymologically signify *to fasten, to tie*, and we should therefore, in all cases, give the preference to *loose*.

§ 358. The second essential quality of style is PROPRIETY: which consists in avoiding *vulgarisms*, or undignified and low expressions; in choosing correctly between words formed from the same radical, which resemble each other in appearance, but differ in application and meaning; and in employing words only in such acceptations as are authorized by good usage.

Vulgarisms are out of place in every variety of composition except low burlesques. Under this head are included, not only coarse expressions, such as, "*to turn up one's nose* at any thing," but also words which are proper enough in conversation but not sufficiently dignified for composition. The latter are technically called *colloquialisms;* "by *dint* of argument," "not a *whit* better," "to *get* a disease," will serve as examples. Young writers naturally express themselves in writing as they would in speaking. Hence colloquialisms, unless they exercise great care, will constantly occur in their compositions.

The second fault which violates Propriety is the confounding of kindred derivatives in the case of which the writer is misled by the resemblance in the appearance of the words, though the difference between their respective meanings may be so great that they can hardly be regarded as synonymes. Thus, from *false* we have three nouns formed, which are too often used without proper discrimination,—*falseness, falsity,* and *falsehood.* The following distinction should be observed in their use:— *falseness* is equivalent to the want of truth, and is applied to persons only: *falsity* and *falsehood* are applied to things alone; the former denotes that abstract quality which may be defined as *contrariety to truth;* the latter is simply an untrue assertion. We speak of the *falseness* of one who tells *falsehoods,* and expose the *falsity* of his pretensions.

So, *observation* and *observance* are often confounded. The radical, to

---

rd rule, should be preferred? Give the substance of the fourth rule, and apply it in the case of *loose* and *unloose*.

§ 358. What is the second essential quality of style? In what does propriety consist? Where alone are vulgarisms admissible? What are included under this head? What writers are apt to fall into colloquialisms? What is the second fault which violates propriety? Give the three nouns derived from *false;* show the proper application, and illustrate the use, of each. Define the two derivatives from the verb *observe*,

observe, signifies both *to note, to mark*, and *to keep, to celebrate*. In its former acceptation, it gives rise to the verbal noun *observation;* in its latter, to *observance*. We say, "a man of *observation*," not *observance;*— "the *observance* [not *observation*] of the Sabbath."

Conscience and *consciousness* are thus distinguished: the former is the moral sense which discerns between right and wrong; the latter is simply knowledge, as used in connection with sensations or mental operations. Dryden, therefore, violates Propriety in the following couplet:—

> "The sweetest cordial we receive at last,
> Is *conscience* of virtuous actions past."

Negligence is often improperly used for *neglect*. The former is a habit; the latter, an act. "His *negligence* was the source of all his misfortunes."—"By his *neglect* he lost the opportunity."

In like manner, *sophism* and *sophistry* are apt to be confounded. The former is a fallacious argument; the latter, a fallacious course of reasoning. "Gorgias, who was noted for his *sophistry*, then had recourse to a transparent *sophism*."

The third fault that violates Propriety is the employment of a word in a sense not authorized by good usage; as when we say a road is *impracticable*, for *impassable;* or speak of *decompounding* a mixture, instead of *analyzing* it.

LESSON LVII.

EXERCISE ON PURITY AND PROPRIETY.

CORRECT the violations of Purity and Propriety in the following sentences:—

PURITY.

1. If the privileges to which he has an undoubted right, and has so long enjoyed, should now be wrested from him, would be flagrant injustice. 2. The religion of these people, as well as their customs and manners, were strangely misrepresented. 3. Removing the term from Westminster, sitting the Parliament, was illegal. 4. This change of fortune had quite transmogrified him. 5. The king soon found reason to

---

and illustrate their use. Show the difference between *conscience* and *consciousness*. How does Dryden violate propriety by the use of the former? Define the difference between *negligence* and *neglect;* between *sophism* and *sophistry*. Define and illustrate the third fault that violates propriety.

repent him of provoking such dangerous enemies. 6. The popular lords did not fail to enlarge themselves on the subject. 7. I shall endeavor to live hereafter suitable to a man in my station. 8. It was thought that the *coup d'état* would have occasioned an *émeute*. 9. The *dernier resort* of the emperor will be to make the *amende honorable*; but *nous verrons*. 10. The queen, whom it highly imported that the two monarchs should be at peace, acted the part of mediator. 11. The wisest princes need not think it any diminution to their greatness, or derogation to their sufficiency, to rely upon counsel. 12. He behaved himself conformable to that blessed example. 13. I should be obliged to him, if he will gratify me in that particular. 14. May is *par excellence* the month of flowers; it is delicious at this season to go stroaming about the fields. 15. You can't bamboozle me with such flimsy excuses. 16. I hold that this argument is irrefragable. 17. Whether one person or more was concerned in the business, does not yet appear. 18. The conspiracy was the easier discovered from its being known to many. 19. These feasts were celebrated to the honor of Osiris, whom the Greeks called Dionysius, and is the same with Bacchus. 20. Such a sight was enough to dumfounder an ordinary man. 21. This will eventuate in jeopardizing the whole party. 22. Firstly, he has conducted matters so illy that his fellow countrymen can hereafter repose no confidence in him. 23. All these things required abundance of *finesse* and *delicatesse* to manage with advantage. 24. When I made some *à propos* remarks upon his conduct, he began to quiz me; but he had better have let it alone. 25. A large part of the meadows and cornfields was overflown. 26. Having finished my chores before sundown, I lit a fire. 27. The pleasures of the understanding are more preferable than those of the senses. 28. Virtue confers the supremest dignity on man, and should be his chiefest desire. 29. Temperance and exercise are excellent preventatives of debility. 30. I admire his amiableness and candidness. 31. It grieves me to think with what ardor two or three eminent personages have inchoated such a course.

PROPRIETY.

1. Every year a new flower, in his judgment, beats all the old ones, though it is much inferior to them both in color and shape. 2. The [ceremonious, or ceremonial?] law is so called in contradistinction to the moral and the judicial law. 3. Come often; do not be [ceremonious, or ceremonial?]. 4. Meanwhile the Britons, left to shift for themselves, were forced to call in the Saxons to their aid. 5. Conscience of integrity supports the misfortunate. 6. His name must go down to posterity with distinguished honor in the public records of the nation. 7. Every thing goes helter-skelter and topsy-turvy, when a man leaves his business to be done by others. 8. The alone principle;—a likely boy;—he is considerable of a man;—the balance of them;—at a wide remove;—I expect he did it;—I learned him the lesson;—to fall trees;—he conducts well;—like he did;—we started directly they came;—I feel as though;—equally as well. 9. What [further, or farther?] need have we of caution? 10. Still [further, or farther?], what evidence have we of this? 11. We may try hard, and still be [further, or farther?] from success than ever. 12. If all men were exemplary in their conduct, things would soon take a new face, and religion receive a mighty encouragement. 13. A reader can often see with half an eye what ails a

sentence, when its author is unable to discover any mistake. 14. He passed his time at the court of St. James, currying favor with the minister. 15. One brave [act, or action?] often turns the fortune of battle. 16. Our [acts, or actions?] generally proceed from instinct or impulse · our [acts, or actions?] are more frequently the result of deliberation. 17. Learning and arts were but then getting up. 18. One is in a bad fix that has to spend a rainy day in the country. It is enough to give most people the blues. 19. I had like to have gotten a broken head. 20. It is difficult for one unaccustomed to [sophism, or sophistry?] to succeed in a [sophism, or sophistry?]. 21. This performance was much at one with the other. 22. I had a great mind to tell him that I set store by him. 23. If we can not beat our adversaries with logic, we should at least not allow them to get the upper hand of us in mildness of temper and properness of behavior.

LESSON LVIII.

PRECISION.

§ 359. THE third essential property of style is PRECISION. This term is derived from the Latin *præcidere, to cut off*; and the property so called consists in the use of such words as exactly convey the meaning, and nothing more. Suppose we mean to say, " Cæsar displayed great courage on the battle-field"; were we to use *fortitude* instead of *courage*, we should violate Precision, because the former quality is displayed in supporting pain, the latter in meeting danger. We should be guilty of the same fault, if we were to employ both words,—" Cæsar displayed great *courage* and *fortitude* on the battle-field,"—because it would be saying more than we mean.

§ 360. Precision is most frequently violated by a want of discrimination in the use of synonymous terms; as in the example above, when *fortitude* is substituted for *courage*. One

---

§ 359. What is the third essential property of style? From what is the word *precision* derived? In what does the quality so called consist? Illustrate this with the sentence, "Cæsar displayed great courage on the battle-field."

§ 360. How is precision most frequently violated? When is one word said to be the

word is said to be the synonyme of another, when it means the same thing or nearly the same: as, *enough*, and *sufficient*, *active*, *brisk*, *agile*, and *nimble*. In such synonymous terms our language abounds, in consequence of its having received additions from many different sources. While a very few of these differ so imperceptibly that they may be regarded as almost identical in signification, by far the greater part are distinguished by delicate shades of meaning; and their discriminate use at once denotes the scholar and imparts the finest effect to composition.

The habit of using words accurately begets the habit of thinking accurately; the student, therefore, when in the act of composing, can not be too careful in the choice of the words he employs,—can not make a better use of his time than in examining and comparing the various synonymous expressions that present themselves to his mind, and in thus enabling himself to select from among them such as exactly convey his meaning, and nothing more or less. As aids in this improving mental exercise, he will find Webster's Quarto Dictionary and Crabb's "English Synonymes" specially useful. To illustrate this subject, a few synonymes are here defined in contrast, from which the importance of using them aright will be apparent.

I. *Custom, habit.* *Custom* is the frequent repetition of the same act; *habit* is the effect of such repetition. By the *custom* of early rising, we form *habits* of diligence. *Custom* applies to men collectively or individually; *habit* applies to them as individuals only. Every nation has its *customs*; every man has his peculiar *habits*.

II. *Surprise, astonish, amaze, confound.* We are *surprised* at what is unexpected; *astonished*, at what is more unexpected, and at what is vast or great; *amazed*, at what is incomprehensible, or what unfavorably affects our interests; *confounded*, at what is shocking or terrible. We are *surprised* to meet a friend, at an hour when he is generally engaged at home; we are *astonished* to meet one whom we supposed to be across the ocean; we are *amazed* to meet a person of whose death we have been informed; we are *confounded* to hear that a family of our acquaintance have been poisoned.

III. *Abhor, detest.* *To abhor* implies strong dislike; *to detest* com

---

synonyme of another? Why are synonymous terms numerous in our language? What is said respecting their shades of meaning? How can an examination into these delicate differences of signification benefit the student? Show and illustrate the difference between *custom* and *habit*; between *surprise*, *astonish*, *amaze*, and *confound*; be

bines with this dislike an equally strong disapprobation. We *abhor* being in debt; we *detest* treachery.

IV. *Only, alone.* *Only* imports that there is no other of the same kind; *alone* imports being accompanied by no other. An *only* child is one that has neither brother nor sister; a child *alone*, is one that is left by itself. There is a difference, therefore, in precise language, between the two phrases, "virtue only makes us happy," and "virtue alone makes us happy." The former implies that nothing else can do it; the latter, that virtue itself, unaccompanied with other advantages, is sufficient to ensure our happiness.

V. *Entire, complete.* A thing is *entire* when it wants none of its parts; *complete*, when it lacks none of its appendages. A man may have an *entire* house to himself, and yet not have one *complete* apartment.

VI. *Enough, sufficient.* *Enough*, properly speaking, has reference to the quantity one wishes to have; *sufficient*, to that which one needs. The former, therefore, generally implies more than the latter. The miser may have *sufficient*, but never has *enough*.

VII. *Avow, acknowledge, confess.* Each of these words implies the admission of a fact, but under different circumstances. *To avow* supposes the person to glory in the admission; *to acknowledge* implies a small fault, for which the acknowledgment compensates; *to confess* is used in connection with greater offences. A patriot *avows* his opposition to a tyrant, and is applauded; a gentleman *acknowledges* his mistake, and is forgiven; a prisoner *confesses* his crime, and is punished.

§ 361. The precise writer rejects all unnecessary words; he does not, for instance, say, that such a thing cannot *possibly* be, or must *necessarily* be, because *possibly* and *necessarily* imply nothing more than *can* and *must*. He does not, after having made a statement, repeat it without any modification of the idea, in several different clauses, imagining that he is thereby adding to what has been said. Such unmeaning repetitions are called *redundancies*, and no other fault so enfeebles style.

Addison, at the beginning of his *Cato*, is guilty of several gross redundancies:—

---

tween *abhor* and *detest;* between *only* and *alone;* between *entire* and *complete;* between *enough* and *sufficient;* between *avow, acknowledge*, and *confess.*

§ 361. What is said of the precise writer? What are redundancies? What is their effect on style? Who is mentioned as guilty of this fault? Repeat the passage, and

> "The dawn is overcast, the morning lowers,
> And heavily in clouds brings on the day,
> The great, the important day, big with the fate
> Of Cato and of Rome."

In the first two lines, the same sentiment is three times repeated in different words. "The dawn is overcast," means no more than "the morning lowers"; and both these expressions denote precisely the same thing as the line that follows. In the third line, three synonymous expressions appear,—" the *great*, the *important* day, *big with the fate.*"

In revising a composition, special regard must be had to Precision. Unnecessary words (and sometimes many will be found) must be unsparingly pruned out. The best method of avoiding such superfluities, or of breaking up a loose style, when once formed, is to endeavor, before writing, to get a well-defined conception of the subject. Redundancies often proceed from the writer's not having any precise idea himself of what he wants to say.

§ 362. Another violation of Precision consists in the affected substitution for the names of persons or the terms which we ordinarily apply to abstract ideas, circumlocutions expressive of some attribute, which may belong to another object, and is therefore liable to be mistaken by the reader. Thus, Shaftesbury, devoting several pages of one of his works to Aristotle, names him only as "the master critic", "the mighty genius and judge of art", "the prince of critics", "the grand master of art", and "the consummate philologist",—leaving the reader to infer who is meant by these high-sounding titles. So, in another passage, without designating them by name, he alludes to Homer, Socrates, and Plato, respectively, as "the grand poetic sire", "the philosophical patriarch", and "his disciple of noble birth and lofty genius".

In like manner, when the proper name has been mentioned, an allusion to the same individual by means of a circumlocution is apt to give the reader a wrong impression; as, "Literary and scientific men hastened to the court of Charlemagne, anxious to secure the favor of the greatest

---

point out the redundancies. In revising a composition, to what must special regard be had? What is the best method of avoiding superfluities and breaking up a loose style? From what do redundancies often proceed?

§ 362. What other violation of precision is here alluded to? Show how Shaftesbury violates this principle. When the proper name has been mentioned, what is the effect of alluding to the same individual by means of a circumlocution? Illustrate this.

monarch of his age." A reader ignorant of history might suppose that it was not Charlemagne's favor, but that of some other monarch residing at his court, that they were desirous of securing. A slight change will prevent the possibility of mistake as to the meaning: "Anxious to secure the favor of Charlemagne, literary and scientific men hastened to his court."

EXERCISE.

In the following sentences, when two synonymes are presented within brackets, select the proper one; when Precision is violated, correct the error :—

1. He [only, or alone?] of all their number had sufficient resolution to declare himself ready to proceed.—This circumstance [only, or alone?] is sufficient to prove the worthlessness of the criticism.—On questioning them, they all denied knowledge of the fact, except one [only, or alone?], in whose countenance I traced evident signs of guilt. 2. As soon as you have heard [enough, or sufficient?] music, we will adjourn to the other apartment.—I am obliged to remain here, because I have not [enough, or sufficient?] money to proceed on my journey. 3. We [avow, acknowledge, or confess?] an omission of duty;—we —— a debt;— the criminal cannot be persuaded to ——; — the martyr ——s his faith. 4. The equipment of the ship is [entire, or complete?]. 5. A being who has nothing to pardon or forgive in himself may reward every man according to his works. 6. The physician enjoined temperance and abstinence on his patient. 7. There was no tenant in the house; it was [vacant, or empty?].—The house was stripped of its furniture; it was entirely [vacant, or empty?].—Mr. D.'s death has left a [vacant, or empty?] seat in the Board. 8. Paley has said that man is a bundle of [customs, or habits?].—Many great men have the [custom, or habit?] of taking snuff.—The [custom, or habit?] of going to church may produce [customs, or habits?] of piety. 9. The general said that he [received, or accepted?] with pride and satisfaction this token of their friendship. 10. Though numerous applications were made for the prisoner's [forgiveness, or pardon?], they were all [unsuccessful, or ineffectual?]. 11. The pleasures of imagination are more preferable than those of sense. 12. This is the chiefest objection that I have to such a course. 13. No man of spirit can acquiesce in, and remain satisfied with, this decision. 14. This wavering and unsettled policy cannot be too strongly condemned. 15. I am certain and confident that the account I have given is correct and true. 16. He then made his statement and related his story. 17. We rested beneath the umbrageous shadow of a shady oak, and then again resumed our journey anew. 18. The brightness of prosperity, shining on the anticipations of futurity, casts the shadows of adversity into the shade, and causes the prospects of the future to look bright. 19. We often conjure up grounds of apprehension, and give ourselves unnecessary uneasiness. 20. The magistrate questioned the prisoner minutely and examined him at length. 21. Now, if the fabric of the mind or temper appeared to us such as it really is; if we saw it impossible to remove hence any one good or orderly affection, or to in-

troduce any ill or disorderly one, without drawing on, in some degree that dissolute state which, at its height, is confessed to be so miserable,— it would then, undoubtedly, be confessed, that since no ill, immoral, or unjust action, can be committed without either a new inroad and breach on the temper and passions, or a further advancing of that execution already done; whoever did ill, or acted in prejudice to his integrity, good nature, or worth, would, of necessity, act with greater cruelty towards himself, than he who scrupled not to swallow what was poisonous, or who, with his own hands, should voluntarily mangle or wound his outward form or constitution, natural limbs, or body. 22. Constantine was constantly receiving presents, which were forwarded from all quarters to the great Christian emperor.

LESSON LIX.

CLEARNESS, OR PERSPICUITY.

§ 363. THE fourth essential property of style is CLEARNESS, or PERSPICUITY; which consists in such a use and arrangement of words and clauses, as at once distinctly indicate the meaning of the writer or speaker. To a certain extent, this quality involves the three already considered; that is, other things being equal, the greater the Purity, Propriety, and Precision, of a sentence, the clearer it will be. Yet these properties may belong, in a high degree, to a style which is far from perspicuous. Something more is necessary to constitute the quality under consideration.

§ 364. The faults opposed to clearness are,
 I. *Obscurity*, which consists in the use of words and constructions from which it is difficult to gather any meaning at all.
 II. *Equivocation*, which consists in the use of words susceptible, in the connection in which they are placed, of more than one interpretation.

---

§ 363. What is the fourth essential property of style? In what does it consist? What does clearness, to a certain extent, involve?
§ 364. Enumerate and define the three faults opposed to clearness.

III. *Ambiguity*, which consists in such an arrangement of words or clauses as leaves the reader in doubt between two different significations.

§ 365. *Obscurity.*—Nothing disgusts us more with a composition than to find difficulty in arriving at its meaning. Whatever effect the thoughts it embodies might have produced had they been clearly expressed, is inevitably lost, while the reader is pondering its intricate periods. Obscurity results from various causes, of which the principal are as follows:—

I. *An improper ellipsis.*

This figure, as we have seen in § 317, authorizes the omission of words necessary to the construction, but not to the sense. Whenever the omission of a word renders the meaning of a sentence unintelligible, the ellipsis becomes improper. A writer in *The Guardian* uses this expression: "He is inspired with a true sense of that function." The meaning is not intelligible till we put in the words improperly left out: "He is inspired with a true sense of *the importance of* that function." "Arbitrary power", says another, "I look upon as a greater evil than anarchy itself, as much as a savage is a happier state of life than a galley-slave." We can not properly call a savage or a galley-slave a state of life, though we may with propriety compare their conditions. The obscurity is removed by doing away with the ellipsis: "as much as *the state of* a savage is happier than *that of* a galley-slave."

II. *A bad arrangement.*

Some sentences have their parts so arranged that, on commencing them, we imagine they will convey a certain meaning, which is quite different from what we find they really signify when we get to their close. Thus, in *The Spectator* the following sentence occurs: "I have hopes that when Will confronts him, and *all the ladies in whose behalf he engages him* cast kind looks and wishes of success at their champion, he will have some shame." On hearing the first part of the sentence, we naturally imagine that Will is to confront all the ladies; but we soon find that it is necessary to construe this clause with the verb *cast*. To

---

§ 365. What feeling is produced in the reader by a composition difficult to be understood? What is the first source of obscurity? When is an ellipsis improper? Give examples of improper ellipses. What is the second source of obscurity? What false impression do we receive from some sentences whose parts are improperly arranged? Illustrate this error from The Spectator, and show how it may be corrected. What

correct the error, the whole sentence must be remodelled, or we may simply introduce the adverb *when* after *and:* "I have hopes that when Will confronts him, and *when* all the ladies," &c.

The words most frequently misplaced in such a way as to involve obscurity are adverbs, particularly *only* and *not only.* If these words are separated from what they are intended to modify, the meaning of the whole sentence is obscured. "He not only owns a house, but also a large farm." *Not only,* as it now stands, modifies the verb *owns;* and from the beginning of the sentence one naturally supposes that another verb is to follow,—that he not only *owns* the house, but *lives* in it, or something of the kind. Whereas, *not only* is intended to modify *house,* and should therefore be placed immediately before it: "He owns. not only a house, but also a large farm."

Sometimes a faulty arrangement of adjuncts or clauses produces a ludicrous combination of ideas; as when we say, "Here is a horse ploughing with one eye", instead of, "Here is a horse with one eye ploughing." From the former sentence we would infer that the horse was turning up the ground with one of his organs of vision. So, in the following: "He was at a window in Litchfield, where a party of royalists had fortified themselves, taking a view of the cathedral." The royalists would hardly go to the trouble of fortifying themselves merely for the purpose of taking a view of the cathedral. It should read thus: "He was at a window in Litchfield, taking a view of the cathedral, where a party," &c.

The sentences given above as examples would be *ambiguous* according to our definition of that term, if there were any other than an absurd meaning to be gleaned from the construction which we first naturally put upon them. As this is not the case, however, they fall under the head we are now considering,—*obscurity.* It may be argued that, in these and similar examples, the obscurity will quickly be removed if the reader uses the least reflection. But this is not sufficient; we must have no obscurity to be removed. Clearness requires, according to Quintilian, "not that the reader *may* understand if he will, but that he *must* understand whether he will or not".

III. *The use of the same word in different senses.*

---

words are most frequently misplaced in such a way as to involve obscurity? What is the effect of separating them from what they are intended to modify? Give an example of this error, show how it occasions obscurity, and correct it. What does a faulty arrangement of adjuncts and clauses sometimes produce? Give examples, and correct the errors they contain. Why do we not rank these cases under the head of ambiguous constructions? What may be argued with respect to them? Is this sufficient? What does Quintilian say respecting clearness? What is the third source of obscurity? Illus-

CLEARNESS, OR PERSPICUITY.

A word should not be used in different senses in the same sentence. Thus, "He presents *more* and *more* convincing arguments than his adversary." Here the word *more* first occurs as an adjective, and is presently, to the great confusion of the reader, repeated as an adverb, the sign of the comparative degree. It should be: "He presents *more numerous* and more convincing arguments than his adversary",—*more* being here in each case an adverb.

The words oftenest used in this way are pronouns, particularly the personals and relatives. Depending for their signification on the substantives for which they stand, if they are used with reference to different objects, their meaning is of course varied, and this should be strictly avoided in the progress of a sentence. Examples of this fault follow. "*They* were persons of moderate intellects, even before *they* were impaired by *their* passions." Here, the first *they* refers to certain persons; the second, to the noun *intellects*, while the same pronoun in the possessive case, *their*, refers again to the persons in question. To correct the error, we must either remodel the whole, or (though it sounds stiff in so short a sentence) alter the second *they* to *the latter :*—"They were persons of moderate intellects, even before *the latter* were impaired by their passions." Again: "Lysias promised *his* father that *he* would never forget *his* advice." There is no equivocation here, for it is evident at once that, though the first *his*, and *he*, refer to Lysias, the second *his* has reference to the father; yet such constructions are highly objectionable. This sentence, as well as others like it, is most neatly corrected by substituting the exact words of the speaker for the substance of what he said; as, "Lysias promised his father, "I will never forget *thy* advice."

Not only does this incorrect use of pronouns produce obscurity, it is also inconsistent with Harmony and Strength. In composing, therefore, it is well constantly to bear in mind the rule,—*Do not make the same pronoun refer to different objects in the same sentence.* This is sometimes a difficult rule to follow, as every careful writer must have found. Reinhard says, in his *Memoirs*, "I have always had considerable difficulty in making a proper use of pronouns. Indeed, I have taken great pains so to use them, that all ambiguity by the reference to a wrong antecedent should be impossible, and yet have often failed in the attempt." Notwithstanding this difficulty, the principle involved is of such importance that it should be carried out, even if the whole train of thought

---

trate this, and show how the error may be corrected. What words are oftenest used in this way? How is it that they may bear different significations? Give an example. When such an error occurs in a sentence containing an indirect quotation, how may it be corrected? What other faults besides obscurity does this incorrect use of pronouns involve? Repeat the rule. What does Reinhard say respecting it? What is the fourth

has to be put in a different form at a considerable expense of time and trouble.

IV. *Complicated sentential structure.*

When the structure of a sentence is much involved, especially when its parts differ in form, or when long or abrupt parentheses are introduced, obscurity is apt to result. This fault is more common with old writers than among those of the present day. It violates, not only the rules of Clearness, but also those of Unity; under which latter subject it will be illustrated, and the best modes of correction will be pointed out.

V. *Long sentences.*

These are always a source of obscurity, unless the members composing them are similar in their structure. There is a tendency in most young writers to make their sentences too long. The other extreme is safer than this; but either is to be avoided. The most pleasing style in this respect is one characterized by variety; one in which long and short sentences are judiciously alternated.

VI. *Technical Terms.*

Terms belonging to a particular trade, business, or science, not being understood by the generality of readers, should be strictly avoided, especially in poetry. Dryden, however, was of the contrary opinion. "As those," says he, "who in a logical disputation keep to general terms would hide a fallacy, so those who do it in any poetical description would veil their ignorance." Accordingly, in his translation of the Æneid, he indulges in the following technicalities:—

> "*Tack* to the *larboard*, and *stand off* to sea,
> *Veer starboard* sea and land."

Technical terms are allowable only in scientific treatises, where we expect to find them; and in comedy and fiction, where they are sometimes introduced into dialogue for the purpose of illustrating individual peculiarities.

§ 366. *Equivocation.*—To avoid this fault, it is not neces-

---

source of obscurity? What is meant by this? What besides a want of clearness results from such involved constructions? What is the fifth source of obscurity? In what case only is a long sentence perspicuous? In whom is there a tendency to long sentences? What is the best rule, as regards length of sentences? What is the sixth source of obscurity? Why should technical terms be avoided? What was Dryden's opinion on this point? Show how he has acted on this opinion in his translation of the Æneid. In what compositions are technical terms allowable?

§ 366. What is meant by an equivocal term? When may such a term be used, and

sary that we reject all words of more than one signification; for, in that case, our vocabulary would become exceedingly limited, and by far the greater part of our language would be utterly useless. But a regard for Perspicuity requires us to reject an equivocal term except when its connection with other words in any particular case distinctly indicates which of its significations, as there used, it bears. This connection will almost always determine the meaning so clearly that the true sense will be the only one suggested. Thus, the word *pound* signifies both the sum of *twenty shillings sterling* and *sixteen ounces avoirdupois*. Yet, if a person tells me that he rents a house for fifty *pounds* a year, or that he has bought fifty *pounds* of meat, there will be no lack of perspicuity,—the idea of weight will not present itself to my mind in the one case, or that of money in the other. Sometimes, however, the connection is insufficient to determine the meaning; and the expression, being thus susceptible of a two-fold interpretation, must be avoided. Examples of the different kinds of equivocation are presented below, together with the best modes of correction

I. "I am persuaded that neither death nor life will be able to separate us from the love of God." Here *of* is equivocal; we cannot tell whether the meaning is the love which we bear to God, or that which He bears to us. If the former is intended, it should be "our love to God"; if the latter, "God's love to us". So, "the reformation of Luther" means either the change wrought *in* him, or that brought about *by* him. The latter signification may be denoted by commencing *reformation* with a capital; as, in this sense, it is an important historical event.

II. "They were both more ancient than Zoroaster, or Zerdusht." Here, *or* is equivocal. This conjunction connects either equivalents or substitutes. Hence, the reader unacquainted with Persian history may be at a loss to know whether Zoroaster and Zerdusht are the same person or different ones. According to the system of punctuation laid down in this volume, the comma before *or* denotes that they are

---

when must it be avoided? What generally determines the meaning of an equivocal word? Give an example.

Quote a sentence in which *of* is equivocal; point out the two interpretations of which it is susceptible; and show what alterations should be made to express each meaning clearly. Treat in this same manner a sentence in which *or* is equivocal; one

one and the same, and its omission would signify that two persons were intended. Yet, as many are unacquainted with punctuation, it is best, when this conjunction is used in the latter sense,—that is, as a connective of substitutes,—to introduce its correlative *either* before the first of the words so connected. " They were both more ancient than *either* Zoroaster *or* Zerdusht ", would denote that they were different persons, beyond the possibility of mistake.

III. " I have long since learned to like nothing but what you do." *Do* is equivocal; we can not tell whether it is an auxiliary or a principal verb,—whether the meaning is *to like nothing but what you* like, or *nothing but what you* do. If the former is intended, we should change *do* to *like*, or else say *nothing but what* pleases you.

IV. " Lysias promised his father that he would never forget his friends." Properly speaking, the last *his* refers to the same antecedent as the first; and the meaning is, that he would never forget his own (Lysias') friends. If this is the author's meaning, the sentence is grammatically correct; yet, as it may be misunderstood by those who do not look closely at grammatical relations, it would be well to alter the form according to the suggestion touching an analogous case in § 365: " Lysias promised his father, ' I will never forget *thy* [or *my*] friends.' "

V. " He aimed at nothing less than the crown." Owing to the equivocal expression *nothing less than*, this sentence may denote either, " Nothing was less aimed at by him than the crown ; " or, " Nothing inferior to the crown could satisfy his ambition."

§ 367. *Ambiguity.*—This fault, also, leaves the reader in doubt between two meanings; but this doubt is occasioned, not by the use of equivocal terms, but by a faulty arrangement of words or clauses. Both equivocation and ambiguity, but particularly the latter, are faults of frequent occurrence in composition; from the fact that a writer whose mind is pre-occupied with one of the significations of an expression, which he designs it to convey, is not likely to notice that it also bears another. The commonest varieties of ambiguity are illustrated in the following examples :—

I. The proper place for a relative pronoun is immediately after its

---

in which *do* is equivocal; one in which *his* is equivocal; one in which the expression *nothing less than* is equivocal.

§ 367. By what is ambiguity occasioned? What renders it a fault of frequent occurrence? What part of speech, improperly placed, often occasions ambiguity? Where should the relative pronoun stand? Correct the sentence, " A servant will obey a mas

antecedent; and, if it occupies any other place, the sentence, as a general rule, should be so changed as to allow it to stand in that position. Thus, instead of, "A servant will obey a master's orders whom he loves," we should have, "A servant will obey the orders of a master whom he loves." Yet, as this principle is constantly violated in composition, we are sometimes at a loss to determine to which of two antecedent substantives a relative belongs. "Solomon, the son of David, *who* built the temple at Jerusalem, was a wise and powerful monarch."—"Solomon, the son of David, *who* was persecuted by Saul, was a wise and powerful monarch."—In these two sentences, *who* is similarly situated; yet in the former it relates to Solomon, and in the latter to David. A perspicuous writer would avoid the possibility of misconception by changing both:—"Solomon, the son of David and builder of the temple at Jerusalem, was a wise and powerful monarch."—"Solomon, whose father David was persecuted by Saul, was" &c.

II. The peculiar position of a substantive sometimes occasions ambiguity, particularly in poetry, when the object is placed before the verb. In the sentence, "And thus the son the fervent sire addressed," we are unable to say whether the son or the sire was the speaker. The meaning may be fixed in either way by substituting *his* for *the*, before the object; for, according to the idiom of our language, the possessive pronoun is, in such cases, more properly joined to the regimen of a verb than to its nominative. If the son was the speaker, the line should run, "And thus the son *his* fervent sire addressed;" if he was the party spoken to, "And thus his son the fervent sire addressed."

LESSON LX.

EXERCISE ON CLEARNESS.

In the following sentences, correct such expressions as are not perspicuous:—

1. He talks all the way up stairs to a visit. 2. God begins His cure by caustics, by incisions and instruments of vexation, to try if the disease that will not yield to the allectives of cordials and perfumes, fric-

---

tor's orders whom he loves." Show how the relative *who*, similarly placed in two different sentences, may refer to different antecedents. How may these sentences be altered, to make the reference clear? In poetry, from what does ambiguity sometimes proceed? Give an example, and show how the meaning may be determined.

tions and baths, may be forced out by deleterics, scarifications, and more salutary, but less pleasing, physic. 3. Some productions of nature rise in value according as they more or less resemble art. 4. The farmer went to his neighbor, and told him that his cattle were in his field. 5. He may be said to have saved the life of a citizen, and consequently entitled to the reward. 6. I perceived it had been scoured with half an eye. 7. The love of a parent is one of the strongest passions implanted in the heart. 8. So obscure are Carlyle's sentences that nine tenths of his readers do not receive any idea from them. [*Equivocal:—does it mean that only one tenth of his readers understand them; or that, though nine tenths may not do so, eight tenths may? Alter the sentence in two ways, so that it may perspicuously express both these ideas.*] 9. Few kings have been more energetic than Menes, or [*equivocal*] Misraim. 10. The young man did not want natural talents; but the father of him was a coxcomb, who affected being a fine gentleman so unmercifully, that he could not endure in his sight, or the frequent mention of, one who was his son, growing into manhood, and thrusting him out of the gay world. 11. We are naturally inclined to praise who praise us, and to flatter who flatter us. 12. The rising tomb a lofty column bore. [*Ambiguous:— which bore the other?*] 13. He advanced against the old man, imitating his address, his pace, and career, as well as the vigor of his horse and his own skill would allow. 14. Their rebuke had the effect intended. [*Equivocal:—did they give the rebuke, or receive it?*] 15. Whom chance misled his mother to destroy. [*Ambiguous:—was the mother the destroyer or the destroyed?*] 16. This work has been overlooked [*equivocal*] by the most eminent critics. 17. You ought to contemn all the wit in the world against you. 18. The clerk told his employer, whatever he did, he could not please him. 19. Claudius was canonized among the gods, who scarcely deserved the name of a man. 20. The Latin tongue, in its purity, was never in England. 21. The lady was sewing with a Roman nose. 22. Here I saw two men digging a well with straw hats. 23. We may have more, but we can not have more satisfactory, evidence. 24. Dr. Prideaux used to relate that, when he brought the copy of his "Connection of the Old and New Testaments" to the bookseller, *he* told *him* it was a dry subject, and the printing could not be safely ventured upon unless he could enliven the work with a little humor. 25. The sharks who prey upon the inadvertency of young heirs are more pardonable than *those who* trespass upon the good opinion of *those who* treat them with respect. 26. Dryden makes a handsome observation on Ovid's writing a letter from Dido to Æneas, in the following words. [*Ambiguous:—were the words here referred to those of Dryden's observation or those of Dido's letter?*] 27. Most of the hands were asleep in their berths, when the vessel shipped a sea that carried away our pinnace and binnacle. Our dead-lights were in, or we should have filled. The mainmast was so sprung, that we were obliged to fish it, and bear away for the nearest port. 28. This occurs in Ben Jonson's works, a prominent dramatist contemporary with Shakspeare. 29. D's fortune is equal to half of E's fortune, which is a thousand dollars. [*Ambiguous:—does E's fortune, or a half of it, amount to a thousand dollars?*] 30. My Christian and surname begin and end with the same letters. [*Ambiguous:—does the Christian name begin with the same letter that the surname begins with; and end with the same letter that the surname ends with; as, in Andrew Askew? or does the Christian name* end with the same letter with which it begins, and the surname also end with the same letter with which it begins; as, in *Hezekiah Thrift?* or, lastly, are all these four letters, the first and the last of each name the same; as, in *Norman Nelson?* 31. The good man not only deserves the respect but the love of his fellow-beings. 32. Charlemagne patronized not only learned men, but also established several educational institutions. 33. Sixtus the Fourth was, if I mistake not, a great collector of books, at least.

LESSON LXI.

STRENGTH.

§ 368. THE fifth essential property of a good style is STRENGTH; which consists in such a use and arrangement of words as make a deep impression on the mind of the reader or hearer.

§ 369. The first requisite of Strength is the rejection of all superfluous words, which constitutes, as we have seen, one of the elements of Precision also. Whatever adds nothing to the meaning of a sentence takes from its Strength; and, whether it be simply a word, a clause, or a member, should be rejected. In the following passages, the words in italics convey no additional meaning, and, consequently, a regard for Strength requires their omission:—" *Being* satisfied with what he has achieved, he attempts nothing further."—" *If I had not been absent* if I had been here, this would not have happened."— " The very first discovery of it strikes the mind with inward joy, *and spreads delight through all its faculties.*"

§ 370. The second principle to be observed by those who aim at Strength of style, has reference to the use of relatives,

---

§ 368. What is the fifth essential property of style? In what does it consist?
§ 369. What is the first requisite of strength? What is the effect of words which add nothing to the meaning of a sentence? Give examples.
§ 370. To what does the second principle refer? By what are parts of sentences

conjunctions, and prepositions, which, indicating the connection and relation of words, are constantly occurring.

I. Parts of sentences are connected by either a conjunction or a relative pronoun, *not by both*. In the following sentence, the connection is made by *and*, and *who* should therefore be rejected: "He was a man of fine abilities, and *who* lost no opportunity of improving them by study." Between two relative clauses, however, a conjunction is generally employed; as, "Cicero, whom the profligate feared, *but* who was honored by the upright," &c. The conjunction is also introduced even when the relative and its verb are suppressed in one of the clauses, as in the commencement of the sentence from Swift, given below. Care must be taken not to use the relative for the conjunction, or the conjunction for the relative; of which latter fault, Swift is guilty in the following sentence:—

"There is no talent so useful towards rising in the world, or which puts men more out of the reach of fortune, than that quality generally possessed by the dullest sort of people, *and* is, in common language, called discretion."

Here *and* should be *which*. It will be observed, also, that the words *which is* are understood after *talent*, near the commencement of the sentence, and that the conjunction *or* is therefore introduced to connect the first clause with that which follows.

II. The too frequent use of *and* must be avoided. Not only when employed to introduce a sentence, but also when often repeated during its progress, this conjunction greatly enfeebles style. Such is its effect in the following sentence from Sir William Temple, in which it is used no less than eight times:—

"The Academy set up by Cardinal Richelieu, to amuse the wits of that age and country, and divert them from raking into his politics and ministry, brought this into vogue; and the French wits have, for this last age, been wholly turned to the refinement of their style and language; and, indeed, with such success that it can hardly be equalled, and runs equally through their verse and their prose."

When the object is to present a quick succession of spirited images, the conjunction is often entirely omitted with fine effect, by a figure called by grammarians *Asyndeton*. This is illustrated in Cæsar's celebrated *veni, vidi, vici*, and constitutes the chief feature of the style of Sallust.

---

connected? Should both the relative and the conjunction be used for this purpose in the same connection? In what case is the relative alone insufficient to make the connection? What is the fault in the sentence quoted from Swift? What conjunction must not be repeated too often? From whom is a sentence quoted, which is faulty in this respect? What is meant by *asyndeton*? When is this figure used with fine

On the other hand, when we are making an enumeration in which it is important that the transition from one object to another should not be too rapid, but that each should appear distinct from the rest and by itself occupy the mind for a moment, the conjunction may be repeated with peculiar advantage. Such repetition is called *Polysyndeton;* it is exemplified in the following sentence of St. Paul's:—

" I am persuaded that neither death, nor life, nor angels, nor principalities, nor powers, nor things present, nor things to come, nor height, nor depth, nor any other creature, shall be able to separate us from the love of God."

III. What is called the splitting of particles,—that is, the separation of a preposition from the noun which it governs,—is always to be avoided. This fault occurs in the following sentence: "Though virtue borrows no assistance from, yet it may often be accompanied by, the advantages of fortune." No one can read these lines without perceiving their decided lack of Strength and Harmony. A slight change will greatly improve their effect: "Though virtue borrows no assistance from the advantages of fortune, yet it may often be accompanied by them."

IV. Avoid, on ordinary occasions, the common expletive *there*, as used in the following sentence:—"There is nothing which disgusts us sooner than the empty pomp of language." The sentiment is expressed more simply and strongly thus: "Nothing disgusts us sooner", &c. This expletive form is proper only when used to introduce an important proposition.

§ 371. A third means of promoting the Strength of a sentence is to dispose of the important word or words in that place where they will make the greatest impression. What this place is, depends on the nature and length of the sentence. Sometimes, it is at the commencement, as in the following from Addison; *" The pleasures of the imagination,* taken in their full extent, are not so gross as those of sense, nor so refined as those of the understanding." In other

---

effect? In what sentence of Cæsar's is it illustrated? In whose writings does it constantly recur? What is *polysyndeton?* When may it be used with advantage? Repeat a sentence from Scripture, in which it occurs. What is meant by the splitting of particles? What effect has it on style? Repeat a sentence in which this fault occurs, and show how to correct it. In what cases is the expletive form *there is* proper, and where should it be avoided?

§ 371. As a third means of promoting strength, where should the important word or words be placed? In what position will they make the greatest impression? Where

cases, it will be found of advantage to suspend the sense for a time, and bring the important term at the close of the period. "On whatever side," says Pope, "we contemplate Homer, what principally strikes us is his *wonderful invention*." No rule can be given on this subject; a comparison of different arrangements is the only means of ascertaining, in any particular case, which is the best. It will, therefore, be well for a writer, when a sentence which he has composed seems weak, to try whether he can not improve it by varying the position of the important words.

But, whatever position the emphatic word or words may occupy, it is of primary importance that they be disencumbered of less significant terms; which, if presented in too close connection, divert the mind from the prominent idea or object on which it should be allowed to dwell. The difference of effect will be evident on comparing one of Shaftesbury's sentences, in which a variety of adverbs and adverbial phrases are skilfully introduced, and a sentence composed of the same words, less forcibly, though not ungrammatically, arranged.

As written.—"If, whilst they [poets] profess only to please, they secretly advise and give instruction, they may now, perhaps, as well as formerly, be esteemed, with justice, the best and most honorable among authors."

As altered.—If, whilst they profess to please only, they advise and give instruction secretly, they may be esteemed the best and most honorable among authors, with justice, perhaps, now as well as formerly.

§ 372. Fourthly, Strength requires that, when the members of a sentence differ in length, the shorter should have precedence of the longer; and, when they are of unequal force, that the weaker be placed before the stronger. Both of these principles are violated in the following sentence: "In this state of mind, every employment of life be-

---

do they stand in the sentence quoted from Addison? Where, in that taken from Pope? What course is suggested to the writer, when he finds that he has composed a feeble sentence? Wherever the emphatic words are placed, what is of primary importance? From whom is a sentence quoted in illustration?

§ 372. What does strength require, as regards the position of members that differ in length or force? Repeat a sentence in which these principles are violated, and show how it may be corrected. What figure consists in an arrangement similar

comes an oppressive burden, and every object appears gloomy.' How much more forcible does it become when the shorter and weaker member is placed first: "In this state of mind, every object appears gloomy, and every employment of life becomes an oppressive burden."

This arrangement of the members of a sentence constitutes what has already been defined among the rhetorical figures as Climax. What is most emphatic is brought last, in order that a strong impression may be left on the reader's mind. From this rule the next naturally follows.

§ 373. Avoid closing a sentence with an adverb, a preposition, or any small unaccented word. Besides the violation of Harmony involved in placing a monosyllable where we are accustomed to find a swelling sound, there is a peculiar feebleness arising from the fact that the mind naturally pauses to consider the import of the word last presented, and is disappointed when, as in the case of a preposition, it has no significance of its own, but merely indicates the relation between words that have preceded it. "He is one whom good men are glad to be acquainted with." It will be readily seen how much is gained by a simple transposition: "He is one with whom good men are glad to be acquainted."

The same principle holds good in the case of adverbs. "Such things were not allowed formerly", is feeble compared with, "Formerly such things were not allowed." When, however, an adverb is emphatic, it is often, according to § 371, introduced at the close of a period with fine effect; as in the following sentence of Bolingbroke's: "In their prosperity, my friends shall never hear of me; in their adversity, always."

This principle, also, requires us to avoid terminating a sentence with a succession of unaccented words; such as, *with it, in it, on it,* &c. "This is a proposition which I did not expect; and I must ask the

---

to that here prescribed? Why is it best to place last that which is most emphatic?

§ 373. With what must we avoid closing a sentence? What is the effect of terminating a period in this way? Give an example of this error, and show how to correct it. With what part of speech, as a general rule, must a sentence not be closed? Exemplify, and then correct, this error. In what case may an adverb close a period? Repeat a sentence of Bolingbroke's, in which one is so placed with fine effect. What else does this principle require us to avoid? Give an example.

privilege of reflecting on it." The last member would be more forcible thus: "and I must ask time for reflection."

§ 374. Lastly, when in different members' two objects are contrasted, a resemblance in language and construction increases the effect. The most striking comparisons are those in which this rule is observed. Thus, Pope, speaking of Homer and Virgil:—" Homer was the greater genius; Virgil the better artist: in the one, we most admire the man; in the other, the work. Homer hurries us with a commanding impetuosity; Virgil leads us with an attractive majesty. Homer scatters with a generous profusion; Virgil bestows with a careful magnificence."

We may further illustrate this point by placing side by side two sentences embodying the same thought, in one of which this rule is observed, while in the other it is disregarded.

Weak.—He embraced the cause of liberty faintly, and pursued it without resolution; he grew tired of it when he had much to hope, and gave it up when there was no ground for apprehension.

Strong.—He embraced the cause of liberty faintly, and pursued it irresolutely; he grew tired of it when he had much to hope, and gave it up when he had nothing to fear.

EXERCISE.

In the following sentences, make such corrections as are required by the rules for the promotion of Strength:—

1. He was a man of fine reputation, and enjoyed a high degree of popularity. 2. I went home, full of *a great many* serious reflections. 3. This is the principle which I referred *to*. 4. Catiline was *not only* an infamous traitor, but a profligate man. 5. We should constantly aim at perfection, though we may have no expectation of ever arriving *at it*. 6. It was a case of unpardonable breach of trust and gross disregard of official duty, *to say the least*. 7. We flatter ourselves with the belief that we have forsaken our passions, when they have forsaken us. 8. Every one that aims at greatness does not succeed (§ 371). 9. He appears to enjoy the *universal* esteem *of all men*. 10. Though virtue borrows no assistance from, yet it may often be accompanied by, the advantages of fortune. 11. As the strength of our cause does not depend upon, so neither is it to be decided by, any critical points of history, chronology, or language. 12. Alfred the Great, of England, was one of the most

---

§ 874. When in different members of a sentence two objects are contrasted, how is the effect increased? Show how Pope applies this principle in comparing Homer and Virgil.

remarkable and distinguished men that we read of in history. Though his efforts were unable and insufficient entirely to banish the darkness of the age he lived in, yet he greatly improved the condition of his countrymen, and was the means of doing much good to them. 13. Sensualists, by their gross excesses and frequent indulgences, debase their minds, enfeeble their bodies, and wear out their spirits (§ 372). 14. Ingratitude is not a crime that I am chargeable *with*, whatever other faults I may be guilty *of*. 15. The man of virtue and of honor will be trusted, and esteemed, and respected, and relied upon. 16. He has talents which are rapidly unfolding into life and vigor, and indomitable energies (§ 372). 17. It is absurd to think of judging either Ariosto or Spenser by precepts which they did not attend *to*. 18. Force was resisted by force, valor opposed by valor, and art encountered or eluded by similar address (§ 374). 19. It is a principle of our religion that we should not revenge ourselves on our enemies or take vengeance on our foes. 20. It is impossible for us to behold the divine works with coldness or indifference, or to survey so many beauties without a secret satisfaction and complacency. 21. The faith he professed, and which he became an apostle *of*, was not his invention. 22. The creed originated by Mohammed, and which almost all the Arabians and Persians believe *in*, is a mixture of Paganism, and Judaism, and Christianity. 23. There is not, in my opinion, a more pleasing and triumphant consideration in religion than this, of the perpetual progress which the soul makes towards the perfection of its nature, without ever arriving at a period *in it*. 24. Their idleness, and their luxury and pleasures, their criminal deeds, and their immoderate passions, and their timidity and baseness of mind, have dejected them to such a degree, that life itself is a burden, and they find no pleasure *in it*. 25. Shakspeare was a man of profound genius, and whose bold and striking thoughts must be admired in every age. 26. Avarice is a crime which wise men are often guilty *of*.

LESSON LXII.

HARMONY.

§ 375. THE sixth essential property of a good style is HARMONY; a term used to denote that smooth and easy flow which pleases the ear. Sound, though less important than sense, must not be disregarded, as a means of increasing the effect of what is spoken or written. Pleasing ideas can hardly be transmitted by harsh and disagreeable words; and, what-

---

§ 375. What is the sixth essential property of style? What does harmony denote?

ever emotion we are endeavoring to excite in the reader, we accomplish our object much more readily and effectually by availing ourselves of the peculiar sounds appropriate thereto.

Harmony consists in,

I. The use of euphonious, or pleasant-sounding, words.
II. The euphonious arrangement of words.
III. The adaptation of sound to the sense it expresses.

§ 376. The following words are to be avoided as inharmonious:—

I. Derivatives from long compound words; such as *barefacedness, wrong headedness, unsuccessfulness.*

II. Words containing a succession of consonant sounds; as, *form'dst, strik'st, flinched.*

III. Words containing a succession of unaccented syllables; as, *meteorological, derogatorily, mercinariness.*

IV. Words in which a short or unaccented syllable is repeated, or followed by another that closely resembles it; as, *holily, farriering.*

It must not be inferred that the writer is required, in all cases, to reject the words embraced under the classes just enumerated. Harsh terms are sometimes adapted to the subject, and express the meaning more forcibly than any others. They should be avoided, however, when euphony is desirable, and there are other terms which express the meaning with equal significance.

Those words are most agreeable to the ear, in which there is an intermixture of consonants and vowels; not so many of the former as to impede freedom of utterance, or such a recurrence of the latter as frequently to occasion hiatus.

§ 377. A regard for harmony also requires us, in the progress of a sentence, to avoid repeating a sound by employing the same word more than once, or using, in contiguous words, similar combinations of letters. This fault is known as *Tauology.* It may be corrected by substituting a synonyme for

---

How does sound compare in importance with sense? In what three particulars does harmony consist?

§ 376. Mention the four classes of words to be avoided as inharmonious. When are such words to be rejected? When may they be employed? What words are most agreeable to the ear?

§ 377. What is tautology? What is its effect? How may it be corrected? Give examples.

one of the words in which the repeated sound occurs. The unpleasant effect of tautology will be readily perceived in the following sentences:—" The general *ordered* the captain to *order* the soldiers to observe good *order*."—" We went *in an enormous* car." By a substitution of synonymes, as above suggested, we avoid the unpleasant repetitions in these passages, and increase their Strength.—" The general *directed* the captain to *command* the soldiers to observe good order."— " We went in *a large* car."

§ 378. Harmony, moreover, is deficient in sentences containing a succession of words of the same number of syllables; thus, " No kind of joy can long please us," is less harmonious than, " No *species* of joy can long *delight* us." So we improve the sound of the following sentence, in which there is a preponderance of dissyllables, by varying the length of the words. " She always displays a cheerful temper and pleasant humor."—" She *invariably exhibits* a *contented* and pleasant *disposition*."

§ 379. The second particular on which the Harmony of a sentence depends, is the proper arrangement of its parts. However well-chosen the words may be, or however euphonious in themselves, if they are unskilfully arranged the music of the sentence is lost.

In the harmonious structure of periods, no writer, ancient or modern, equals Cicero. It was a feature which he regarded as of the utmost importance to the effect of a composition, and to ensure the perfection of which he spared no labor. Indeed, his countrymen generally were more thorough in their investigations of this subject, and more careful in their observance of the rules pertaining thereto, than are the most polished of modern writers. Not only was their language susceptible of more melodious combinations than ours, but their ears were more delicately attuned, and were thus the means of affording them livelier pleasure from a well-rounded period. " I have often," says Cicero, " been witness to bursts of acclamation in the public assemblies when sentences

---

§ 378. In what sentences is harmony deficient? Give examples.
§ 379. What is the second particular on which the harmony of a sentence depends? Who surpasses all writers in the harmonious structure of his periods? How, as regards this property, do the ancient Romans compare with the moderns? What does Cicero

closed musically; for that is a pleasure which the ear expects." Elsewhere, alluding to a sentence of the eloquent Carbo, he tells us, "So great a clamor was excited on the part of the assembly that it was altogether wonderful." At the present day, we can not, even with the most harmonious style, hope to produce such effects. It is sufficient if the ear is pleased; it need not be transported. There is danger, moreover, if a swelling tone is continued too long, of giving to what is composed an air of tumid declamation. The ear of a reader, becoming familiar with a monotonous melody, is apt to be cloyed with it, and to convey to the mind but a slight impression compared with that produced by variety. Contiguous sentences must be constructed differently, so that their pauses may fall at unequal intervals. Even discords properly introduced, and abrupt departures from regularity of cadence, have, at times, a good effect. Above all, there must be no appearance of labored attempts at Harmony; no sacrifice of Perspicuity, Precision, or Strength, to sound. All unmeaning words introduced merely to round a period must be regarded as blemishes. When the meaning of a sentence is expressed with clearness, force, and dignity, it can hardly fail to strike the ear agreeably; at most, a moderate degree of attention will be all that is required for imparting to such a period a pleasing cadence. Labored attempts will often result in nothing more than rendering the composition languid and enervated.

§ 380. The first thing requiring attention in the arrangement of sentences, is that the parts be disposed in such a way as to be easily read. What the organs of speech find no difficulty in uttering, will, as a general rule, afford pleasure to the ear. In the progress of a sentence, the voice naturally rests at the close of each member; and these pauses should be so distributed as neither to exhaust the breath by their distance from each other, nor to require constant cessations of voice by the frequency of their recurrence. Below are presented in contrast a harmonious sentence from Milton, and one of an opposite character from Tillotson; the former of which pleases the

---

say that he has witnessed? What does he state with respect to a sentence of Carbo's? Why should we not, at the present day, aim at a similar degree of harmony? What is recommended with respect to the construction of contiguous sentences? What is sometimes the effect of discords? What periods will generally strike the ear agreeably? What is the effect of labored attempts at harmony?

§ 380. What first requires attention in the arrangement of sentences? Where does the voice, in reading, naturally rest? How should these pauses be distributed? From

ear with its well-arranged succession of pauses; while the latter offends this organ by reason of the length of its members, particularly the closing one, in which the reader finds no opportunity for taking breath.

From Milton.—" We shall conduct you to a hill-side, laborious, indeed, at the first ascent; but else, so smooth, so green, so full of goodly prospects, and melodious sounds on every side, that the harp of Orpheus was not more charming."

From Tillotson.—" This discourse concerning the easiness of God's commands, does, all along, suppose and acknowledge the difficulties of the first entrance upon a religious course; except only in those persons who have had the happiness to be trained up to religion by the easy and insensible degrees of a pious and virtuous education."

On this same account, a want of skill in the distribution of pauses, the example given "*as altered*" in § 371 is singularly inharmonious; as, also, are many sentences in which there are long parentheses.

§ 381. The next thing to be considered is the cadence of periods. The rule bearing on this point is, that when we aim at dignity or elevation the sound should be made to swell to the last. Herein the requirements of Strength and Harmony agree,—that the longest members and the fullest and most sonorous words be retained for the conclusion. To end a sentence, therefore, with a preposition, or a succession of unaccented words, is as disagreeable to the ear as it is enfeebling. Observe the admirable cadence of the following fine sentence of Sterne's:—

" The accusing spirit which flew up to Heaven's Chancery with the oath, blushed as he gave it in; and the recording angel, as he wrote it down, dropped a tear upon the word, and blotted it out forever."

A slight change at the close of the sentence will mar its melody.

" The accusing spirit which flew up to Heaven's Chancery with the oath, blushed as he gave it in; and the recording angel, as he wrote it down, dropped a tear, and blotted it out."

§ 382. Finally, as the highest kind of Harmony,—most difficult to attain, and, when attained, most effective,—we have to

---

what authors are examples quoted, and wherein lies the harmony of the one, and the harshness of the other? What is said of sentences containing long parentheses?

§ 381. What is the rule for giving an effective cadence to a sentence? With what do both strength and harmony require us to avoid closing a period? Repeat a musical sentence from Sterne, point out wherein its harmony consists, and show how a slight change will destroy its cadence.

consider the adaptation of sound to sense. This is two-fold first, the natural adaptation of particular sounds to certain kinds of writing; and, secondly, the use of such words in the description of sound, motion, or passion, as, either in reality or by reason of imaginary associations, bear some resemblance to the object described.

§ 383. Certain currents of sound, it has been said, are adapted to the tenor of certain varieties of composition. Sounds have, in many respects, a correspondence with our ideas, partly natural, and partly the effect of artificial associations. Hence, any one modulation continued impresses a certain character on style. Sentences constructed with the Ciceronian swell are appropriate to what is grave, important, or magnificent; for this is the tone which such sentiments naturally assume: but they suit no violent passion, no eager reasoning, no familiar address. These require sentences brisker, easier, and more abrupt. No one current of sounds, therefore, will be found appropriate to different compositions, or even to different parts of the same production. To use the same cadence in an oration and letter would be as absurd as to set the words of a tender love-song to the air of a stately march. There is thus much room for taste and judgment in forming such combinations of words as are suited to the subject under consideration.

§ 384. Not only is a general correspondence of the current of sound with that of thought to be maintained in composition, but, in particular cases, the words, either by their length, their rapidity of movement, or some other peculiarity, may be made to resemble the sense with the happiest effect. This can sometimes be accomplished in prose, but is to be looked

---

§ 382. What is the highest kind of harmony? Under what two heads do we consider the adaptation of sound to sense?

§ 383. To what are certain currents of sound adapted? Explain the reason. What is the result of continuing any one modulation? To what are sentences constructed with the Ciceronian swell appropriate? To what are they unsuited? In what, then, is there much room for taste and judgment?

§ 384. How may words be made to resemble the sense? In what department of

for chiefly in poetry, where inversions and other licenses give us a greater command of sound.

The sounds of words are employed for representing, chiefly, three classes of objects : first, other sounds; secondly, different kinds of motion; thirdly, the passions of the mind.

The simplest variety of this kind of Harmony is the imitation, by a proper choice of words, of striking sounds which we wish to describe; such as the noise of waters, or the roaring of winds.

This imitation is not difficult. No great degree of art is required 'n a poet, when he is describing sweet and soft sounds, to use words that are composed principally of liquids and vowels, and therefore glide easily along; or, when he is speaking of harsh noises, to throw together a number of rough syllables of difficult pronunciation. This is, in fact, no more than a continued onomatopœia, a rhetorical figure already defined; it is simply carrying out a principle which has operated in the formation of many words in our language. In common conversation we speak of the *whistling* of winds, the *shriek* of the eagle, the *whoop* of the Indian, the *buzz* of insects, and the *hiss* of serpents. These sounds we express respectively by articulate sounds which resemble them; and this is just what the poet seeks to do, only at greater length, and by combinations instead of individual words.

The first two examples are passages from Paradise Lost, representing respectively the sounds made by the unclosing of the gates of Hell, and the opening of the portals of Heaven. Observe how admirably these sentences are adapted, each to its subject; how harsh the one, how harmonious the other.

> "On a sudden, open fly,
> With impetuous recoil, and jarring sound,
> The infernal doors; and on their hinges grate
> Harsh thunder."

> "Heaven opened wide
> Her ever-during gates, harmonious sound,
> On golden hinges turning."

None knew better than Pope the effect of this higher kind of Har-

---

composition, chiefly, is this beauty to be looked for, and why? What three classes of objects are oftenest thus represented by sounds? What is the simplest variety of this kind of harmony? How may sweet and soft sounds be represented? How, harsh noises? What figure is thus carried out? Give examples of words formed in imitation of the sounds which they denote. What do the first two examples represent? How do they compare with each other? What poet, in particular, has attained this higher

mony. He thus, in the Odyssey (xxi., 449), represents the sound of a bow-string:—

"The string, let fly,
Twanged short and sharp, like the shrill swallow's cry."

So, in his Iliad (xxiii., 146), he imitates the noise of **axes** and **falling oaks**:—

"Loud sounds the axe, redoubling strokes on strokes,
On all sides round the forest hurls her oaks
Headlong. Deep echoing groan the thickets brown,
Then, *rustling, crackling, crashing, thunder down*."

The roaring of a whirlpool he describes in the following terms:—

"Dire Scylla there a scene of horror forms,
And here Charybdis fills the deep with storms;
When the tide rushes from her *rumbling* caves,
The rough rock roars: tumultuous boil the waves."

In allusion to the very subject before us,—i. e. making the sound in poetry, resemble the sense,—the same author gives a precept, and strikingly illustrates it, in a single line:—

"But, when loud surges lash the sounding shore,
The hoarse rough verse should like the torrent roar."

In the second place, the sound of words is often employed to imitate motion, whether swift or slow, violent or gentle, equable or interrupted. Though there is no natural affinity between sound and motion, yet in the imagination they are closely connected, as appears from the relation subsisting between music and dancing.

Long syllables naturally give the impression of slow and difficult motion, as in these lines of Pope:—

"A needless Alexandrine ends the song;
That, like a wounded snake, drags its slow length along.

"Just writes to make his barrenness appear,
And strains from hard-bound brains eight lines a year."

A succession of short syllables containing but few consonants denotes rapid motion, as in the last of the following lines from Cowley,

---

kind of harmony? Repeat the lines in which he represents the sound of a bow-string; those in which he imitates the noise of axes and falling oaks; those in which he describes the roaring of a whirlpool; those in which he alludes to the subject under consideration.

What is the second variety of this kind of harmony? What is said of the connection between sound and motion? How is the impression of slow and difficult motion conveyed? Illustrate this from Pope. How is rapid motion denoted? Quote, in illus-

which Johnson says, as an example of representative versification, "perhaps no other English line can equal."

> "He who defers this work from day to day,
> Does on a river's bank expecting stay,
> Till the whole stream that stopped him shall be gone,—
> *Which runs, and, as it runs, forever shall run on.*"

Pope furnishes an example of easy metrical flow, which admirably represents the gentle motion of which he speaks.

> "Soft is the strain when Zephyr gently blows,
> *And the smooth stream in smoother numbers flows.*"

A sudden calm at sea is well painted in the following lines:—

> "Then the shrouds drop;
> The downy feather, on the cordage hung,
> Moves not: the flat sea shines like yellow gold
> Fused in the fire, or like the marble floor
> Of some old temple wide."

Sounds are also capable of representing the emotions and passions of the mind: not that there is, logically speaking, any resemblance between the two; but inasmuch as different syllabic combinations awaken certain ideas, and may thus predispose the reader's mind to sympathy with that emotion on which the poet intends to dwell. Of this, Dryden's Ode on St. Cecilia's Day is a striking exemplification; as, also, is Collins' Ode on "The Passions." An extract or two from the latter poem will sufficiently illustrate the subject; it will be observed that the words, the metre, and the cadence, admirably correspond with the emotion in each case depicted.

> "Next Anger rushed, his eyes on fire,
> In lightnings owned his secret stings;
> In one rude clash he struck the lyre,
> And swept with hurried hand the strings."

> "With woful measures wan Despair—
> Low sullen sounds his grief beguiled;
> A solemn, strange, and mingled air,
> 'Twas sad by fits, by starts 'twas wild!"

---

tration, a line from Cowley, highly commended by Johnson. Quote a couplet of Pope's, which represents gentle motion. Repeat the example in which a sudden calm at sea is described. What else are sounds capable of representing? Explain how this is possible. What poems afford examples? Repeat the passages quoted from Collins' Ode, and show how the sound corresponds with the emotion denoted.

"But thou, O Hope, with eyes so fair,
  What was thy delighted measure?
Still it whispered promised pleasure,
And bade the lovely scenes at distance hail!
Still would her touch the strain prolong,
  And from the rocks, the woods, the vale,
She called on Echo still through all her song;
  And where her sweetest theme she chose,
A soft responsive voice was heard at every close,
And Hope, enchanted, smiled, and waved her golden hair!"

LESSON LXIII.

EXERCISE ON HARMONY.

CORRECT the following sentences according to the rules for the promotion of Harmony:—

1. No mortal author, in the ordinary fate and vicissitude of things, knows to what use his works, whatever they are, may, some time or other, be applied (§ 381). 2. It is likewise urged, that there are, by computation, in this kingdom, above ten thousand parsons, whose revenues, added to those of my Lords the Bishops, would suffice to maintain, at their present rate of living, half a million, if not more, poor men. 3. Study to unite with firmness gentle pleasing manners (§ 378). 4. He was mortifyingly rebuked for the mischievousness of his behavior. 5. There are no persons, or, if there are any, assuredly they are few in number, who have not, at some time of life, either directly or indirectly, with or without consciousness on their part, been of service to their fellow-creatures, or at least a portion of them. 6. Thou rushedst into the midst of the conflict and swervedst not. 7. I have just made arrangements *for forw*arding *four* bales of goods. 8. A mild child is liked better than a wild child. 9. St. Augustine lived holily and godlily. 10. Notwithstanding the barefacedness of his conduct, we could not help pitying the miserableness of his condition. 11. The slow horse that keeps on his course may beat the fast horse that stops to eat or sleep by the way (§ 378). 12. It is he that has committed the deed, at least accessorily. 13. Sobermindedness and shamefacedness are by some considered evidences of virtue. 14. Generally speaking, a prudent general will avoid a general engagement unless his forces are equal in bravery and discipline to those of his opponent. 15. This is distinctly stated in an encyclical letter of that age. 16. Energy, industry, temperance, and handiness, recommend mechanics. 17. Hydrophobia (which is derived from two Greek words, meaning *fear of water*, and is so called from the aversion to that element which it produces in human patients suffering from its attack, though it seldom causes a similar aversion in the animal from whose bite it originates) sometimes does not

display itself for months after the poison has been received into the system. 18. To two tunes I have made up my mind never to listen. 19. Days, weeks, and months, pass by; the rocks shall waste and man shall turn to dust. 20. *In an analogous* case, this might be different. 21. Should liberty continue to be abused, as it has been for some time past, (and, though demagogues may not admit it, yet sensible and observing men will not deny, that it has been,) the people will seek relief in despotism or in emigration. 22. We should carefully examine into, and candidly pass judgment on, our faults. 23. In a few years, the hand of industry may change the face of a country, so that one who was familiar with it may be unable to recognize it as that which he once knew; but many generations must pass before any change can be wrought in the sentiments or manners of a people, cut off from intercourse with the rest of the world, and thereby confined to the sphere of their own narrow experience (§ 380). 24. Confident as you are now in your assertions, and positive as you are in your opinions, the time, be assured, approaches, when things and men will appear in a different light to you. 25. Some *chroniclers*, by an injudicious use of familiar phrases, express themselves *sillily*. 26. The scene is laid *on an inland* lake.

LESSON LXIV.

UNITY.

§ 385. The last essential property of a good style is Unity; which consists in the restriction of a sentence to one leading proposition, modified only by such accessories as are materially and closely connected with it. The very nature of a sentence implies that it must contain but one proposition. It may, indeed, consist of parts; but these must be so bound together as to convey to the mind the impression of one fact, and one alone.

§ 386. The first requirement of Unity is, that during the course of the sentence the scene and the subject be changed as little as possible. The reader must not be hurried by sud-

---

§ 385. What is the last essential property of a good style? In what does unity consist? What does the nature of a sentence imply? If it consists of parts, what must be their character?

§ 386. What is the first requirement of unity? What is the effect of sudden transi-

den transitions from place to place, or from person to person. One leading subject at a time is enough for the mind to contemplate; when more are introduced, the attention is distracted, the Unity destroyed, and the impression weakened. This, it will be seen, is the effect in the following sentence, which contains no less than four subjects,—*friends, we, I, who* [that is, *passengers*]. Observe how a slight change in the construction gets rid of two of the subjects and thus insures the Unity of the sentence.

"My friends turned back after we reached the vessel, on board of which I was received with kindness by the passengers, who vied with each other in showing me attention."

Corrected.—" My friends having turned back after we reached the vessel, the passengers received me on board with kindness, and vied with each other in showing me attention."

§ 387. A second rule is, do not crowd into one sentence things that have no connection.

This rule is violated in the following passage:—"Archbishop Tillotson died in this year. He was exceedingly beloved both by King William and Queen Mary, who nominated Dr. Tennison, Bishop of Lincoln, to succeed him." Who, from the beginning of this sentence, would expect such a conclusion? When we are told that he was loved by the king and queen, we naturally look for some proof of this affection, or at least something connected with the main proposition; whereas we are suddenly informed of Dr. Tennison's nomination in his place. To correct such an error, we must remove the discordant idea, and embody it, if it is essential that it be presented, in a distinct sentence:—" He was exceedingly beloved by King William and Queen Mary. Dr. Tennison, Bishop of Lincoln, was nominated to succeed him."

The following sentence, from a translation of Plutarch, is still worse. Speaking of the Greeks, under Alexander, the author says:—

"Their march was through an uncultivated country, whose savage inhabitants fared hardly, having no other riches than a breed of lean sheep, whose flesh was rank and unsavory, by reason of their continual feeding upon sea-fish."

Here the scene is changed again and again. The march of the

---

tions in a sentence from place to place or from person to person? Illustrate this with a sentence containing four subjects, and show how the fault may be corrected.

§ 387. What is the second rule for the preservation of unity? Repeat a passage in which it is violated. Show wherein the error lies, and correct it. Give the substance of the passage quoted from a translation of Plutarch. What is objectionable in it? In

Greeks, the description of the inhabitants through whose country they travelled, the account of their sheep, and the reason why these animals made unsavory food, form a medley which can not fail to be distasteful in the highest degree to an intelligent reader.

A violation of this rule is fatal to Unity even in periods of no great length, as is apparent from the examples just given; in sentences unduly protracted, however, there is a still greater liability to err in this particular. The involved style of Clarendon furnishes numerous examples. Nor does he stand alone; many of the old writers are, in this respect, equally faulty. From Shaftesbury we shall quote a sentence in point. He is describing the effect of the sun in the frozen regions; beginning with this orb as his prominent subject, he soon proceeds to certain monsters and their exploits; whence, by an unexpected and unaccountable transition, he suddenly brings man into view, and admonishes him at some length as to his religious duties. The only way to correct such an involved period as this, is to break it up into several smaller sentences.

"It breaks the icy fetters of the main, where vast sea-monsters pierce through floating islands, with arms which can withstand the crystal rock; whilst others, who of themselves seem great as islands, are by their bulk alone armed against all but man; whose superiority over creatures of such stupendous size and force, should make him mindful of his privilege of reason, and force him humbly to adore the great composer of these wondrous frames, and the author of his own superior wisdom."

It may be contended that, in passages like the above, punctuation will bring out the meaning by showing the relation between the various parts; and that, therefore, if commas, semicolons, and colons, are properly used, a violation of Unity may be tolerated. It is true that punctuation does much to remedy even faults as gross as those in the last paragraph; but it must be remembered that the points it employs do not make divisions of thought, but merely serve to mark those already existing, and are therefore proper only when they correspond with the latter. Let those who think that a proper distribution of points will

---

what sentences is a want of unity most likely to occur? Whose long and intricate periods furnish examples? From whom is a sentence in point quoted? Give its substance. What mistaken view do some take with respect to the correction of sentences deficient in unity, by means of punctuation? Show why this view is mistaken.

make up for the want of Unity, try the experiment in the last example. The ideas it contains are so foreign to each other that we must have at least three distinct sentences to express them properly; yet it is evident that, as the members now stand, periods between them are inadmissible, on account of the closeness of their connection.

§ 388. In the third place, a regard for Unity requires that we avoid long parentheses. We have already alluded to their effect as prejudicial to Clearness, Strength, and Harmony. In the old writers they are of frequent occurrence, and constitute so palpable a fault that in later times it has been thought the safest course to reject parentheses of every kind. Passages in which they occur, must be divided into as many sentences as there are leading propositions.

EXAMPLE.—The quicksilver mines of Idria, in Austria (which were discovered in 1797, by a peasant, who, catching some water from a spring, found the tub so heavy that he could not move it, and the bottom covered with a shining substance which turned out to be mercury) yield, every year, over three hundred thousand pounds of that valuable metal.

Corrected.—The quicksilver mines of Idria, in Austria, were discovered by a peasant in 1797. Catching some water from a spring, he found the tub so heavy that he could not move it, and the bottom covered with a shining substance which turned out to be mercury. Of this valuable metal, the mines in question yield, every year, over three hundred thousand pounds.

EXERCISE.

Correct the following sentences so that their Unity may be preserved, altering the punctuation as may be required by the changes made:—

1. The usual acceptation takes profit and pleasure for two different things, and not only calls the followers or votaries of them by the several names of busy and idle men, but distinguishes the faculties of the mind, that are conversant about them; calling the operations of the first, wisdom; and of the other, wit;—which is a Saxon word, used to express what the Spaniards and Italians call *ingenio*, and the French, *esprit*, both from the Latin: though I think wit more particularly signifies that of poetry, as may occur in remarks on the Runic language.— SIR WILLIAM TEMPLE. 2. To this succeeded that licentiousness which entered with the Restoration, and from infecting our religion and morals fell to corrupt our language; which last was not likely to be much improved by those who at that time made up the court of King Charles the Second; either such as had followed him in his banishment, or who

---

§ 388. What is the third rule? What is the effect of long parentheses?

nad been altogether conversant in the dialect of these fanatic times; or young men who had been educated in the same country; so that the court, which used to be the standard of correctness and propriety of speech, was then, and I think has ever since continued, the worst school in England for that accomplishment; and so will remain, till better care be taken in the education of our nobility, that they may set out in the world with some foundation of literature, in order to qualify them for patterns of politeness.—SWIFT. 3. We left Italy with a fine wind, which continued three days; when a violent storm drove us to the coast of Sardinia, which is free from all kinds of poisonous and deadly herbs, except one; which resembles parsley, and which, they say, causes those who eat it to die of laughing. 4. At Coleridge's table we were introduced to Count Frioli, a foreigner of engaging manners and fine conversational powers, who was killed the following day by a steamboat explosion. 5. The lion is a noble animal, and has been known to live fifty years in a state of confinement. 6. Haydn (who was the son of a poor wheelwright, and is best known to us by a noble oratorio called "The Creation," which he is said to have composed after a season of solemn prayer for divine assistance) wrote fine pieces of music when he was no more than ten years old. 7. The famous poisoned valley of Java (which, as Mr. Loudon, a recent traveller in that region, informs us, is twenty miles in length and is filled with skeletons of men and birds; and into which it is said that the neighboring tribes are in the habit of driving criminals, as a convenient mode of executing capital punishment) has proved to be the crater of an extinct volcano, in which carbonic acid is generated in great quantities, as in the Grotto del Cane at Naples. 8. The Chinese women are for the most part industrious; and use, as embellishments of their beauty, paint, false hair, oils, and pork fat. 9. London, which is a very dirty city, has a population of two millions and a quarter. 10. We next took the cars, which were filled, to overflowing, and brought us to a landing, where a boat was in waiting that looked as if it were a century old; but which, while we were examining its worm-eaten sides, put off at a rate which soon showed us that its sailing qualities were by no means contemptible, and taught us the practical lesson that it is unsafe to judge of the merits of a thing by its external appearance.

LESSON LXV.

THE FORMING OF STYLE.

§ 389. As we have now considered the various kinds of style, and the essential properties which should be preserved in them all, it may not be out of place to add a few practical suggestions respecting the best mode of forming a characteristic manner of expressing one's thoughts. Whether a young composer's style is to be concise or diffuse, simple or labored, nervous or feeble, will depend, of course, in a great measure, on the bent of his mind when he shall have attained mature years; but, as it is necessary to begin composing at an early age, it is unsafe to trust to the vicissitudes of natural temperament, and run the risk of contracting bad habits, which, when discovered, it may be hard to lay aside. These difficulties it is best to avoid by employing, from the outset, such aids as reason and experience recommend. The object in so doing is not to sacrifice nature to art, to restrain the flow of genius, or to destroy individuality of manner: but, on the other hand, to promote the healthy development of this individuality; to modify its extravagances, suppress those of its features which are objectionable, and cultivate with the utmost care such as are meritorious and pleasing.

§ 390. In the first place, *give careful and earnest thought to the subject about which you propose to write.*

Though at first sight this may seem to have little to do with the formation of style, the relation between the two is in reality extremely close. Before we have ourselves obtained a full, clear, and decided, view of a subject, we can not hope to communicate such an impression of it to others. The habit of writing without first having distinct ideas of what we intend to say, will inevitably produce a loose, confused, and slovenly, style.

§ 391. Secondly, *compose frequently.* Rules are of service, but they are not intended to take the place of practice. Nothing but exercise will give facility of composition.

§ 392. In the third place, *compose slowly and with care* It is to hasty and careless writing that a bad style may gene-

---

§ 389. On what will the characteristics of a young composer's style, in a great measure, depend? What is said of the necessity of using aids in the formation of style? What is the object in so doing?

§ 390. What is the first rule relating to the formation of style? What is said of the connection between style and thought? What will inevitably result from writing without having distinct ideas of what we intend to say?

§ 391. What is the second rule?

rally be traced. Faults are thus contracted which it will cost infinite trouble to unlearn.

Quintilian (bk. x., ch. 3) alludes to this point in the following terms:—" I enjoin that such as are beginning the practice of composition write slowly and with anxious deliberation. Their great object, at first, should be to write as well as possible; practice will enable them to write quickly. By degrees, matter will offer itself still more readily; words will be at hand; composition will flow; every thing, as in the arrangement of a well-ordered family, will present itself in its proper place. The sum of the whole is this: by hasty composition we shall never acquire the art of composing well; by writing well, we shall soon be able to write speedily."

§ 393. Fourthly, *revise carefully*. Nothing is more necessary to what is written, or more important to the writer "Condemn," says Horace, in his Epistle to the Pisos, v. 292–294, " condemn that poem which many a day and many a blot have not corrected, and castigated ten times to perfect accuracy."

Even the most experienced writers are apt to commit oversights, for which revision is the only remedy. If we put aside what has been written till the expressions we have used are forgotten, and then review our work with a cool and critical eye, as if it were the performance of another, we shall discern many imperfections which at first were overlooked. This is the time for pruning away redundancies; for seeing that the parts of sentences are correctly arranged and connected by the proper particles; for observing whether the requirements of grammar are strictly complied with; and for bringing style into a consistent and effective form. Disagreeable as this labor of correction may be, all must submit to it who would attain literary distinction, or even express their thoughts with ordinary propriety and force. A little practice will soon create a critical taste, and render the work if not pleasant, at least easy and tolerable.

§ 394. In the fifth place, *study the style of the best authors*. Notice their peculiarities; observe what gives effect

---

§ 392. What is the third rule? To what is a bad style generally traceable? What is Quintilian's advice on this point?

§ 393. What is the fourth rule? What does Horace say on this point? Describe the most effective method of revising. To what, in this process, must the author's attention be directed? What is said of the necessity of this labor of correction?

§ 394. What is the fifth rule? Explain what is meant by this. What is said of ser

to their writings; compare one with another; and, in composing, endeavor to avoid their faults and imitate their beauties.

No servile imitation is here recommended. This is in the highest degree dangerous, generally resulting in stiffness and artificiality of manner, and a lack of self-confidence, which is fatal to success in composition. Avoid adopting a favorite author's peculiar phrases or constructions. "It is infinitely better," says Blair, "to have something that is our own, though of moderate beauty, than to affect to shine in borrowed ornaments, which will, at last, betray the utter poverty of our genius." Modifying our style by assimilating it to one which we particularly admire, or which the world has stamped with its approval, is quite a different thing from laying aside our own individuality entirely, to adopt another's, which we have but a slight chance of being able to maintain.

No exercise is likely to aid us more in acquiring a good style than to translate frequently from the writings of some eminent English author into our own words; to take, for instance, a page of Addison or Goldsmith, and, having read it over until we have fully mastered the meaning, to lay aside the book and attempt to reproduce the passage from memory. A comparison of what we have written with the original will then show us in what the faults of our style consist, and how we may correct them; and, among the different modes of expressing the same thought, will enable us to perceive which is the most beautiful.

§ 395. *Avoid such mannerism as would prevent you from adapting your style to your subject and to the capacity of those you address.* Keep the object proposed in view, and let your mode of expression be strictly consistent therewith. Nothing is more absurd than to attempt a florid, poetical style, on occasions when it is our business only to reason; or to speak with elaborate pomp of expression, before persons to whom such magnificence is unintelligible.

MISCELLANEOUS EXERCISE ON THE ESSENTIAL PROPERTIES OF STYLE.

In the following sentences, make such corrections as are required by the rules for Purity, Propriety, Precision, Clearness, Strength, Harmony, and Unity :—

---

vile imitation? What does Blair say on this subject? Show the difference between a servile imitation and the course here advised. What exercise is likely to aid us in acquiring a good style?

§ 395. What is the last rule, relating to the adaptation of the style to the subject? What advice is given on this head?

1. Misfortunes never *arrive* singly, but crowd upon us *en masse* when we are least able to resist them. 2. A [peaceable, or peaceful?] valley; —a [peaceable, or peaceful?] disposition. 3. I decline accepting *of* the situation. 4. Petrarch was much esteemed by his countrymen, who, even at the present day, mention with reverence *the poet of Vaucluse and the inventor of the sonnet.* 5. This is *so*; and *so* cruel an [act, or action?] has rarely been heard *of.* 6. The lad can not leave his father; for, if *he* should leave *him, he* would die. 7. The works of art receive a great advantage from the resemblance which they have to those of nature, because her3 the similitude is *not only* pleasant, but the pattern is perfect. 8. A friend exaggerates a man's virtues; *one who is hostile endeavors to magnify* his crimes (§ 374). 9. This is not a principle that we can act *on* and adhere *to.* 10. Diana of the Ephesians is great. 11. We do things frequently that we repent of afterwards. 12. Great and rich men owe much to chance, which gives to one what it takes from others. 13. There are *those who* allow their envy of *those who* are more fortunate than themselves to get the better of *them* to such an extent that *they* try to injure *them* all *they* can. 14. [Classic, or classical?] and English school;—a [classic, or classical?] statue. 15. Running out to see whether there was a new *émeute*, which the *hauteur* of the new governor rendered very *plausible*, I *came within an ace of being done for*. 16. They attempted to remain *incog.* 17. If a man have little merit, he *had need have* much modesty. 18. The laws of nature are truly what Lord Bacon styles his aphorisms,—laws of laws. Civil laws are always imperfect, and often false deductions from *them*, or applications of *them;* nay, *they* stand, in many instances, in direct opposition to *them.* 19. *Being* content with deserving a triumph, he refused the honor *of it.* 20. That *temperamental dignotions*, and conjectures of prevalent humors, may be collected from spots in our nails, we are not averse to concede. 21. It cannot be impertinent or ridiculous, therefore, in such a country, whatever it might be in the Abbot of St. Real's, which was Savoy, I think; or in Peru, under the Incas, where Garcilasso de la Vega says it was lawful for none but the nobility to study—for men of all degrees to instruct themselves in those affairs wherein they may be actors, or judges of those that act, or controllers of those that judge. 22. The moon was casting a pale light on the numerous graves that were scattered before me, as it peered above the horizon when I opened the little gate of the church-yard. 23. This work, having been fiercely attacked by critics, he proposes for the present to lay aside. 24. Men look with an evil eye upon the good that is in others, and think that *their* reputation obscures *them*, and that *their* commendable qualities do stand in *their* light; and therefore *they* do what they can to cast a cloud over *them*, that the bright shining of *their* virtues may not obscure *them.* 25. In this uneasy state, both of his public and private life, Cicero was oppressed by a new and cruel affliction, the death of his beloved daughter, Tullia, which happened soon after her divorce from Dolabella, whose manners and humors were entirely disagreeable *to her.* 26. The erroneous judgment of parents concerning the conduct of schoolmasters, has crushed the peace of many an ingenious man who is engaged in the care of youth; and paved the way to the ruin of hopeful boys. 27. The discontented man (as his spleen irritates and sours his temper, and leads him to discharge its venom on all with whom he stands connected) is never found without a great share of malignity. 28. We have been *choused* out of our

rights by these *clod-polls* and *blackguards*. 29. As no one is free from faults, so few want good qualities (§378). 30. No man of *feeling* can look upon the *ocean* without *feeling* an *emotion* of grandeur. 31. The *mercenariness* of many tradesmen leads them to speak *derogatorily* of their neighbors. 32. With Cicero's *writ*ings, it is *right* that young divines should be conversant; but they should not give them the preference to Demosthenes, who, by many degrees, excelled the other; *at least as an orator*. 33. After he has finished his elementary studies, which will discipline his mind, and fit it for the pursuit of more advanced branches, I advise him to commence with the ancient languages, which will, by easy stages, prepare him for the acquisition of the modern tongues; whence he may with propriety proceed to the careful study of the higher departments of mathematics and belles-lettres, which form an important part of every scholar's education. 34. Such were the prudence and energy of Cicero's course during this critical state of affairs, that his countrymen overlooked his *self-conceitedness*, and vied with each other in testifying their respect to "the father of his country" 35. He *used* to *use* many expressions, which, though *useful*, are not *usually used*, and have not come into general *use*.

LESSON LXVI.

CRITICISM.

§ 396. *Definition.*—Criticism (from the Greek κρίνω, *judge*) may be defined as the art of judging with propriety concerning any object or combination of objects. In the more limited signification in which it is generally used, its province is confined to literature, philology, and the fine arts, and to subjects of antiquarian, scientific, or historical investigation. In this sense, every branch of literary study, as well as each of the arts, has its proper criticism.

§ 397. *Rules.*—It is criticism that has developed the rules and principles of Rhetoric. As was remarked when we first entered on the study of this subject, its rules are not arbitrary, but have been deduced from a careful examination of

---

§ 396. From what is the term *criticism* derived? What does it signify? As generally used, to what is it confined?

§ 397. How have the rules and principles of rhetoric been developed? What be-

those great productions which have been admired as beautiful in every age. Nor has beauty been the sole object of the critic's search. Truth, particularly in history and the sciences, it has been his province not only to seek out, but, when found, to use as a balance in weighing the objects on which he passes judgment. The office of criticism, therefore, is, first to establish the essential ideas which answer to our conceptions of the beautiful or the true in each branch of study; and next to point out, by reference to these ideas, the excellencies or deficiencies of individual works, according as they approach, or vary from, the standard in question.

Thus historical criticism teaches us to distinguish the true from the false, or the probable from the improbable, in historical works: scientific criticism has in view the same object in each respective line of science: literary criticism, in a general sense, investigates the merits and demerits of style or diction, according to the received standard of excellence in every language; while, in poetry and the arts, it develops the principles of that more refined and exquisite sense of beauty which forms the ideal model of perfection in each.

§ 398. *Relation between its ancient and its present character.*—Criticism originated among the Greeks and Romans at an early day, and was carried by them to a high degree of perfection. Aristotle, Dionysius Halicarnasseus, and Longinus, among the former, and, among the latter, Cicero and Quintilian, did much towards awakening a critical taste in their respective countrymen; enabling them to appreciate propriety of diction, and making them acquainted with those minute matters, which, however insignificant they may appear, are essential to effective composition.

The classical critics, however, confined themselves mainly to that department of their art which has reference to the principles of beauty. Their sphere of knowledge being more limited than ours, their minds

---

sides beauty has been the object of the critic's search? What, then, is the office of criticism? What does historical criticism teach us? What is the object of scientific criticism? What, of literary criticism?

§ 398. What is said of criticism among the ancient Greeks and Romans? What authors are mentioned as distinguished in this department? What effect did their efforts produce on their countrymen? To what did the classical critics confine them-

were more sedulously exercised in reflecting on their own perceptions. Hence the astonishing progress they made in the fine arts; and hence, in literature, beauty of language and sentiment was their highest aim. Accordingly, the criticisms of antiquity relate almost exclusively to literature and the arts; and the term is, therefore, still confined, in its most popular signification, to those provinces of research.

The criticism of Truth, which pertains chiefly to history and science, was of later origin; but may be regarded as closely allied to the criticism of beauty, inasmuch as it is regulated by analogous principles, and minds which possess a high degree of judgment in the one are generally capable of forming right apprehensions in the other. One principle, important to be noted, is equally true of each: that, whether beauty or truth is the aim, extensive knowledge of the subject, as well as education and practice, is necessary in the sound critic;—yet knowledge alone is not sufficient; the ability to discriminate and judge correctly is still more important, and this no knowledge, however great, can supply. To be acquainted with a rule, and to be able to apply it in difficult cases, are entirely different things.

§ 399. *Literary Criticism.*—We have here to do with criticism, only so far as it pertains to the works of literature. The rules of good writing having been deduced in the manner above described, it is the business of the critic to employ them as a standard, by a judicious comparison with which he may distinguish what is beautiful and what is faulty in every performance. He must look at the sentiments expressed, and judge of their correctness and consistency; he must view the performance as a whole, and see whether it clearly and properly embodies the ideas intended to be conveyed; he must examine whether there is sufficient variety in the style, must note its beauties, and show, if it is susceptible of improvement, in what that improvement should consist; he must see whether the principles of syntax or rhetoric are violated; and, finally, must extend his scrutiny even to the individual words

---

selves? How is the astonishing progress of the ancients in the fine arts explained? In literature, what was their highest aim? Accordingly, to what did their criticisms relate? To what does the criticism of truth chiefly refer? What is the connection between it and the criticism of beauty? What important principle is equally true of both?

§ 399. With what department of criticism have we here to do? Point out the various duties of the literary critic. By what must he be guided? To what should his

employed. And all this must be done without allowing prejudice to bias his decisions, or the desire of displaying his own knowledge to lead him from the legitimate pursuit of his subject.

The critic must be guided by feeling as well as rules; otherwise, his efforts will result in a pedantry as useless as it is distasteful. He should not, on account of minor imperfections, condemn, as a whole, a performance which evinces in its author deep and correct feeling, or possesses other merits equally important. He should carefully draw a distinction between what is good and what is bad, giving full credit for the one and showing how to correct the other. His criticisms should not be confined to little faults and errors, which no writer, however careful, has been able entirely to avoid. A true critic will rather dwell on excellencies than on imperfections; will seek to discover the concealed beauties of a writer, and communicate to the world such things as are worthy of their observation. This, indeed, is a more difficult task, and involves a more delicate taste and a profounder knowledge, than indiscriminate fault-finding. As Dryden has justly remarked,

"Errors, like straws, upon the surface flow;
He who would search for pearls, must dive below."

§ 400. *Abuse.*—The most exquisite words and finest strokes of an author are those which often appear most exceptionable to a man deficient in learning or delicacy of taste; and it is these that a captious and undistinguishing critic generally attacks with the greatest violence. In this case, recourse is often had to ridicule. A little wit is capable of making a beauty as well as a blemish the subject of derision. Though such treatment of an author may have its effect with some, who erroneously think that the sentiment criticised is ridiculous instead of the wit with which it is attacked, yet in the intelligent reader it will naturally produce indignation or disgust.

When, moreover, a critic frequently indulges in such a course, he is apt to find fault with every thing against which he can bring this fa-

---

criticisms not be confined? On what will the true critic dwell? Is the discovery of beauties or defects the more difficult task? What couplet of Dryden's illustrates this point?

§ 400. What is said of an author's most exquisite words and finest strokes? To what does the malicious critic often have recourse? What is said of the use of wit or ridicule in criticism? What habit is a critic who indulges in ridicule apt to form? How is pleasantry of this kind characterized?

vorite weapon to bear; and often censures a passage, not because there is any thing wrong in it, but merely from the fact that it affords him an opportunity of being merry at another's expense. Such pleasantry is unseasonable, as well as disingenuous and unfair.

§ 401. *Objections.*—The objection most commonly urged against criticism is that it abridges the natural liberty of genius, and imposes shackles which are fatal to freedom of thought and expression. This argument has been noticed before. It is sufficient here to say that the cutting off of faults cannot be called an abridgment of freedom; or, if it can, it is well that such freedom should be abridged. The reasonable author is not unwilling to have his work examined by the principles of good taste and sound understanding; and this is all that the true critic proposes to do. There may, indeed, be some unreasonable critics who carry their strictures to the verge of personal abuse; but their violence gives no more ground for objecting to healthy and proper criticism than the fact that there are unsound reasoners affords for inveighing against all logic.

A more specious objection is sometimes made, which is aimed particularly at the principles on which criticism is founded. These, it is charged, are arbitrary and untrue, because it sometimes happens that what the critic condemns the public receive with approbation. Were this often the case, there would be ground to doubt whether the art of the critic, and indeed all the departments of rhetoric, are not resting on a false foundation. Such instances, though very rare, do sometimes occur. It must be admitted that works containing gross violations of the rules of art have attained a general and even a lasting reputation. Such are the plays of Shakspeare, which, considered as dramatic poems, are irregular in the highest degree. But it must be observed that they have gained public admiration, not by their transgressions of the

---

§ 401. What is most commonly urged as an objection against criticism? How is this objection answered? What more specious objection is sometimes advanced? What admission is made? Explain how this fact furnishes no argument in favor of the

laws of criticism, but in spite of such transgressions. The beauties they possess, in points where they conform to the rules of art, are sufficient to overshadow their blemishes and inspire a degree of satisfaction superior to the disgust arising from the latter. Shakspeare pleases, not by bringing the transactions of many years into one play, not by his mixture of tragedy and comedy in the same piece, nor by his strained thoughts and affected witticisms. These we regard as blemishes, traceable to the tone of the age in which he lived. But these faults are forgotten in his animated and masterly representations of character, his lively descriptions, his striking and original conceptions, and above all his nice appreciation of the emotions and passions of the human heart; beauties which true criticism teaches us to value no less than nature enables us to feel.

We have not here the space for an example of extended criticism. Blair, whose lucid pen, correct taste, sound judgment, and extensive reading, eminently fitted him for the task, furnishes in his lectures (xx–xxiv) several admirable papers on the style of Addison and Swift. To these, the student who wishes specimens of critical writing extended to some length, will do well to refer. We here present a brief examination of two passages in which verbal criticism is exemplified.

SPECIMENS OF VERBAL CRITICISM.

1. "Man, considered in himself, is a very helpless and a very wretched being. Launched alone on the sea of life, he would soon suffer shipwreck."

We have here a proposition strikingly true, expressed in clear and forcible terms. The first word, "man", is universally employed by the best authors as an appellative for the human race. "Man, considered in himself", signifies, the human family viewed as individuals independent of each other. In this state, says the author, he is "a very helpless being". The term "helpless" here implies the want of power to succor himself: and it is evident that, if man were left to himself in infancy, he would perish; and that, if altogether detached from society in manhood, it would be only with great difficulty that he could procure for himself either the comforts or the necessaries of life.

---

objector. Whose productions are instanced as having gained a world-wide popularity in spite of their irregularities? To what is this popularity attributable?

But man, "considered in himself", is not only a very helpless, but also "a very wretched being". It will be observed that additional emphasis is here communicated by the repetition of the article and the adverb. He is not merely a very helpless and wretched being, but "a very helpless and *a very* wretched being". The term "wretched" is generally used as synonymous with *unhappy* or *miserable*; but, in this passage, it expresses the meaning of the author more precisely than either of these words would have done. *Unhappy* may denote merely the uneasiness of a man who may be happy if he pleases; the discontented are unhappy, because they think others more prosperous than themselves. *Miserable* is applied to persons whose minds are tormented by the stings of conscience, agitated by the violence of passion, or harassed by worldly vexations; and, accordingly, we say that wicked men are miserable. But, "wretched", derived from the Saxon word for an *exile*, literally signifies *cast away*, or *abandoned*. Hence appears the proper application of the word in this sentence: man, if left to himself, might indeed exist in a solitary state without being either unhappy or miserable, provided his bodily wants were supplied; though he certainly would be a very "wretched" being, when deprived of all the comforts of social life, and all the endearments of friends and kindred.

Having thus stated his proposition, the author illustrates it with a metaphor. The figure, though appropriate, is trite; life has, from time immemorial, been compared to a sea, and man to a voyager. An original comparison, which a little thought could hardly have failed to suggest, would have been more striking and effective.

2. "Education is the most excellent endowment, as it enlarges the mind, promotes its powers, and renders a man estimable in the eyes of society."

This sentence, though it contains many pompous words, is a remarkable example of a style which lacks propriety. Education is not an "endowment"; for an endowment is a natural gift, such as taste or imagination. Education does not "enlarge" the "mind"; though it may, in a figurative sense, enlarge its capacities. Neither can it "promote" the mental "powers" themselves; but it may promote their improvement. Nor does it follow, that, because a man has improved his mind by education, he is on that account "estimable", *esteem* being produced only by intrinsic worth; but a good education may render a man *respectable*. The sentiment which the author intended to convey should have been expressed thus: "Education is the most excellent attainment, as it enlarges the capacities of the mind, promotes their improvement, and renders a man respectable in the eyes of society."

PART IV

PROSE COMPOSITION.

LESSON LXVII.

INVENTION.—ANALYSIS OF SUBJECTS.

§ 402. Up to the present point, the attention of the student has been directed chiefly to the dress in which he should clothe his thoughts; we now proceed to the thoughts themselves, and those practical exercises in composition, to prepare for which has been the object of the preceding pages.

The process of evolving thoughts in connection with any particular subject is known as INVENTION. It is this that furnishes the material of composition, and on which, in a great measure, its value depends.

Here, moreover, lies most of the difficulty which the young experience in writing. Let them have definite thoughts, and they will generally find it easy to express themselves. But how are they to deal with intangible things; to form the necessary conceptions; and to insure that, when formed, they will be worthy of being embodied and

---

§ 402. Up to the present point, to what has the student's attention been directed? To what do we now proceed? What is Invention? What does it furnish? What is said of the difficulty which the young experience in writing?

preserved in language? This question we now proceed to answer; not claiming that the want of intellectual ability can be supplied by this or any other course; yet believing that those to whom composition is distasteful, will, by pursuing the plan here prescribed, find most of their difficulty vanish, and that all who fairly test the system will improve more rapidly than they could do if left to chance or their own unaided efforts.

§ 403. As soon as a subject has been selected, the first thing required is thought,—careful, deliberate, concentrated, thought. When Newton was asked how he had succeeded in making so many great discoveries, he replied, "By thinking." This labor the composer must undergo; no instruction or aid from foreign sources can take its place. It must be patient and deliberate thought, moreover, not hasty or superficial; it must be original thought, not a reproduction of the ideas of others; it must be well-directed thought, fixed on a definite object, and not allowed to wander from one thing to another; it must be exhaustive thought, embracing the subject in all its relations.

When this task has been fairly performed, the next step is in order. This is an *Analysis* of the subject, or a drawing out of the various heads which suggest themselves to the mind as appropriate to the theme of discourse. Such heads will of course differ according to the subject under consideration, as will appear when we treat in turn of the different kinds of composition. There is so general a resemblance between them, however, that from an example or two there will be no difficulty in understanding what is here meant.

Suppose, for instance, that ANGER is the subject. On a little reflection, such questions as the following will suggest themselves to the composer; and, as they occur, he notes them down.

What is meant by the term Anger?—What visible effect does this passion produce on the person indulging in it?—How does he feel, when his fit of passion has subsided?—Morally speaking, what is the charac-

---

§ 403. When a subject has been selected, what is the first thing required? What kind of thought is here referred to? To what did Newton attribute his discoveries? What step is next in order? What is meant by analyzing a subject? Suppose *Anger* to be the theme, what questions will suggest themselves to the composer? What will

ter of this passion?—What are its usual effects on individuals?—To what may the angry man be compared?—What examples does history afford?—What has been said by others respecting Anger?—What are the best modes of regulating this passion, or of avoiding its occasions?—What are its effects on society?—Draw a contrast between a man of calm, placid, temper, and one of a hasty, irritable, disposition.—Show the advantage, under as many heads as possible, of regulating angry feelings.

Here then is the germ of a composition. Abundant material is now at hand. Thoughts beget thoughts; from these ideas, others will naturally spring during the process of writing. Before proceeding to this, however, it will be necessary to arrange these heads in their proper order, so that a logical connection may be preserved throughout the whole. The leading subject of inquiry must be kept constantly in view, and all thoughts must be rejected that do not bear directly upon it. Unity is as necessary in an extended composition as in a single sentence. The time to ensure sequence and unity of parts is when the Analysis is being revised. Beginning with a general introduction, arranging properly, enlarging on some of the heads by following out the trains of thought suggested, and closing with practical reflections, the analysis, as improved by the writer, would stand as follows:—

ANALYSIS OF AN ESSAY ON ANGER.

I. *Introduction.* The passions in general; relation which anger sustains to the rest.

II. *Definition.* What anger is. A proverb found in various languages says it is "a short-lived madness." Show why.
  1. A man in a violent fit of anger looks as if he were insane; show in what respects.
  2. His mind is beyond the control of reason and judgment; it is like a chariot without a driver, or a ship in a storm without a pilot.
  3. He says and does things so unreasonable that they must be the result of temporary derangement. He may be compared to a tornado, a mountain torrent, or a conflagration, to whose fury none can set bounds, and whose disastrous effects are visited even on the innocent.
  4. The world, and even the law, in a measure, deal with him as if he were a maniac.
  5. Even the angry man himself admits that he has no control over his reason, deeming it sufficient apology for the most unseemly blow or word to say that it was done in a passion.

---

these questions furnish? Before proceeding to write out the matter they suggest, what is it necessary to do? What must be kept in view? What is essential in an extended composition, as well as in a single sentence? What is the time for insuring sequence and unity of parts? As properly arranged and ready for the writer, give an analysis of an Essay on *Anger.*

III. *Feelings which follow its indulgence.* Mortification; humiliation regret at what may have been done under the influence of passion. "An angry man," says Publius Syrus, "is again angry with himself when he returns to reason." He may be likened to a scorpion which stings itself as well as others.

IV. *Historical Illustrations.* Cain and Abel; Alexander the Great and Clitus; &c.

V. *Moral Character of Anger.* At variance with the principles of the Gospel. "Wrath is cruel, and anger is outrageous." Prov. xxvii., 4.

VI. *Quotations.* What do others say of anger?
A passionate man rides a horse that runs away with him.
Maunder's Proverbs.
Anger begins with folly, and ends with repentance.—*Ibid.*
Rage is the mania of the mind.—*Ibid.*
A passionate man scourgeth himself with his own scorpions.
Ray's Proverbs
An angry man opens his mouth and shuts his eyes.—*Cato.*
Anger is certainly a kind of baseness, as it appears well in the weakness of those subjects in whom it reigns, children, old folks, sick folks.—*Lord Bacon.*
When passion enters at the fore-gate, wisdom goes out at the postern.—*Fielding's Proverbs.*
Anger and haste hinder good counsel.—*Ibid.*
No man is free who does not command himself.—*Pythagoras.*

VII. *Effects of Anger on Society.*
1. In individuals, leads to crime, as in the above examples. Makes one enemies, and becomes a source of adversity. Draw a contrast between a man of placid temper and one of hasty disposition.
2. In families and communities, produces hard feelings and unhappiness.
3. In nations, causes war and all its attendant evils.

VIII. *Best Modes of regulating this passion.*

IX. *Conclusion.* Our own duty in this respect, and what we shall gain by controlling our angry feelings.

Here, in its proper form, is an abstract of what the writer intends to say. Of course, the words and formal divisions used above will not appear in his composition. They are merely the means of ensuring a proper arrangement and exhaustive examination of the subject. The Invention is now in a great measure done; all that remains is to embody these thoughts in proper language, according to the rules and principles already considered at length, and to interweave with them such further matter as presents itself. This is called Amplification, and will be con-

---

In a composition from this analysis, what will not appear? For what are they used? What now remains? What is the process called? By what must it be followed? Enumerate the three steps to be taken in composing. What may some

sidered in the next lesson. Followed by a careful revision, it completes the process of composing; which consists, to sum up our remarks, of three steps:—

    I. Roughly drafting all the thoughts suggested by the subject.
    II. Arranging and enlarging these into a formal Analysis.
    III. Amplifying this Analysis into a composition.

To some, this three-fold process may seem to involve unnecessary labor; but experience proves that these steps can all be properly taken, and the composition written in less time than by the common method of attempting to write without any guide of the kind here proposed. It will, at the same time, be found a far more satisfactory and interesting mode of proceeding; and will result in the production of a more meritorious composition. Those who are in the habit of writing much, almost invariably make a preliminary Analysis of their subject, no matter what they are about to compose. The lawyer always draws up a brief of his points; and the minister, a corresponding abstract of his sermon. It is expected, therefore, that, in every case, the student, before attempting to write his exercise, will draw up the two Analyses, as here suggested.

EXERCISE.—Draw up careful and exhaustive Analyses, on the plan here described, of the subjects, EDUCATION and DEATH.

LESSON LXVIII.

AMPLIFICATION.

§ 404. THE analysis completed, the next step is AMPLIFICATION. This, as already explained, consists in enlarging on the ideas before expressed under the various heads, throwing in appropriate additional matter, and forming a complete and consistent whole.

---

think of this three-fold process? What does experience prove with regard to it? What is said of those who are in the habit of writing? What is expected of the student?

§ 404. After analyzing the subject and properly arranging the heads, what is the

The following example will serve to illustrate the process to which we refer. A brief and simple proposition is here made the basis of several successive amplifications, in each of which some new fact or circumstance is added.

1. Alexander conquered the Persians.
2. Alexander the Great, the son of Philip of Macedon, conquered the Persians.
3. Alexander the Great, the son of Philip of Macedon, being chosen generalissimo of the Greeks, destroyed the empire of the Persians.
4. Alexander the Great, the son of Philip of Macedon, being chosen generalissimo of the Greeks, destroyed the empire of the Persians, the inveterate enemies of Greece.
5. About 330 years before Christ, Alexander the Great, the son of Philip of Macedon, being chosen generalissimo of the Greeks, destroyed the empire of the Persians, the inveterate enemies of Greece.
6. About 330 years before Christ, Alexander the Great, the son of Philip of Macedon, after a long series of splendid victories, succeeded in demolishing the empire of the Persians, the ancient and inveterate enemies of Grecian liberty.

Analogous to such an amplification of a simple proposition, is the production of a composition from an analysis like that furnished in the last lesson. When the writer passes from one head to another, he should commence a new paragraph; that is, leaving blank the remainder of the line on which he has been writing, he should pass to the next, and commence about an inch from the left edge of the page. This division is important. A distinct portion of a composition relating to a particular point, whether consisting of one sentence or of more, should invariably constitute a distinct paragraph.

Of course, different writers, in the expression of their ideas, will amplify in different ways, according to their respective turns of mind and the amount of thought they bestow on the subject. Yet the general principles stated below will apply in a majority of cases, and may be found of service.

§ 405. As regards the introduction, it must be short, pointed, and appropriate. On this part of the composition much depends, for it is all-important that a good impression be made at the outset. The reader's mind, not yet occupie with facts, or fairly engaged in the consideration of the subject, is directed chiefly to the words and constructions employed;

---

next step? In what does amplification consist? Give an example in which a simple proposition is made the basis of five successive amplifications. To such an amplification what is analogous? What is the meaning of *commencing a new paragraph?* When should a new paragraph be commenced?

§ 405. What must be the character of introductions? Why is it important that they

and, if it finds ground for severe criticism, will naturally be prejudiced against the author and his work. If the composition is to be short, the introduction should be brief in proportion. In some cases, a formal introduction is unnecessary, and the author at once lays down the proposition he intends to prove, or defines the subject of which he proposes to treat. In this case, the first sentence should be brief, forcible, and striking.

§ 406. An effective introduction is frequently made by commencing with a general proposition, proceeding thence to a particular statement, and following this with an individual application; as in the following paragraph from The Spectator, which would be an appropriate introduction for an essay on "The Art of Music, as practised by the Ancient Hebrews:"—

(*General Assertion.*) "Music, among those who were styled the chosen people, was a religious art. (*Particular assertion.*) The songs of Sion, which we have reason to believe were in high repute among the courts of the Eastern monarchs, were nothing else but psalms, and pieces of poetry, that adored or celebrated the Supreme Being. (*Individual assertion.*) The greatest conqueror in this holy nation, after the manner of the old Grecian lyrics, did not only compose the words of his divine odes, but generally set them to music himself; after which, his works, though they were consecrated to the tabernacle, became the national entertainment, as well as the devotion, of his people."

§ 407. The commonest and easiest introduction, however, is one in which a remark is made respecting the general class to which the object under consideration belongs; from which remark there is an easy transition to an analogous statement respecting the particular case in question. An example of such an introduction follows:—

(*General Statement.*) "Few institutions can contribute more to preserve civilization, and promote moral and intellectual improvement among all ranks of people, than the establishment of public lectures in every part of the kingdom, periodically repeated after a short interval. (*Particular Statement.*) Such is the light in which are to be considered

---

should be well written? To what must the length of the introduction be proportioned? Instead of presenting a formal introduction, to what does the writer sometimes proceed? In this case, what should be the character of the first sentence?

§ 406. How is an effective introduction frequently made? Give an example.

§ 407. Describe the commonest introduction. Give an example. Give the substance of an introduction appropriate to the essay on *Anger* analyzed in the last lesson.

the discourses appointed by the wisdom of the Church to be everywhere held on the recurrence of the seventh day. By these, the meanest and most illiterate are enabled to hear moral and philosophical treatises on every thing which concerns their several duties, without expense, and without solicitation."

An introduction of this character would be appropriate to the essay on Anger, analyzed in the last lesson; something, for instance, like the following:—

Every passion in the breast of man, when allowed to control his action, unrestrained by the conservative power of reason, is attended with the unhappiest consequences, both to himself and the community in which he lives. If this is true of the passions in general, even of those which are comparatively mild in their nature, how emphatically is it the case with Anger, which, more than all others, disdains the control of good sense and a sound understanding.

§ 408. A happy allusion to some story, tradition, or historical fact, is among the most pleasing, and therefore successful, introductions that can be employed. When the circumstance to which reference is made is well known, the mere allusion is sufficient; as when we say, "There are some to whose charity ties of blood are the only *open sesame*." The story of "The Forty Thieves," in which these words occur as the charm used in opening the door of the robbers' cave, is familiar to every one, and therefore an explanation is unnecessary. If, however, there is a likelihood that some may be ignorant of the subject alluded to, it is well briefly to tell the story, and then to apply it in the case in question. This is gracefully done in the following example, which would be an admirable introduction for the subject, "Liberty to be cherished, under whatever form it may appear":—

"Ariosto tells a pretty story of a fairy, who, by some mysterious law of her nature, was condemned to appear at certain seasons in the form of a foul and poisonous snake. Those who injured her during this period of her disguise were forever excluded from participation in the blessings she bestowed. But to those, who, in spite of her loathsome aspect, pitied and protected her, she afterwards revealed herself in the beautiful and celestial form which was natural to her; accompanied their footsteps, granted all their wishes, filled their houses with wealth, made them happy in love, and victorious in war. Such a spirit is Lib-

---

§ 408. What is mentioned as one of the most pleasing introductions? In what case is the mere allusion sufficient? When is an explanation necessary? Give an example of a happy introductory allusion.

erty. At times she takes the form of a hateful reptile. She grovels, she hisses, she stings. But woe to those who in disgust shall venture to crush her! And happy are those, who, having dared to receive her in her degraded and frightful shape, shall at length be rewarded by her in the time of her beauty and glory."

§ 409. A definition may be amplified by presenting the meaning of the term defined under different forms, if there is danger of its being misunderstood; by stating any erroneous impression respecting it against which it may be necessary to guard; or, negatively, by pointing out in what it does not consist. Historical illustrations and quotations may be multiplied according to the reading of the student. Arguments for or against a proposition may be extended by enumerating the particular instances from which the general truth has been deduced, in which case the process is known as Induction; or by an appeal to the statements of others,-which is called the argument from Testimony; or by referring to what is proved or acknowledged to be true in similar cases, which is the argument from Analogy. Under the head of effects, we may extend our observations to collateral consequences; or contrast the subject under discussion with its opposite, as regards the results which follow from each. The conclusion, in many cases, makes a practical application of the subject; which may be diversified by appealing to the conscience, or sense of right and wrong; to the selfish propensities, on which considerations of expediency act; to the common sense, which weighs what is said, and opens the mind of the candid enquirer to conviction; or to the feelings, which awaken the sympathy, and persuade, though they may fail to convince.

---

§ 409. How may a definition be amplified? What is said of historical illustrations and quotations? In what three ways may arguments be extended? Under the head of effects, how may we amplify? What does the conclusion in many cases do? How may it be diversified?

LESSON LXIX.

REVISION AND CORRECTION OF COMPOSITIONS.

§ 410. *Revision of Compositions.*—When a composition has been prepared according to the suggestions in the last two lessons, the next thing is to revise it. Before this is attempted, a short interval should be allowed to elapse, so that the writer may, in a measure, forget the expressions he has used, and criticise his work as severely and impartially as if it were the production of another.

To ensure time for this important examination, at least a week should be allowed for the preparation of each exercise; the first part of which should be appropriated by the student to its composition, and the remainder to its careful correction. In revising, each sentence should be read aloud slowly and distinctly, that the ear may aid the eye in detecting faults. The principles laid down for the promotion of Propriety, Precision, Strength, &c., should be strictly followed. Whatever violates them must be altered, no matter what the expense of time or trouble. Even such passages as seem doubtful to the writer, although he may be unable to detect in them any positive error, it will be safest to change. The commonest faults are solecisms, tautologies, redundancies, and a want of unity; for the detection of these, therefore, the reviser should be constantly on the alert. Having satisfied himself that, in these particulars, his sentences will pass criticism, he should next seek to increase their effect and enhance their beauty, by improving, polishing, and ornamenting his style, when this can be done without the appearance of affectation. He should ensure that a proper connection is maintained between the parts, supplying omitted matter that may be essential to a proper understanding of the train of thought, and omitting whatever of a foreign nature he may at first inadvertently have introduced.

A clean copy is now to be made, in doing which regard must be had to neatness of chirography. A careless habit of writing is apt to lead to a careless habit of composing, a careless habit of study, and a careless habit of life. What is worth doing at all, it has been remarked is worth doing well; and, therefore, though it may seem to some a tri-

---

§ 410. After a composition is written, what is next necessary? What is said with respect to allowing an interval between the act of composing and revising? Describe the process of revision. In making a clean copy, what must be regarded? What is

fling matter, the careful student will see that his exercise is presented in the neatest possible form. The most convenient paper, as regards size, is the ordinary letter sheet. A margin of an inch and a half should be allowed on each side for the remarks of the teacher. The subject should occupy a line by itself, should be equally distant from both margins, and should be written in a larger hand than the rest. Attention must be paid to the spelling and punctuation. When there is not room for the whole of a word at the end of a line, it must be divided after one of its syllables, and the hyphen must connect the separated parts as directed in § 202.

SUGGESTIONS TO THE TEACHER.

§ 411. *Correction of Compositions.*—Most teachers have their own system of examining and correcting compositions: those who have not, may find the following suggestions of service :—

I. Read the exercises presented in the presence of the class, and invite criticism from all. The credits allowed should be based, as well on the promptitude and soundness of the remarks thus made, as on the merits of the performances submitted. It is surprising to see how soon this simple exercise develops a critical taste, and what a salutary effect this taste in turn produces on the style of those in whom it is awakened. Underline words in which errors of any kind occur, and require the student to correct them himself. Remarks on the style may with advantage be made by the teacher, and their substance embodied in the margins left for that purpose.

II. In certain words, errors in orthography are very common; *business* is apt to be written *buisness; separate, seperate; believe, beleive,* &c. When such errors occur, let the words be spelled by the whole class in concert. If, as is often the case, special difficulty is found in spelling particular words, it is well for the teacher to keep a record of the latter, and to give them to the class from time to time as a lesson in orthography.

III. In correcting compositions, do not criticise so closely or severely as to discourage the pupil; but adapt your remarks to his degree of advancement. Let your corrections, in every case, be in harmony with

---

said of a careless habit of writing? What suggestions are made with respect to paper, &c.?

the scope and style of the exercise. With beginners, it is well to make no other alterations than such as are absolutely required. As the composer advances, his performances may be more closely criticised, and his attention may be directed to those nicer points, to which, at an earlier period, it would be injudicious to refer.

IV. After a criticism by the class and remarks by the teacher, the student should make the required corrections, and submit them for approval. He should then copy his exercise in a book provided for the purpose, a comparison of the different parts of which will at any time show what progress he has made.

V. In correcting, the student will save time and trouble by availing himself of some of the marks used in the correction of proof, and exhibited on a specimen sheet at the close of this volume.

EXERCISE IN AMPLIFICATION.

I. Amplify, according to the example in § 404, in five or more successive sentences, each of the following simple propositions:—

    1. Alfred the Great died.
    2. Richard Cœur de Lion engaged in one of the Crusades.
    3. A storm wrecked the Spanish Armada.
    4. Cornwallis surrendered at Yorktown.
    5. Can we doubt the immortality of the soul?

II. According to the example in § 406, construct an introduction asserting,

(*Generally*) that a knowledge of music is becoming rapidly extended in this country; (*Particularly*) that singing and instrumental music are studied in different sections and by all grades of society; and (*Individually*) that almost every household contains some performer. These propositions must be amplified, and constitute not less than three distinct sentences.

III. Write, on the same plan, an introduction laying down the proposition that dissimulation is one of the prominent faults of the present generation.

IV. According to the example in § 407, write introductions stating,

1. That a virtue carried to an extreme becomes a fault; and that, therefore, by those who do not look closely enough to discern the line which distinguishes the two, they are apt to be confounded: apply this in the case of *frugality* and *parsimony*.
2. The general consequence of becoming familiar with any thing, and the particular consequence of becoming familiar with vice.
3. The fact that every tongue may be regarded as an index to the peculiarities of the people speaking it, and that this is the case with the English language.

LESSON LXX.—EXERCISE IN AMPLIFICATION.

Prepare an Essay on ANGER from the analysis in Lesson LXVII.

LESSON LXXI.—EXERCISE IN AMPLIFICATION.

Write an Essay on EDUCATION from the analysis already prepared.

LESSON LXXII.—EXERCISE ON PLAIN AND FIGURATIVE LANGUAGE.

Compose two sentences for each of the following words, one of which shall contain it in its literal, the other in its figurative, signification:—

EXAMPLES.—WEIGH. [*Literal.*] On *weighing* the goods he had purchased that morning at the market, he found they were deficient by at least two pounds.

[*Figurative.*] After well *weighing* the matter in his mind, he determined upon pursuing the plan he had first intended.

BITTER. [*Literal.*] Among the fruits we met with in this country, was a sort of *bitter* apple, very disagreeable to the taste.

[*Figurative.*] He is now no longer the gay, thoughtless creature of former years his face is furrowed, his look haggard and anxious, and his heart a prey to the *bitterest* anguish.

Rest—stand—watch—cover—mask—idle—deep—sleep—monument—constellation—refulgent—overwhelm—sepulchre—response—burn—discover—observation—entertain—carnation—illuminate—eradicate—torment—labyrinth—emanate—pliable.

LESSON LXXIII.—Exercise in Extended Simile.

Trace, at length, the points of resemblance between the given subjects that follow, carrying out the comparison as in the Example:—

EXAMPLE.—OLD AGE, *Sunset.* Old age has been called the sunset of life; it is then that the mind, free from the agitation and tumult of the passions, is calm and tranquil, like the still serenity of the evening, when the busy sound of labor is hushed, and the glare of the meridian sun has passed away. The soul of the just man, conscious of his own integrity, like the glorious orb enveloped in those mellow tints which are then reflected from it in a thousand hues, sinks into a peaceful slumber, again to rise in brighter splendor, and renew in another world the course destined for it by the Almighty Ruler of the universe.

1. *Youth*—morning. 2. *Life*—an ocean. 3. *Joy and sorrow*—light and shade. 4. *Knowledge*—a hill. 5. *Earth*—a mother. 6. *Uncultivated genius*—an unpolished diamond. 7. *Neglected talent*—a flower in the desert. 8. *Death of a child*—blighting of a blossom. 9. *Charity diffusing its blessings*—the sun imparting light and heat. 10. *Honor appearing through a mean habit*—the sun breaking through clouds.

LESSON LXXIV.—Exercise in Extended Simile.

Select natural objects to which the following abstract qualities may be compared, and carry out the simile as in the Example in the last Lesson:—

ADVERSITY.	AMBITION.	PEACE.	DEATH.
PROSPERITY.	IGNORANCE.	WAR.	MEMORY.
MELANCHOLY.	CALUMNY.	SIN.	JUSTICE.

LESSON LXXV.—Exercise in Metaphorical Language.

Compose sentences containing the following words used, metaphorically, in the sense of the words placed after them in italics:—

EXAMPLE.—PATH, *Career.* Notwithstanding all the temptations held out to him, he resolutely pursued the *path* of integrity, untouched alike by the follies and licentiousness of a corrupt court.

1. Crown—*glory.* 2. Dregs—*vice.* 3. Cloak—*covering.* 4. Yoke—*power.* 5. Abyss—*ruin.* 6. Spring—

source. 7. Fruits — *results*. 8. Curb — *restraint*. 9. Blow — *affliction*. 10. Rod — *tyranny*. 11. Veil — *conceal*. 12. Paint — *describe*. 13. Blush — *become red*. 14. Drink — *absorb*. 15. Seal — *close*. 16. Dance — *move gracefully*. 17. Steal — *move silently*. 18. Frown upon — *testify disapprobation of*. 19. Fly — *move swiftly*. 20. Scum — *unworthy portion*.

LESSON LXXVI.—EXERCISE IN ALLEGORY.

Two examples of Allegory, extracted from The Spectator, are presented below. The one is an apologue, or fable, which, to convey a great moral truth, represents the lower animals as possessing reason, and inanimate objects as endowed with life and intelligence; the second is an allegory proper, which, with the same end in view, personifies the abstract qualities. Imitate the latter model in allegories representing,

I. TRUTH and FALSEHOOD.
II. DILIGENCE and IDLENESS.
III. MODESTY and ASSURANCE.
IV. Man, a voyager, addressed on the one hand by PLEASURE, on the other by VIRTUE.

THE COMPLAINING DROP.

"A drop of water fell out of a cloud into the sea; and, finding itself lost in such an immensity of fluid matter, broke out into the following reflection:—'Alas! what an inconsiderable creature am I in this prodigious ocean of waters! My existence is of no concern to the universe; I am reduced to a kind of nothing, and am less than the least of the works of God.' It so happened that an oyster, which lay in the neighborhood of this drop, chanced to gape and swallow it up in the midst of this its humble soliloquy. The drop lay a great while hardening in the shell, until by degrees it was ripened into a pearl; which, falling into the hands of a diver, after a long series of adventures, is at present that famous pearl which is fixed on the top of the Persian diadem."

THE PALACE OF VANITY.

(From an Allegory entitled " The Paradise of Fools.")

"At last we approached a bower, at the entrance of which Error was seated. The trees were thick woven, and the place where he sat artfully contrived to darken him a little. He was disguised in a whitish robe, which he had put on that he might appear to us with a nearer resemblance to Truth; and as she has a light whereby she manifests the beauties of nature to the eyes of her adorers, so he had provided himself with a magical wand, that he might do something in imitation of it, and please with delusions. This he lifted solemnly, and, muttering to himself, bid the glories which he kept under enchantment to appear before us. Immediately we cast our eyes on that part of the sky to which he pointed, and observed a thin blue prospect; which cleared as mountains in a summer morning when the mist goes off, and the palace of Vanity appeared to sight. * * * * *

"At the gate, the travellers neither met with a porter, nor waited till one should appear; every one thought his merits a sufficient passport, and pressed forward. In the hall we met with several phantoms, that roved amongst us and ranged the company according to their sentiments. There was decreasing Honor, that had nothing to show but an old coat of his ancestor's achievements. There was Ostentation, that made himself his own constant subject; and Gallantry, strutting upon his tiptoes. At the upper end of the hall stood a throne, whose canopy glittered with all the riches that gayety could contrive to lavish on it; and between the gilded arms sat Vanity, decked in the peacock's feathers, and acknowledged for another Venus by her votaries. The boy who stood beside her for a Cupid, and who made the world to bow before her, was called Self-Conceit. His eyes had every now and then a cast inwards, to the neglect of all objects about him; and the arms which he made use of for conquest, were borrowed from those against whom he had a design. The arrow which he shot at the soldier was fledged from his own plume of feathers; the dart he directed against the man of wit, was winged from the quills he writ with; and that which he sent against those who presumed upon their riches, was headed with gold out of their treasuries. He made nets for statesmen from their own contrivances; he took fire from the eyes of the ladies with which he melted their hearts; and lightning from the tongues of the eloquent, to inflame them with their own glories. At the foot of the throne sat three false Graces; Flattery with a shell of paint, Affectation with a mirror to practise at, and Fashion ever changing the posture of her clothes. These applied themselves to secure the conquests which Self-Conceit had gotten, and had each of them their particular polities. Flattery gave new colors and complexions to all things; Affectation, new airs and appearances, which, as she said, were not vulgar; and Fashion both concealed some home defects, and added some foreign external beauties."

LESSON LXXVII.—EXERCISE IN HYPERBOLE.

Represent the following subjects by Hyperbole.

EXAMPLE.—*An impressive speech.* His speech was so deeply interesting and impressive, that the very walls listened to his arguments, and were moved by his eloquence.

1. The brightness of a lighted room.
2. The splendor of a dress ornamented with jewels.
3. The number of persons in a crowd.
4. The quantity of rain which has fallen in a shower.
5. The thirst of an individual (by the quantity of liquid he consumes).
6. The size of a country (by the rising and setting of the sun).
7. The affliction caused by the death of a distinguished individual.
8. The depth of a precipice.
9. The waves of the ocean in a storm.
10. The heat of a summer day.
11. The refreshing effects of a shower.
12. The excitement of city life.
13. The darkness of night.
14. The selfishness of a miser.
15. Vegetation in the torrid zone.

LESSON LXXVIII.—Exercises in Vision and Apostrophe.

I. Employ Vision in brief descriptions of the following scenes:—

    I. A Battle-scene.   III. An Earthquake.
    II. A Storm at Sea.   IV. A Thunder-storm.

II. Alter the following passages, so that they may contain examples of Apostrophe:—

1. I cannot but imagine that the virtuous heroes, legislators, and patriots of every age and country, are bending from their elevated seats to witness this contest, as if they were incapable, till it be brought to a favorable issue, of enjoying their eternal repose. Let these illustrious immortals enjoy that repose! Their mantle fell when they ascended; and thousands, inflamed with their spirit, and impatient to tread in their steps, are ready to swear by Him that sitteth upon the throne and liveth for ever and ever, that they will protect Freedom in her last asylum, and never desert that cause, which they sustained by their labors, and cemented with their blood.

2. Thus passes the world away. Throughout all ranks and conditions, "one generation passeth, and another generation cometh;" and this great inn is by turns evacuated and replenished by troops of succeeding pilgrims. The world is vain and inconstant. Life is fleeting and transient. When will the sons of men learn to think of it as they ought? When will they learn humanity from the afflictions of their brethren; or moderation and wisdom from the sense of their own fugitive state?

LESSON LXXIX.—Exercise in Personification.

I. Introduce into sentences the following expressions illustrative of Personification:—

Sleep embraces—Nature speaks—The evening invites—The moon gilds—The morning smiles—The sun climbs—Care keeps watch—Night spreads—Vengeance bares his arm—Time has tamed—Years had ploughed—Britain saw—Death prepared his dart—Memory wept—Freedom shrieked—Rapine prowls—Murder stalks—The vessel cleaves—Wisdom strays—Hope fled—Love watches.

II. Write sentences containing the following subjects personified:—

Example.—*Contentment.* If Contentment, the parent of Felicity and the faithful companion of Hope, would whisper her consolations in our ears, in vain might Fortune wreck us on inhospitable shores.

Eternity.	Pity.	Charity.	Folly.
Idleness.	Hope.	Disease.	Peace.
The Grave.	Faith.	Mirth.	Light.

LESSON LXXX.—Exercises in Climax and Antithesis.

I. In each of the following passages, arrange the parts so as to form a Climax :—

EXAMPLE.—*Improperly arranged.* What a piece of work is man! in action how like an angel! how noble in reason! in apprehension how like a god! how infinite in faculties! in form and motion how expressive and admirable

Arranged in the form of a Climax. What a piece of work is man! how noble in reason! how infinite in faculties! in form and motion how expressive and admirable! in action how like an angel! in apprehension how like a god!

1. Nothing can be more worthy of us than to contribute to the happiness of those who have been once useful and are still willing to be so; to be a staff to their declining days; to make the winter of old age wear the aspect of spring; to prevent them from feeling the want of such pleasures as they are able to enjoy; and to smooth the furrows in their faded cheeks.

2. The history of every succeeding generation is this. New objects attract the attention; new intrigues engage the passions of man; new actors come forth on the stage of the world; a new world, in short, in the course of a few years, has gradually and insensibly risen around us; new ministers fill the temples of religion; new members, the seats of justice.

3. It is pleasant to command our appetites and passions, and to keep them in due order, within the bounds of reason and religion, because that is empire; it is pleasant to mortify and subdue our lusts, because that is victory; it is pleasant to be virtuous and good, because that is to excel many others; it is pleasant to grow better, because that is to excel ourselves.

II. Represent the following subjects in Antithesis, remembering the principle stated in § 374 :—

EXAMPLE.—*A Wise Man and a Fool.* A wise man endeavors to shine in himself; a fool, to outshine others. The former is humbled by the sense of his own infirmities, the latter is lifted up by the discovery of those which he observes in others. The wise man considers what he wants; the fool, what he abounds in. The wise man is happy when he gains his own approbation; and the fool, when he recommends himself to the applause of those about him.

Summer and Winter.
Modesty and Prudery.
Gratitude and Ingratitude.
Morality and Religion.
Knowledge and Ignorance.
Geography and History.

Pride and Humility.
Moderation and Intemperance.
Peace and War.
Discretion and Cunning.
Cheerfulness and Melancholy.
Spring and Autumn.

LESSON LXXXI.—Parallels.

A Parallel is a comparison showing the points of similitude and difference between two persons, characters, or objects that resemble each other either in appearance or in reality. In this variety of composition, individual peculiarities are often contrasted by means of Antitheses with fine effect. From Dr. Johnson's Life of Pope, we extract the following fine specimen of the Parallel:—

DRYDEN AND POPE.

"In acquired knowledge, the superiority must be allowed to Dryden, whose education was more scholastic, and who, before he became an author, had been allowed more time for study, with better means of information. His mind has a larger range, and he collects his images and illustrations from a more extensive circumference of science. Dryden knew more of man in his general nature, and Pope in his local manners. The notions of Dryden were formed by comprehensive speculation, and those of Pope by minute attention. There is more dignity in the knowledge of Dryden, and more certainty in that of Pope. Poetry was not the sole praise of either, for both excelled likewise in prose; but Pope did not borrow his prose from his predecessor. The style of Dryden is capricious and varied; that of Pope is cautious and uniform. Dryden obeys the motions of his own mind; Pope constrains his mind to his own rules of composition. Dryden is sometimes vehement and rapid; Pope is always smooth, uniform, and gentle. Dryden's page is a natural field, rising into inequalities, and diversified by the varied exuberance of abundant vegetation; Pope's is a velvet lawn, shaven by the scythe, and levelled by the roller.

"Of genius,—that power which constitutes a poet; that quality without which judgment is cold, and knowledge is inert; that energy which collects, combines, amplifies, and animates;—the superiority must, with some hesitation, be allowed to Dryden. It is not to be inferred, that of this poetical vigor Pope had only a little, because Dryden had more; for every other writer, since Milton, must give place to Pope: and even of Dryden it must be said, that if he has brighter paragraphs, he has not better poems. Dryden's performances were always hasty, either excited by some external occasion, or extorted by domestic necessity; he composed without consideration, and published without correction. What his mind could supply at call, or gather in one excursion, was all that he sought, and all that he gave. The dilatory caution of Pope enabled him to condense his sentiments, to multiply his images, and to accumulate all that study might produce, or chance might supply. If the flights of Dryden, therefore, are higher, Pope continues longer on the wing. If of Dryden's fire the blaze is brighter, of Pope's the heat is more regular and constant. Dryden often surpasses expectation, and Pope never falls below it. Dryden is read with frequent astonishment, and Pope with perpetual delight."

Draw Parallels, in the style of the example just given between,

   1. Napoleon and Washington.
   2. Lafayette and Howard.

LESSON LXXXII.—EXERCISE IN PARALLELS.

Draw Parallels between,

1. Queen Elizabeth and Queen Victoria.
2. The United States and England.

LESSON LXXXIII.—Exercise in Parallels.

Draw Parallels between,
1. The Torrid and the Temperate Zone.
2. The European and the Oriental.
3. The Eloquence of the Bar and that of the Pulpit.
4. A Plain and a Florid Style.

LESSON LXXXIV.—Exercise in Defining Synonymes.

Analogous to the drawing of Parallels is the defining of the shades of difference between synonymous terms, models of which will be found on pp. 280, 281. In a similar manner, show the distinction between the following synonymes, and illustrate their use in different sentences:—

1. Invention, Discovery.
2. Genius, Talent.
3. Pride, Vanity.
4. Handsome, Pretty.
5. Wit, Humor.
6. Poison, Venom.
7. Peaceful, Peaceable.
8. Continuation, Continuance.

LESSON LXXXV.—Exercise in Defining Synonymes.

Show the difference between the following synonymous terms:—

1. Associate, Companion. 2. Idle, Lazy, Indolent. 3. Great, Large, Big. 4. Sick, Sickly, Diseased. 5. Contemptible, Despicable, Pitiful. 6. Right, Claim, Privilege.* 7. Disregard, Slight, Neglect. 8. Anecdote, Tale, Story, Novel, Romance.

LESSON LXXXVI.—Exercise in Paraphrasing.

A Paraphrase is the amplified explanation of a passage in clearer terms than those employed by its author. Paraphrases frequently occur in versions from foreign languages; when, instead of a literal translation of the original text, the substance is given in an amplified form and in a style which is regarded as more intelligible.

Maxims, Aphorisms, Proverbs, and Saws, are often paraphrased. A Maxim is a proposition briefly expressed, which teaches a moral truth and is susceptible of practical application. An Aphorism (which corresponds with the Apophthegm of the ancients) is a speculative rather than a practical proposition, embodying a doctrine or the principles of a science. A Proverb or Saying (the Adage of the ancients) is a terse proposition current among all classes, relating to matters of worldly wisdom as well as moral truth. A Saw is a vulgar proverb. The following examples will show the difference between them.

Maxim.—Forgiveness is the noblest revenge.
Aphorism.—Originality in Art is the individualizing of the universal.
Proverb.—A word to the wise is sufficient.
Saw.—A nod is as good as a wink to a blind horse.

Paraphrase the following Maxims, Proverbs, &c..—

EXAMPLE.—*Wealth begets want.*

Paraphrase.—The desires of man increase with his acquisitions. Every step that he advances, brings something within his view, which he did not see before, and which, as soon as he sees it, he begins to want. When necessity ends, curiosity begins; and no sooner are we supplied with every thing that nature can demand, than we sit down to contrive artificial appetites.

1. Either never attempt, or persevere to the end.
2. Poor and content is rich, and rich enough.
3. Good news doeth good like medicine.
4. No pains, no gains.
5. Fear is the mark of a mean spirit.
6. One swallow does not make a summer.
7. Nothing venture, nothing have.
8. Between two stools one comes to the ground.
9. One good turn deserves another.
10. Money makes the mare go.
11. It never rains but it pours.
12. Penny wise, pound foolish.

LESSON LXXXVII—EXERCISE IN PARAPHRASING.

Paraphrase the following passages :—

1. Make no man your idol, for the best man must have faults; and his faults will insensibly become yours, in addition to your own.

2. He that argues for victory is but a gambler in words, seeking to enrich himself by another's loss.

3. Distress and difficulty are known to operate in private life as the spurs of diligence.

4. The love of gain never made a painter; but it has marred many.

5. Complaints and murmurs are often loudest and most frequent among those who possess all the external means of temporal enjoyment.

6. The want of employment is one of the most frequent causes of vice.

7. A wound from a tongue is worse than a wound from the sword: for the latter affects only the body; the former, the soul.

8. Trust him little who praises all; him less, who censures all; and him least, who is indifferent about all.

9. He that finds truth, without loving her, is like a bat; which, though it hath eyes to discern that there is a sun, yet hath so evil eyes, that it can not delight in the sun.

10. They who have never known prosperity, can hardly be said to be unhappy; it is from the remembrance of joys we have lost, that the arrows of affliction are pointed.

11. Every man has just as much vanity as he wants understanding.

12. The strongest passions allow us some rest, but vanity keeps us in perpetual motion. "What a dust do I raise!" says the fly upon a coach-wheel. "At what a rate do I drive!" says the fly upon the horse's back.

LESSON LXXXVIII—Exercise in Abridging.

Abridging (sometimes called Epitomizing) is the opposite of Amplification, and consists in expressing the substance of a passage, article, or volume, in fewer words.

Example.—Tradition says, that Foo-tsze, the Chinese philosopher, was in his youth of so impatient a temper, that he could not endure the drudgery of learning, and determined to give up literary pursuits for some manual employment. One day, as he was returning home with a full determination to go to school no longer, he happened to pass by a half-witted old woman, who was rubbing a small bar of iron on a whetstone. When the young student asked her the reason of this strange employment, she replied, "Why, sir, I have lost my knitting-needle, and just thought I would rub down this bar to make me another." The words acted like magic on the young philosopher, who returned to his books with tenfold diligence; and, whenever he felt impatient and despondent, would say to himself, "If a half-witted old woman has resolution enough to rub down a bar of iron into a needle, it would be disgraceful in me to have less perseverance, when the highest honors of the empire are before me." He lived to see the justice of these reflections. His acquirements, in process of time, made his name a proverb, and procured for him those very honors, which, but for this fortunate incident, he would have thrown away, and which without exertion none can hope to attain.

Abridged.—Foo-tsze, the Chinese philosopher, was possessed of so little diligence in his youth that he determined to abandon literary pursuits. Returning from school with the resolution of at once seeking some manual employment, he observed a half-witted old woman rubbing a bar of iron on a whetstone. Asking the reason of this strange proceeding, he learned from her that she had lost her knitting-needle and was endeavoring to make another by rubbing down the bar. The words acted like magic on the young philosopher. "Shall an old woman," he said to himself, ' have more resolution and perseverance than I, within whose reach are the highest honors of the empire?" Inspired with new vigor, he returned to his books; his good resolutions were kept; and history still names him as among the wisest of philosophers.

LESSON LXXXIX.—Exercise in Abridging.

Abridge, and present in your own words, the matter contained in Lesson XXXIX. of this volume, on " The Sublime ".

LESSON XC.—Exercise in Abridging.

Abridge, and present in your own words, the matter contained in Lesson LXVI., on Criticism.

LESSON XCI.—Exercise in Criticism.

In the style of the Examples presented in Lesson LXVI., write a criticism on the Allegory entitled "The Palace of Vanity," quoted in Lesson LXXVI.

LESSON XCII.—Exercise in Criticism.

Questions on the Remarks in the Preceding Lessons.—What is an apologue, or fable? What is an allegory proper? What is a parallel? What figure is used with advantage in parallels? What is a paraphrase? In what do paraphrases frequently occur? What are often paraphrased? What is a maxim? What is an aphorism? What was it called by the ancients? What is a proverb? What is a saw? Give examples of each. What is meant by abridging? What other name is sometimes given to this process?

Write a criticism on Dr. Johnson's Parallel between Dryden and Pope, quoted in Lesson LXXXI.

LESSON XCIII.

DESCRIPTION OF MATERIAL OBJECTS.

§ 412. *Composition* is the art of inventing ideas and expressing them by means of written language.

A composition is a written production on any subject, and of any length or style.

§ 413. There are two great divisions under which all compositions may be classed,—Prose and Poetry.

Those compositions are embraced under the head of Prose, in which a natural order and mode of expression are employed, without reference to an exact arrangement of syllables or the recurrence of certain sounds.

Poetry embraces such compositions as are characterized by a departure from the natural order and mode of expression; or, by an exact arrangement of syllables or the recurrence of certain sounds.

§ 414. The parts of composition, whether Prose or Poetry, are five; Description, Narration, Argument, Exposition, and Speculation. Either of these may separately constitute the bulk of a written production; or, they may all, as is frequently the case, enter, in a greater or less degree, into the same composition.

§ 415. *Description* consists in delineating the characteristics of any object by means of words. It forms an important part of almost every variety of composition; and allows the widest scope for ornament and beauty of language. The style used in description should correspond with the character

---

§ 412. What is composition? What is meant by a composition?
§ 413. What are the two great divisions under which all compositions are classed? Which are embraced under the head of Prose? Which, under Poetry?
§ 414. Enumerate the parts which enter, in a greater or less degree, into different compositions.
§ 415. In what does description consist? For what does it allow wide scope? What

of the object treated. If the latter is grand, the language in which it is described should be elevated in proportion. If beauty is the leading characteristic of the one, it should distinguish the other also. Whatever the nature of the object described, the style, to be effective, should be adapted to it, according to the principle stated under the head of Harmony.

Writers are most frequently called on to describe material objects, natural scenery, and persons.

§ 416. In the description of material objects, such heads as the following will generally be found appropriate; and, in drawing up an analysis for any particular subject, a selection may be made from them, and such new divisions introduced as are suggested:—

    I. The place where, and the circumstances under which, the object was seen; the time when it was made, invented, or discovered; the changes which time may have produced in it.
    II. Its history; traditions or reminiscences connected with it.
    III. The materials of which, and the persons by whom, it was made.
    IV. Its form, size, and general appearance.
    V. Comparison of it with any similar object.
    VI. The feelings excited by beholding it.
    VII. The purpose for which it was designed.
    VIII. The effects it has produced.

§ 417. As a specimen of this kind of description, we extract from Forsyth's "Remarks on Antiquities, Arts, and Letters," a passage on

THE COLISEUM.

A colossal taste gave rise to the Coliseum. Here, indeed, gigantic dimensions were necessary for, though hundreds could enter at once, and fifty thousand find seats, the space was still insufficient for Rome, and the crowd for the morning games began at midnight. Vespasian and Titus, as if presaging their own deaths, hurried the building, and left several marks of their precipitancy behind. In the upper walls they have inserted stones which had evidently been dressed for a different purpose. Some of the arcades are grossly unequal; no moulding preserves the same level and form round the whole ellipse, and every order is full of license.

Happily for the Coliseum, the shape necessary to an amphitheatre has given it a stability of construction sufficient to resist fires, and earthquakes, and lightnings, and

---

    is said of the style to be used in description? What are writers most frequently called on to describe?

    § 416. In the description of material objects, what heads will generally be found appropriate?

sieges. Its elliptical form was the hoop which bound and held it entire till barbarians rent that consolidating ring; popes widened the breach; and time, not unassisted, continues the work of dilapidation. At this moment, the hermitage is threatened with a dreadful crash; and a generation not very remote must be content, I apprehend, with the picture of this stupendous monument.

When the whole amphitheatre was entire, a child might comprehend its design in a moment, and go direct to his place without straying in the porticoes; for each arcade bears its number engraved, and opposite to every fourth arcade was a staircase. This multiplicity of wide, straight, and separate passages, proves the attention which the ancients paid to the safe discharge of a crowd; it finely illustrates the precept of Vitruvius, and exposes the perplexity of some modern theatres.

Every nation has undergone its revolution of vices; and, as cruelty is not the present vice of ours, we can all humanely execrate the purpose of amphitheatres, now that they lie in ruins. Moralists may tell us that the truly brave are never cruel; but this monument says, "No." Here sat the conquerors of the world, coolly to enjoy the tortures and death of men who had never offended them. Two aqueducts were scarcely sufficient to wash off the human blood which a few hours' sport shed in this imperial shambles. Twice in one day came the senators and matrons of Rome to the butchery; a virgin always gave the signal for slaughter; and, when glutted with bloodshed, those ladies sat down in the wet and streaming arena to a luxurious supper! Such reflections check our regret for its ruin.

As it now stands, the Coliseum is a striking image of Rome itself; decayed, vacant, serious, yet grand; half-gray and half-green; erect on one side and fallen on the other with consecrated ground in its bosom; inhabited by a beadsman; visited by every caste; for moralists, antiquaries, painters, architects, devotees, all meet here to meditate, to examine, to draw, to measure, and to pray. "In contemplating antiquities," says Livy, "the mind itself becomes antique." It contracts from such objects a venerable rust, which I prefer to the polish and the point of those wits who have lately profaned this august ruin with ridicule.

EXERCISE.

Write a Criticism on the above extract.

LESSON XCIV.

DESCRIPTION OF NATURAL SCENERY, AND PERSONS.

§ 418. In descriptions of natural scenery, a selection may generally be made from the following heads. The order in which they should be treated depends somewhat on the nature of the subject.

---

§ 418. In descriptions of natural scenery, what heads will generally be found appropriate?

I. Circumstances under which it was seen; whether at sunrise, at noon, or by moonlight.
II. Natural features of the scene; level or undulating; fertile or barren; vegetation, trees, mountains, streams, &c., within view.
III. Improvements of art; whether well cultivated; buildings, and other productions of human industry.
IV. Living creatures that animate the scene; human beings.
V. Neighboring inhabitants; peculiarities, &c.
VI. Sounds; murmur of a stream; noise of a waterfall; rustling of leaves; lowing of cattle; barking of dogs; singing of birds; cries of children; noise of machinery, &c.
VII. Distant prospect.
VIII. Comparison with any other scene.
IX. Historical associations.
X. Feelings awakened in the mind.

§ 419. For an example of this kind of description, the student is referred to the following extract from Sir Walter Scott. He will find other specimens, of a different style, inasmuch as they treat of individual curiosities of scenery rather than extended landscapes, in Willis's description of the Grotto of Adelsburg, quoted in p. 90 of this volume, and Campbell's Account of Fingal's Cave in a Letter to the poet Thomson, Lesson XCVI.

A YORKSHIRE FOREST SCENE.

The sun was setting upon one of the rich grassy glades of this forest. Hundreds of broad-headed, short-stemmed, wide-branched, oaks, which had witnessed, perhaps, the stately march of the Roman soldiery, flung their gnarled arms over a thick carpet of the most delicious greensward. In some places, they were intermingled with beeches, hollies, and copsewood of various descriptions, so closely as totally to intercept the level beams of the sinking sun; in others, they receded from each other, forming those long sweeping vistas, in the intricacy of which the eye delights to lose itself, while imagination considers them as the paths to yet wilder scenes of sylvan solitude. Here, the red rays of the sun shot a broken and discolored light that partially hung upon the shattered boughs and mossy trunks of the trees; and there, they illuminated, in brilliant patches, the portions of turf to which they made their way.

A considerable open space in the midst of this glade seemed formerly to have been dedicated to the rites of Druidical superstition; for, on the summit of a hillock so regular as to seem artificial, there still remained part of a circle of rough unhewn stones of large dimensions. Seven stood upright; the rest had been dislodged from their places, probably by the zeal of some convert to Christianity, and lay, some prostrate near their former site, and others on the side of the hill. One large stone only had found its way to the bottom; and, in stopping the course of a small brook which glided smoothly round the foot of the eminence, gave, by its opposition, a feeble voice of murmur to the placid, and elsewhere silent, streamlet.

§ 420. Descriptions of persons are often required in composition. In writing them, such heads as the following are generally taken:—

I. Form; whether tall or short, fleshy or thin, &c.
II. Face, features, hair, expression, &c.
III. Manners; dignified, graceful, awkward, haughty, or affable.
IV. Dress.
V. Any peculiarity of appearance.
VI. Character, disposition, mental abilities, &c.

§ 421. Two graphic specimens of this kind of description are given below: one from Cooper, representing a well-drawn character in his "Last of the Mohicans"; the other, from the elegant pen of Bulwer.

DAVID GAMUT, THE SINGING-MASTER.

The person of this remarkable individual was to the last degree ungainly, without being in any particular manner deformed. He had all the bones and joints of other men, without any of their proportions. Erect, his stature surpassed that of his fellows; though, seated, he appeared reduced within the ordinary limits of our race. The same contrariety in his members seemed to exist throughout the whole man. His head was large; his shoulders, narrow; his arms, long and dangling; while his hands were small, if not delicate. His legs and thighs were thin nearly to emaciation, but of extraordinary length; and his knees would have been considered tremendous, had they not been outdone by the broader foundations on which this false superstructure of blended human orders was so profanely reared. The ill-assorted and injudicious attire of the individual only served to render his awkwardness more conspicuous. A sky-blue coat, with short and broad skirts and low cape, exposed a long thin neck, and longer and thinner legs, to the worst animadversions of the evil-disposed. His nether garment was of yellow nankeen, closely fitted to the shape, and tied at his bunches of knees by large knots of white ribbon, a good deal sullied by use. Clouded cotton stockings, and shoes, on one of the latter of which was a plated spur, completed the costume of the lower extremity of this figure, no curve or angle of which was concealed, but, on the other hand, studiously exhibited, through the vanity or simplicity of its owner. From beneath the flap of an enormous pocket of a soiled vest of embossed silk, heavily ornamented with tarnished silver lace, projected an instrument [a tuning fork], which, from being seen in such martial company, might have been easily mistaken for some mischievous and unknown implement of war. Small as it was, this uncommon engine had excited the curiosity of most of the Europeans in the camp, though several of the provincials were seen to handle it, not only without fear, but with the utmost familiarity. A large civil cocked hat, like those worn by clergymen within the last thirty years, surmounted the whole, furnishing dignity to a good-natured and somewhat vacant countenance, that apparently needed such artificial aid to support the gravity of some high and extraordinary trust.

NINA DI RASELLI.

At once vain, yet high-minded,—resolute, yet impassioned,—there was a gorgeous magnificence in her very vanity and splendor, and ideality in her waywardness: her defects made a part of her brilliancy; without them she would have seemed less woman, and, knowing her, you would have compared all women by her standard. Softer qualities beside her seemed not more charming, but more insipid. She had no vulgar ambition, for she had obstinately refused many alliances which the daughter of Raselli could scarcely have hoped to form. The untutored minds and savage power of the Roman nobles seemed to her imagination, which was full of the *poetry* of rank (its luxury and its graces), as something barbarous and revolting, at once to be dreaded and despised. She had, therefore, passed her twentieth year unmarried, but not, perhaps, without love. The faults themselves of her character, elevated that ideal of love which she had formed. She required some being round whom all her vainer qualities could rally; she felt that where she loved she must adore; she demanded no common idol before which to humble so strong and imperious a mind. Unlike women of a gentler mould, who desire for a short period to exercise the caprices of sweet empire, when she loved she must cease to command, and ride, at once, be humbled to devotion. So rare were the qualities that could attract her, so imperiously did her haughtiness require that those qualities should be above her own, yet of the same order, that her love elevated its object like a god. Accustomed to despise, she felt all the luxury it is to venerate! And if it were her lot to be united to one thus loved, her nature was that which might become elevated by that it gazed on.

For her beauty, reader, shouldst thou ever go to Rome, thou wilt see in the capitol the picture of the Cumæan Sibyl, which, often copied, no copy can even faintly represent; why this is so called I know not, save that it has something strange and unearthly in the dark beauty of the eyes. I beseech thee, mistake not this sibyl for another, for the Roman galleries abound in sibyls. The sibyl I speak of is dark, and the face has an Eastern cast; the robe and turban, gorgeous though they be, grow dim before the rich but transparent roses of the cheek; the hair would be black save for that golden glow which mellows it to a hue and lustre never seen but in the South, and even in the South most rare; the features, not Grecian, are yet faultless; the mouth, the brow, the ripe and exquisite contour, all are human and voluptuous; the expression, the aspect, is something more; the form is, perhaps, too full for the ideal of loveliness, for the proportions of sculpture, for the delicacy of Athenian models; but the luxuriant fault has a majesty. Gaze long upon that picture: it charms, yet commands, the eye. While you gaze, you call back five centuries. You see before you the breathing image of Nina di Raselli.

EXERCISE.

Write a Criticism on either of these extracts.

LESSON XCV.

NARRATION.—ARGUMENT.—EXPOSITION.—SPECULATION.

§ 422. *Narration* is the account of real or imaginary facts or events. A neat or an elegant style is most effective for this kind of writing, in which too much ornament is out of place. Events should be related in the order of their occurrence, and in such a way that the interest of the reader may be kept alive.

§ 422. What is narration? What style is recommended for this kind of writing? In what order should events be related?

§ 423. *Argument* is the statement of reasons for or against a proposition, made with the view of inducing belief in others. Clearness and strength are essential to its success. Little, if any, ornament is necessary; to this element of composition, a neat, diffuse style is appropriate.

§ 424. *Exposition* consists in explaining the meaning of an author, in defining terms, setting forth an abstract subject in its various relations, or presenting doctrines, precepts, principles, or rules, for the purpose of instructing others. A treatise on grammar, for instance, consists principally of exposition. Clearness being the chief object, and the nature of the subject in most cases almost entirely excluding ornament, this kind of matter should be presented in a neat, concise, style.

§ 425. *Speculation* is the expression of theoretical views not as yet verified by fact or practice. It enters largely into works on metaphysics, and is best understood through the medium of a neat, simple, style.

§ 426. A specimen of narration follows:—

THE FIELD OF THE PIOUS.

In one of those terrible eruptions of Mount Etna which have often happened, the danger of the inhabitants of the adjacent country was uncommonly great. To avoid immediate destruction from the flames and the melted lava which ran down the sides of the mountain, the people were obliged to retire to a considerable distance. Amidst the hurry and confusion of such a scene, every one fleeing and carrying away whatever he deemed most precious, two brothers, in the height of their solicitude for the preservation of their wealth and goods, suddenly recollected that their father and mother, both very old, were unable to save themselves by flight. Filial tenderness triumphed over every other consideration. "Where," cried the generous youths, "shall we find a more precious treasure than they are, who gave us being, and who have cherished and protected us through life?" Having said this, the one taking up his father on his shoulders, and the other his mother, they happily made their way through the surrounding smoke and flames. All who were witnesses of this dutiful and affectionate conduct were struck with the highest admiration; and they and their posterity ever after called the plain through which these young men made their retreat, "The Field of the Pious".

---

§ 423. What is argument? In what style is it best presented?

§ 424. In what does exposition consist? Of what, for instance, does it form the principal part? What is the chief object in exposition? What style is appropriate to it?

§ 425. What is speculation? Into what does it largely enter? Through what style is it best understood?

EXERCISE.

I. Amplify the above specimen of narration, presenting it entirely in your own language.

II. Amplify the following heads into a specimen of narration, in the style of the above model, using your own language throughout:—

THE SWORD OF DAMOCLES.

Dionysius, tyrant of Sicily, though surrounded by riches and pleasures, was far from being happy. [Why?]

Damocles, one day, complimented him on his power, and affirmed that no monarch was ever greater or happier than he.

Dionysius asked him whether he would like to make trial of this happiness, and see whether it was as great as he imagined.

On Damocles' gladly consenting, the king ordered a gilded couch to be brought in for him, a splendid banquet to be prepared, and the royal pages to wait on him as if he were their monarch. [Describe the banquet.]

Damocles was intoxicated with pleasure. But, chancing to look up, as he lay luxuriously pillowed on his royal couch, he saw a glittering sword suspended from the ceiling, by a single hair, exactly over his head.

This sight put an end to his joy. The rare perfumes and inviting dishes had lost their charm. [Describe his feelings in detail.] Finally, leaping from the couch, he besought the king to allow him to return to his former humble position. [Moral which Dionysius, in his answer, drew from this act of his courtier, with respect to the happiness of kings.]

LESSON XCVI.

LETTERS.

§ 427. There are six leading divisions of Prose Composition; Letters, Narratives, Fiction, Essays, Theses or Argumentative Discourses, and Orations.

LETTERS.

§ 428. *Definition.*—A Letter is a written communication on any subject from one person to another.

---

§ 427. Enumerate the six leading divisions of prose composition.
§ 428. What is a letter? What is letter-writing commonly called? What is said

Letter-writing is commonly called Epistolary Correspondence. It is one of the most important branches of composition, entering more largely than any other into the daily business of life.

The form of the letter has often been used for essays, novels, histories, &c.; that is, these productions have been divided into parts, each of which commences with an address to some friend of the author or imaginary personage, as if it had passed as an actual communication. Such compositions, however, should be classed under the divisions to which, according to their matter, they respectively belong. The letter proper is one intended for the person to whom it is addressed.

§ 429. *Varieties.*—The principal kinds of letters are,

I. News Letters, or communications to papers or periodicals, containing accounts of what has happened or is happening elsewhere than at the place of publication.

Such communications have lately become popular, and now form a feature of almost all leading newspapers. In these letters, profundity is not expected, unless they treat of political, religious, or other serious topics. They should rather be characterized by brilliancy of thought, and an original, striking, mode of expression. Their effect may often be increased by strokes of humor, and what is commonly called *piquancy*, or a pleasing vein of sarcasm on persons and things in general. Taste and judgment are required for a proper selection of subjects. The space allowed, being generally limited, should be filled to the best advantage. Local matters should be avoided; it is well to introduce no topics but those of general interest.

II. Letters of business. In these, brevity and clearness are all-important. The writer should aim at the greatest degree of conciseness consistent with perspicuity, and should confine himself strictly to the business in hand.

III. Official letters, or such as pass between men in office, respecting public affairs. These are always formal, and

---

of its importance? For what is the form of the letter often used? How should such compositions be classed? What is the letter proper?

§ 429. What are the principal kinds of letters? What are news letters? What is said of the popularity of news letters? What is not expected in them? By what should they be characterized? What often increases their effect? What topics should be selected for such letters? What are required in letters of business? To what must they be confined? What is meant by official letters? Describe them? In letters

abound in phrases of courtesy. Their style should be firm and dignified.

IV. Letters of friendship.

In these, a tendency to diffuseness, arising in young writers from a fear that they may not have enough matter to fill the sheet, must be avoided. "There is hardly any species of composition, in my opinion," says Kirke White, "easier than the epistolary." There is an off-hand ease about the letter which renders its production a work of but little time or difficulty; and, by reason of this very facility of composition, the writer is apt to express himself carelessly and without proper thought. Time and labor should be bestowed on this, as well as every other, department of composition.

Flippancy, also, should be carefully avoided. It must be remembered that what is committed to paper does not, like conversation, pass into forgetfulness; it is preserved, and may, at any time, be made public. We should therefore never write, even to the most intimate friend, any thing which we would be ashamed that the world should see.

The commonest fault, perhaps, of letters of friendship, is egotism. This cannot but be distasteful to the person addressed, no matter how great his interest in the writer. A friend, of course, expects from his correspondent some personal intelligence, but he looks for other matter along with it; and will inevitably be struck with the bad taste of one who confines his letter to an enumeration of his own exploits or those of the limited circle to which he belongs. In like manner, we should avoid filling a letter with details relating to parties with whom the person addressed is unacquainted.

V. Letters of condolence, written to persons in affliction for the purpose of expressing sympathy with their misfortunes. In these, great tact is necessary; for ill-judged consolation, instead of healing the wound, opens it afresh. In this, as well as the two classes which follow, the writer should confine himself to the leading subject of his communication.

VI. Letters of congratulation, or those in which the writer

---

of friendship, to what is there a tendency? What does Kirke White say of epistolary correspondence? To what is this facility of composition apt to lead? What else must be carefully avoided? Why? What should we never write, even to the most intimate friend? What is the commonest fault of letters of friendship? What is the effect of egotism on the person addressed? With what, in like manner, should we avoid filling a letter? What are letters of condolence? Why should they be written with great tact? To what should the writer confine himself? What are letters of con-

professes his joy at the success or happiness of another, or at some event deemed fortunate for both parties or for the community at large. They should be brief, sincere, and to the point.

VII. Letters of introduction, in which the writer commends a friend to the kind offices of some third party.

It is customary to leave such letters unsealed, and to put on the back, besides the superscription, the name of the party introduced. In giving letters of introduction, it is of primary importance to adhere strictly to the truth. It is false kindness to exaggerate the merits of the bearer, or to recommend in high terms a person but partially known. Such a course often places all parties concerned in an unpleasant position.

§ 430. *Style.*—The style of letters (with the exception of official communications, which require a studied and formal elegance) should be simple, easy, and natural. All appearance of effort, far-fetched ornaments, and attempts at display, are fatal to their effect. Puerilities and affected simplicity, on the other hand, are equally objectionable.

A good letter bears the same relation to other kinds of writing, that friendly conversation does to the more dignified varieties of spoken language. "I love talking letters dearly," said the poet Cowper, and the majority of correspondents will agree with him. A letter of friendship should be a mirror of the writer's mind, and nothing is so likely to ensure this as a conversational style. We should write as we would speak were the friend we addressed suddenly to make his appearance,— yet, of course, with more deliberation and care. If his stay were to be brief, we would naturally touch only on the more interesting topics; and so, in a letter, where we are necessarily limited, we should give preference to those subjects that are most important.

§ 431. *Answers.*—Every letter, not insulting, merits a rompt reply; and such a reply is called an Answer. In

---

gratulation? What should be their character What is meant by letters of introduction? What is customary with respect to such letters? What caution is given?

§ 430. What style is most effective for letters? What exception is made? What must be avoided? To what is the relation which a good letter bears to other kinds of writing compared? What kind of letters did Cowper like? How should we write to a friend? What subjects should we select?

§ 431. What is meant by an *answer?* What letters merit answers? In answering.

answering, it is proper always, at the outset, to acknowledge the receipt of your correspondent's communication, in some such words, for instance, as the following : " Yours of the 15th inst. came safely to hand yesterday; and I am glad to learn from it," &c. ; or, " Your welcome letter of the 10th ult. was received in due course of mail, and would have been answered sooner had it not been," &c.

Besides this, it is customary for a person answering a business or official letter to embody in his opening sentence a statement of what he understands it to contain ; as in the following, which also illustrates the profuse use of form and titles in official communications :—

DEPARTMENT OF STATE,
Washington, April 28, 1854.

The undersigned, Secretary of State of the United States, has had the honor to receive the note of Mr. ———, her Britannic Majesty's Envoy Extraordinary and Minister Plenipotentiary, of the 21st instant, accompanied by the declaration of her Majesty the Queen of the United Kingdom of Great Britain and Ireland, in regard to the rule which will for the present be observed towards those Powers with which she is at peace, in the existing war with Russia.

§ 432. *Manual Execution.*—By complying with the following suggestions, the student will ensure neatness in making copies of his letters and other compositions :—

Draw two light pencil lines parallel with the left edge of the page, the first about half an inch, the second an inch and a half, distant from it. Commence your composition, and every successive paragraph, on the inner marginal line; but let the body of your writing rest on the outer one. When you have completed a page, erase the marginal lines neatly with india-rubber. When a letter is not long enough to fill a page, it should not be commenced on the first line, but at such a distance from it as will leave an equal space above and below.

§ 433. *Date.*—The date of a letter, which should always be distinctly stated, must stand at the right of the first line. It consists of the name of the place where it is written, the

---

what is always proper at the outset? Give examples. Besides this, what is it customary for a person answering a business or official letter to embody in the opening sentence? Give an example.

§ 432. What suggestions are made, for the purpose of ensuring neatness?

§ 433. Describe the date of a letter. Where does it stand?

month, day of the month, and year; as, *Mobile, August* 26, 1854.

§ 434. *Address.*—The address of a letter is found on the next line below the date, at the left side. It contains, in the first line, the name and title of the party written to; and, on the second, the words, "Sir," "Dear Sir," "My dear Sir," for a gentleman,—or, "Madam," "Dear Madam," "My dear Madam," for a married lady,—according to the degree of intimacy.

An unmarried lady is best addressed in a single line: "Miss ——;" "Dear Miss ——;" or, "My dear Miss ——."

In addressing a business firm, place on the first line its proper style and title; and, on the second, the word "Gentlemen" or "Ladies," according to the sex of the parties composing it.

A relative is properly addressed by the name that indicates the relationship; as, "My dear Father," "My dear Grandson," "My dear Sister;" or, a relative of the same age, or a friend, may be addressed by the Christian name, if intimacy will allow it; as, "My dear William," "My dear Julia."

Some prefer placing the first line, containing the name and title of the party addressed, at the bottom of the letter instead of the top, as above suggested.

Examples of proper forms of date and address follow; the pupil will do well to observe their punctuation:—

173 Greenwich St., New-York,
Sept. 1, 1854.

Messrs. Davis & Clapp:
   Gentlemen,

Jackson, N. C.,
2d Sept., 1854.

Hon. E. S. Norton,
   Canal Com. of the State of N. Y.:
     Sir,

---

§ 434. Where is the address of a letter found? Describe it. How is an unmarried lady best addressed? Describe the address of a business firm? How is a relative properly addressed? Where do some prefer placing the first line containing the name and title of the party addressed? Give some examples of proper forms of date and address.

Haskins P. O., Tenn.,
September 3, 1854.

Rev. James Norton, D. D.:
Rev. and dear Sir,

Steamer Washington,
Miss. River, Sept. 4th, '54.

Stewart L. Roy, Esq.:
Dear Sir,

Boston, Aug. 20, '54.

Mesdames E. & J. Lacretelle:
Ladies,

N. O., Aug. 26, 1854.

Miss R. A. Tompkins:
My dear Friend,

§ 435. *Subscription.*—By the subscription of a letter is meant that clause or sentence at the end which contains the terms of affection or respect, and the signature. Different forms are appropriate, according to the relative position of the writer and the person addressed. A few of the most common are subjoined. It will be seen at once in what case each is appropriate. Observe the punctuation, as before.

I remain, dear Sir,
Your obedient servant,
Geo. H. Smith.

Allow me to subscribe myself
Your obliged & obt. servt.,
Thomas Dean.

With my best wishes for your welfare, I remain
Your sincere friend,
Reuben H. S. Wells.

Hoping to hear from you without delay, I remain
Yours &c.,
S. Wellman Brown.

---

§ 435. What is meant by the subscription of a letter? To what must the subscription be appropriate? Give examples.

With my best love to all, I am, as ever,
Your affectionate daughter,
Helen.

———

Rest assured, dear madam, that your long continued kindness will not be forgotten, but will ever command the gratitude and service of
Yours most respectfully & truly,
Horace H. Hinman.

———

Whatever may betide, you have the warm and earnest sympathy of
Your faithful & affectionate cousin,
Jane.

———

The undersigned has the honor to avail himself of this opportunity to renew to the Secretary of State of the United States the assurance of his distinguished consideration.
John F. Crampton.
Hon. W. L. Marcy, Secretary of State, &c.

§ 436. We subjoin four specimens of the different kinds of letters. The first is a business letter, given by a person of known responsibility to a friend, to enable the latter to procure goods on time. It is commonly called a letter of credit. The second is a letter of introduction. The third is a letter of friendship, from Campbell to the poet Thomson, descriptive of a visit to Fingal's Cave. The fourth is in a more familiar style, being one of Moore's letters to his mother. The student is particularly requested to notice their characteristics.

No. 1. LETTER OF CREDIT.

Coburg, Canada West, }
September 15, 1854. }

Gentlemen,

Please deliver to Richard Berry, of this place, goods, silks, and merchandise, to any amount not exceeding five thousand dollars; and I will hold myself accountable to you for the payment of the same, in case Mr. Berry should fail to make payment therefor.

You will please to notify me of the amount for which you may give him credit and, if default should be made in the payment, let me know it immediately.

I am, gentlemen, your most obt. servant,
John Anderson.

Messrs. Isaac Smith & Co.,
No. 25 Broadway, N. Y.

No. 2. LETTER OF INTRODUCTION.

St. Louis, Jan. 3, 1854.

My dear Sir,

Allow me to introduce to you my friend, Cyrus Johnson, a distinguished teacher of this place, who visits your city for the purpose of making himself acquainted with the system of instruction pursued in your common schools. He is one whose life thus far has been devoted to the cause of education, and whose efforts have already been signally blessed to hundreds of our youth. Any aid, therefore, that you may be able to render him in the prosecution of his inquiries, will be a service to our whole community, as well as a personal favor to

Yours very truly,
Henry F. Quinn.

Joseph B. Stacy, Esq.,
14 Fifth Avenue, N. Y.

No. 3

Thule's Wildest Shore, 15th day of the Harvest Storm; Sept. 16, 1795.

My dear Friend,

I have deferred answering your very welcome favor till I could inform you of the accomplishment of my long meditated tour through the Western Isles. Though I have been disappointed in my expectations of seeing St. Kilda, yet I have no reason to be dissatisfied with my short voyage, having visited the famous Staffa and Icolmkill, so much admired by your countrymen. I had formed, as usual, very sanguine ideas of the happiness I should enjoy in beholding wonders so new to me. I was not in the least disappointed. The grand regularity of Staffa, and the venerable ruins of Iona, filled me with emotions of pleasure to which I had been hitherto a stranger. It was not merely the gratification of curiosity; for these two islands are marked with a grand species of beauty, besides their novelty, and a remarkable difference from all the other islands among the Hebrides. In short, when I looked into the cave of Staffa, I regretted nothing but that my friend was not there too.

Staffa, the nearest to Mull, and the most admirable of all the Hebrides, is but a small island, but exceedingly fertile. From one point to another, it is probably an English mile. The shore is boisterous and rocky near the sea; but at the distance of twenty yards from its rugged base, it rises for thirty or forty feet into a smooth, stony, plain, gradually sloping to the bottom of the rocks, which rise perpendicularly to a vast height, and form the walls of the island. On the top of these are rich plains of grass and corn, in the centre of which stands a lonely hut, in appearance very like the abode of a hermit or savage.

The walls of the island (for so I beg leave to denominate the rocks that form its sides) are truly wonderful. They are divided into natural pillars, of a triangular shape. These pillars are not a random curiosity, broken and irregular. They are as exactly similar and well proportioned, as if the hand of an artist had carved them out on the walls with a chisel. The range of them is so very long and steep that we cannot admit the idea of their being wrought by human hands. There is a wildness and sublimity in them beyond what art can produce; and we are so struck with its regularity that we can hardly allow Nature the merit of such an artificial work. Certain it is, if Art accomplished such a curiosity, she has handled instruments more gigantic than any which are used at present; and if Nature designed the pillars, she has bestowed more geometry on the rocks of Staffa, than on any of her works so stupendous in size. The cave of Staffa is at least three hundred feet long, lined with long stripes of pillars of the same kind, and hung at the top with stones of an exact figure of five sides. The height is seventy feet, so that, being very wide, it appears like a very large Gothic cathedral. Its arch is gradually narrowed at the top, and its base, except the footpath on one side, is the sea which comes in. We entered the mouth of the cave with a peal of bagpipes, which made a most tremendous echo.

Icolmkill is venerable for being the burial-place of forty-eight Scotch, and eight Danish kings, whose tombs we saw. Our voyage lasted three days. I slept the first night at Icolmkill, the second at Tiree, and the third again at Mull.

If I had room, I would scribble down an olegy, composed a few days after my arrival in Mull from Glasgow; but you see I have clattered away all my paper upon Staffa. I depend upon your good-nature to excuse my prolix description, and the illegibl scrawling of your very sincere friend,

LE CAMILLE.

Mr. James Thomson, London.

No. 4

Aboard the Boston,
Sandy Hook, thirty miles from New York,
Friday, May 11, 1804.

My darling Mother,

I wrote to you on my arrival at New York, where I have been nearly a week, and am now returned aboard the frigate, which but waits a fair wind to sail for Norfolk. The Halifax packet is lying alongside of us, and I shall take the opportunity of sending this letter by her. At New York, I was made happy by my father's letter of the 25th January, and dear Kate's of the 30th, which make four in all that I have received from home. I had so very few opportunities at Bermuda, and they were attended with so much uncertainty, that I fear you may have suffered many an anxious moment, darling mother, from the interruption and delay of the few letters I could despatch to you. But, please Heaven! we shall soon have those barriers of distance removed; my own tongue shall tell you my "travel's history," and your heart shall go along with me over every billow and step of the way. When I left Bermuda, I could not help regretting that the hopes which took me thither could not be even half realized; for I should love to live there, and you would like it too, dear mother: and I think if the situation would give me but a fourth of what I was so deludingly taught to expect, you should all have come to me; and, though set apart from the rest of the world, we should have found in that quiet spot, and under that sweet sky, quite enough to counterbalance what the rest of the world could give us. But I am still to seek, and can only hope that I may find at last.

The environs of New York are pretty, from the number of little, fanciful, wooden houses that are scattered, to the distance of six to eight miles, round the city; but when one reflects upon the cause of this, and that these houses are the retreat of the terrified, desponding, inhabitants, from the wilderness of death which every autumn produces in the city,* there is very little pleasure in the prospect · and, notwithstanding the rich fields, and the various blossoms of their orchards, I prefer the barren breezy, rock of Bermuda, to whole continents of such dearly purchased fertility.

While in New York, I employed my time to advantage in witnessing all the novelties possible. I saw young M. Buonaparte, and felt a slight shock of an earthquake which are two things I could not often meet with upon Usher's Quay. From Norfolk I intend going to Baltimore and Washington; if possible, also to Philadelphia and Boston, from thence to Halifax. From Halifax I hope to set sail, in the cabin where I now

---

* Reference is here made to the yellow fever, which, at the time this letter was written, prevailed in New York, to a greater or less extent, every year.

write this letter for the dear old Isles of the Old World again; and I think it probable that twelve months from the time I left England, will very nearly see me on its coasts once more. * * * Your own,

T. M.

EXERCISE.

Somewhat in the style of the above models, write a LETTER OF CREDIT, and a LETTER OF INTRODUCTION.

LESSON XCVII.

LETTERS (CONTINUED).

§ 437. *Folding and Sealing.*

As envelopes are now generally used for enclosing letters, the most convenient mode of folding is as follows:—As the sheet lies before you, turn up the bottom until its edge exactly lies upon the edge at the top, and make a fold in the middle. The sheet is now in an oblong form. Bring the side at your right hand to your body, and fold over about one third of the letter towards the top. Finally, turn as much of the upper part over in the opposite direction.

Most envelopes are self-sealing; that is, are furnished with a glutinous substance, which, on being moistened, answers the purpose of a seal. When this convenience is wanting, a wafer is generally used; in which case, care must be taken not to make it so wet as to spread and soil the adjacent parts. The use of the wafer, however, implies haste; and those who study etiquette, almost without exception, give the preference to sealing-wax. Indeed, according to Lord Chesterfield, the use of the wafer is open to a still more serious objection than the mere implying of haste. This nobleman is said, on having received a letter sealed with the obnoxious article in question, to have remarked with some indignation, "What does the fellow mean *by sending me his own spittle?*"

If no envelope is used, but the old-fashioned mode of folding is follow-

---

§ 437. What are now generally used for enclosing letters? Describe the most convenient mode of folding. With what are most envelopes furnished? When this convenience is wanting, what is generally used? In the use of the wafer, what must be avoided? To what do those who study etiquette give the preference? Why? What was Lord Chesterfield's objection to the wafer? If the old-fashioned mode of folding is followed, what must be avoided in putting on the seal?

ed. be careful that the seal, whether wax or wafer, is so placed, that the opening of the letter will not render any part of the writing illegible.

§ 438. *Superscription.*—The superscription of a letter is the direction on the outside, consisting of the name of the person addressed, and the place and state in which he lives.

In directing, be careful not to apply to a person two titles that mean the same thing; as, *Mr.* Robert Jones, *Esq.*; *Dr.* Edward Sayre, *M. D.* In the first example, either *Mr.* or *Esq.* should be omitted; and, in the last, either *Dr.* or *M. D.*

When a letter is not sent by mail, but is taken by private hand, it is customary to acknowledge the favor by placing on the outside, at the lower corner on the left, the bearer's name, in some such expression as the following:—"*Politeness of Mr. ——*"; "*Courtesy of Mrs. ——*"; "*Favored by Miss ——*".

A letter of introduction should contain, in the same position as the above, the name of the person introduced, in some such form as the following:—"Introducing Mr. ——"; "To introduce Mr. ——".

§ 439. A short letter is called a *Note.*

Business notes have the same form as letters. Notes of invitation should be written on small sheets, called, from the use to which they are appropriated, note-paper.

It is customary, in writing notes, to use the 3d person instead of both the 1st and 2d, as in the example given below. Care must be taken to avoid the common error of introducing the 1st or 2d person, after the 3d has been thus employed; as in the following: "*Mrs. White presents her compliments to Mr. Roy, and solicits the pleasure of your* [instead of *his*] *company on Monday evening, the 4th inst.*

In notes, the oldest or only daughter of a family is addressed as Miss ——, no other name being used; when there are other daughters, they are distinguished by their Christian names. If Mr. David Temple, for instance, has three daughters, Caroline, Mary, and Cornelia, the first is properly addressed as Miss Temple; the second, as Miss Mary Temple; and the third, as Miss Cornelia Temple. On the death or marriage of

---

§ 438. What is meant by the superscription of a letter? In directing, what must we avoid? Give examples. When a letter is taken by private hand, how is it customary to acknowledge the favor? What should a letter of introduction contain on the back, besides the superscription?

§ 439. What is a note? What form have business notes? On what should notes of invitation be written? In what person does the writer speak of himself? In what of the person addressed? Against what common error is the writer cautioned? In notes, how is the oldest daughter of a family addressed? How, the other daughters?

Caroline, Mary becomes Miss Temple; and, on that of both Caroline and Mary, Cornelia assumes the title in question.

A few forms, with their appropriate replies, may be of service.

INVITATIONS.	REPLIES.
No. 1.	*No.* 1.
Mrs. Dunn presents her compliments to Mr. and Mrs. Baker, and solicits the pleasure of their company on Tuesday evening, the 12th inst. 23 Broadway, Sept. 8.	Mr. and Mrs. Baker accept with pleasure Mrs. Dunn's polite invitation for the 12th inst. Jay st., Sept. 9.
No. 2.	*No.* 2.—*A Regret.*
Mr. Bristow requests the pleasure of the Hon. Mr. Marshall's company at dinner on Wednesday next, at 4 o'clock. 7 Greene st., Sept. 4.	Mr. Marshall regrets that a previous engagement will deprive him of the pleasure of accepting Mr. Bristow's invitation to dinner for Wednesday next. Astor House, Sept. 5.
No. 3.	*No.* 3.—*A Regret.*
Mr. W. F. Cameron presents his respects to Miss Lydia Bryant, and begs that he may be allowed to wait on her this evening to the Italian Opera. Liberty st., Sept. 8.	Miss Lydia Bryant presents her compliments to Mr. W. F. Cameron, and regrets that sickness in her family will prevent her acceptance of his invitation for this evening. Montague square, Sept. 8.

EXERCISE.

I. Write a letter to a friend in the city from some country retreat which you may have lately visited, remembering to draw up a preliminary analysis, and to follow the models in the last lesson, as regards date, address, &c.

II. Write a note requesting the loan of a volume from a friend.

III. Write a note accepting a friend's invitation to tea.

LESSON XCVIII.

NARRATIVES.

§ 440. A NARRATIVE is a composition which consists, for the most part, of an account of real facts or events; but into

---

Give an example. On the death or marriage of the oldest daughter, how is the second daughter addressed? Give the form of a note of invitation, and the reply.

which, description, argument, exposition, or speculation, may also be introduced.

§ 441. Narratives are divided into Histories Biographies Obituaries, Voyages, Travels, and Anecdotes.

§ 442. A History is an account of facts or events pertaining to distinguished places or objects, to communities, nations or states. A detached portion of history, confined to any particular era or event, is known as an Historical Sketch.

The difference between a history and annals is, that the latter merely enumerate events in chronological order, without admitting any observations on the part of the writer; whereas history has less regard to the order of time, and allows the writer to investigate causes and effects, and to introduce other matter connected with the subject.

§ 443. A history, to be good, must be true and interesting.

The first essential is truth. The writer must present a faithful account of what has taken place, or his work is valueless. All prejudice must be laid aside. Nothing must be concealed, nothing exaggerated. All available sources of information must be explored, and whatever bears on the subject in hand must be brought to light. In cases of doubtful or conflicting testimony, the rules of evidence must be carefully weighed, and truth ensured at the expense of every other consideration.

In the second place, a good history must be interesting. Much depends on the manner of the historian. Whatever the nature of the events he records, however great his research or accurate his statements, if his style is dry, dull, or lifeless, he can not hope to gain the favor of his readers. He should aim at simplicity, clearness, and strength; but, when he is dwelling on those splendid achievements which at intervals have spread a glorious refulgence over the page of history, with his subject he naturally rises to sublimity.

The English language has produced many historians of the first ank; among whom, Robertson, Hume, and Gibbon, are worthy of spe-

---

§ 440. What is a narrative?
§ 441. Into what are narratives divided?
§ 442. What is a history? What is an historical sketch? Define the difference between a history and annals.
§ 443. What two things are essential to a good history? To ensure truth, what must the writer do? What is the second essential of a good history? On what does much depend? At what should the historian aim? When does he naturally rise to sublimity? Mention some of the prominent English historians. Mention those dis-

cial mention. American literature can boast of three names equally great,—Bancroft, Hildreth, and Prescott. The style of the latter is justly regarded as a model of historical writing, as well from its purity and beauty as from the absorbing interest with which it invests whatever he treats.

The North American Review makes the following remarks on Prescott's style, which are worthy of being added, as likely to convey a just idea of what a good historical style should be:—

"Mr. Prescott is not a mannerist in style, and does not deal in elaborate, antithetical, nicely-balanced periods. His sentences are not cast in the same artificial mould, nor is there a perpetual recurrence of the same forms of expression, as in the writings of Johnson or Gibbon; nor have they that satin-like smoothness and gloss for which Robertson is so remarkable. The dignified simplicity of his style is still farther removed from any thing like pertness, smartness, or affectation; from tawdry gum-flowers of rhetoric, and brass-gilt ornaments; from those fantastic tricks with language which bear the same relation to good writing that vaulting and tumbling do to walking. It is perspicuous, flexible, and natural, sometimes betraying a want of high finish, but always manly, always correct,—never feeble, and never inflated. He does not darkly insinuate statements, or leave his reader to infer facts. Indeed, it may be said of his style, that it has no marked character at all. Without ever offending the mind or the ear, it has nothing that attracts observation to it, simply as a style. It is a transparent medium, through which we see the form and movement of the writer's mind. In this respect, we may compare it with the manners of a well-bred gentleman, which have nothing so peculiar as to awaken attention, and which, from their very ease and simplicity, enable the essential qualities of the understanding and character to be more clearly discerned."

§ 444. A Biography is an account of the life of an individual. When the chief incidents only are touched upon, it is called a Biographical Sketch. The style recommended in the last paragraph for history is also appropriate to biography. The writer should avoid a tendency to minuteness of uninteresting detail, and exaggerated praise of the person of whose life he is treating.

§ 445. The third variety of narrative is the Obituary, which is a notice of a person's death, accompanied with a brief sketch of his life and character. Obituaries are generally written by friends of the deceased, in whom, as in the

---

tinguished in American literature. What is said of Prescott's style? In what terms does the North American Review speak of it?

§ 444. What is a biography? What is a biographical sketch? What style is appropriate to biography? Against what tendency should the biographer be on his guard?

§ 445. What is the third variety of narrative? What is an obituary? By whom are obituaries generally written? What, therefore, is the natural tendency in the

biographer, there is a natural tendency to exaggerate the abilities and virtues of those whose memory they would preserve. Such exaggeration fails of its object, being readily detected, and in that case not only losing its effect, but actually offending the reader. In this, as in every other species of narrative, *truth* should be the primary object.

§ 446. Travels constitute the fourth kind of narrative. They may be defined as an account of incidents that have happened, and observations that have been made, during a journey; and form one of the most entertaining and popular departments of literature.

Narration constitutes the greater part of a book of travels; but description and the other elements of composition may also be introduced, in a greater or less degree. Keen powers of observation are essential to the writer in this department of composition. His style should be varied to suit the different objects and incidents he is called on successively to describe; ornamented or simple, sublime or sparkling with humor, as occasion may require. To awaken interest in his readers, he should select new and important subjects only, and exhibit them in their most striking light.

§ 447. The fifth class comprises Voyages; which resemble travels in every respect, except that the incidents they relate are such as have happened to one passing by water between countries remote from each other. As regards style, the same principles apply as in the case of travels.

§ 448. The last variety of narrative we shall here mention, is the Anecdote. This term is derived from two Greek words (α privative and ἔκδοτος, *given out, made public*); and was originally applied to an historical fact not generally known,

---

writers of obituaries? What is said of such exaggeration? In all the varieties of narrative, what should be the primary object?

§ 446. What constitute the fourth kind of narrative? What is meant by *travels?* What constitutes the greater part of a book of travels? What else may be introduced? What is essential to success in the writing of travels? What style is most effective for them? What subjects should be selected by the writers of travels?

§ 447. What is the fifth division of narratives? In what do voyages differ from travels? What style is recommended for voyages?

§ 448. What is the last variety of narrative mentioned? From what is the word

when promulgated for the first time. As now used, however, this term signifies an account of an interesting detached incident, particularly one connected with the career of some distinguished person. The point of an anecdote should not be obscured by too many words.

§ 449. The only example it is thought necessary to present, is one of the anecdote. The other varieties form so considerable a portion of the current literature of the day that the student can hardly go amiss for suitable models.

ANECDOTE OF DR. FRANKLIN.

Long after the victories of Washington over the French and English had made his name familiar to all Europe, Dr. Franklin chanced to dine with the English and French ambassadors; when, as nearly as the precise words can be recollected, the following toasts were drunk:—

"ENGLAND—The *Sun* whose bright beams enlighten and fructify the remotest corners of the earth."

The French ambassador, filled with national pride, but too polite to dispute the previous toast, drank the following:—

"FRANCE—The *Moon* whose mild, steady, and cheering rays, are the delight of all nations, consoling them in darkness, and making their dreariness beautiful."

Dr. Franklin then arose, and, with his usual dignified simplicity, said:—

"GEORGE WASHINGTON—The *Joshua* who commanded the Sun and Moon to stand still; and they obeyed him."

EXERCISE.

I. Write, in your own language, an Anecdote of Richard the Lion-hearted.

II. Write, in your own language, an Anecdote of Philip of Macedon, from the following heads:—

A Macedonian soldier had so distinguished himself by extraordinary acts of valor as to gain the favor of King Philip and many marks of royal approbation.

This soldier was once shipwrecked; and, being cast ashore with scarcely a sign of life, was revived only by the care and tenderness of a Macedonian, whose lands were contiguous to the sea, and who hastened to his relief. Placed in this good man's bed, carefully nursed, and freely supplied with the necessaries of life, the shipwrecked soldier found himself, at the expiration of forty days, sufficiently recovered to be able to resume his journey. He left with loud protestations of gratitude to his kind host; and, informing the latter of his influence with the king, promised that his first care should be to secure from the royal bounty a munificent reward for one who had so generously befriended him in time of need.

---

anecdote derived? To what was this term originally applied? As now used, what does it signify? What is the effect of too many words in an anecdote?

In reality, however, he was filled with base cupidity, and ungratefully resolved to procure for himself the grounds of his benefactor. Shortly after, he presented himself before the king; and, recounting his misfortunes and at the same time his services, begged that Philip would give him an estate, and specified that of his entertainer as one which would be peculiarly acceptable. Ignorant of the circumstances, Philip inconsiderately granted the request.

The soldier immediately returned, and, driving out his preserver with violence, seized on the property in question. The latter, stung to the heart by this unparalleled ingratitude, boldly approached the king, and laid the whole case before him. Philip, finding, on examination, the story to be true, lamented his own inconsiderate act, ordered the property to be restored, made the suffering complainant a munificent present, and, seizing the base soldier, confiscated his goods, and had the words THE UNGRATEFUL GUEST branded on his forehead.

[Close with remarks on the king's justice.]

LESSON XCIX.

EXERCISE IN BIOGRAPHY.

FROM the following points, draw up two Biographical Sketches, one of Alfred the Great, and the other of William the Conqueror. If further information is needed, any history will supply it.

ALFRED THE GREAT.

Introduction—Responsibility resting on kings—How much the happiness or misery of their subjects depends on them—How some kings abuse their opportunities of doing good, while others are incalculable blessings to the lands they rule—How it was in the case of Alfred.

Born 849, at Wantage in Berkshire—son of Ethelwolf, his mother was Osburgh, daughter of Oslac, butler to Ethelwolf, but well descended.

His early education neglected—his natural thirst for knowledge—skilled in bodily exercises.

His enemies, the Danes : *i. e.* the people of Scandinavia (Sweden, Denmark, and Norway). Commander of his brother's armies—recommends a navy.

Losses and reverses of fortune—anecdote of the burnt cakes—visit in disguise to the Danish camp—defeat of the Danes—baptism of Guthrum—Alfred's power increases.—Peace during the last two years of his reign—dies 901.

His character—learning—piety—habits—political institutions—patronage of learned men—division of England into counties, hundreds, tithings, &c.

WILLIAM THE CONQUEROR.

Introduction—some kings seem to have been chosen by Providence as instruments for effecting mighty changes in nations—the case with William the Conqueror—intermixture of Normans with Saxons produced the English nation of the present day.

Whose son?—his title to the English throne—his rival—the invasion of England—the number of William's army—where he landed.

Harold's title to the crown—proposals made by William to Harold the night before the battle.

The battle and its circumstances—death of Harold, and victory of William—14th October, 1066. Extinction of the Saxon rule—submission of the clergy.

Coronation—oath—return to Normandy—Effects of his absence—Conspiracy of the English—return of William, and treatment of the rebels and English clergy.

Destined to vexation and trouble—his children—anecdote of their quarrels.

Insurrection in Normandy—conduct of the queen, daughter of Baldwin, Earl of Flanders—rebellion quelled by an English army.

Death of Queen Matilda—insurrection in Maine aided by the King of France.

Invasion of France by William—accident which caused the death of the king in 1087.

Character—changes produced in England during his reign—Relations between the Saxons and the Normans—changes in the language.

LESSON C.

FICTION.

§ 450. FICTION is that branch of composition which consists in the narration of imaginary incidents. With this narration, descriptions of material objects, of natural scenery, and of persons, are generally combined.

It will be seen that the difference between the narrative and the fiction lies in the character of the incidents they respectively relate; the former being limited to such as are true, while those of the latter are created either wholly or in part by the imagination. We say in part, for fictions may be founded on fact, historical events being often taken as the basis of such compositions. If the details have been invented by the author, if imaginary conversations, characters, or scenes, are introduced, it is sufficient to constitute a fiction.

§ 451. The chain of incidents on which a fiction is founded, is called its Plot. A plot should not be glaringly improbable; it should be moral, consistent in all its parts, and so managed as to keep alive the reader's interest throughout. This is often ensured by reserving some important denouement for the last.

§ 452. Next to a good plot, nothing is more necessary to success in fictitious composition than a striking and life-like portraiture of character. Individual peculiarities of mind and manners must be carried out. Whatever the personages introduced say or do, must strictly harmonize with the character assigned them by the writer.

§ 453. Fictitious compositions constitute one of the most

---

§ 450. What is fiction? With this narration, what are generally combined? What constitutes the difference between a narrative and a fiction? On what may fictions be founded? What are often taken as a basis for them? In such cases, what is sufficient to constitute a fiction?

§ 451. What is meant by the plot of a fictitious composition? What is essential with respect to a plot? How is the reader's interest often kept alive to the end?

§ 452. Next to a good plot, what is most important to success in fictitious composition? What is meant by this?

§ 453. Explain how fictitious compositions exert a powerful influence on the morals

important departments of literature. Obtaining greater currency than almost any other kinds of writing, and furnishing food, as they do, to a great extent, for the imaginations of the young, they exert a powerful influence on the morals and taste of a nation. That this influence should be cast on the side of morality and truth, is all-important.

In the hands of judicious writers who feel the responsibility of their position, fiction becomes an important instrument of good. It furnishes one of the best channels for conveying instruction, for showing the errors into which we are betrayed by our passions, for rendering virtue attractive and vice odious. Accordingly, we find that the wisest of men, in all ages, have used fables and parables as vehicles of moral instruction. It must be observed, however, that, while fiction, as shown above, may be an effective instrument of good, it is no less powerful an agent of evil, when diverted from its proper use, and made to teach a false moral or pander to the baser passions. No ordinary responsibility, therefore, rests on the writer in this department of composition.

§ 454. The principal forms in which fiction appears are Tales, Novels, Romances, and Dialogues.

The first three of these are closely related; the difference between them is as follows. The Tale is short and simple, and admits of comparatively few characters; it is told without much regard to keeping the reader in suspense, and often has but little depth of plot or importance of denouement. The Novel and the Romance, on the contrary, admit of every possible variety of character, and afford the greatest scope for exciting the interest of the reader by a rapid succession of events, an involvement of interests, and the unravelling of intricacies of plot. The Novel, though thus like the Romance in its main features, differs from the latter in that it aims at the delineation of social manners, or the development of a story founded on the incidents of ordinary life, or both together; whereas the Romance is based on incidents, not mere-

---

and taste of a nation. In the hands of judicious writers, what does fiction become? Show how it is made an instrument of good. On the other hand, show how it may be attended with the most pernicious effects.

§ 454. What are the principal forms in which fiction appears? What are the distinguishing features of the tale, the novel, and the romance? What word is commonly

ly improbable, but altogether wild and out of the common course of life at the present day,—on legends of bygone ages, heroic exploits of former times, supernatural events, and vagaries of the imagination in general. In all three, the plot may be unfolded, at least in a measure, by means of conversations between the characters introduced.

The word *story* is commonly used as synonymous with *tale*. Properly speaking, however, this term is applied to any narrative of past events, real or fictitious. We speak of " the story of Joseph," and " the story of the Forty Thieves."

A Dialogue is a fictitious conversation between two or more persons.

Dialogues have been used with great success, particularly by the ancients, as a convenient form for the discussion of serious topics connected with criticism, morals, and philosophy. Well conducted, they are peculiarly entertaining to the reader; as they not only afford him a full view of the subject in all its relations, but at the same time please him with their easy conversational style, and their display of well-supported characters. But, to be thus effective, a dialogue must show in a striking light the character and manners of the several speakers, must adapt to these their thoughts and expressions respectively,—in a word, must be a spirited representation of a real conversation.

In this difficult branch of composition, few have equalled Plato, in whose mind soundness of judgment seems to have been combined in an unprecedented degree with richness of imagination. Socrates is one of his prominent characters. This sage, whom he reveres as a philosopher and loves as his master, is represented as conversing with the sophists on various topics; as asking them questions which bear on the point without their perceiving it, founding new interrogatories on the answers received, and thus leading them on until they suddenly find themselves involved in difficulties and absurdities, and are obliged, by the admissions they have made, to own the falsity of their own position and the correctness of their adversary's. This mode of reasoning has

---

used as synonymous with *tale ?* What two-fold signification has this term *story ?* Illustrate each. What is a dialogue ? For what have dialogues been used ? What renders them, when well conducted, peculiarly entertaining to the reader. To be effective, what is essential with respect to a dialogue ? Who is distinguished for his skill in this department of composition ? Who constitutes one of Plato's prominent characters ? Describe the Socratic mode of reasoning as represented in Plato's dialogues. What is meant by a Socratic dialogue ? What other kind of dialogue is mentioned ? What

hence been called Socratic; and a Socratic dialogue is one in which it is pursued.

There are also lighter dialogues, in which wit and humor play an important part, and which are designed principally to satirize the follies of the day. These, Lucian, among the ancients, carried to a high degree of perfection. In modern times, we have few specimens either of the lighter or the graver kind, that can be said to possess superior merit; the difficulty of this style of composition seems to have brought it into disfavor with the majority of writers.

§ 455. An extended dialogue, consisting of different scenes accommodated to action, and participated in by a number of characters, who appear and disappear at intervals as may be necessary for the development of the plot, is called a Drama. Dramas are written in either prose or poetry, but generally the latter; for which reason, we shall at present postpone their consideration.

§ 456. We subjoin a specimen of the tale,—one, however, in which, by reason of its brevity, there is necessarily but little plot. In tales of any length, description may be introduced with effect.

CARDINAL RICHELIEU'S GUEST.

Cardinal de Richelieu has always been considered a great minister, and on some accounts he well deserved the name. He rendered an immense service to monarchy in despatching the last heads of the feudal hydra, and literature owes him much for the establishment of the French Academy. Although himself but an indifferent writer, he was ever ready to encourage the arts, and paid liberally for the efforts of others. The Cardinal, however, could not endure that his acts should be made the subject of comment, particularly since some of them were of a character not calculated to elicit very warm commendation from lovers of morality. The more powerful, indeed, occasionally indulged in freedom of speech; but woe to the humble individual that was indiscreet enough publicly to find fault with the peccadilloes of his Eminence. With such he had a summary way of privately dealing which effectually closed their lips for the future.

M. Dumont, a small merchant of the Rue St. Denis, received one morning a letter dated Ruell, a little village on the outskirts of Paris, where the Cardinal had a country-seat. This letter contained an invitation to supper for the next day with his Eminence. M. Dumont could not believe his eyes; he read the letter several times, looked at the direction, and finally concluded that he must be indeed the person to whom it was addressed. Amazed beyond expression, he called his wife and daugh-

---

ancient writer excelled in it? What has brought this kind of composition into disfavor with the majority of writers?

§ 455. What is a drama? Are dramas generally written in prose, or poetry?

ters, to communicate to them his good fortune. You may imagine the joy and pride of the three women!

About four o'clock he mounted his horse, and started for Rueil. He had scarcely passed the suburbs, when the clouds assumed a threatening look, and the sound of distant thunder announced the approach of a violent storm. The merchant, having neglected to provide himself with a cloak, doubled the speed of his horse. But the storm travelled faster than his steed; flashes of lightning succeeded each other with frightful rapidity, and the rain fell in torrents. Assailed by the tempest, our hero put his horse to the gallop; but at length, unable to continue his journey, he stopped at a small tavern in Manterre. He alighted, sent his horse to the stable, and took refuge in a low room, where the servants lighted a blazing fire to dry his clothes. While he was warming himself, the door opened, and another person, also drenched with rain, entered, and seated himself in the opposite corner.

The two travellers looked at each other for some time in silence. At last, M. Dumont addressed his companion with the words: "What detestable weather!"

"It is very bad indeed," replied the stranger. "But it is only a shower, which, I hope, will soon pass over."

"Hear," continued M. Dumont; "the storm increases; peals of thunder shake the house; the rain falls in torrents: and yet I must go on."

"Sir," said the unknown, "it must be important business that can induce you to proceed on your journey in this weather."

"It is, indeed," said Dumont; "I will tell you: it is no secret. I am invited to a supper, this evening, with the Cardinal de Richelieu."

"Ah! I know it is a difficult matter to decline such an invitation. But you have still a long way to go, and how can you present yourself before his Eminence in the state in which you now are?"

"His Eminence will, perhaps, appreciate my eagerness to accept his kind invitation."

"If I did not fear to appear indiscreet, I would ask you if you ever had any thing to do with the Cardinal."

"Nothing at all. I must even say that I can not account for the favor which I have received."

"The Cardinal is very jealous of his authority; he does not like to have his actions judged. One word sometimes is sufficient to excite his suspicion; think well. Have you never given his Eminence any cause for complaint against you?"

"I think not. I have been constantly occupied with my business. I have no interest in what they call politics. However, I believe that, before two or three friends only, I censured the death of the Duke of Montmorency, and you would have done the same, had your grandfather been the steward of that illustrious noble."

"My dear sir, you look like an honest man. You have inspired me with much interest for you; will you listen to me then? Do not go to Rueil."

"Not go to Rueil! I shall set out this instant, in spite of the storm."

"One word more, my friend, for your position interests me exceedingly; you really believe that the Cardinal is expecting you to supper? Well, let me undeceive you. You are expected, it is true,—but to be hung!"

"Oh, merciful Heaven! what do you mean? It is impossible."

"I tell you again," said the stranger, "to be hung!"

At these words, Dumont, shuddering with terror, drew himself near to the unknown.

"For Heaven's sake, how do you know?"

"I am sure of it."

"But what have I done to deserve such a fate?"

"I don't know; but I am sure of what I say, for I am the one who has been sent for to hang you."

The poor merchant, pale as a corpse, drew back several steps, and, scarcely able to speak, said:

"Pray tell me, sir—who are you?"

"The hangman of Paris, called by his Eminence to despatch you. Think of the service I have rendered you, and remember that the least indiscretion on your part will be my ruin."

The merchant remounted his horse without waiting for the storm to abate; and, drenched to the bone, he reached Paris. Instead of repairing to his own house, he sought shelter with an old friend, to whom he related his adventure and wonderful escape. With the aid of money, he obtained a passport, under a false name; and, well disguised, started for England. There he remained till the death of the Cardinal, which occurred two years after.

EXERCISE.

Write a Tale, founded on incidents of your own invention, and conveying the moral that *appearances are deceitful*.

LESSON CI.

ESSAYS.

§ 457. Essays constitute the fourth division of prose compositions.

The term *essay* literally signifies an attempt; and is generally applied, in literature, to productions in which a writer briefly sets forth his views on the leading points connected with a subject, without pausing to consider them carefully or minutely. Some writers, however, in a spirit of modesty, have thought proper to characterize as *essays* their most profound and elaborate compositions, following the example of Locke in his celebrated "*Essay* on the Human Understanding." The term has thus come to have a widely extended signification; and is now equally applicable to the crude exercise of the school-boy and the sublimest effort of the man of letters.

---

§ 457. What constitute the fourth division of prose compositions? What does the term *essay* literally signify? To what is it generally applied in literature? What have some writers, in a spirit of modesty, used this term to denote? What is the consequence, as regards the present acceptation of the word *essay*? What, for the most part

The themes of essays are, for the most part, either abstract subjects or topics connected with life and manners.

§ 458. The term *essay* being thus comprehensive, the compositions so designated are susceptible of division into a variety of classes distinguished by particular names; the principal of which are Editorials, Reviews, Treatises, Tracts, Dissertations, and Disquisitions.

An Editorial is a short essay on some current topic of the day, presented in a newspaper or periodical as embodying the views of its conductors.

A Review is a critical essay on some literary production, in which its beauties and defects are pointed out.

A Treatise is a methodical and elaborate essay, generally on some ethical, political, or speculative, subject.

A Tract is a brief essay, generally on some religious or political theme, called forth by the events of the day, and seldom possessing sufficient general interest to survive the occasion which gave it birth.

A Dissertation is an essay of some length, investigating, in all its relations, some disputed subject; and written, not for the purpose of establishing a given position, but of fairly presenting the arguments on all sides, and arriving at the truth.

A Disquisition has the same object in view as a dissertation,—that is, the eliciting of truth; it differs from the latter only in being more brief, and being confined more strictly to the particular point under consideration.

§ 459. In the conduct of the essay, great latitude is allowed. Its subjects are so various that no uniform mode of treatment can be recommended or followed. The heads to be taken will of course differ according to the character of the topics treated; yet, in most compositions of this class,

---

constitute the themes of essays? Enumerate the classes into which essays are divided. What is an editorial? a review? a treatise? a tract? a dissertation? a disquisition?

§ 459. What is allowed in the conduct of an essay? Why cannot a uniform mode of treatment be followed? According to what will the heads to be taken differ? What

the following will be found appropriate. They may be amplified according to the suggestions in § 409.

    I. *Introduction.*—Suggestions respecting it will be found in § 405, 406, 407, 408.
    II. *Definition.*
    III. *Origin.*
    IV. *History.*
    V. *Historical Illustrations.*
    VI. *Advantages.* Similes and Quotations.
    VII. *Disadvantages.* Similes and Quotations.
    VIII. *Practical Conclusion.*

If the subject is one on which there is a difference of opinion, it may be well, in place of the fourth and the fifth head, given above, to substitute the following:—

    IV. *Statement of Views.*
        I. *General view.* What has been thought on this subject by all nations, and in all ages?
        II. *Local view.* What opinions are entertained on it in the age and country to which the writer belongs?

        Or the following division may be preferable:—

        I. *Ancient view,* or that held by the ancients generally, and especially their philosophers.
        II. *Modern view.* Causes which may have operated to produce a change of opinion.

    V. *Author's View.* Arguments to sustain it. The negative argument, or proving the truth of what is advanced by showing the absurdity of the contrary, is often introduced with fine effect.

It will be seen from the above heads that the essay may contain all the parts of composition,—description, narration, argument, exposition, and speculation.

§ 460. As a specimen of the essay, in the brief form in which, as a school or college exercise, it generally appears, we subjoin a composition on *Friendship*, which may be supposed to have been written from the following

ANALYSIS.

    I. Definition. What is friendship?
    II. Origin and necessity.
    III. Estimation in which it was formerly held. Examples.
    IV. Universality; extends to all ranks of life.
    V. Benefits of true, and evils of false, friendship?
    VI. Conclusion. Practical reflections.

---

heads will generally be found appropriate? If the subject is one on which there is a difference of opinion, what heads will it be well to take?

FRIENDSHIP.

Friendship is an attachment between persons of congenial dispositions, habits, and pursuits.

It has its origin in the nature and condition of man. He is a social creature, and naturally loves to frequent the society, and enjoy the affections, of those who are like himself. He is also, individually, a feeble creature; and a sense of this weakness renders friendship indispensable to him. Though he may have all other enjoyments within his reach, he still finds his happiness incomplete, unless participated by one whom he considers his friend. When in difficulty and distress, he looks around for advice, assistance, and consolation.

No wonder, therefore, that a sentiment of such importance to man should have been so frequently and so fully considered. We can scarcely open any of the volumes of antiquity without being reminded how excellent a thing is friendship. The examples of David and Jonathan, Achilles and Patroclus, Pylades and Orestes, Nisus and Euryalus, Damon and Pythias, all show to what a degree of enthusiasm it was sometimes carried. Even the great Cicero deemed it of sufficient importance to form the subject of one of his masterly essays. But it is to be feared that, in modern times, friendship is seldom remarkable for similar devotedness. With some, it is nominal rather than real; and, with others, it is regulated entirely by self-interest.

Yet it would, no doubt, be possible to produce, from every rank in life, and from every state of society, instances of sincere and disinterested friendship, creditable to human nature, and to the age in which we live. We can not think so ill of our species as to believe that selfishness has got the better of their nobler feelings sufficiently to destroy their sympathy with their fellow-creatures, and their love towards those whom God hath given them for neighbors and brethren.

After these remarks, to enlarge on the benefits of possessing a real friend appears unnecessary. What would be more intolerable than the consciousness that in all the wide world, not one heart beat in unison with our own, or cared for our welfare? What indescribable happiness must it be, on the other hand, to possess a real friend;—a friend who will counsel, instruct, assist; who will bear a willing part in our calamity, and cordially rejoice when the hour of happiness returns!

Let us remember, however, that all who assume the name of friends are not entitled to our confidence. History records many instances of the fatal consequences of infidelity in friendship; and it cannot be denied that the world contains men who are happy to find a heart they can pervert, or a head they can mislead, if thus their unworthy ends can be more surely attained. Caution in the formation of friendships is, therefore, in the highest degree necessary. We should admit none to the altar of our social affections without closely scrutinizing their lives and characters. We must assure ourselves of the uprightness and truth of those to whom we open our hearts in friendship, if we would not have a pernicious influence exerted on our own dispositions; if we would not, in the hour of trial, find ourselves forgotten and abandoned to the old charities of an unsympathizing world.

EXERCISE.

Write an Essay from the following extended Analysis :—

A GOOD CAUSE MAKES A STOUT HEART.

I. *Introduction.* Courage is a natural quality, yet it is often increased or lessened by circumstances. Among the considerations which tend to confirm this quality on particular occasions, is the consciousness that we have right on our side, that we are engaged in a just and honorable cause.

II. *Reasons why this is the case.*
1. A mind conscious of right is not ashamed; and, as shame is always cowardly, so the absence of it conduces to moral courage.
2. A mind conscious to itself of honest intentions is not paralyzed by any fear of being detected in what it is doing.
3. Conscious rectitude gives confidence to the heart, from a conviction of being in the path of duty.
4. A good cause makes a stout heart, from a persuasion that God will maintain the right; and, "if God be for us, who can be against us?"
5. A desire for the approbation of men will encourage those who are engaged in the cause of truth and justice.
6. The just man will be further emboldened by the reflection that his adversary's cause is a bad one, and can not prevail against him.
7. Even to fail in a good cause is honorable; and, therefore, the upright mind is sustained by the double assurance mentioned by St. Paul, "Whether we live, we live unto the Lord; or whether we die, we die unto the Lord: living or dying, we are the Lord's."

III. *Contrast.*—While he who feels he is in the right is thus fearless, one who is doing what he knows to be wrong is afraid to be seen: his heart is paralyzed by a constant dread of detection, disgrace, and punishment; and the conviction that he is maintaining the wrong against an adversary who is armed with the consciousness of rectitude, will have a most pernicious influence upon both his moral and physical courage.

IV. *Similes.*—As bright armor will resist a musket ball far better than a rusty suit of mail, so a good cause is far stronger than a puissant arm raised to uphold what is wrong.

A good foundation makes a building firm; and when the rain descends and the floods come, and the winds blow and beat upon that house, it will not fall, because its foundation is secure: whereas, a house built upon the sand cannot resist the rain, the floods, and the wind, but will fall when they beat against it, and great will be the fall thereof.

A ship built of sound timber may weather the roughest sea; but one made of rotten planks can not ride in safety through the smoothest water.

A dog stealing a bone is alarmed at the slightest sound, and will run away; while the same dog, guarding a house at night, can not be terrified by threats or danger.

A "thief doth fear each bush an officer"; but a soldier in the battle-field will stand fearlessly at the cannon's mouth.

Boys engaged upon their duty are not afraid of the eye of their master; but every sound alarms them when they are doing what they know to be wrong.

A dying man who has endeavored to discharge his duty, is not afraid to meet his Maker; but one whose conscience tells him that he has been an evil-doer, is in an agony of fear when he finds himself on his death-bed.

V. *Historical Illustrations.*—According to Shakspeare's representation, Richard III., at the battle of Bosworth Field, was weighed down with the oppression of conscious guilt; but Richmond, being buoyed up with the conviction of the justness of his cause, fought like a lion, and prevailed.

Macbeth started at every whisper of the wind, or shriek of the night-hawk, when he went to murder Duncan; but stood as an "eagle against a sparrow, or a lion against a hare," in the fierce contest with the Norwegian rebels.

Siccus Dentatus resisted a hundred adversaries sent to assassinate him, with considerable success; killing fifteen, and wounding thirty others.

A usurper is in constant fear of conspiracies: common tradition says that Cromwell wore armor under his clothes, and never went and returned by the same route.

Leonidas, at the straits of Thermopylæ, was not afraid with four hundred men to oppose Xerxes, the invader of Greece, at the head of a million troops.

William Tell, with a handful of adherents, boldly resisted the Austrian multitude, and even repulsed it.

David, with a simple sling and stone, encountered Goliath, the giant of Gath, and slew him.

VI. *Quotations.* Honor shall uphold the humble in spirit.—*Prov.* XIX., 23.

The wicked flee when no man pursueth: but the righteous are bold as a lion.—*Prov.* XXVIII., 1.

Virtue is bold, and goodness never fearful.—*Shakspeare.*

Thrice is he armed that hath his quarrel just;
And he but naked, though locked up in steel,
Whose conscience with injustice is corrupted.
Shakspeare.

Conscience makes cowards of us all.—*Shakspeare.*

Conscience is a dangerous thing, it makes a man a coward; a man can not steal, but it accuseth him; a man can not swear, but it checks him. 'Tis a blushing shamefaced spirit, that mutinies in a man's bosom, and fills one full of obstacles.—*Shakspeare.*

When the mind proposes honorable ends, not only the virtues, but the deities also, are ready to assist.—*Lord Bacon.*

Innocence is the best armor.—*Proverb.*

VII. *Conclusion.*

1. When we feel ill at ease and afraid to persevere in an enterprise or take a bold part against our adversaries, let us carefully examine whether our cause is just.
2. If we would not be cowards, we must be sure that we have right on our side; for, if we have not, we will inevitably distrust our own success and be unable to do justice to the cause in which we are engaged.

LESSON CII

EXERCISES IN ESSAY-WRITING

1. DRAW up an analysis, and write an essay, from the following suggestions:—

What is Society?—When did it begin to exist?—Under what forms did it at first appear?—What are its benefits?—What is the effect of society on the human mind?—What is its effect on the arts and sciences?—Show the difference between a state of barbarism and one of civilization.—What are the disadvantages of society?—Mention some of the vices engendered by an over-refined state of society—and the pernicious effects resulting to the community from them.—Give historical examples of these effects.

2. Draw up an analysis, and write an essay, from the following suggestions:—

What does the word *government* signify?—Show the origin and necessity of government.—Show the effects of anarchy.—Which was the earliest form of government?—Describe this patriarchal form of government.—What qualities naturally give one man a power over others?—Which are, or have been, the prevailing forms of government?—Enumerate the advantages and disadvantages of each.—Which is the most stable?—What is the form of government in this country?—Show the advantages of the government of the United States.—Conclusion; how thankful we should be that our lots are cast in a country which enjoys so liberal a government, and how careful we should be not to abuse the blessings thus placed within our reach.

LESSON CIII.

THESES, OR ARGUMENTATIVE DISCOURSES.

§ 461. THE fifth form in which prose compositions appear is that of the Thesis, or Argumentative Discourse.

A Thesis, or Argumentative Discourse, is a composition in which the writer lays down a proposition, and endeavors to persuade others that it is true. The statements or reasons

---

§ 461. What is the fifth form in which prose compositions appear? What is a thesis, or argumentative discourse? What are arguments? In what case does a thesis become an oration?

used for this purpose are called Arguments. When intended for delivery, or written in a suitable style for that purpose, a thesis becomes an Oration.

§ 462. In the conduct of orations and argumentative discourses, six formal divisions were adopted by the ancients, the Exordium or Introduction, the Division, the Statement, the Reasoning, the Appeal to the Feelings, and the Peroration. It is by no means necessary, however, that these six parts should enter into every discourse. To employ them all would inevitably, in some cases, produce an appearance of stiffness and pedantry. Yet, as any of them may be used, we proceed to define and treat briefly of each.

§ 463. The object of the Exordium or Introduction is to render the reader or hearer well-disposed, attentive, and open to persuasion.

To accomplish the first of these ends, the writer must make a modest opening, and convey to his readers the impression that he is candidly maintaining a position of the truth of which he is himself assured. To awaken attention, he should hint at the importance, novelty, or dignity of the subject. Finally, to make his readers open to conviction, he should endeavor to remove any prejudices they may have formed against the side of the question he intends to espouse.

The introduction of a discourse is its most difficult part. If, as we have seen, it is important in other compositions to make a good impression at the outset, it is doubly so when we are endeavoring to persuade. The following suggestions will be found generally applicable:—

I. An introduction must be easy and natural. It must appear, as Cicero says, " to have sprung up of its own accord from the matter under consideration". To ensure these qualities, it is recommended hat the introduction should not be composed until the other parts of

---

§ 462. In the conduct of argumentative discourses, what formal divisions were adopted by the ancients? · In some cases, what would result from employing all these divisions?

§ 463. What is the object of the exordium? What must the writer do, in order to accomplish these three ends? What is said of the importance of having an effective introduction? What is the first essential of an introduction? What does Cicero say on this head? To ensure this, when is it recommended that the introduction should be

the discourse are written, or at least until its general scope and bearing are digested. Cicero, though in treating of the subject he distinctly approves of this plan, did not see fit in his own case to follow it. It was his custom, as we learn from one of his Letters to Atticus, to prepare, at his leisure, a variety of introductions, that he might have them in readiness for any work which he should afterwards write. In consequence of this singular mode of proceeding, he happened unwittingly to employ the same introduction in two different works. Atticus informed him of the fact, and Cicero, acknowledging the mistake, sent him a new exordium.

II. In the second place, modesty is essential in an introduction; it must not promise too much, and thus raise expectations in the reader which may be disappointed.

III. An introduction is not the place for vehemence and passion. The minds of the readers must be gradually prepared before the writer can venture on strong and animated outbursts. An exception, however, may be made when the subject is of such a nature that the very mention of it naturally awakens passionate emotion.

IV. Introductions, moreover, should not anticipate any material part of the subject. If topics or arguments afterwards to be enlarged upon are hinted at or partially discussed in the introduction, they lose, when subsequently brought forward, the grace of novelty, and thereby a great portion of their effect.

V. Lastly, the introduction should be accommodated, both in length and character, to the discourse that is to follow: in length, as nothing can be more absurd than to erect an immense vestibule before a diminutive building; and in character, as it is no less absurd to overcharge with superb ornaments the portico of a plain dwelling-house, or to make the entrance to a monument as gay as that to an arbor.

§ 464. The Division is that part of a discourse in which the writer makes known to his readers the method to be pursued, and the heads he intends to take, in treating his subject. There are many cases in which the division is unnecessary; some, in which its introduction would even be improper: as, for instance, when only a single argument is to be used.

---

composed? What was Cicero's practice? Into what difficulty did it once lead him? In the second place, what is essential in an introduction? Thirdly, for what is an introduction not the place? What exception is made? What is the effect of anticipating in the introduction any material part of the subject? Lastly, to what should the introduction be accommodated? How is this illustrated?

§ 464. What is the division? In what compositions is it most frequently used?

A formal division is used more frequently in the sermon than in any other species of composition; but it has been questioned by many whether the laying down of heads, as it is called, does not lessen, rather than add to, the effect. The Archbishop of Cambray, in his Dialogues on Eloquence, strongly condemns it: observing that it is a modern invention, which took its rise only when metaphysics began to be introduced into preaching; that it renders a sermon stiff and destroys its unity; and is fatal to oratorical effect. It is urged, on the other hand, however, that a formal division renders a sermon more clear by showing how all the parts hang on each other and tend to one and the same point, and thus makes it more impressive and instructive. The heads of a sermon, moreover, are of great assistance to the memory of a hearer; they enable him to keep pace with the progress of the discourse, and afford him resting-places whence he can reflect on what has been said, and look forward to what is to follow.

When the division is employed, care should be taken,

I. That the several parts into which the subject is divided be really distinct; that is, that no one include another.

II. That the heads taken be those into which the subject is most easily and naturally resolved.

III. That the several members of the division exhaust the subject.

IV. That there be no unnecessary multiplication of heads, to distract and weary the reader.

V. That a natural order be followed; that is, that the simplest points be first discussed, and afterwards the more difficult ones that are founded on them.

VI. That the terms in which the division is expressed be as concise as possible. That there be no circumlocution, no unnecessary words.

§ 465. The third division of a discourse is the Statement, in which the facts connected with the subject are laid open This generally forms an important part of legal pleadings. The statement should be put forth in a clear and forcible style. The writer must state his facts in such a way as to

---

What has been questioned by many? What is the opinion of the Archbishop of Cambray? What advantages, on the other hand, does a formal division possess? When the division is employed, what six points should be attended to?

§ 465. What is the third division of a discourse? What is the statement? Of what compositions does it form an important part? In what style should it be written? How must the writer state his facts?

keep strictly within the bounds of truth, and yet to present them under the colors that are most favorable to his cause; to place in the most striking light every circumstance that is to his advantage, and explain away, as far as possible such as make against him.

§ 466. The fourth division is the Reasoning; and on this every thing depends. It is here that the arguments are found which are to induce conviction, and to prepare for which is the object of the parts already discussed. The following suggestions should be regarded :—

I. The writer should select such arguments only as he feels to be solid and convincing. He must not expect to impose on the world by mere arts of language; but, placing himself in the situation of a reader, should think how he would be affected by the reasoning which he proposes to use for the persuasion of others.

II. When the arguments employed are strong and satisfactory, the more they are distinguished and treated apart from each other, the better; but, when they are weak or doubtful, it is expedient rather to throw them together, than to present each in a clear and separate light.

III. When we have a number of arguments of different degrees of strength, it is best to begin and close with the stronger, placing the weaker in the middle, where they will naturally attract least attention.

IV. Arguments should not be multiplied too much, or extended too far. Besides burdening the memory, and lessening the effect of individual points, such diffuseness renders a cause suspected.

§ 467. The fifth division is the Appeal to the Feelings. This should be short and to the point. All appearance of art should be strictly avoided. To move his readers, the writer must be moved himself.

§ 468. The last division of a discourse is the Peroration;

---

§ 466. What is the fourth division? Of what does it consist? What arguments should be selected? When the arguments employed are strong and satisfactory, how should they be treated? How, when they are weak or doubtful? When we have a number of arguments of different degrees of strength, how is it best to arrange them? What is the effect of multiplying arguments too much, or extending them too far?

§ 467. What is the fifth division of a discourse? What should be the character of an appeal to the feelings?

§ 468. What is the last division of a discourse? In it, what does the writer do?

in which the writer sums up all that has been said, and endeavors to leave a forcible impression on the reader's mind.

§ 469. As examples, two argumentative discourses are presented below, supporting, respectively, the affirmative and the negative of the question, " Does virtue always ensure happiness ? "

[*Affirmative.*]
VIRTUE ALWAYS ENSURES HAPPINESS.

Selfishness exerts a powerful influence over the actions of all men. Even when we least suspect that we are complying with its dictates, if we closely examine the springs of our action, we shall find that we are instinctively following the promptings of our own tastes and propensities. We can hence perceive the wisdom of Providence, who, to win men to virtue even against their own will, has annexed to it an invariable reward. Happiness He has made depend solely and exclusively on uprightness; and this proposition it is the object of the present discourse to establish.

It would seem as if this were so palpable a truth that it would require no demonstration, but would be at once universally admitted. Yet there are some, who, despite the teachings of moralists of every age, deeming themselves wiser in their generation than the children of light, have thought proper to deny it, and thus have sought to overthrow the strongest bulwark on which society depends. Whatever the scoffer may say, however confidently he may point to individual instances as contradicting the position here maintained, it becomes the candid examiner not to be driven from the truth by ridicule or sophistry; not to let sneers prevail against the weight of testimony that ancient sages, as well as modern philosophers, have borne on this subject; and, finally, to consider with care before he ventures to disbelieve a doctrine which is at the foundation of all morality.

In the first place, it is necessary to define virtue; we regard it as consisting in the discharge of our duty to God and our neighbor, despite all temptations to the contrary. Our first argument is, that a virtuous course is so consonant to the light of reason, is so agreeable to our moral sentiments, and produces such peace of mind, that it may be said to carry its reward along with it, even if unattended by that recompense which it ought to receive from the world.

This is evident in the very nature of things. The all-wise and beneficent Author of nature has so framed the soul of man that he can not but approve of virtue, whether in himself or in others, and has annexed to the practice of it an inward satisfaction that surpasses all the blessings of earth. The goods of fortune, wealth, rank, external prosperity,—all these may take to themselves wings and fly away; but of the happiness which springs from the consciousness of a proper discharge of duty, no thief can rob us, no stroke of adversity can deprive us.

But the reward of virtue is not always confined to this internal peace and happiness. As, in the works of nature and art, whatever is really beautiful is generally useful, so in the moral world, whatever is truly virtuous, is at the same time so beneficial to society that it seldom goes without some external recompense. Men know that they can depend on one who acts from principle; they have confidence in his words and representations, and give him the preference in all matters of business. Thus, even in a worldly point of view, the virtuous man has an advantage over those of loose principles or immoral lives.

In the third place, nothing is so liable to create in our behalf firm and lasting friendship on the part of the good, as virtuous practices. The associations of the wicked are undeserving of the name of friendship; it is only to the elevated fellowship of upright minds that this term is applied. Now, that friendship is a source of the purest happiness none will deny; and for the blessings resulting from it we are thus indebted, in great measure, to virtue.

But there is another important consideration that we should not forget. Few men are so constituted as to be insensible to the approbation or censure of the world. To many, its smile is alone sufficient to constitute happiness; its frown is a source of misery. Now, this smile is gained in no way so readily as by a course of integrity.

How has the approbation of all ages rewarded the virtue of Scipio! That great warrior had taken a beautiful captive, with whose charms he was greatly enamored; but, finding that she was betrothed to a young nobleman of her own country, he, without hesitation, generously delivered her up to his rival. This one act of the noble Roman has, more than all his conquests, shed an imperishable lustre around his character.

Nor has the approbation of society been limited to the virtuous actions of individuals. The loveliness of virtue generally has been the constant topic of all moralists, ancient and modern. Plato remarks, that, if virtue were to assume a human form, it would command the admiration of the whole world. A late writer has said, "In every region, every clime, the homage paid to virtue is the same. In no one sentiment were ever mankind more generally agreed."

If, therefore, virtue is in itself so lovely; if it is accompanied with an inward peace and satisfaction; if it is a source of temporal advantages; if it is the spring from which flow the blessings of friendship; if it wins for those who practise it the approbation of the world;—it must be admitted by every candid enquirer that the proposition with which we started is true, that virtue always ensures happiness. Though it must be acknowledged that it is frequently attended with crosses in this life, and that something of self-denial is implied in its very idea; yet the wise will admit the truth of the poet's words, will consider

"The broadest mirth unfeeling folly wears,
Less pleasing far than virtue's very tears."

Our own experience, no less than the arguments here adduced, must convince us that

"Guilt ever carries his own scourge along;
Virtue, her own reward".

[*Negative.*]

VIRTUE DOES NOT ALWAYS ENSURE HAPPINESS.

In contemplating the maxims of the ancient Stoic philosophers, we cannot help being struck with the soundness of their principles, and the stern requirements of their moral code. Yet there is one of their propositions to which we cannot yield assent; and that is, that temporal happiness is the necessary consequence of virtue. So important a question,—one on which so many issues, and those the practical issues of life, are staked,—is well worthy of discussion.

It is well understood that, in treating this question, prejudices will have to be combated and removed: for there are many who, without having looked closely at the subject, have followed the ancient Stoics; and, because it is a convenient creed to teach, and one which it is believed will lead to the practice of virtue, have sought to inculcate this selfish principle. A regard for virtue should be instilled by higher arguments than this; virtue should be practised because it is a duty,—because it is the command of God.

In the first place, we lay down the proposition that there is no necessary connection between virtue and happiness. To the ancients, who knew not that the soul was immortal, it may have seemed necessary that the patient self-denial, the forgiving charity, and the active benevolence, of virtue, should be rewarded in this world; but we, who live in the light of a revelation from on high, know that there is a hereafter, and look to that infinite cycle of ages, not to this finite state of probation, for the reward to which virtue may be entitled.

Again: no one can deny that it is an important principle of our religious system that the virtuous and the pious should be put to the trial, and that afflictions and crosses are sent by the Omnipotent to test the stability of their faith and practice. As Job, a man that "feared God and eschewed evil," was tried by visitations from on high; so have the good of all ages been obliged to submit to similar probation. Viewed in this light, it would seem that trial is peculiarly, in this world, the lot of virtue; the necessary preparation to be made, in time, by those who would enjoy a blissful eternity.

But those who, with the poet, believe that

"Virtue alone is happiness below",

point us to the pleasures of a quiet conscience, and the peace which a knowledge of the performance of duty brings with it. It is admitted that these are great blessings, and that without them happiness cannot exist; but are they alone sufficient to make a man happy? Can the quietest conscience in the universe remove the pangs of hunger, alleviate the sufferings of the sick, or comfort the mourner? The experience of the world will answer, *no*. There are many Jobs; there are many good, but unhappy, men.

To go a step further; to say what is necessary to ensure happiness; to point to religion, the hope of that which is to come, as an anchor to which the soul may cling "amid a sea of trouble,"—would be foreign to the question. In view of the arguments we have advanced, in view of the striking argument furnished by our own experience, we think we may fairly conclude that

"Virtue alone is" *not* "happiness below".

EXERCISE.

Write an argumentative discourse supporting either the affirmative or the negative of the question, "Do public amusements exercise a beneficial influence on society?"

LESSON CIV.

ORATIONS.—SERMON-WRITING.

§ 470. An Oration is a discourse intended for public delivery, and written in a style adapted thereto. At the present day, this term is generally applied to discourses appropriate to some important or solemn occasion; such as a funeral, an anniversary, a college commencement, &c. It is a speech of an elevated character, and differs in this respect from the harangue

---

§ 470. What is an oration? To what is the term generally applied at the present day? How does the oration differ from the harangue and the address?

and the address: the former of which implies a noisy and declamatory manner in the speaker; the latter, a less formal and stately style than characterizes the oration.

§ 471. The ancients recognized three classes of orations; the demonstrative, the deliberative, and the judicial. The scope of the first was to praise or to censure; that of the second, to advise or to persuade; that of the third, to accuse or to defend. The chief subjects of demonstrative eloquence, for instance, were panegyrics, invectives, gratulatory and funeral orations; deliberative eloquence was displayed chiefly in the senate-house and assembly of the people; while judicial eloquence was confined to the courts of law.

In modern times, also, a three-fold division has been adopted, though one different from that just described. Orations are now distinguished as,

I. Speeches to be delivered in deliberative public assemblies; as in Congress, at popular meetings, &c.

II. Speeches at the bar.

III. Sermons, or discourses to be delivered from the pulpit.

§ 472. The style of an oration should be elevated and forcible. It should not lack ornament; and whatever embellishments are introduced must be of the most exalted character.

An argumentative discourse, written in the style just described, and intended for delivery in public, becomes an oration. To the latter, therefore, the principles laid down for such discourses in the last lesson are equally applicable. The same formal divisions may be adopted, either in whole or in part, as occasion may require.

§ 473. Sermons constitute the most important class of orations. For the benefit of those who desire brief and practical directions for the preparation of such discourses, we condense the following remarks from Hannam's valuable "Pulpit Assistant":—

---

§ 471. How many classes of orations did the ancients recognize? Name them, and state what was the scope of each. In modern times, what division has been adopted?

§ 472. What should be the style of an oration? What should be the character of the ornaments introduced? What divisions may be adopted in the preparation of orations?

PRACTICAL HINTS ON SERMON-WRITING.

Choice of Texts.

1. Never choose such texts as have not complete sense; for only impertinent and foolish people will attempt to preach from one or two words, which signify nothing.

2. Not only words which have a complete sense of themselves must be taken, but they must also include the complete sense of the writer; for it is his language and sentiments that you aim to explain. For example, if you take these words of 2 Cor. i., 3, "Blessed be God, the Father of our Lord Jesus Christ, the Father of mercies, and the God of all comfort," and stop here, you will have complete sense; but it is not the Apostle's sense. If you go further, and add "who comforteth us in all our tribulation", it will not then be the complete sense of St. Paul, nor will his meaning be wholly taken in, unless you go to the end of the fourth verse. When the complete sense of the sacred writer is taken, you may stop; for there are few texts in Scripture which do not afford matter sufficient for a sermon, and it is as inconvenient to take too much text as too little; both extremes must be avoided.

General Suggestions.

1. A sermon should clearly explain a text; that is, should place things before the people's eyes in such a way that they may be understood without difficulty. Bishop Burnett says, "a preacher is to fancy himself as in the room of the most unlearned man in the whole parish, and must therefore put such parts of his discourses as he would have all understand in so plain a form of words that it may not be beyond the meanest of them. This he will certainly study to do if his desire be to edify them, rather than to make them admire himself as a learned and high spoken man."

2. A sermon must give the entire sense of the whole text, to ensure which, it must be considered in every view. This rule condemns dry and barren explications, wherein the preacher discovers neither study nor invention, and leaves unsaid a great number of beautiful things with which his text might have furnished him. In matters of religion and piety, not to edify much is to destroy much; and a sermon cold and poor, will do more mischief in an hour, than a hundred of the other kind can do good.

3. The preacher must be discreet, in opposition to those impertinent people who utter jests, comical comparisons, quirks, and extravagances; sober, in opposition to those rash spirits who would curiously dive into mysteries beyond the bounds of modesty; chaste, in opposition to those bold and imprudent geniuses who are not ashamed of saying many things which beget unclean ideas. The preacher must be simple and grave. Simple, speaking things of good natural sense, without metaphysical speculations; grave, because all sorts of vulgar and proverbial sayings ought to be avoided.

4. The understanding must be informed, but in a manner which affects the heart; either to comfort the hearers, or to excite them to acts of piety and repentance.

5. Above all things, avoid excess. There must not be too much genius; too many brilliant, sparkling, and shining, things. Over-abundant ornaments lead the hearer to say, "The man preaches himself, aims to display his genius, and is animated by the spirit of the world rather than the Spirit of God."

6. A sermon must not be overcharged with doctrine, because the hearers' memories can not retain it all; and by aiming to keep all, they will lose all.

Reasoning must not be carried too far. Long trains of argument, composed of a number of propositions chained together, with principles and consequences dependent on them, are always embarrassing to the auditor.

Connection.

By this is meant the relation of the text to the foregoing or following verses. This must be found by deliberate thought, with the aid of good commentaries. The connection often contributes much to the elucidation of the text; and, in this case, should always be alluded to in the discourse. The beginning of the sermon seems to be the best place for treating it; it often affords good material for an introduction.

Division

Four or five heads are generally sufficient; a greater number are embarrassing to the hearer.

There are two sorts of divisions which we may properly make: the first, which is the most common, is the division of the text into its parts; the other is a division of the discourse, or sermon itself.

The division of the sermon itself is proper in the following cases:—

1. When a prophecy of the Old Testament is handled; for, generally, the understanding of these prophecies depends on many general considerations, which, by exposing and refuting false senses, open a way to the true explication.

2. When a text is connected with a disputed point, the understanding of which must depend on the state of the question, and the arguments that have been advanced. All these lights are previously necessary, and they can be given only by general considerations. For example, Rom. iii. 28,—" We conclude that a man is justified by faith without the deeds of the law." Some general considerations must precede, which clear up the state of the question between St. Paul and the Jews, touching justification, which mark the hypothesis of the Jews upon that subject, and which discover the true principle that St. Paul would establish; so that, in the end, the text may be clearly understood.

3. In a conclusion drawn from a long preceding discourse; as, for example, Rom. v., 1. "Therefore, being justified by faith, we have peace with God, through our Lord Jesus Christ." The discourse must be divided into two parts: the first consisting of some general considerations on the doctrine of justification, which St. Paul establishes in the preceding chapters; and the second, of his conclusion, that, being thus justified, we have peace with God, &c.

4. In the case of texts quoted in the New Testament from the Old. Prove by general considerations that the text is properly produced, and then proceed clearly to its explication. Of this kind are Hebrews i., 5, 6, "I will be to him a Father," &c. "One in a certain place testified," &c., ii. 6. "Wherefore, as the Holy Ghost saith," &c., iii. 7.

5. In this class must be placed divisions into different views. These, to speak properly, are not divisions of a text into its parts; but rather different applications, which are made of the same texts to divers subjects. Typical texts should be divided thus; and a great number of passages in the Psalms, which relate not only to David, but also to Jesus Christ: such should be considered first literally, as they relate to David; and then in the mystical sense, as they refer to the Lord Jesus.

There are also typical passages, which, besides their literal sense, have figurative meanings, relating not only to Jesus Christ, but also to the church in general, and to every believer in particular. For example, Dan. ix., 7, "O Lord, righteousness belongeth unto thee, but unto us confusion of faces as at this day," must not be divided into parts, but considered in different views: 1. In regard to all men in general. 2. In regard to the Jewish Church in Daniel's time. 3. In regard to ourselves at the present day. So, again, Heb. iii. 7, 8, "To-day if ye will hear his voice," which is taken from Psalm xcv., cannot be better divided than by referring it, 1. To David's time. 2. To St. Paul's. 3. To our own.

As to the division of the text itself, sometimes the order of the words is so clear and natural, that no division is necessary; we need only follow the order in question. As, for example, Eph. i., 3. "Blessed be the God and Father of our Lord Jesus Christ, who hath blessed us with all spiritual blessings in heavenly places in Christ." Here the words divide themselves, and to explain them we need only follow them. A grateful acknowledgment, "Blessed be God". The title under which the Apostle blesses God, "The Father of our Lord Jesus Christ". The reason for which he blesses him, because "he hath blessed us". The plenitude of this blessing, "with all blessings". The nature or kind signified by the term *spiritual*. The place where he hath blessed us, "in heavenly places". In whom he hath blessed us, "in Christ".

Most texts, however, ought to be formally divided; for which purpose we must regard chiefly the order of nature: put that division which naturally precedes, in the first place, and let the rest follow in its proper order.

There are two natural orders: one natural in regard to subjects themselves; the other natural in regard to us. Though in general you may follow which of the two you please, yet there are some texts that determine the division; as Phil. ii., 13. "It is God which worketh effectually in you both to will and to do of his good pleasure." There are, it is plain, three things to be discussed; the action of God's grace upon men, "God worketh effectually in you"; the effect of this grace, "to will and to do"; and the spring or source of the action, according to "his good pleasure". I think the division would not be proper, if we were to treat, 1. Of God's good pleasure; 2. Of his grace; and 3. Of the will and works of men.

Above all things, in divisions, avoid introducing anything in the first part which implies a knowledge of the second, or which obliges you to treat of the second to make the first understood; otherwise you will be obliged to make many tedious repetitions. Endeavor to separate your parts from each other as well as you can. When they are very closely connected, place the most detached first, and make that serve for a foundation to the explication of the second, and the second to the third; so that, at the conclusion, the hearer may at a glance perceive, as it were, a perfect body, a well-finished building. One of the greatest merits of a sermon is harmony in its component parts; that the first lead naturally to the second, the second to the third, &c.; that what goes before excite a desire for what is to follow.

When, in a text, there are several terms which need a particular explanation, and which can not be explained without confusion; or without dividing the text into too many parts, then do not divide the text at all, but divide the discourse into two or three parts. First explain the terms, and then proceed to the subject itself.

There are many texts, in discussing which it is not necessary to treat of either subject or attribute; but all the discussion turns on words that convey no meaning independently of other terms, and which are called in logic *syncategorematica*. For example, John iii., 16, "God so loved the world, that he gave his only begotten Son, that whosoever believeth in him, should not perish, but have everlasting life." The categorical proposition is, God loved the world; yet, it is necessary neither to insist much upon the term *God*, nor to speak in a common-place way of the divine love. The text should be divided into two parts: first, the gift which God in his love hath made of his Son; secondly, the end for which this gift was bestowed, "that whosoever believeth in him should not perish, but have everlasting life".

There are texts of reasoning which are composed of an objection and an answer. These are naturally divided into the objection and the solution. As, Romans vi., 1, 2, "What shall we say then," &c.

There are some texts of reasoning which are extremely difficult to divide, because they cannot be extended into many propositions without confusion. As, John iv., 10 "If thou knewest the gift of God," &c. Here we may take two heads: the first including the general proposition contained in the words; the second, the particular application of these to the Samaritan woman.

There are some texts which imply many important truths without expressing them. These should be alluded to and enlarged upon. In such cases, the text may be divided into two parts; one referring to what is implied, and the other to what is expressed.

Subdivisions also should be made, for they are of great assistance to the writer; they need not, however, be mentioned in the discourse, for there is a risk of overburdening the hearer's memory.

Methods of Discussion.

These are four in number. According to the nature of the subject, one or more may be employed. Clear subjects must be discussed by observation or continued application; difficult and important ones, by explication.

EXPLICATION.—This consists in explaining the terms used, or the subject, or both. There are two sorts of explications: the one, simple and plain, needs only to be proposed, and agreeably elucidated; the other must be confirmed, if it speak of fact, by proofs of fact; if of right, by proofs of right; if of both, by proofs of both. A great and important subject, consisting of many branches, may be reduced to a certain number of propositions or questions, and these may be discussed one after the other.

I. *Explication of Terms.*—The difficulties of these arise from three causes; either the terms do not seem to make any sense; or they are equivocal, forming different senses; or the sense they seem to make at first appears perplexed, improper, or contradictory; or the meaning, though clear, may be controverted, and is exposed to cavil. First propose the difficulty: then solve it as briefly as possible.

What we have to explain in a text consists of one or more simple terms; of ways of speaking peculiar to Scripture; or of particles called *syncategorematica*.

1. Simple terms are the divine attributes, goodness, &c., man's virtues or vices, faith, hope, &c. These are either literal or figurative; if figurative, give the meaning of the figure, and, without stopping long, pass on to the thing itself. Some simple terms should be explained only so far as they bear on the meaning of the sacred author. Sometimes the simple terms in a text must be discussed at length, in order to give a clear and full view of the subject.

2. Expressions peculiar to Scripture deserve a particular explanation, because they are rich in meaning; such as, "to be *in* Christ," "come *after* Christ," &c.

3. Particles called *syncategorematica* (such as *none, some, all, now, when,* &c. which augment, or limit the meaning of the proposition, should be carefully examined for often the whole explication depends upon them.

2. *Explication of the Subject.*—If the difficulty arise from errors, or false senses, refute and remove them; then establish the truth. If from the intricacy of the subject itself, do not propose difficulties, and raise objections, but enter immediately into the explication of the matter, and take care to arrange your ideas well.

In all cases, illustrate by reasons, examples, comparisons of the subject; their relations, conformities, or differences. You may do it by consequences; by the person, his state, &c., who proposes the subject; or the persons to whom it is proposed; by circumstances, time, place, &c.

OBSERVATION.—This method is best for clear and historical passages. Some texts require both explication and observation. Sometimes an observation may be made by way of explication. Observations, for the most part, ought to be theological; historical, philosophical, or critical, very seldom. They must not be proposed in a scholastic style, or common-place form; but in an easy, familiar, manner.

CONTINUAL APPLICATION.—This method may be entirely free from explanations and observations; it is appropriate to texts exhorting to holiness and repentance.

PROPOSITION.—Texts may be reduced to two propositions at least, and three or four at most, having a mutual dependence and connection. This method opens the most extensive field for discussion. In the former modes of discussion you are restrained to your text but here your subject is the matter contained in your proposition.

The way of explication is most proper to give the meaning of Scripture: this, of systematic divinity; and it has this advantage, it will equally serve either theory or practise.

Peroration, or Conclusion.

This ought to be short, lively, and animating; full of great and beautiful figures; aiming to move Christian affections,—to confirm our love of God, our gratitude, zeal, repentance, self-condemnation, consolation, hope of felicity, courage, constancy in affliction, and steadiness in temptation. Let some one or more striking ideas, not mentioned in the discussion, be reserved for this part, and applied with vigor.

ANALYSIS OF A SERMON.

The Existence of God.

"The fool hath said in his heart, there is no God." Psalms xiv., 1.

"The fool hath said,"—it is evident that none but a fool would have said it.

The fool, a term in Scripture signifying a wicked man; one who hath lost his wisdom, and right apprehension of God; one dead in sin.

"Said in his heart"; i. e., he thinks, or he doubts, or he wishes. He dares not openly publish it, though he dares secretly think it; he doubts, he wishes, and sometimes hopes.

"There is no God,"—no judge, no one to govern, reward, or punish. Those who deny the providence of God, do in effect deny his existence; they strip him of that wisdom, goodness, mercy, and justice, which are the glory of the Deity.

The existence of God is the foundation of all religion. The whole building totters, if the foundation be out. We must believe that he is, and that he is what he has declared himself, before we can seek him, adore him, or love him.

It is, therefore, necessary we should know why we believe, that our belief be founded on undeniable evidence, and that we may give a better reason for his existence, than that we have heard our parents and teachers tell of it. It is as much as to say, "There is no God," when we have no better arguments than those. Let us look at the evidences which should establish us in the truth.

I. *All nature* shows the existence of its Maker. We cannot open our eyes but we discover this truth shining through all creatures. The whole universe bears the character and stamp of a First Cause, infinitely wise, infinitely powerful. Let us cast our eyes on the earth which bears us, and ask, "Who laid the foundation?" Job xxxviii., 4. Let us look on that vast arch of skies that covers us, and inquire, "Who hath thus stretched it forth?" Isaiah xl., 21, 22. "Who is it also who hath fixed so many luminous bodies with so much order and regularity?" Job xxvi., 13. Every plant, every atom, as well as every star, bears witness of a Deity. Whoever saw statues, or pictures, but concluded there had been a statuary and limner? Who can behold garments, ships, or houses, and not understand there was a weaver, a carpenter, an architect? A man may as well doubt whether there be a sun, when he sees his beams gilding the earth, as doubt whether there be a God, when he sees his works. Psalms xix., 1–6. The Atheist is, therefore, a fool, because he denies that which every creature in his constitution asserts. Can he behold the spider's net, or the silk-worm's web, the bee's closets, or the ant's granaries, without acknowledging a higher being than a creature, who hath planted that genius in them? Job xxxix. Psalms civ., 24. All the stars in heaven and the dust on earth, oppose the Atheist. Romans i., 19, 20.

II. *The power of conscience* is an argument to convince us of this truth. "Every one that findeth me shall slay me," Genesis iv., 14, was the language of Cain; and similar apprehensions are frequent in those who feel the fury of an enraged conscience. The psalmist tells us concerning those who say in their heart "There is no God ", that "they are in fear where no fear is." Psalms liii., 5. Their guilty minds invent terrors, and thereby confess a Deity, while they deny it,—that there is a sovereign Being who will punish. Pashur, who wickedly insulted the prophet Jeremiah, had this for his reward, "that his name should be Magor-missabib," i. e., "fear round about". Jeremiah xx., 3, 4. When Belshazzar saw the handwriting, "his countenance was changed," Daniel v., 6. The apostle who tells us that there is a "law written in the hearts cf men ", adds, their "consciences also bear witness." Romans ii., 15.

III. *Universal consent* is another argument. The notion of a God is found among all nations; it is the language of every country and region; the most abominable idolatry argues a Deity. All nations, though ever so barbarous and profligate, have confessed some God.

IV. *Extraordinary judgments*. When a just revenge follows abominable crimes, especially when the judgment is suited to the sin; when the sin is made legible by the inflicted judgment. "The Lord is known by the judgment which he executeth." Psalms ix., 16. Herod Agrippa received the flattering applause of the people, and thought himself a God; but was, by the judgment inflicted upon him, forced to confess another. Acts xii., 21-28; Judges i., 6, 7; Acts v., 1-10.

V. *Accomplishment of Prophecies*. To foretell things that are future, as if they already existed or had existed long ago, must be the result of a mind infinitely intelligent. "Show the things that are to come hereafter." Isaiah xli., 23. "I am God, declaring the end from the beginning." Isaiah xlvi., 9, 10. Cyrus was prophesied of, Isaiah xliv., 28, and xlv., 1, long before he was born; Alexander's sight of Daniel's prophecy concerning his victories, moved him to spare Jerusalem. The four monarchies were plainly deciphered in Daniel, before the fourth rose up. That power, which foretells things beyond the wit of man, and orders all causes to bring about those predictions, must be an infinite and omniscient power.

What folly, then, for any to shut their eyes, and stop their ears; to attribute those things to blind chance, which nothing less than an infinitely wise and powerful Being could effect!

Peroration, or Conclusion.

I. If God can be seen in creation, study the creatures; the creatures are the heralds of God's glory. "The glory of the Lord shall endure." Psalms civ., 31. The world is a sacred temple; man is introduced to contemplate it. As grace does not destroy nature, so the book of redemption does not blot out the book of creation.

II. If it be a folly to deny or doubt the being of God, is it not a folly also not to worship God when we acknowledge his existence? ' To fear God, and keep his commandments, is the whole duty of man." We are not reasonable if we are not religious. Romans xii., 1.

III. If it be a folly to deny the existence of God, will it not be our wisdom, since we acknowledge his being, often to think of him? It is said of the fool only, "God is not in all his thoughts." Psalms x., 4.

IV. If we believe the being of God, let us abhor practical atheism. Men's practices are the best indexes to their principles. "Let your light shine before men." Matthew v., 16.

PART V:

POETICAL COMPOSITION

LESSON CV.

VERSE.—QUANTITY.—FEET.—METRES.

§ 474. STRICTLY speaking, those compositions only fall under the head of poetry, into which the language of the imagination largely enters; which abound in metaphors, similes, personifications, and other rhetorical figures. Such writings, even if they have the form of prose, must be regarded as poems; while, on the other hand, prosaic matter, even if put into the form in which poetry generally appears, is still nothing more than prose. The distinction between prose and poetry, therefore, has reference to the matter of which they are respectively composed.

Poetry being the language of imagination and passion, we naturally expect to find in it more figures than in prose. These, having been already fully treated, need no further consideration here. As regards its form, poetry is generally characterized by deviations from the natural

---

§ 474. What compositions fall under the head of poetry? To what does the distinction between prose and poetry refer? What do we naturally expect to find in

order and mode of expression, which are known as poetical licenses. Examples of some of these follow :—

I. Violent inversions.

"Now storming fury rose,
And clamor such as *heard in Heaven till now
Was never.*"

II. Violent ellipses.

"While all those souls [*that*] have ever felt the force
Of those enchanting passions, to my lyre
Should throng attentive."

III. The use of peculiar words, idioms, phrases, &c., not generally found in prose; as, *morn, eve, o'er, sheen, passing rich.*

IV. Connecting an adjective with a different substantive from that which it really qualifies; as in the following lines, in which *wide* is joined to *nature* instead of *bounds* :—

"Through wide nature's bounds
Expatiate with glad step."

V. Using a noun and a pronoun standing for it [in violation of a syntactical rule] as subjects or objects of the same verb; as,

The *boy*—oh! where was *he!*"

VI. The use of *or* for *either*, and *nor* for *neither*.

"Whate'er thy name, *or* Muse or Grace."
"*Nor* earth nor Heaven shall hear his prayer."

VII. The introduction of an adverb between *to*, the sign of the infinitive, and the verb with which it is connected; as,

"To *slowly* trace the forest's shady scene."

VIII. Making intransitive verbs transitive; as,

"Still, in harmonious intercourse, they *lived*
The rural day, and *talked* the flowing heart."

IX. The use of foreign idioms; as,

"To some she *gave*
To *search* the story of eternal thought."

§ 475. Verse is the form in which poetry generally appears. It consists of language arranged into metrical lines, called verses, of a length and rhythm determined by rules

---

poetry? What is meant by poetical licenses? Enumerate the poetical licenses mentioned in the text, and give an example of each.

§ 475. What is verse? Of what does it generally consist? What is the difference

which usage has sanctioned. The distinction between prose and verse is, therefore, a matter of form.

Verse is merely the dress which poetry generally assumes. The two are entirely independent of each other: all poetry is not verse, as we see in the case of Fénélon's Telemachus and Ossian's Poems; nor, on the other hand, is all verse by any means poetry, as nine tenths of the fugitive pieces given to the world under the latter name abundantly show.

Versification is the art of making verses.

A Verse, as we have seen, is a metrical line of a length and rhythm determined by rules which usage has sanctioned.

A Hemistich is half of a verse.

Rhyme is a similarity of sound in syllables which begin differently but end alike. It is exemplified at the close of the following lines:—

> "Self-love, the spring of motion, acts the *soul;*
> Reason's comparing balance rules the *whole.*"

A Distich, or couplet, consists of two verses rhyming together; the lines just given are an example.

A Triplet consists of three verses rhyming together; as,

> "Souls that can scarce ferment their mass of clay,—
> So drossy, so divisible, are they,
> As would but serve pure bodies for allay."

A Stanza [often incorrectly called a *verse*] is a regular division of a poem, consisting of two or more lines, or verses. Stanzas are of every conceivable variety, their formation being regulated by the taste of the poet alone. The stanzas of the same poem, however, should be uniform.

§ 476. Syllables occurring in verse are distinguished as long and short, according to the time occupied in uttering them. A long syllable is equivalent to two short ones.

---

between verse and poetry? What is versification? What is a verse? What is a hemistich? What is rhyme? What is a distich? What is a triplet? What is a stanza? What is it often incorrectly called? By what is the formation of the stanza regulated? What is said of the stanzas of the same poem?

§ 476. How are syllables occurring in verse distinguished? On what is this distinc

QUANTITY.

When it is desired to indicate the quantity, the macron [−] is placed over a long syllable, and the breve [˘] over a short one; as, *thĕ mān*.

In words of more than one syllable, accent, whether primary or secondary, constitutes length; syllables that are unaccented are short. In the case of monosyllables, nouns, adjectives, verbs, adverbs, and interjections, are for the most part long; articles are always short; prepositions and conjunctions are generally short; pronouns are long when emphasized,—when not, short. This will appear from the following lines:—

> Thĕ gŏddĕss hēard, ănd bāde thĕ Mūsĕs rāise
> Thĕ gōldĕn trŭmpĕt ŏf ĕtērnăl prāise:
> Frŏm pōle tŏ pōle thĕ wīnds diffūse thĕ soūnd,
> Thăt fĭlls thĕ cīrcuĭt ŏf thĕ wōrld ăroūnd.

In Latin and Greek, each syllable has a definite quantity, without reference to accent. This is not the case in English. Our vowel sounds have nothing to do with the length or shortness of syllables. *Fat*, in which *a* has its flat or short sound, is as likely to be accented, and therefore long, in poetry, as *fate*, in which the sound of the vowel is generally called long.

§ 477. A **Foot** is a division of a verse, consisting of two or three syllables.

The dissyllabic feet are four in number, as follows:—

Iambus ˘ —, rĕmōve.	Spondee, — —, dărk nīght.
Trochee — ˘, mōvĭng.	Pyrrhic, ˘ ˘, hap-|pĭly̆.

The trisyllabic feet are eight in number, as follows:—

Anapest ˘ ˘ —, ĭntĕrvēne.	Bacchius ˘ — —, thĕ dārk nīght.
Dactyl — ˘ ˘, hăppĭly̆.	Antibacchius — — ˘, ēye-sērvănt.
Amphibrach ˘ — ˘, rĕdūndănt.	Molossus — — —, lōng dārk nīght.
Amphimacer — ˘ —, wīndĭng-shēet.	Tribrach ˘ ˘ ˘, insu-|pĕrăblĕ.

Of these twelve feet, the iambus, the trochee, the anapest, and the dactyl, are oftenest used; and are capable, respective-

---

tion founded? How is the quantity of a syllable indicated? In words of more than one syllable, which syllables are long, and which short? In the case of monosyllables which of the parts of speech are generally long, and which are short? What is the case in Latin and Greek, with respect to the quantity of syllables? What relation subsists in English between the quantity of syllables and the sound of the vowels they contain? Illustrate this.

§ 477. What is a foot? How many dissyllabic feet are there? Enumerate them, state of what syllables they are respectively composed, and give an example of each. How many trisyllabic feet are there? Enumerate them, state of what syllables they are composed, and give an example of each. Of these twelve feet, which are oftenest

ly, without the assistance of the rest, of forming distinct orders of numbers. They are, therefore, called *primary* feet and the measures of which they respectively form the chief component part, are known as *iambic, trochaic, anapestic*, and *dactylic*. A line which consists wholly of one kind of foot is called *pure:* that is, a line containing nothing but iambi is a pure iambic; one into which no foot but the trochee enters is a pure trochaic. Verses not consisting exclusively of one kind of foot are said to be *mixed*. Examples follow:—

1. *Pure Iambic.*—Thĕ rŭl-|ĭng păs-|sĭon cŏn-|quĕrs rēa-|sŏn still.
2. *Pure Trochaic.*—Sĭstĕr | spĭrĭt | cŏme ȃ-|wāy.
3. *Pure Anapestic.*—Frŏm thĕ plāins, | frŏm thĕ wōod-|lănds ănd grōves.
4. *Pure Dactylic.*—Bĭrd ŏf thĕ | wĭldĕrnĕss.

1. *Mixed Iambic.*—Nŏ crīme | wăs thĭne | ĭll-fă-|tĕd fāir.
2. *Mixed Trochaic.*—Trĕmblĭng, | hōpĭng, | lĭngĕrĭng, | flȳĭng.
3. *Mixed Anapestic.*—Dĕar rĕ-|gĭons ŏf sī-|lĕnce ănd shāde.
4. *Mixed Dactylic.*—Mĭdnĭght ăs-|sĭst oŭr mŏan.

The remaining eight feet are called *secondary*, and are occasionally admitted for the sake of preventing monotony and allowing the poet freer scope.

§ 478. By Metre, or Measure, is meant the system according to which verses are formed. The metre depends on the character and number of the feet employed. According to the character of the feet, metres, we have already seen, are distinguished as iambic, trochaic, anapestic, and dactylic. According to the number of the feet, the varieties of metre are as follows: Monometer, or a measure composed of one foot; Dimeter, of two feet; Trimeter, of three; Tetrameter, of four; Pentameter, of five; Hexameter, of six; Heptameter of seven; Octometer, of eight.

A line at the end of which a syllable is wanting to complete the measure, is said to be *catalectic*. One in which there

---

used? What name is given to these four? Why? What are the measures of which they respectively form the chief component part, called? What is meant by a pure iambic line? What, by a mixed? Enumerate the secondary feet. For what purpose are they occasionally admitted?

§ 478. What is meant by metre, or measure? On what does the metre depend? According to the character of the feet, what are the varieties of metre? What, accord-

is a syllable over at the end, is called *hypercatalectic.* When there is neither deficiency nor redundancy, a line is said to be *acatalectic.*

Scanning is the process of dividing a line into the feet of which it is composed.

§ 479. Examples of the different measures follow. Some of the lines are pure, and some are mixed. The figures 1, 2, 3, &c., respectively denote monometer, dimeter, trimeter, &c. Vertical lines mark some of the divisions into feet. Scanning is performed by pronouncing the syllables which constitute the successive feet, and after each mentioning its name. Thus, in scanning the fifth line, the following words would be employed: "*Honor*, trochee; *and shame*, iambus; *from no*, iambus; *condi-*, iambus; *tion rise*, iambus." The line is *mixed iambic pentameter acatalectic.* The student is requested to scan the following lines, and name the measure of each:—

IAMBIC MEASURES

1. Lŏchĭĕl!
2. Thĕ māin | | thĕ māin!
3. Fŏr ŭs | thĕ sŭm- | mĕrs shīne.
4. Fīrst stănds | thĕ nŏ- | blĕ Wăsh- | ĭngtŏn.
5. Honor | and shame | from no | condi- | tion rise.
6. With his sharp-pointed head he dealeth deadly wounds.
7. Over the Alban mountains high, the light of morning broke.
8. O all ye people clap your hands, and with triumphant voices sing.

TROCHAIC MEASURES.

1. Tūrnĭng.
2. Fēar sŭr- | roŭnds mĕ.
3. Dēarĕr | frĭĕnds cā- | rĕss theĕ.
4. Honor's | but an | empty | bubble.
5. Chains of care to lower earth enthral me.
6. Up the dewy mountain, Health is bounding lightly.
7. Hasten, Lord, to rescue me, and set me safe from trouble.
8. Once upon a midnight dreary, while I pondered weak and weary.

ANAPESTIC MEASURES.

1. Whĕn hĕ wĭnks.
2. Lĕt 'hŏ stŭ- | pĭd bĕ grāve.
3. Hŏw thĕ nĭght- | ĭngāles wăr- | blĕ their lōves!
4. Thĕ plĕn- | tĭfŭl moĭst- | ūre ĕncŭm- | bĕred thĕ flōwer!

DACTYLIC MEASURES.

1. Think ǒf ĭt.
2. Rāsh ănd ŭn-|dūtĭfŭl.
3. Brīghtĕr thăn | sŭmmĕr's greēn | cārpĕtĭng.
4. Cold is thy heart, and as frozen as charity.
5. Land of the beautiful, land of the generous, hail to thee.
6. Land of the beautiful, land of the generous, hail to thee heartily.
7. Out of the kingdom of Christ shall be gathered by angels victorious.

CATALECTIC MEASURES.

Almost any of the above metres may be made a syllable shorter and thus become catalectic. The following will serve as specimens:—

1. *Iamb. Tetram. Cat.*—Tŏ-dāy | nŏ āxe | ĭs rīng-|ĭng.
2. *Tro. Tetram. Cat.*—Mōthĕr | dārksōme, | mōthĕr | *drĕad*.
3. *Dact. Tetram. Cat.*—Hārk, hŏw Crĕ-|ātĭŏn's deĕp | mŭsĭcăl | *chŏrds*.
4. *Tro. Tetram. Cat.*—Hĕavĭng, | ūpwărd | tŏ thĕ | lĭght.

HYPERCATALECTIC MEASURES.

The addition of a syllable to any of the acatalectic varieties of metre makes them hypercatalectic. Specimens follow. From the first two lines it will be seen, that, in iambic and trochaic metres, a verse ending with an odd syllable may be regarded either as a higher measure catalectic, or a lower measure hypercatalectic.

1. *Iamb. Trim. Hyp.*—Tŏ-dāy | nŏ āxe | ĭs rīng-|ĭng.
2. *Tro. Trim. Hyp.*—Mōthĕr | dārksōme, | mōthĕr | *drĕad*.
3. *Anap. Tetram. Hyp.*—'Tĭs thĕ chĭĕf | ŏf Glŏnă-|ră lămŏnts | fŏr hĭs dăr-|*ĭng*.
4. *Dact. Mon. Hyp.*—Lĭft hĕr wĭth | *cāre*.

LESSON CVI.

STANZAS.—SONNETS.—HEROIC VERSE.—BLANK VERSE.

§ 480. IAMBIC measures constitute the great body of our poetry, both from the fact that they are easier of construction than any other, and because there is no emotion, which they are not adapted to express. Trochaic measures are peculiarly appropriate to gay and tender sentiments; anapestic, to what is animated, forcible, or heart-stirring. Dactylic verse is

---

§ 480. Of what measures does the great body of our poetry consist? What reasons are given for this? To what are trochaic measures appropriate? To what, anapestic? What is said of dactylic verse?

the most difficult to write, and enters into our poetical literature to such a limited extent that its capacities can hardly be properly estimated. It is effective whenever a rapid movement is desirable, and has been used with success in humorous poetry.

§ 481. It was observed in the last lesson that lines may be combined into an infinite variety of stanzas, according to the poet's taste. To illustrate all of these with examples is impracticable; we can allude only to those that most frequently occur.

The commonest stanza, perhaps, consists of four lines, of which either the first and third, and the second and fourth, rhyme together; or, the first and second, and the third and fourth: as follows:—

> "The curfew tolls the knell of parting day,
> The lowing herd winds slowly o'er the lea;
> The ploughman homeward plods his weary way,
> And leaves the world to darkness and to me."—GRAY.

> "The Assyrian came down like a wolf on the fold,
> And his cohorts were gleaming in purple and gold;
> And the sheen of their spears was like stars on the sea,
> When the blue wave rolls nightly on deep Galilee."—BYRON.

This stanza, when composed of iambic tetrameters, rhyming either consecutively or alternately, is known as Long Metre.

> "O all ye people, clap your hands,
> And with triumphant voices sing;
> No force the mighty power withstands
> Of God, the universal King."—PSALMS OF DAVID.

When the first and third lines are iambic tetrameters, and the second and fourth iambic trimeters, the rhyme being alternate or confined to the two last mentioned, this four-lined stanza becomes Common Metre

> "Over the Alban mountains high
> The light of morning broke;
> From all the roofs of the Seven Hills
> Curled the thin wreaths of smoke."—MACAULAY.

When all the lines of this stanza are iambic trimeters except the third,

---

§ 481. Describe the commonest stanza met with in poetry. Give examples of it from Gray and Byron. Describe long metre; common metre; short metre. To what are these three metres peculiarly adapted, and for what are they therefore employed? In what other way may long and common metre be written? What is the regular ballad-measure of our language? How are stanzas of eight and twelve lines formed?

and that is tetrameter, the rhyme being the same as in the last case, we have Short Metre.

> "The day is past and gone;
> The evening shades appear;
> Oh! may we all remember well
> The night of death draws near."—HYMN-BOOK.

These three metres are peculiarly adapted to slow and solemn music, and hence are generally employed, in preference to others, in the composition of psalms and hymns. By a comparison of the two last examples but one, with numbers 7 and 8 of the iambic measures presented at the close of the preceding lesson, it will be seen that long metre is simply iambic octometer divided into two equal parts, while common metre is iambic heptameter divided after the first four feet. The latter is the regular ballad-measure of our language. Octometer and heptameter, on account of their length, are generally thus divided into two separate lines.

The four-lined stanza doubled and trebled makes effective and common stanzas of eight and twelve lines respectively.

Six-lined stanzas are often used. Some of these have their first and second lines rhyme, their third and sixth, and their fourth and fifth. In others, the first four lines rhyme as in the four-lined stanza, and the last two rhyme with each other; as, in the following:—

> "Friend after friend departs;
> Who has not lost a friend?
> There is no union here of hearts,
> That finds not here an end;
> Were this frail world our final rest,
> Living or dying, none were blest."—MONTGOMERY.

The most noted of all stanzas is the Spenserian, so called from the author of "The Faery Queen", by whom it was borrowed from Italian poetry. Though highly artificial, in the hands of a master it has a fine effect. Its difficulty has deterred most of our later poets from attempting it in pieces of any length; Thomson, however, in his "Castle of Indolence", Beattie in "The Minstrel", and Byron in "Childe Harold", have used it with success. The following from Byron will serve as a specimen; it will be seen that it consists of nine lines, of which eight are iambic pentameter, while the last is a hexameter:—

What are the different ways of rhyming in six-lined stanzas? Repeat a six-lined stanza from Montgomery. What is the most noted of all stanzas? Whence was it borrowed? What is said of its effect? What has deterred our later poets from attempting it? Who have used it with the best success? Of how many lines does it consist? What measure are they? Repeat one of Byron's Spenserian stanzas.

> "To sit on rocks, to muse o'er flood and fell,
>   To slowly trace the forest's shady scene,
>   Where things that own not man's dominion dwell,
>   And mortal foot hath ne'er or rarely been;
> To climb the trackless mountain all unseen
>   With the wild flock, that never needs a fold;
> Alone, o'er steeps and foaming falls to lean;—
>   This is not solitude; 'tis but to hold
> Converse with nature's charms, and view her stores unrolled."

§ 482. The Sonnet, though not a stanza, inasmuch as it is a complete poem in itself, will next be considered; its distinguishing features having reference, not so much to the matter it contains, as to the form it assumes, and the peculiar manner in which its lines rhyme.

Everett, in his comprehensive and thorough "System of English Versification", thus describes the Sonnet. "The Sonnet, like the Spenserian stanza, was borrowed from the Italians. Petrarch is reckoned the father of it. It is still more difficult of construction than the Spenserian stanza; for, besides requiring a great number of rhymes, it demands a terseness of construction, and a point in the thought, which that does not. In the Sonnet, no line should be admitted merely for ornament, and the versification should be faultless. Sonnets, like Spenserian stanzas, are somewhat affected; and this is to be attributed to the age in which they were introduced, when far-fetched thoughts and ingenious ideas were more in vogue than simplicity and natural expression.—The Sonnet is subject to more rigorous rules than any other species of verse. It is composed of exactly fourteen lines, so constructed that the first eight lines shall contain but two rhymes, and the last six but two more. The most approved arrangement is that in which the first line is made to rhyme with the fourth, the fifth, and the eighth,—the second rhyming with the third, the sixth, and the seventh." With respect to the last six lines, Hallam observes:—"By far the worst arrangement and also the least common in Italy is that we usually adopt, the fifth and sixth rhyming together, frequently after a full pause; so that the sonnet ends with the point of an epigram. The best form, as the Italians hold, is the rhyming together of the three uneven and the three even lines; but, as our language is less rich in consonant terminations,

---

§ 482. What is said of the sonnet? From whom was it borrowed? What renders it difficult of construction? To what is the artificial character of the sonnet to be attributed? What is said of the rules of the sonnet? Of how many lines is it composed? In these fourteen lines, how many rhymes are there? As regards the rhyming of the first eight lines, what is the most approved arrangement? With respect to the last six lines, what does Hallam pronounce the worst arrangement? What, the best?

there can be no objection to what has abundant precedents even in theirs, the rhyming of the first and fourth, second and fifth, third and sixth lines." The following is an example of the best arrangement:—

AUTUMN.

"The blithe birds of the summer-tide are flown;
   Cold, motionless, and mute, stands all the wood,
   Save as the restless wind, in mournful mood,
Strays through the tossing limbs with saddest moan.
The leaves it wooed with kisses, overblown
   By gusts, capricious, pitiless, and rude,
   Lie dank and dead amid the solitude;
Where-through it waileth desolate and lone.
But with a clearer splendor sunlight streams
   Athwart the bare, slim, branches· and on high
   Each star, in Night's rich coronal that beams,
Pours down intenser brilliance on the eye;
   Till dazzled Fancy finds her gorgeous dreams
   Outshone in beauty by the autumn sky!"—PIKE.

§ 483. Iambic tetrameter is a favorite measure, and may be used with advantage, not only in small fugitive pieces, but also, without any division into stanzas, throughout a long poem. It is thus employed by Byron in his *Mazeppa*, and Scott in his *Lady of the Lake* and *Marmion*. It is the easiest of all measures to write in; and this very facility is apt to betray a poet, unless he is on his guard, into commonplace expressions, and a careless habit which is fatal to the effect of his verses.

§ 484. Iambic pentameter constitutes what is called the Heroic Line. It is the most dignified of measures, and is peculiarly adapted to grave, solemn, or sublime, subjects. Heroic lines are frequently combined in the quatrain, or stanza of four lines rhyming alternately, as in the specimen from Gray's "Elegy in a Country Church-yard", quoted in § 481. They are also, as we have seen, used in the Spenserian stanza. But they appear most commonly in the form of

---

What other arrangement does he say has precedents in the Italian language, and is not objectionable? Repeat a sonnet constructed according to the best arrangement.

§ 433. What is said of iambic tetrameter? In what long poems has it been employed? Why is it apt to betray a poet into a careless habit of expression?

§ 484. What name is given to iambic pentameter? What is the character of this measure? In what stanza does it frequently appear? What is its commonest form

the couplet, and in poems which have no division into stanzas but are written continuously. They are thus employed by Pope in his "Essay on Criticism", his "Essay on Man", and his translations of the Iliad and the Odyssey.

The pentameter couplet should have complete sense within itself, and is most effective when enlivened with an epigrammatic turn. "It is formed", says Webb, in his "Beauties of Poetry", "to run into points: but above all it delights in the antithesis; and the art of the versifier is complete when the discordance in the ideas is proportioned to the accordance in the sounds. To jar and jingle in the same breath is a master-piece of Gothic refinement." The epigrammatic tendency alluded to is illustrated in the opening lines of the "Essay on Criticism", which constitute a fair specimen of Pope's delicate skill in the management of this his favorite metre:—

> "'Tis hard to say if greater want of skill
> Appear in writing, or in judging, ill;
> But, of the two, less dangerous is the offence
> To tire our patience, than mislead our sense.
> Some few in that, but numbers err in this;
> Ten censure wrong for one who writes amiss:
> A fool might once himself alone expose;
> Now one in verse makes many more in prose."

§ 485. The line of six iambi is called the Alexandrine, from a poem on Alexander the Great, in which it is said to have been first employed. It is a majestic line occasionally used as the third of a triplet, and at the close of Spenserian and other stanzas, for the purpose of imparting additional weight or solemnity. Thus, from Dryden's Æneid:—

> "Their fury falls; he skims the liquid plains,
> High on his chariot, and, with loosened reins,
> Majestic moves along, and awful peace maintains."

The Alexandrine is peculiarly effective when the poet desires to express by the sound of his verse a slow or difficult motion. When the line is so constructed as to admit of a pause in the middle, or at the

---

Who has thus employed it? What is said of the sense of the couplet? To be most effective, with what should it be enlivened? What does Webb say respecting it? Quote a passage from Pope illustrating this epigrammatic turn.

§ 485. Of what is the Alexandrine composed? Whence is its name derived? Where is it used and for what purpose? Scan the lines quoted from Dryden in illustration. In what case is the Alexandrine peculiarly effective? Where should it admit of a pause? How should it be used?

close of the first hemistich, it is by no means inharmonious, yet it is too cumbrous to be carried through an entire piece. It should be used sparingly; and that only in a livelier metre, for the sake of an occasional contrast.

§ 486. Heroic lines,—that is, iambic pentameters,—when constructed without rhyme, constitute what is called Blank Verse. This is the most elevated of all measures, and is the only form in which epic poetry should appear. At the same time, to succeed in it is more difficult than in any other kind of verse. The reason is evident; the effect, having no assistance, as in most cases, from rhyme, is produced entirely by a musical disposition of the feet, frequent inversions, and the constant introduction of those other peculiarities which have been already enumerated as constituting the distinction between the outward form of prose and that of poetry. A correct ear, a delicate taste, and true poetical genius, are essential to success in blank verse.

Milton has made a more effective use of blank verse than any other poet in our literature. It has been employed to a considerable extent in tragedy, to which, as Addison says, "it seems wonderfully adapted"; but even Shakspeare himself has not attained the harmony and effect which characterize the author of "Paradise Lost". Notwithstanding Milton's success, the older critics seem, in general, to have looked on blank verse with disfavor. Dr. Johnson, in his life of the poet just mentioned, pronounces against it in the following terms:—"Poetry may subsist without rhyme; but English poetry will not often please, nor can rhyme ever be safely spared, but where the subject is able to support itself. Of the Italian writers without rhyme whom Milton alleges as precedents, not one is popular · what reason could urge in its defence has been confuted by the ear. * * Like other heroes, Milton is to be admired rather than imitated. He that thinks himself capable of astonishing, may write blank verse; but those that hope only to please, must condescend to rhyme."

Yet, in spite of this verdict from a master-critic, it is evident that blank verse has many advantages. It certainly allows the poet a far

---

§ 486. What is meant by blank verse? What is its character? What renders it difficult to succeed in blank verse? What are essential to success in this measure? In whose hands has the most effective use been made of it? To what department of literature does Addison declare blank verse adapted? Notwithstanding this, how does Shakspeare himself compare with Milton? How did the older critics regard

freer scope: both from the fact that the sense is not, as in rhymed pentameters, confined to the couplet, and also because it does away with the necessity which rhyme too often imposes on the versifier, of putting in superfluous matter simply for the purpose of filling out the sound. "What rhyme adds to sweetness", says Dryden, "it takes away from sense; and he who loses least by it may be called a gainer."

For a choice specimen of blank verse, the pupil is referred to p. 224.

§ 487. Whatever may be the effect of dispensing with rhyme in the case of iambic pentameters, there can be no question as to its inexpediency in other measures. It has occasionally been attempted; but never, perhaps, with success, except in the case of Southey's "Thalaba", for which, despite this drawback, its author's genius has procured an honorable place in our literature.

LESSON CVII.

RHYMES.—PAUSES.

§ 488. RHYME has been already defined. As we have seen, it enters largely into English verse. The following principles are to be observed respecting it:—

I. The more numerous the letters that make the rhyme, the better it is. The French designate as *rich rhymes* those into which a number of consonants enter. Thus the rhyme of the first couplet given below is fuller, and therefore better, than that of the second:—

    1. "True wit is nature to advantage *dressed;*
       What oft was thought, but ne'er so well ex*pressed.*"

    2. "Whoever thinks a faultless piece to *see,*
       Thinks what ne'er was, nor is, nor e'er shall *be.*"

II. No Syllable must rhyme with itself. Hence there is a fault in the following couplet:—

---

blank verse? What does Johnson say about it? With what advantages is blank verse attended? What does Dryden say respecting rhyme?

§ 487. What is the effect of dispensing with rhyme in measures other than iambic pentameter?

§ 488. What rhymes are considered the best? What name is applied to such by the French? Illustrate this by means of the two given couplets. What is the second prin

"We go from Ilium's ruined walls *away*,
Wherever favoring fortune points the *way*."

III. Rhyme speaks to the ear, and not to the eye. If, therefore, the concluding sound is the same, no matter what the spelling, the rhyme is perfect. This is the case in the following couplet, though the combinations of letters in the rhyming syllables are quite different:—

"The increasing prospect tires our wandering *eyes*;
Hills peep o'er hills, and Alps on Alps *arise*."

Vice versa, though the concluding letters be the same, if the sound is different the rhyme is imperfect; as in the following:—

"Encouraged thus, wit's Titans braved the *skies*;
And the press groaned with licensed blasphemies."

IV. In lines terminating with trochees or amphibrachs, the last two syllables must rhyme; in such as close with dactyls, the last three.

"In the dark and green and gloomy *valley*,
Satyrs by the brooklet love to *dally*."

"Take her up *tenderly*,
Fashioned so *slenderly*."

§ 489. Rhymes are divided into two classes; perfect, and admissible. In the former, as we have seen, the closing vowel sounds are the same (without reference to spelling), while the consonant sounds that precede them are different; in the latter, the closing vowel sounds, though not the same, closely resemble each other. In either case, if the closing vowel sounds are followed by consonant sounds, the latter must correspond, or the rhyme is inadmissible. Examples follow:—

1. Perfect.—"Be thou the first true merit to be*friend*;
His praise is lost who stays till all com*mend*."
2. Admissible.—"Good nature and good sense must ever *join*;
To err is human; to forgive, di*vine*."
3. Inadmiss.—"Yet he was kind; or, if severe in *aught*,
The love he bore to learning was in *fault*."

§ 490. With respect to the number of lines that may rhyme together in a stanza, there is no definite rule. Two is

ciple with respect to rhymes? To what does rhyme speak? What is necessary to make a perfect rhyme? What is the character of the rhyme, if the sound is different though the concluding letters be the same? In what lines must the last two syllables rhyme? In what, the last three?

§ 489. Into what two classes are rhymes divided? When is a rhyme said to be perfect? When, admissible? When is a rhyme inadmissible? Give examples.

§ 490. What is said of the number of lines that may rhyme together? What is the

the most common; though we often have three, and even four in the sonnet and the Spenserian stanza. Other things being equal, the difficulty of constructing a stanza is proportioned to the number of lines made to close with the same sound.

Though there is no rule as to the number of lines that may rhyme together, it is a general principle, that, throughout the same poem, those which do rhyme should stand at regular intervals. This the ear expects, and it is disappointed when it finds the regularity disturbed. A capricious disposition of rhymes may surprise the reader, but it rarely pleases him.

§ 491. Ease of utterance requires that every line of ten or more syllables should be so constructed, with regard to its sense, as to admit of at least one cessation of voice, which is known as the Primary Pause. Some lines admit of several; in which case, the inferior or shorter ones are denominated Secondary Pauses. Whether primary or secondary, these pauses must not contravene the sense; and, therefore, it is clear,

I. That they must not divide a word.

II. That they must not separate an adjective and its noun, or an adverb and its verb, when, in either case, the latter immediately follows the former.

§ 492. Heroic lines, or iambic pentameters, are most melodious when the primary pause comes after the fourth or the fifth syllable. Pope, whose accurate ear rarely allowed him to err in matters of euphony, generally brings the pause in question in one of these positions; as in the following lines :—

---

commonest number? How many do we sometimes have? To what is the difficulty of constructing a stanza proportioned? What principle prevails with respect to the regular occurrence of rhymes?

§ 491. What does ease of utterance require? What is a primary pause? What is a secondary pause? With what must these pauses be consistent? What two principles, therefore, are established respecting them?

§ 492. Where does the primary pause occur in the most harmonious heroic lines. What poet generally brings his pauses in one of these positions? Show how they fall in the passage quoted.

"Thee, bold Longinus! || all the Nine inspire,
And bless their critic || with a poet's fire:
An ardent judge, || who, zealous to his trust,
With warmth gives sentence, || yet is always just
Whose own example || strengthens all his laws,
And is himself || that great sublime he draws."

§ 493. The alexandrine, or iambic hexameter, requires its primary pause, after the third foot.

"The cruel, ravenous, hounds || and bloody hunters near,
This noblest beast of chase, || that vainly doth but fear,
Some bank or quick-set finds; || to which his haunch opposed,
He turns upon his foes, || that soon have him enclosed."

§ 494. Secondary pauses may occur in any part of a line, but contribute most to its melody when they stand at a short distance from the primary. Observe how they fall in the following passages: the secondary pause is denoted by a single vertical line; the primary, by parallels.

"Two principles || in human nature | reign;
Self-love | to urge, || and reason | to restrain:
Nor this | a good, || nor that a bad, | we call,
Each works its end, || to move | or govern | all;
And | to their proper operation || still
Ascribe all good, || to their improper, | ill."

"The dew was falling fast, || the stars | began to blink;
I heard a voice; | it said, || 'Drink, | pretty creature, | drink!'
And, | looking o'er the hedge, || before me I espied
A snow-white mountain lamb, || with a maiden at its side."

EXERCISE.

I. Each of the following lines contains its own words; but they are misplaced, so that there is neither rhyme nor rhythm. Restore the order, so as to make the verses *anapestic tetrameter acatalectic,* rhyming consecutively.

THE ALBATROSS.

Where, in magnificence, the fathomless waves toss,
The wild albatross soars, high and homeless;
Unshrinking, alone, undaunted, unwearied,
The tempest his throne, his empire the ocean.

§ 493. Where does the Alexandrine require its primary pause?
§ 494. Where may secondary pauses occur? In what position do they contribute most to the melody of a line?

When, o'er the surge, the wild terrible whirl-wind raves,
And the hurricane hurls the mariner's dirge out,
The dark-heaving sea thou in thy glory spurnest,
Proud, free, and homeless, bird of the ocean-world.
When the winds are at rest and in his glow the sun,
And below the glittering tide in beauty sleeps,
Above, triumphant, in the pride of thy power,
Thou, with thy mate, thy revels of love art holding
Unconfined, unfettered, untired, unwatched,
In the world of the mind, like thee be my spirit;
No leaning for earth, its flight e'er to weary,
And in regions of light fresh as thy pinions.

II. Restore the words in the following lines to their order so that they may rhyme as required in the best form of the *Sonnet* :—

THE AUTUMN OF LIFE.

Flown are the songs of buoyant youth's swift hours;
   And through his heart whose locks are white and thin
   With rime of age, the Spirit of Delight
With a melancholy moan goes wailing.
For all the joys, that, with winning tone, Hope
   Proclaimed should linger, dear, bright, and deathless,
   Around the day which to night now waneth,
Alone, the spirit fruitless search maketh.
Yet to the soul, aspiring and trustful,
   Are given visions exalting of its home:
And its lofty goal grander glory clothes,
   Than, in cloudless autumn's even, stars assume.
In dole and in darkness Earth slowly sinks,
   While the auroral, pure, light of Heaven breaks.

III. Restore the words in the following lines to their order, so that they may rhyme, and form alternately *trochaic tetrameter acatalectic*, and *trochaic tetrameter catalectic* :—

IRON.

While stronger grows our faith in good,
   Means of greater good increase;
No longer slave of war, iron
   The march of peace onward leads.
Still finding new modes of service,
   It moves air, earth, and ocean;
And, binding the distant nations,
   It proves like the kindred tie;
Sharing, with its Atlas-shoulder,
   Loads of toil and human care;
Bearing, on its wing of lightning,
   Through the air swift thought's mission.

IV. Restore the words in the following lines to their order, so that they may form *dactylic tetrameters acatalectic,* and rhyme consecutively:—

> For human fraternity one more new claimant,
>   Swelling the flood that on to eternity sweeps.
> I, who have filled the cup, to think of it tremble,
>   For I must drink of it yet, be it what it may.
> Into the ranks of humanity, room for him!
>   In your kingdom of vanity, give him a place!
> With kindly affection welcome the stranger,
>   Not with dejection, hopefully, trustfully.

LESSON CVIII.

VARIETIES OF POETRY.

§ 495. The principal varieties of poetry are Epic, Dramatic, Lyric, Elegiac, Pastoral, Didactic, and Satirical. Each of these classes has its distinctive features; yet the characteristics of several varieties may enter into the same poem, and sometimes do so to such an extent that it is difficult to decide to which it belongs.

§ 496. Epic Poetry is that which treats of the exploits of heroes. It generally embraces a variety of characters and incidents; but must be so constructed that *unity of design* may be preserved,—that is, one leading and complete action should be carried through the work, with the distinctness and prominence of which the less important stories, or episodes, as they are called, should not be allowed to interfere. Epic is universally admitted to be the most elevated and majestic department of poetry. It is, at the same time, the most dif-

---

§ 495. Enumerate the principal varieties of poetry.

§ 496. What is epic poetry? How does it compare with the other varieties? What must be preserved throughout? What is meant by unity of design? What is said of the difficulty of writing epics? What are the great master-pieces of ant'quity in this department of poetry? Of modern literatures, which has produced the greatest

ficult, and that in which mediocrity is least endurable ; hence few have attempted it, and a still smaller number have attained success. There are few literatures that can boast of more than one great epic. Homer's *Iliad* and Virgil's *Æneid* are the master-pieces of antiquity in this department of poetry. In modern times, English literature has produced, in Milton's *Paradise Lost*, incomparably the greatest epic; in Italian, Tasso's *Jerusalem Delivered*,—in Spanish, the *Romance of the Cid*,—in German, the *Niebelungen-Lied*,—and, in French, the *Henriade*, —are generally ranked by critics in this class of poems.

An epic is also technically termed an Epopea or Epopœia.

The word *epic* is derived from the Greek ἔπος, *a heroic poem;* and the species of poetry so called claims a very ancient origin. History has generally furnished its themes: but a strict regard for historical truth in the development of the story is by no means requisite. Fiction, invention, imagination, may be indulged in to an almost unlimited extent, provided the unity be preserved. According to Aristotle, the plot of an epic must be important in itself and instructive in the reflections it suggests; must be filled with suitable incidents, as well as enlivened with a variety of characters and descriptions; and must maintain throughout propriety of character and elevation of style. Besides these essentials, there are generally episodes, formal addresses, sustained pomp, and machinery. This last term, as used by critics, signifies the introduction of supernatural beings; without which the French maintain that no poem can be admitted as an epic.

§ 497. Dramatic Poetry is closely allied to epic. Like the latter, it generally relates to some important event, and for the most part appears in the form of blank, or heroic, verse. The term *drama* [derived from the Greek verb δράω, *I do* or *act*] is applied to compositions, whether prose or

---

*epic? Enumerate the epics of different literatures. What other name is sometimes given to an epic poem? From what is the word *epic* derived? What is said of the origin of epic poetry? Whence are its themes, for the most part, taken? In carrying out an historical event, what may be indulged in? According to Aristotle, what are the essentials of an epic? Besides these essentials, what are generally found in a poem of this class?

§ 497. To what is dramatic poetry closely allied? To what does it generally relate? In what form does it, for the most part, appear? From what is the word *drama* de-

poetry, in which the events that form their subjects are not related by the author, but are represented as actually taking place by means of dialogue between the various characters, who speak the poet's language as if it were their own. The principles here laid down respecting poetical dramas are equally applicable to compositions of the same class in prose.

In dramatic, as in epic, poetry, strict regard must be had to *unity.* The Dramatic unities are three:—1. *Unity of action;* which requires that but one leading train of events be kept in view, and forbids the introduction of all underplots except such as are closely connected with the principal action and are calculated to develop it. 2. *Unity of time,* which limits the action to a short period, generally a single day. 3. *Unity of place,* which confines the action to narrow geographical bounds. In addition to this, regard should be had to what is termed *poetical justice;* that is, the plot should be so constructed that the different characters, whether good or bad, may, at the termination of the piece, obtain their respective deserts.

The great dramatists of antiquity are Æschylus, Sophocles, and Euripides,—all ornaments of Grecian literature. Of these, Æschylus is the most sublime: Sophocles, the most beautiful; Euripides, the most pathetic. The first displays the lofty intellect; the second exercises the cultivated taste; the third indulges the feeling heart. Among moderns, the first place belongs to Shakspeare. In French literature, Racine, Molière, and Corneille, are the leading dramatists; in German, Schiller and Kotzebue; in Spanish, Lope de Vega and Calderon.

The leading divisions of dramatic poetry are two; Tragedy and Comedy. The former embraces those compositions which represent some great or sublime action, attended with a fatal catastrophe and calculated to awaken in the reader or spectator strong emotions of pity or horror. Its diction is elevated; and it is generally written in blank, or heroic, verse. Comedy, on the other hand, is that species of drama in which the incidents and language resemble those of ordinary life and the plot has a happy termination.

---

rived? To what compositions is the term applied? What must be strictly regarded in dramatic poetry? How many dramatic unities are there? Define them. Who are the great dramatists of antiquity? Mention the characteristics of each. Among moderns, to whom does the first place belong? Who are the leading dramatists of French literature? of German? of Spanish? What are the leading divisions of dramatic poetry? What compositions are embraced under the head of tragedy? What s said of the diction of tragedy? In what is it generally written? Define comedy

The great divisions of dramas are called Acts, and these are sub divided into Scenes. Regular tragedies and comedies are limited to five acts. The division must in a great measure be arbitrary, though rules have been laid down by various writers to define the portion of the plot which should be contained in each. According to Vossius, the first act must present the intrigue; the second must develop it; the third should be filled with incidents forming its complication; and the fourth should prepare the means of unravelling it, which is finally accomplished in the fifth.

A Farce is a short piece of low comic character. Its object being simply to excite mirth, there is nothing too unnatural or improbable for it to contain. The farce is restricted to three acts as its greatest limit, but is often confined to two, and sometimes even to one. In England, it seems to have risen to the dignity of a regular theatrical entertainment, about the beginning of the last century; since which time, it has maintained a high degree of popularity, being usually performed, by way of contrast, after a tragedy.

A Burlesque is a dramatic composition, the humor of which consists in mixing things high and low,—clothing elevated thoughts in low expressions, or investing ordinary topics with the artificial dignity of poetic diction. A Parody, or Travestie, is a species of Burlesque in which the form and expressions of serious dramas are closely imitated in language of a ridiculous character.

A Melodrama is a short dramatic composition into which music is introduced. Its plot is generally of an insignificant character, the display of gorgeous scenery being its chief object.

A Burletta is a short comic musical drama.

A Prologue is a short composition in verse, used to introduce a drama and intended to be recited before its representation.

An Epilogue is a closing address to the audience at the conclusion of a drama. It sometimes recapitulates the chief incidents of the piece and draws a moral from them.

§ 498. Lyric Poetry is that variety which is adapted to singing and an accompaniment of the lyre or other musical instrument.

Of lyric compositions, the Ode is the most elevated. It

What are *acts* and *scenes*? To how many acts are regular tragedies and comedies confined? What is said of the division into acts? What rule does Vossius lay down? What is a farce? Of how many acts does it consist? At what time, in England, did it rise to the dignity of a regular theatrical entertainment? What is a burlesque? What a parody or travestie? What is a melodrama? What is a burletta? What is a prologue? What is an epilogue?

§ 498. What is meant by lyric poetry? What is the most elevated of lyric compo-

is characterized by length and variety, and is for the most part confined to the expression of sentiment or imaginative thought, admitting of narrative only incidentally. In ancient literature, it was sometimes distinguished by a high degree of sublimity, as in the case of the odes of Pindar. Previously to the discoveries which have been recently made by scholars in the science of Greek metres, the Pindaric ode was supposed to admit of the most capricious irregularity in the length and measure of its lines; and hence our modern compositions which were imitated from those ancient models were constructed on a system of absolute license in this respect. In point of fact, however, a scheme of perfect metrical regularity pervades the Greek ode of both Pindar and the dramatic choruses. In English literature, Collins' "Ode on the Passions", and Dryden's on "St. Cecilia's Day", are among the finest specimens of this variety of composition.

A Song differs from an ode in being shorter, having greater uniformity of metre, and treating rather of tender and melancholy, than of sublime, subjects.

A Ballad is a popular species of lyric poem which records in easy and uniform verse some interesting incident or romantic adventure. Our most approved ballad measure is iambic heptameter, often written, however, in two lines, tetrameter and trimeter alternately.

Odes sung in honor of the gods were anciently called Hymns; and this term has been applied, in modern times, to the spiritual songs used in church-worship. The term Psalm, originally applied to the lyric compositions of King David and others of the Hebrew poets, is now used as synonymous with hymn.

The Madrigal generally consists of less than twelve lines, and is often constructed without strict reference to rule, according to the fancy of the poet, rhymes and verses of different species being frequently intermingled. The subjects are generally of a tender or amorous character; and the expressions used in it are simple and often quaint.

---

sitions? Describe the ode. By what, in ancient literature, was it characterized? How is the irregularity of metre in our modern odes accounted for? What odes are mentioned as among the finest specimens in our language? In what respects does a song differ from an ode? What is a ballad? What is our most approved ballad measure? What was formerly meant by the term *hymn*? To what is this term now applied? What was the original meaning of the term *psalm*? With what is it now synonymous? What is a madrigal? What is said of the subjects of madrigals?

The Epigram closely resembles the madrigal in form, though it is written without reference to musical adaptation. It consists of a few lines embodying a lively or ingenious thought concisely expressed. Its point often consists in a verbal pun; but the higher species of epigram is rather characterized by fineness and delicacy.

§ 499. Elegiac Poetry is that variety which treats of mournful subjects. Gray's "Elegy in a Country Church-Yard" is the most noted poem of this description in the whole range of our literature. A short elegy, commemorative of the dead and expressive of the sorrow of surviving friends, is called an Epitaph.

§ 500. Pastoral Poetry depicts shepherd-life by means of narratives, songs, and dialogues. An Idyl is a short descriptive pastoral poem. An Eclogue is a pastoral in which shepherds are represented as conversing. The art of the pastoral poet lies in selecting for his descriptions the beauties of rural life, and carefully avoiding all its repulsive features.

§ 501. Didactic Poetry aims to instruct rather than to please. Generally devoted to the exposition of some dry abstract subject, it fails to interest the reader unless replete with ornament. Of this species of poetry, Pollok's "Course of Time", Young's "Night Thoughts", and Pope's "Essay on Man", will serve as specimens.

§ 502. Satirical Poetry is that in which the weaknesses, follies, or wickedness, of men, are held up to ridicule, or rebuked with serious severity.

A Satire is general in its character, and is aimed at the weakness, folly, or wickedness, rather than the individual. Its object is the reformation of the abuses it attacks. A Lampoon, or Pasquinade, on the other hand, is personally offensive, assailing the individual rather than his fault. It employs abuse in preference to argument, and aims rather to annoy or injure than to reform.

---

§ 499. What is elegiac poetry? What is the most noted poem of this description in our literature? What is an epitaph?

§ 500. What does pastoral poetry depict? What is an idyl? What is an eclogue In what does the art of the pastoral poet consist?

§ 501. What is the aim of didactic poetry? Why should it be replete with ornament? What works are mentioned as specimens of didactic poems?

§ 502. What is satirical poetry? What is a satire? What is a lampoon?

SPECIMEN PROOF-SHEET,

EXHIBITING THE MARKS USED IN THE CORRECTION OF ERRORS.

WILLIAM FALCONER.

William Falconer was the son of a barber in Edinburgh, and was born in 1730. He had very few avantages of education, and went to sea in early life in the merchant service. He afterwards became mate of a vessel that wrecked in the Levant and was saved with only two of his crew: this catastrophe formed the subject of his poem entitled "The Shipwreck, on which his reputation as a writer chiefly rests. Early in 1769, his "*Marine Dictionary*" appeared, which hasbeen highly spoken of by those capable of estimating its merits.

In this seam year, he embarked on the AURORA but the vessel was never heard of after she passed the Cape; the poet of the Shipwreck is therefore supposed to have perish'd by the same disaster he had himself so graphically described. ¶ The subject of the "Shipwreck" and its authors fate demand our interest and sympathy. If we pay respect to the ingenyous scholar who can produce agreeable verses in leisure and retirement, how much more interest must we take in the "shipboy on the high and giddy mast' cherishing the hour which he may casually snatch from danger and fatigue.

refined visions of fancy at/

SPECIMEN PROOF-SHEET,

AS CORRECTED.

WILLIAM FALCONER.

WILLIAM FALCONER was the son of a barber in Edinburgh, and was born in 1730. He had very few advantages of education, and in early life went to sea in the merchant service. He afterwards became mate of a vessel that was wrecked in the *Levant*, and was saved with only two of his crew. This catastrophe formed the subject of his poem entitled "The Shipwreck", on which his reputation as a writer chiefly rests. Early in 1769, his "Marine Dictionary" appeared, which has been highly spoken of by those capable of estimating its merits. In this same year, he embarked on the Aurora; but the vessel was never heard of after she passed the Cape: the poet of the Shipwreck is therefore supposed to have perished by the same disaster he had himself so graphically described.

The subject of the "Shipwreck" and its author's fate demand our interest and sympathy.—If we pay respect to the ingenious scholar who can produce agreeable verses in leisure and retirement, how much more interest must we take in the "ship-boy on the high and giddy mast", cherishing refined visions of fancy at the hour which he may casually snatch from danger and fatigue!

EXPLANATION OF MARKS USED ON THE SPECIMEN PROOF-SHEET.

If it is desired to change any word to capitals, small capitals, Roman text (the ordinary letter), or italics, draw a line beneath it, and write in the margin, *Caps., S. caps., Rom.*, or *Ital.*, as the case may be. See corrections 1, 2, 14, and 8, on the specimen sheet.

When it is necessary to expunge a letter or word, draw a line through it, and place in the margin a character resembling a *d* of current hand, which stands for the Latin word *dele (erase)*; as in No. 3.

When a wrong letter or word occurs in the proof-sheet, draw a line through it, and place what must be substituted for it in the margin, with a vertical line at the right; as in the corrections marked 4.

Attention is drawn to an inverted letter by underscoring it, and writing opposite the character used in No. 5.

An omitted word, letter, comma, semicolon, colon, exclamation-point, or interrogation-point, as well as brackets and parentheses, are written in the margin, with a vertical line at the right; as in the various corrections marked 6: a caret shows where to introduce what is thus marked in. When there is so much omitted that there is not room for it in the margin, it is written at the top or bottom of the page, and a line is used to show where it is to be introduced; as at the bottom of the specimen sheet.

A period is marked in by placing it in the margin inside of a circle, as in No. 9.

Apostrophes and quotation-points are introduced in a character resembling a V, and a caret is placed in the text to show where they are to be inserted. This is illustrated in No. 11.

No. 22 shows how the dash and hyphen are introduced.

When a letter or word should be transposed, a line is drawn around it and carried to the place where it should stand, and the letters *tr.* are placed opposite, as in No. 7.

No. 10 shows how to mark out a quadrat or space which improperly appears.

If a broken or imperfect letter is used, draw a line through or beneath it, and make an inclined cross in the margin, as in No. 12.

Sometimes a letter of the wrong size will be used by mistake; in such a case, underline it and place the letters *w. f. (wrong font)* in the margin, as in No. 13.

If the letters of a word stand apart from each other, draw a curved line beneath the space which separates them, and two curves in the margin, as in 15. If the proper space is wanting between two contiguous words, place a caret where the space should be, and opposite to them make a character like a music sharp, as shown in No. 16.

Two parallel horizontal lines, as in No. 17, are used when the letters of a word are not all in the same level, and a horizontal line is also drawn under such as are out of place.

When a new paragraph has been improperly begun, a line is drawn from its commencement to the end of the previous paragraph, and the words *no break* are written in the margin; see No. 18. When it is desired to commence a new paragraph the paragraph mark (¶) is introduced at the place, and also in the margin.

When letters at the commencement of a line are out of the proper level, a horizontal line should be drawn beneath them, and a similar one placed in the margin; as in No. 21. When any portion of a paragraph projects laterally beyond the rest, a vertical line should be drawn beside it, and a similar one must stand opposite to it in the margin; see No. 23.

When a lead has been improperly omitted, the word *Lead* is written at the side of the page, and a horizontal line shows where it is to be introduced, as in No. 25. If a lead too many has been introduced, the error is corrected as in No. 24.

When uneven spaces are left between words, a line is drawn beneath, and *space better* is written opposite; see 26.

If it is desired to retain a word which has been marked out, dots are placed beneath it, and the word *stet (let it stand)* is written in the margin; as in 27.

A LIST OF SUBJECTS.

The student will find it to his advantage always to prepare a preliminary analysis. To aid him in this, models in the principal departments of prose composition are first presented.

1. A Parallel.—*The Old and the New Testament.*
I. Their respective writers.
II. The parties to whom they are each addressed.
III. The languages in which they are respectively written.
IV. Comparison of their style.
V. Authenticity of each, by whom acknowledged.
VI. Tone of the teachings of each.

2. A Descriptive Letter.—*Dated Niagara Falls.*
I. Acknowledge receipt of a friend's letter, and offer to give an account of a summer tour which you are supposed to have taken.
II. Preparations for leaving home.
III. Incidents on the way to Niagara.
IV. General remarks on the pleasures, fatigues, and advantages, of travelling.
V. Description of the Falls and the surrounding places.
VI. Comparison with any other scene.
VII. Emotions awakened by sublime scenery.
VIII. General remarks about returning, and the anticipated pleasure of rejoining friends.

3. Historical Narrative.—*The Spanish Armada.*
I. Introductory Remarks on the great expeditions of which history tells us.
II. Causes that led to the outfit of the Armada.
III. General description of the Spanish vessels of that age.
IV. Strength of the Armada.
V. Consternation in Britain, and preparations to meet it.
VI. Fate of the Armada.
VII. Political Consequences.
VIII. General reflections. History shows that divine interference often frustrates the greatest human efforts.

4. Biographical Sketch.—*Julius Cæsar.*
I. State of Rome at the time of Cæsar's birth.
II. Cæsar's birth and parentage.
III. Incidents of his youth. Came near falling a victim to Sylla's cruelty.
IV. His first military exploits.
V. Means which he took to attain popularity.
VI. Rapid political advancement. Mighty conquests.
VII. His fate; the causes that led to it, and its consequences.
VIII. Cæsar's character, as a general; as an author; as a man.

5. ESSAY.—*Ships.*

I. Origin. When and by whom first made?
II. Appearance. Original form and subsequent improvements.
III. Inventions. Mariners' compass; application of steam.
IV. Objects for which they are used.
V. Usefulness, as compared with other means of transportation.
VI. Effects that ships have produced on mankind.
VII. Feelings excited by seeing a ship under full sail.

PARALLELS.

6. Character of Columbus and that of Sir Isaac Newton.
7. The character of St. John and that of St. Paul.
8. Luther and Calvin.
9. Cæsar and Alexander.
10. Firmness and Obstinacy.
11. Physical and Moral Courage.
12. Ancient and Modern Literature.
13. Invention of the Mariner's Compass and Application of Steam to Navigation.
14. Ancient and Modern Greece.
15. Ancient and Modern Rome.
16. A Concise and a Diffuse Style.
17. Prose and Poetry.
18. Beauty and Sublimity.
19. The Man of Talent and the Man of Genius.
20. Wit and Humor.
21. French and English Character.
22. Courage and Rashness.
23. Theory and Practice.
24. The Ideal and the Real.
25. Ancient and Modern Patriotism.
26. The Sacred and the Profane Poets.

HISTORICAL NARRATIVES.

27. The Deluge.
28. The Crossing of the Red Sea. (Exodus, chap. XIV.)
29. Naaman, the Leper. (II. Kings, chap. v.)
30. The History of Jonah.
31. Jephthah's Daughter. (Judges, chap. XI, v. 29.)
32. David and Goliath. (I. Samuel, chap. XVII.)
33. The Reign of the Emperor Nero.
34. The Era of Haroun Al Raschid.
35. The Norman Conquest.
36. The Crusades.
37. Granting of the Magna Charta.
38. The Discovery of America.
39. The Settling of America.
40. The Reformation.
41. Luther at the Diet of Worms.
42. The Thirty Years' War.
43. The Reign of Queen Anne.
44. The Era of Louis XIV.
45. The American Revolution.
46. The Battle of Bunker Hill.
47. The Reign of Terror.
48. The Invasion of Russia by Napoleon.
49. The Hungarian Revolution.
50. The Russo-Turkish War.

BIOGRAPHICAL SKETCHES.

51. Moses.
52. Ruth.
53. Solomon.
54. Homer.
55. Daniel.
56. Alexander the Great.
57. Cicero.
58. Mark Antony.
59. Mohammed.
60. Charlemagne.
61. Richard Cœur de Lion.
62. Petrarch.
63. Tasso.
64. Columbus.
65. Henry VIII.
66. Erasmus.
67. Bloody Mary.
68. Sir Isaac Newton.
69. Queen Elizabeth.
70. Shakspeare.
71. Maria Theresa.
72. Peter the Great.
73. Voltaire.
74. Patrick Henry.
75. Washington.
76. Franklin.
77. Robespierre.
78. Aaron Burr.
79. Howard, the philanthropist.
80. Mungo Park.

FICTION.

81. Adventures in California.
82. An Encounter with Pirates.

LIST OF SUBJECTS.

83. A Lion Hunt in Southern Africa.
84. The Indian's Revenge.
85. The History of a Pin.
86. The History of a Bible.
87. The History of a Cent.
88. The History of a Shoe.
89. The History of a Looking-Glass.
90. The History of a Belle.
91. The History of a School-room.
92. The Story of an Old Soldier.
93. Robinson Crusoe.
94. A Hurricane in the Torrid Zone.
95. Visit to Mount St. Bernard.
96. The victim of Intemperance.
97. Incidents of a Whaling Voyage.
98. Adventures in Australia.
99. The Prisoner of the Bastile.
100. The Smugglers.
101. The Alchemist.
102. The Flower-Girl.
103. A Voyage to the Mediterranean.
104. Visit to an Almshouse.
105. Encounter with Robbers.

ESSAYS.

106. Spring.
107. A Thunder-storm.
108. Flowers.
109. The Beauties of Nature.
110. Snow.
111. Mountains.
112. Forests.
113. A Lake Scene.
114. A Storm at Sea.
115. Our Country.
116. Thanksgiving Day.
117. The Study of History.
118. The Advantages of Education.
119. Peace.
120. War.
121. An Earthquake.
122. Chivalry.
123. Scene in an Auction-Room.
124. The Ruins of Time.
125. The Fickleness of Fortune.
126. Disease.
127. The Cholera.
128. Prayer.
129. Death.
130. Life.
131. Youth.
132. Old Age.
133. Morning.
134. Evening.
135. Day.
136. Night.
137. Summer.
138. Autumn.
139. Winter.
140. The Mission of the Dew-drop
141. Truth.
142. Honesty.
143. Earth's Battle-fields.
144. Gambling.
145. Echo.
146. Anger.
147. Self-government.
148. Ambition.
149. Contentment.
150. The Love of Fame.
151. Palestine and its Associations.
152. City Life.
153. The West Indies.
154. Melancholy.
155. Life in the Country.
156. Purity of Thought.
157. Patience.
158. The Life of the Merchant.
159. The Life of the Sailor.
160. The Life of the Soldier.
161. The Mariners' Compass.
162. The Spirit of Discovery.
163. Pride.
164. The Art of Printing.
165. The Third Commandment.
166. Mirrors.
167. Newspapers.
168. Jerusalem.
169. Novelty.
170. The Bible.
171. The Sun.
172. The Starry Heavens.
173. Astronomy.
174. The Rainbow.
175. The Moon.
176. The Aurora Borealis.
177. The Stars.
178. Comets.
179. The Earth.
180. The Study of Geography.
181. The Province of Rhetoric.
182. The Mystic Seven.
183. The Pleasures of Travelling.
184. The Congress of the United States
185. The Applications of Steam.
186. Public Libraries.
187. Rain.
188. The Fourth Commandment.
189. Rivers.

190. To-morrow.
191. The Russian Empire.
192. The Ocean.
193. True Politeness.
194. Icebergs.
195. The Pearl Fishery.
196. Early Piety.
197. The Arctic Regions.
198. The Wrongs of the Indian.
199. Egyptian Pyramids.
200. Government.
201. Manufactures.
202. Character of the Ancient Romans.
203. The Influence of Woman.
204. The Schoolmaster Abroad.
205. The Pleasures of Memory.
206. Humility.
207. Natural History.
208. Music.
209. The Hypocrite.
210. The Art of Composition.
211. The Invisible World.
212. Poetry.
213. Man's True Greatness.
214. Virtue.
215. Vice.
216. The Sabbath.
217. Jealousy.
218. The Fifth Commandment.
219. A Volcanic Eruption.
220. Oriental Countries.
221. Deserts.
222. Egypt.
223. The Mohammedan Religion.
224. Paganism.
225. Industry.
226. Idleness.
227. Flattery.
228. Intemperance.
229. Excelsior.
230. Courage.
231. Duplicity.
232. Early Impressions.
233. Perseverance.
234. Silent Cities.
235. Riches and Poverty.
236. Eloquence.
237. The Miser.
238. Fireside Angels.
239. Conscience and Law
240. Taste.
241. Tyranny.
242. Smuggling.
243. The Evils of Extravagance.
244. The Inquisition.
245. Revenge.
246. The Attraction of Gravitation.
247. The Tempter and the Tempted.
248. The Art of Writing.
249. Advantages of Studying the Classics.
250. Female Character.
251. Knowledge is Power.
252. The Trials of the Teacher.
253. The March of Intellect.
254. The Revival of Learning.
255. Gratitude.
256. Modesty.
257. Benevolence.
258. Genius.
259. The Power of Conscience
260. The Orator.
261. Aristocracy.
262. Ancient Travellers.
263. Dreams.
264. Magic and Magicians.
265. Twilight.
266. Horace and his Friends.
267. Formality.
268. The Rhine.
269. Legendary Poetry.
270. Clemency.
271. Parental Affection.
272. The Spirit of Song.
273. Hope.
274. Where is thy Home?
275. Love.
276. Forgiveness.
277. Earth's Benefactors.
278. Peasant Life.
279. The Power of Association.
280. Missionary Enterprise.
281. The Lord's Prayer.
282. The Jews.
283. The End not yet.
284. The Feudal System.
285. The Progress of Civilization.
286. The Dark Ages.
287. Monastic Institutions.
288. Generosity.
289. The Hermit.
290. Philanthropy.
291. The Good Part.
292. Patriotism.
293. Freedom.
294. The Fourth of July.
295. Honor.
296. A Republican Government.
297. Old things have passed away.

LIST OF SUBJECTS.

298. Hero-worship.
299. The True Hero.
300. Happiness.
301. Sources of a Nation's Wealth.
302. The English Noble.
303. Commerce.
304. The Art of Painting.
305. "Let there be Light."
306. Early Rising.
307. Candor.
308. Dissipation.
309. The Proselyting Spirit.
310. Envy.
311. The Evils of Anarchy.
312. College Life.
313. Cheerfulness.
314. Fashion.
315. The Uses of Biography.
316. Party-spirit.
317. Atheism.
318. Polytheism.
319. Physical Education.
320. The Opening of Japan.
321. Pastoral Poetry.
322. Election-Day.
323. The Pleasures of the Antiquarian.
324. The Backwoodsman.
325. Punctuality.
326. The Great West.
327. Cruelty to Animals.
328. Curiosity.
329. Foppery.
330. Concentration of Mind.
331. Gardening.
332. Christmas Day.
333. Modern Delusions.
334. Young America.
335. The Multiplication of Books.
336. The Philosopher's Stone.
337. Poetesses of Ancient Greece.
338. The Insolence of Office.
339. Authorship.
340. Affectation.
341. The Standard of Taste.
342. The Mind.
343. The Stoic Philosophy.
344. The Drama.
345. The Bulwarks of Despotic Power.
346. Eden.
347. Nature and Art.
348. The True.
349. The Good.
350. The Ludicrous.
351. Epicurus and his Followers.
352. Reformation.
353. The Freedom of the Press.
354. The Present.
355. The Past.
356. The Future.
357. Rome under Augustus.
358. Criticism.
359. Silent Influence.
360. The Immortality of the Soul.
361. Martyrdom for Truth.
362. The Monuments of Antiquity.
363. The Power of Verse to Perpetuate.
364. Rome was not built in a Day.
365. The First Stroke is Half the Battle.
366. Make Hay while the Sun shines.
367. Order is Needful for Improvement.
368. Resist the Beginnings of Evil.
369. Necessity is the Mother of Invention.
370. A Soft Answer turneth away Wrath.
371. Familiarity begets Contempt.
372. Refinement, a National Benefit.
373. A Rolling Stone gathers no Moss.
374. Only a Fool turns aside to Deceit.
375. Avoid Extremes.
376. Cast not Pearls before Swine.
377. Study to mind your own Business.
378. Hunger is the Best Sauce.
379. Fools make a Mock of Sin.
380. A Fault confessed is half redressed.
381. Necessity has no Law.
382. The Face is an Index of the Mind.
383. Science, the Handmaid of Religion.
384. Fortune favors the Brave.
385. Love thy Neighbor as thyself.
386. Many Men of Many Minds.
387. Opportunity makes the Thief.
388. What can't be cured must be endured.
389. Grasp All, lose All.
390. New Brooms sweep Clean.
391. Where there's a Will there's a Way.
392. The Race is not to the Swift.
393. The Burnt Child dreads the Fire.
394. Good Wine needs no Bush.
395. Time brings All Things to Light.
396. Look before you leap.
397. It never rains but it pours.
398. Out of Debt out of Danger.
399. Whatever is, is right.
400. Political Parties at Athens in the Time of Demosthenes.
401. The Literary Character of Julius Cæsar.
402. Influence of Shakspeare's Plays on Popular Estimation of Historical Characters.

403. The Nobility and Responsibility of the Teacher's Vocation.
404. Independence of Thought in America.
405. Great Men, as Types and as Individuals.
406. The Love of Money, the Root of All Evil.
407. By Others' Faults Wise Men correct their own.
408. The Perfection of Art is to conceal Art.
409. A Bird in the Hand is Worth Two in the Bush.
410. Economy, the Philosopher's Stone.
411. Many a Slip 'twixt the Cup and the Lip.
412. Treason does never prosper.
413. Honesty is the best Policy.
414. Great talkers, little doers.
415. Decision of Character.
416. National Prejudice.
417. Horrors of Civil War.
418. The Passion for Dress.
419. Our Duties as Citizens.
420. Never too old to learn.
421. Contrivance proves Design.
422. The Necessity of Relaxation.
423. Example, Better than Precept.
424. Popular Clamor.
425. The Dress is not the Man.
426. Herculaneum and Pompeii.
427. Contemplation.
428. Nature, the Source of Poetic Inspiration.
429. The Conflict of Duties.
430. Infirmities of Men of Genius.
431. The Antediluvians.
432. The Ingratitude of Republics.
433. Domestic Life of the Ancient Greeks.
434. Sir Walter Raleigh and his Age.
435. Political Economy.
436. The Fate of Reformers.
437. Idolatry.
438. Evidences of Revealed Religion.
439. The Pleasures of Imagination.
440. Comparison of Classical with Modern Literature.
441. The Decline of the Roman Empire.
442. Literary Empiricism.
443. The Examples of Great Men.
444. Bacon and Aristotle.
445. Speculation in Philosophy.
446. Fanaticism.
447. Progress versus Conservatism.
448. Radicalism.
449. Intellectual Excitement.
450. Mesmerism.
451. Psychology.
452. Spiritualism.
453. The Force of Prejudice.
454. The Moral Sublime.
455. The Moral Beautiful.
456. Permanence of Literary Fame.
457. Roman Eloquence.
458. Grecian Mythology.
459. The Scholar's Hope.
460. American Literature.
461. The Tendency of American Institutions.
462. The Revolutionary Spirit.
463. Romance of the American Revolution.
464. Magazine Literature.

465. The Satisfaction resulting from a Conscientious Discharge of Duty.
466. The Necessity for Conventional Laws and Forms in Society.
467. The Fatal Results arising from an Early Neglect of the Mental Powers.
468. The Folly of expecting too much from our Fellow-creatures.
469. The Duty of Patient Resignation to Misfortunes.
470. The Necessity of Examining into our Secret Motives of Action.
471. The Advantages to be derived from an Acquaintance with Modern Languages
472. The Difficulty of Conquering Bad Habits.
473. The Happy Results arising from the Cultivation of Taste.
474. The Soothing Power of Music.
475. The Importance of early cultivating the Affections.
476. The Beneficial Effects of Constant Intercourse with our Fellow-creatures.
477. Charity, an Essential Part of True Religion.
478. Religious Enthusiasm, frequently made a Mask for the Basest Purposes.
479. The Danger of forming Hasty Judgments.
480. The Importance of an Early Observance of Religious Duties.
481. The Folly of devoting too much Time to Accomplishments.

LIST OF SUBJECTS.

482. The Feelings with which we should regard Death.
483. The Danger of indulging in a Habit of Exaggeration.
484. The Possession of a Lively Imagination, a Great Misfortune.
485. The Necessity of repressing Idle Curiosity in Youth.
486. The Wisdom of not giving Free Expression to all our Thoughts.
487. The Folly of blindly following the Judgment and Opinions of Others.
488. The Vanity of Human Grandeur.
489. Religion, as a civilizing Agent.
490. The Danger of becoming too much addicted to the Pleasures of the World.
491. Our Duties to our Inferiors.
492. The Folly of striving to please every one.
493. Innovation, as regarded by the Young and by the Old.
494. The Prospects of a Young Professional Man in the United States.
495. Reading, a Means of Intellectual Improvement.
496. The Use and Abuse of Worldly Advantages.
497. Life is Short and Art is long.
498. No one lives for himself alone.
499. Independence must have Limits.
500. Man and Government, as found in the Savage, the Pastoral, the Agricultural, and the Commercial, State.
501. How far the Right should be controlled by the Expedient.
502. Color, as an Element of Beauty.
503. Poetry, Painting, Architecture, and Sculpture, as Means of Refining Taste.
504. The Good and Bad Effects of Emulation.
505. The Influence of Greek, Latin, French, and English, Literature, on Taste.
506. Ancient and Modern Notions of Liberty.
507. Personal Beauty, Rank, and Wealth, as Passports in Society.
508. The Study of Logic, as a Mental Discipline.
509. The respective Effects of Agriculture and Manufactures on the Morals of the Community.
510. An Old and a New Country, as Fields of Enterprise.
511. Patronage, Emulation, and Personal Necessity, as Promotive of Literary Exertion.
512. The Views taken of a Nation by itself and Others.
513. Ancient and Modern Views of Death.
514. The Comparative Influence of Individuals and Learned Societies in forming the Literary Character of a Nation.
515. Proofs afforded by Astronomy of an intelligent Creator.
516. Beware of desperate steps ; the darkest day,
Live till to-morrow, will have passed away.
517. There's a Divinity that shapes our ends,
Rough hew them how we may.
518. Health is the vital principle of bliss.
519. Heaven from all creatures hides the book of fate.
520. Be it ever so humble, there's no place like home.
521. The bolt that strikes the towering cedar dead,
Oft passes harmless o'er the hazel's head.
522. Who by repentance is not satisfied,
Is nor of Heaven, nor earth.
523. Honor and shame from no condition rise;
Act well your part; there all the honor lies.
524. Good name, in man or woman,
Is the immediate jewel of their souls.

525. Sweet are the uses of adversity.
526. Justice may sleep, but never dies.
527. Man yields to custom as he bows to fate;
In all things ruled—mind, body, and estate.
528.   Experience is the school
Where man learns wisdom.
529. All is not gold that glitters.
530. One to-day is worth two to-morrows.
531. Birds of a feather flock together.
532.   All the world's a stage,
And all the men and women merely players.

ARGUMENTATIVE DISCOURSES.

533. Was Napoleon greater in the field than in the cabinet?
534. Is conscience in all cases a correct moral guide?
535. Do inventions improve the condition of the laboring classes?
536. Is the expectation of reward a greater incentive to exertion than the fear of punishment?
537. Would it be right for Congress to pass an international copy-right law?
538. Is it expedient for Congress to pass an international copy-right law?
539. Is the penal transportation of convicts as effective in preventing crime as solitary confinement?
540. Is the country a better place for a University than a large city?
541. Are increased facilities of intercourse with Europe an advantage to us?
542. Has popular superstition a favorable effect on a nation's literature?
543. Do savage nations possess a right to the soil?
544. Ought capital punishment, as a matter of right, to be abolished?
545. Ought capital punishment, as a matter of expediency, to be abolished?
546. Is the mind of woman inferior to that of man?
547. Is it expedient that a new version of the Bible should be made?
548. Is the pen mightier than the sword?
549. Has increased wealth a favorable effect on the morals of a people?
550. Is a nation's literature affected by its form of government?
551. Ought there to be a property qualification for suffrage?
552. Does the study of the classics afford better discipline to the mind than that of mathematics?
553. Is truth invincible, if left to grapple with falsehood on equal terms?
554. Is a monarchy the strongest and most stable form of government?
555. Is it beneficial to a country to have a union between Church and State?
556. Did the Crusades have a beneficial influence on Europe?
557. Is a man justified in obeying a law of his country which he feels to be morally wrong
558. Is it best for judges to be elected by the people?
559. Do the learned professions offer as promising an opening to a young man as mercantile life?
560. Had the Olympic and other games a favorable effect on the ancient Greeks?
561. Is the existence of political parties beneficial to a state?
562. Do parents exercise a greater influence than teachers in forming the character of the young?
563. Is a general war in Europe favorable to the interests of America?
564. Does climate have any effect on the character of a nation?
565. Is a lawyer justified in defending a bad cause?
566. Does the pulpit afford a better field for eloquence than the bar?

TABLE OF ABBREVIATIONS.

A., acre or acres.
A. A. S., *Academiæ Americanæ Socius*, Fellow of the American Academy.
A. B., *Artium Baccalaureus*, Bachelor of Arts.
A. B. C. F. M., American Board of Commissioners for Foreign Missions.
A. C., *ante Christum*, before Christ.
Acct., account.
A. D., *anno Domini*, in the year of our Lord.
Ad lib., *ad libitum*, at pleasure.
Adj., adjective.
Adjt., Adjutant.
Adjt.-Gen., Adjutant General.
Admr., Administrator.
Admx., Administratrix.
Adv., adverb.
Æt., *ætatis*, of age.
A. & F. B. S., American and Foreign Bible Society.
Agt., agent.
Ala. or Al., Alabama.
Ald., Alderman or Aldermen.
Alex., Alexander.
Alt., altitude.
A. M., *Artium Magister*, Master of Arts.
A. M., *anno mundi*, in the year of the world.
A. M., *ante meridiem*, morning.
Am., American.
Amer., America.
And., Andrew.
Anon., anonymous.
Ans. or A., answer.
Anth., Anthony.
Apoc., Apocalypse.
Apr., April.
Arch., Archibald.
Archb. or Apb., Archbishop.
Ark., Arkansas.

Art., Article.
Assist. Sec., Assistant Secretary.
A. S. S. U., American Sunday School Union.
Atty., Attorney. Attys., Attorneys.
Atty.-Gen., Attorney-General.
A. U. C., *anno urbis conditæ*, in the year after the building of the city.
Aug., August.
Auth. Ver., Authorized Version.
B., Book or Books.
B. A., *Baccalaureus Artium*, Bachelor of Arts.
B. A., British America.
Bar. or bl., barrel.
Bar., Baruch.
Bart., Baronet.
B. C., before Christ.
B. D., *Baccalaureus Divinitatis*, Bachelor of Divinity.
Benj., Benjamin.
B. L., *Baccalaureus Legum*, Bachelor of Laws.
Bls. or bbl., barrels.
B. M., *Baccalaureus Medicinæ*, Bachelor of Medicine.
B. M., British Mail.
B. M. or Brit. Mus., British Museum.
Bp., Bishop.
B. R., *Banco Regis*, King's Bench.
Br., brig.
Brig., Brigade; Brigadier.
Brig.-Gen., Brigadier-General.
Bro., Brother. Bros., Brothers.
Bu., bushel or bushels.
B. V., *Beata Virgo*, Blessed Virgin.
Cæt. par., *cæteris paribus*, other things being equal.
Cal., *Calendæ*, the Calends.
Cal., California.
Can., Canada.
Cap. or c., *caput*, chapter.

ABBREVIATIONS.

Cap., Capital. Caps., Capitals.
Capt., Captain.
Capt.-Gen., Captain-General.
Cash., Cashier.
Cath., Catharine; Catholic.
C. B., Companion of the Bath.
C. C. P., Court of Common Pleas.
C. E., Canada East.
Cf., *confer*, compare.
Ch., chaldron or chaldrons.
Ch., Church. Chs., Churches.
Chanc., Chancellor.
Chap., c., or ch., chapter.
Chas., Charles.
Chron., Chronicles.
Cl. Dom. Com., Clerk of the House of Commons.
Cld., cleared.
Co., County; Company.
Coch., *cochleare*, a spoonful.
Col., *Collega*, Colleague.
Col., Colonel; Colossians.
Cold., colored.
Coll., *Collegium*, College.
Com., Commodore; Committee; Commissioner.
Com. Arr., Committee of Arrangements.
Comdg., Commanding.
Comp., Company (Military).
Comp., compare.
Com. Ver., Common Version.
Conj., conjunction.
Conn. or Ct., Connecticut.
Const., Constable; Constitution.
Contr., contraction.
Cor., Corinthians.
Cor. Sec., Corresponding Secretary.
C. P., Common Pleas.
C. P., Court of Probate.
C. P. S., *Custos Privati Sigilli*, Keeper of the Privy Seal.
C. R., *Custos Rotulorum*, Keeper of the Rolls.
Cr. Creditor.
C. S., Court of Sessions.
C. S., *Custos Sigilli*, Keeper of the Seal.
Ct., Count.
Ct. or c., cent. Cts., cents.
Curt., current (month).
C. W., Canada West.
Cwt., hundred weight.
D., day or days; dime or dimes.
D., *denarius*, a penny; *denarii*, pence.
Dan., Daniel.

D. C., District of Columbia.
D. C. L., Doctor of Civil Law.
D. D., Doctor of Divinity.
Dea., Deacon.
Dec., December.
Deg., degree or degrees.
Del., Delaware.
Del., *delineavit*, drew.
Dem., Democrat.
Dep., Deputy; Department.
Deut., Deuteronomy.
Dft., Defendant.
D. G., *Dei Gratia*, by the grace of God.
Dist. Atty., District Attorney.
Div., Division.
Do. or ditto, the same.
Doll., dollar. Dolls., dollars.
Doz., dozen.
D. P., Doctor of Philosophy.
Dr., dear; drachm or drachma.
Dr., Doctor; Debtor.
D. V., *Deo volente*, God willing.
Dwt., pennyweight.
E., East.
Eben., Ebenezer.
Eccl., Ecclesiastes.
Eccles., Ecclesiasticus.
Ed., Editor; Eds., Editors.
Edin., Edinburgh.
Edit. or Ed., edition.
Edm., Edmund.
Edw., Edward.
E. E., errors excepted.
E. E., ell or ells English.
E. Fl., ell or ells Flemish.
E. Fr., ell or ells French.
E. G. or ex. g., *exempli gratia*, for example.
E. I., East Indies.
Eliz., Elizabeth.
Eng., England.
Engd., engraved.
Ep., Epistle.
Eph., Ephraim; Ephesians.
E. S., ell or ells Scotch.
Esq., Esquire. Esqrs., Esquires.
Esth., Esther.
Et al., *et alibi*, and elsewhere; *et alii*, and others.
Etc., *et cæter-i-æ-a*, and so forth.
Et seq., *et sequentia*, and what follows.
Ex., Example.
Exc., Exception.
Exec. or Exr., Executor.
Exec. Com., Executive Committee.

ABBREVIATIONS.

Execx., Executrix.
Exod., Exodus.
Ezd., Ezdra.
Ezek., Ezekiel.
Fahr., Fahrenheit.
F. A. S., Fellow of the Antiquarian Society.
Fath., fathom or fathoms.
F. D., *Fidei Defensor*, Defender of the Faith.
Feb., February.
F. E. S., Fellow of the Entomological Society.
F. G. S., Fellow of the Geological Society.
F. H. S., Fellow of the Horticultural Society.
Fig., figure or figures.
Fir., firkin or firkins.
Fla., Flor., Florida.
F. L. S., Fellow of the Linnæan Society.
F. M., *fiat mixtura*, let a mixture be made.
Fol., fo., or f., folio or folios.
Fred., Frederick.
F. R. S., Fellow of the Royal Society.
F. S. A., Fellow of the Society of Arts.
Ft. or f., foot or feet.
Fur., furlong or furlongs.
Fut., Future.
Ga., Georgia.
Gal., Galatians.
Gal., gallon. Gals., gallons.
G. B., Great Britain.
G. C. B., Grand Cross of the Bath.
Gen., General; Genesis.
Gent., Gentleman.
Geo., George.
Gov., Governor.
Gov.-Gen., Governor-General.
G. R., *Georgius Rex*, King George.
Gr., grain or grains.
Guin. or G., guinea or guineas.
H. or hr., hour or hours.
Hab., Habakkuk.
Hag., Haggai.
H. B. M., His or Her Britannic Majesty.
Heb., Hebrews.
Hd., hogshead. Hhd., hogsheads.
H. E. I. C., Honorable East India Company.
H. M., His or Her Majesty.
H. M. S., His or Her Majesty's Ship or Service.
Hon., Honorable.
Hon. Gent., Honorable Gentleman.
Hon. Mem., Honorable Member.
Hon. Sec., Honorary Secretary.

Hos., Hosea.
H. P., half-pay.
H. R. H., His Royal Highness.
Hund., hundred or hundreds.
I., island. Is., islands.
Ibid. or Ib., *ibidem*, in the same place.
Id., *idem*, the same.
I. e., *id est*, that is.
I. H. S., *Jesus Hominum Salvator*, Jesus the Saviour of Men.
Ill., Illinois.
Imp., Imperfect.
In., inch or inches.
Incog., *incognito*, unknown.
Ind. or Ia., Indiana.
In lim., *in limine*, at the outset.
In loc., *in loco*, in or at the place.
I. N. R. I., *Jesus Nazarenus Rex Judæorum*, Jesus of Nazareth King of the Jews.
Ins., Inspector.
Ins.-Gen., Inspector General.
Inst., instant, of this month.
Int., interest; interjection.
In trans., *in transitu*, on the passage.
Io., Iowa.
I. O. O. F., Independent Order of Odd Fellows.
Irreg., Irregular.
Isa., Isaiah.
Jan., January.
Jas., James.
J. D., *Jurum Doctor*, Doctor of Laws.
Jer., Jeremiah.
Jno., John.
Jona., Jonathan.
Jos., Joseph.
Josh., Joshua.
J. P., Justice of the Peace.
Jud., Judith.
Judg., Judges.
Judg. Adv., Judge Advocate.
Jun. or Jr., Junior.
Just., Justice.
J. V. D., *Juris utriusque Doctor*, Doctor of each Law (of the Canon and the Civil Law).
Kan., Kansas.
K. B., King's Bench.
K. B., Knight of the Bath.
K. C., King's Counsel.
K. C. B., Knight Commander of the Bath.
Ken. or Ky., Kentucky.
K. G., Knight of the Garter.

ABBREVIATIONS.

Kil., kilderkin or kilderkins.
K. M., Knight of Malta.
K. P., Knight of St. Patrick.
K. T., Knight of the Thistle.
Kt. or Knt., Knight.
L., line.
La., Louisiana.
Lam., Lamentations.
Lat., latitude.
Lb., pound or pounds (weight).
L. C., Lower Canada.
L. D., Lady Day.
Ld., Lord. Ldp., Lordship.
Leag., lea., or L, league or leagues.
L. I., Long Island.
Lib. or L., *liber*, Book.
Lieut., Lieutenant.
Lieut.-Col., Lieutenant-Colonel.
Lieut. Comdg., Lieutenant Commanding.
Lieut.-Gen., Lieutenant-General.
Lieut.-Gov., Lieutenant-Governor.
Liv., Liverpool.
LL. B., *Legum Baccalaureus*, Bachelor of Laws.
LL. D., *Legum Doctor*, Doctor of Laws.
Lon. or Lond., London.
Lon. or long., longitude.
L. S., *Locus Sigilli*, Place of the Seal.
Lt., Light.
Lt. In., Light Infantry.
L X X., Septuagint (Version).
M., *mille*, one thousand.
M., *manipulus*, a handful.
M., *meridie*, meridian, noon.
M., *misce*, mix.
M., mile or miles.
M. or Mons., *Monsieur*, Mr., Sir.
Macc., Maccabees.
Mag., Magazine.
Maj., Major.
Maj.-Gen., Major-General.
Mal., Malachi.
Man., Manasses.
Mar., March.
Mass. or Ms., Massachusetts.
Math., Mathematics.
Matt., Matthew.
M. B., *Medicinæ Baccalaureus*, Bachelor of Medicine.
M. B., *Musicæ Baccalaureus*, Bachelor of Music.
M. C., Member of Congress.
M. D., *Medicinæ Doctor*, Doctor of Medicine.

Md., Maryland.
Me., Maine.
Mem., *memento*, remember; memorandum.
Messrs., *Messieurs*, gentlemen.
Mic., Micah.
Mich., Michigan; Michael.
Mid., Midshipman.
Miss., Mississippi.
Mo., Missouri.
Mo., month. Mos., months.
M. P., Member of Parliament.
M. P., Member of Police.
Mr., Mister.
M. R. A. S., Member of the Royal Asiatic Society.
M. R. C. S., Member of the Royal College of Surgeons.
M. R. I. A., Member of the Royal Irish Academy.
Mrs., Mistress.
MS., *manuscriptum*, manuscript.
MSS., manuscripts.
Mus. D., Doctor of Music.
M. W., Most Worthy.
N., North.
N., note or notes.
N. A., North America.
Nah., Nahum.
Nath., Nathaniel.
N. B., *nota bene*, mark well.
N. B., New Brunswick.
N. C., North Carolina.
N. E., New England.
Neb., Nebraska.
Neh., Nehemiah.
Nem. con., *nemine contradicente*; Nem. diss., *nemine dissentiente*, unanimously.
N. F., Newfoundland.
N. H., New Hampshire.
N. J., New Jersey.
Nl., nail. Nls., nails.
N. M., New Mexico.
N. O., New Orleans.
No., *numero*, in number; number.
Nos., numbers.
Nov., November.
N. S., Nova Scotia; New Style.
N. T. or New Test., New Testament.
Num., Numbers.
N. Y., New York.
O., Ohio.
Ob., objection.
Obad., Obadiah.

ABBREVIATIONS. 439

Obt., obedient.
Oct., October.
Olym., Olympiad.
Or., Oregon.
O. S., Old Style.
O. T. or Old Test., Old Testament.
O. T., Oregon Territory.
O. U. A., Order of United Americans.
Oxon., Oxford.
Oz., ounce or ounces.
P., page. Pp., pages.
P., pole or poles.
P. æq., *partes æquales*, equa. parts.
Par., paragraph.
Part., participle
Payt., payment.
Pd., paid.
Penn. or Pa., Pennsylvania.
Per an., *per annum*, by the year.
Perf., Perfect.
Pet., Peter.
Ph. D., *Philosophiæ Doctor*, Doctor of Philosophy.
Phil., Philippians.
Phila. or Phil., Philadelphia.
Philem., Philemon.
Pinx. or pxt., *pinxit*, painted.
Plff., Plaintiff.
P. M., Post Master.
P. M., *post meridiem*, evening.
P. M. G., Post Master General.
P. O., Post Office.
Pop., population.
Prep., preposition.
Pres., President; present.
Prob., Problem.
Prof., Professor.
Prop., Proposition.
Prot., Protestant.
Pro tem., *pro tempore*, for the time being.
Prov., Proverbs.
Prox., *proximo*, of next month.
P. R. S., President of the Royal Society
P. S., *Post scriptum*, Postscript.
P. S., Privy Seal.
Ps., Psalm or Psalms.
Pt., pint. Pts., pints.
Pub. Doc., Public Documents.
Pun., puncheon or puncheons.
Q., Queen.
Q. or Ques., Question.
Q., *quadrans*, farthing; *quadrantes*, farthings.
Q. B., Queen's Bench.

Q. C., Queen's Counsel.
Q.E.D., *quod erat demonstrandum*, which was to be proved.
Q. E. F., *quod erat faciendum*, which was to be done.
Q. l. or q. p., *quantum libet* or *placet*, as much as you please.
Qr., quarter.
Q. S., *quantum sufficit*, a sufficient quantity.
Qt., quart. Qts., quarts.
Qy., Query.
R., *Rex*, King; *Regina*, Queen.
R., rood or roods; rod or rods.
R. A., Royal Academician.
R. A., Royal Artillery.
R. A., Russian America.
R. E., Royal Engineers.
Recd., Received.
Rec. Sec., Recording Secretary.
Rect., Rector.
Ref., Reformed; Reformation.
Reg., Register.
Regt., Regiment.
Rep., Representative.
Rev., Reverend; Revelations.
R. I., Rhode Island.
Richd., Richard.
R. M., Royal Marines.
R. N., Royal Navy.
Robt., Robert.
Rom., Roman; Epistle to the Romans.
R. R., Railroad.
R. S. S., *Regiæ Societatis Socius*, Fellow of the Royal Society.
Rt. Hon., Right Honorable.
Rt. Rev., Right Reverend.
Rt. Wpful., Right Worshipful.
R. W., Right Worthy.
S., South.
S., shilling or shillings.
S. or sec., second or seconds.
S. A., South America.
Sam., Samuel (Book of).
Saml., Samuel.
S. A. S., *Societatis Antiquariorum Socius*, Fellow of the Society of Antiquarians.
S. C., South Carolina.
Sc., *sculpsit*, engraved.
Sc., scruple or scruples.
S. caps., small capitals.
Schr., Schooner.
Scil., sc., or s., *scilicet*, namely.

Sec., Secretary.
Sect., sec., or s., section or sections.
Sen., Senior; Senate; Senator.
Sept., September.
Serg., Sergeant.
Serg.-Maj., Sergeant-Major.
Servt., servant.
S. J. C., Supreme Judicial Court.
Sol., solution; Solomon.
Sol., Solicitor.
Sol. Gen., Solicitor General.
S. P. Q. R., *Senatus populusque Romanus*, the Senate and people of Rome.
Sq. m., square mile or miles.
S. S., Sunday School.
S. S., *sequentia*, what follows.
St., Saint; street.
S. T. D., *Sanctæ Theologiæ Doctor*, Doctor of Divinity.
Ster., Sterling.
S. T. P., *Sanctæ Theologiæ Professor*, Professor of Divinity.
S. T. T. L., *sit tibi terra levis*, may the earth be light to thee.
Sup., Supplement; Supernumerary.
Surg., Surgeon.
Surg.-Gen., Surgeon-General.
Sus., Susannah.
T., ton or tons.
Tenn., Tennessee.
Tex., Texas.
Text. Rec., *Textus Receptus*, the Received Text.
Theo., Theodore.
Theor., Theorem.
Thess., Thessalonians.
Thos., Thomas.
Tier., tierce or tierces.
Tim., Timothy.
Tit., Titus.
T. O., turn over.
Tob., Tobit.

Tr., transpose.
Tr., Trustee. Trs., Trustees.
Trans., translation; translator.
Treas., Treasurer.
U. C., Upper Canada.
U. E. I. C., United East India Company.
U. J. C., *Utriusque Juris Doctor*, Doctor of each Law (Canon and Civil).
U. K., United Kingdom.
Ult., ultimo, of last month.
Univ., University.
U. S., United States.
U. S. A., United States of America.
U. S. A., United States Army.
U. S. M., United States Mail.
U. S. N., United States Navy.
V. or vid., *vide*, see.
Va., Virginia.
Ver. or v., verse or verses.
Vers., vs., or v., *versus*, against.
V. g., *verbi gratia*, for example.
Viz., *videlicet*, namely.
Vol. or v., volume. Vols., volumes.
V. Pres. or V. P., Vice President.
V. R., *Victoria Regina*, Queen Victoria.
Vt., Vermont.
W., West.
W. f., wrong font.
W. I., West Indies.
Wis., Wisconsin.
Wisd., Wisdom (Book of).
Wk. or w., week.
Wm., William.
W. T., Washington Territory.
Wt., weight.
Xmas, Christmas.
Xn., Christian.
Xnty., Christianity.
Xt., Christ.
Yr., year. Yrs., years.
&c., *et cætera-t-æ-a*, and so forth.

INDEX

A.

Abbreviations, to be followed by periods, 89. Table of, 435.
Abridging, in what it consists, 346.
Accent (character), acute, where used, 149. Grave, where used, 149. Circumflex, where used, 149.
Accent (stress of the voice), tendency to throw it back in polysyllables, 60. In poetry, constitutes length, 403.
Adage, the, 345.
Addison, his illustration of delicacy of taste, 175. His style, 264.
Adjectives, origin of, 30. Definition of, 63.
Adjunct, definition of, 69.
Adverbs, origin of, 32. Definition of, 64. When misplaced, are often a source of obscurity, 286.
Agreeableness, held by some to constitute beauty, 215.
Alexandrine, the, of what it consists, 411. Where used, 411. Too cumbrous for an entire piece, 412.
Alison, his view of taste, 171.
Allegory, what it is, 248.
Allusions, often form pleasing introductions, 832.
Alphabet, derivation of the word, 24. The Phœnician, supposed to have been derived from the Hebrew, 27. The Greek, and its derivatives, 28. The Latin, derived from the Greek, 28. The English, derived from the Latin, 28. Number of letters in different alphabets, 29.

Ambiguity, in what it consists, 285. A fault of frequent occurrence, 290. Its commonest varieties, 290.
Amphibrach, the, 408.
Amphimacer, the, 408.
Amplification, in what it consists, 829. Of definitions, 833. Of arguments, 833.
Analogy, argument from, 833.
Analysis, of subjects, 326—328. Should invariably be drawn up, 329.
Anapest, the, 408.
Anecdote, the, 870.
Angles, the, united with the Saxons in invading England, 44. Who they were, 44. Outnumbered by the Saxons on the continent, 45. Gave their name to Britain, 44, 45.
Anglo-Saxon Language, an offshoot of Gothic, 46. Modified but little by the Danish invasions, 47. Changes by which it was converted into English, 51.
Antibacchius, the, 408.
Anticlimax, 251.
Antithesis, 250. Used in Proverbs, 251. Often employed in parallels, 843.
Aphæresis, 236.
Aphorism, the, 345.
Apocope, 286.
Apologue, the, 339.
Apophasis, 252.
Apophthegm, the, 345.
Apostrophe, meaning of the word, 142. Form and position of the character so called, 142. Rules for the, 142. When used to denote the omission of letters

142. Used to form the plural of letters, &c., 143. The figure so called, 250.
Appeal to the feelings, in an argumentative discourse, 389.
Archaism, 236.
Argument, what it is, 354.
Argumentative Discourse, the, 385. Formal divisions of, 385.
Arguments, proper arrangement of, 389.
Aristotle, his rules for unity of action, 169.
Armorican Language, its wonderful resemblance to Welsh, 88.
Art, its relation to science, 165.
Article, the, definition of, 63. The definite, 63. The indefinite, 63.
Associations, instrumental in increasing the pleasures of the imagination, 186. Personal, 187. National, 187. Historical, 187. Source of sublimity in sounds, 200. Source of beauty in sounds, 223.
Asterisk, the, where used, 151.
Asterism, the, where used, 150.
Asyndeton, 294.

B.

Bacchius, the, 403.
Ballad, the, defined, 422.
Barbarisms, of what they consist, 271.
Battles, sublime descriptions of, 202.
Beauty, character of the emotions it excites, 214. Variety of its applications, 215. Theories as to its source, 215. Color, one of its chief elements, 216. Regularity of figure, one of its elements, 217. Hogarth's line of, 217. Smoothness, essential to it, 218. Gentle motion, an element of, 218. Smallness and delicacy, elements of, 219. Design, a source of, 219. Moral beauty, 221. Beauty of the human countenance, 221; depends mainly on the expression, 222. Beautiful sounds, 223. The beautiful in writing, 223.
Belles-lettres, its meaning in the French language, 166. Its general acceptation in English, 167.
Bible, sublimity of the, 210.
Biography, what it is, 369. Style appropriate to, 369.
Blank Verse, a favorable medium for expressing sublime ideas, 212. Of what it consists, 412. The most elevated of all measures, 412. Most difficult to write, 412.

Bombast, 218.
Brace, the, for what used, 151.
Brackets, for what they are used, 139, 140. How to punctuate matter within brackets, 140.
Bretagne, tradition respecting its settlement, 89.
Breve, the, 150.
Britain, state of, before the Roman conquest, 34. Settled by Celts, 35. German colonies planted there at an early date, 42. Invasion of, by the Saxons, 43. Invasion of, by the Danes, 46. Conquest of, by the Normans, 48.
Burlesque, a species of wit, 227. A burlesque, what it is, 421.
Burletta, the, defined, 421.

C.

Cadence, of periods, 303.
Cadmus, the introducer of letters into Greece, 25.
Cambrian, a branch of the Celtic tongue, 38.
Capitals, 74. Rules for, 74—78. Small 78. Too free use of, to be avoided, 78. When used for figures, to be followed by periods, 69.
Captions, what they are, 155.
Caret, the, for what used, 152.
Catch-words, what they are, 155.
Cedilla, the, where used, 152.
Celtic Language, the parent of many tongues, 86. An offshoot from the Hebrew, or Phœnician, 87. Branches of, 88. Its peculiar features, 39. Celtic of Britain, how far modified during the period of Roman supremacy, 40; superseded by Saxon, 44. English words derived from it, 55.
Characters, astronomical, 153.
Chaucer, writings of, 50.
Cicero, the most harmonious of writers, 301.
Circumlocutions, indefinite, violate precision, 282.
Clarendon, the style of, often violates unity, 311.
Clause, definition of, 69. Relative, 69. Participial, 69. Adverbial, 69. Vocative, 70. Adjective, 70. Appositional, 70. Causal, 70. Hypothetical, 70. Dependent, 70. Independent, 70. Vocative and

INDEX. 443

causal, never restrictive, 110 Participial, when restrictive, 111. Appositional, rule for punctuating, 113. Absolute, to be set off by the comma, 116.
Clearness, in what it consists, 284. Involves purity, propriety, and precision, 284. Faults opposed to it, 284.
Climax, what it is, 251. Derivation of the term, 251. Climax of sound, 251.
Coining, of words, forbidden except to those who are unfolding a new science, 272. Of compound words, 272.
Colloquialisms, to be avoided, 276.
Colon, derivation of the word, 97. Its first use, 97. Formerly much used, 97. Its place at the present day usurped by the semicolon, 97. Rules for the, 97, 98, 99. When to be followed by a dash, 98.
Color, one of the chief elements of beauty, 216. Peculiarities which enhance its beauty, 216.
Comedy, defined, 420.
Comedy English, too often disgraced by obscenity, 283.
Comma, meaning of the word, 104. Degree of separation it denotes, 104. Not found in early manuscripts, 104. How previously denoted, 104. General rule for the, 104. Special rules for the, 106—126. Cautions in the use of, 128. Not to be introduced simply because a sentence is long, 128. Not to be used after a grammatical subject when immediately followed by its verb, 128. Not to be used before *and* connecting two words only, 128. To be omitted when there is doubt as to the propriety of using it, 129.
Communication, media of, 18.
Composition, successive steps of, 322. The art defined, 348.
Compositions, revision of, 334. Suggestions as to the correction of, 335.
Conciseness, essential to sublimity in writing, 207. Carried to excess, produces obscurity, 266.
Conjunctions, origin of, 82. Definition of, 64. List of, 64.
Connection of words, clauses, and members, general principles relating to the, 87, 88.
Contrast, a, heightened by a resemblance in language and construction, 298.
Correspondence epistolary, 356.
Countenance beauty of the, 222.

Couplet, the, of what it consists, 402. The heroic should have complete sense with in itself, 411. Delights in antitheses, 411.
Cousin, his view of taste, 171.
Criticism, fatal to the pleasures of the imagination, 185. Reason why it is seldom correct in the case of young persons, 185. Definition of, 318. Developed the rules of rhetoric, 318. Beauty and truth, its objects, 319. Relation between its ancient and its present character, 319. Literary, 320; its office, 320; should be based on feeling as well as rules, 321; abuse of, 821; objections to, 322; its principles not arbitrary, 322.
Curiosity, a universal passion, 191.

D.

Dactyl, the, 408.
Darkness, a source of sublimity, 197.
Dash, but lately introduced, 131. Too freely used at the present day, 131. Rules for the use of, 131—134. When to be used after other points, 132, 133 When used to denote the omission of letters, 142.
Dates, how to be written, 126.
Definitions, how they may be amplified, 333.
Delicacy, an element of beauty, 219.
Description, in what it consists, 348. Of material objects, 349. Of natural scenery, 350. Of persons, 351.
Design, an element of beauty, 219. Unity of, essential to the effect of a composition, 220.
Diæresis, the, for what used, 151. Meaning of the word, 152. The figure so called, 236.
Dialogue, the, 376. Used for the discussion of serious topics, 376.
Didactic Poetry, 423.
Diffuseness, too great, to be avoided, 266.
Dimeter, of what it consists, 404.
Diminutives, origin of, 219.
Disorder, a source of sublimity, 198.
Disquisition, the, 380.
Dissertation, the, 380.
Distich, the, what it is, 402.
Division, the, of an argumentative discourse, 387.
Division-Marks, 150.
Double Comma, the, for what used, 152.
Double Dagger, the, 151.

Dramas, of what they consist, 377. Derivation of the term, 419. Division of, into acts and scenes, 421.
Dramatic Poetry, closely allied to Epic, 419. Three dramatic unities, 420. Leading divisions of, 420.
Dramatists, the distinguished, of antiquity, 420. The distinguished, in modern literatures, 420.

E.

Eclogue, the, 423.
Editorial, the, 380.
Elegiac Poetry, of what it treats, 423.
Ellipsis, marks of, 151. The figure so called, 237. Improper, a cause of obscurity, 285.
Emphasis-Marks, 150.
Ems, what they are, 154.
Enallage, what it is, 238. Does not justify a violation of syntactical rules, 238.
England, a corruption of Angleland, 44.
English Language, the, formation of, 49. First book in, 50. Its forms settled by Wicliffe's translation of the Bible, 50. Its Saxon derivatives, 52, 53. Its Norman French derivatives, 53. Its modern French derivatives, 54. Its Latin derivatives, 54. Its Celtic derivatives, 55. Its Greek derivatives, 56. Its miscellaneous elements, 56. Four fifths of its current words, of Saxon origin, 57. Its characteristics, 57. Its orthography, 58. Its syntactical constructions, 58. Its variety, 58. Its poetical terms, 58. Its strength, 59. Its flexibility, 60. Its harmony, 60. Its simplicity, 61.
Epic Poetry, of what it treats, 418. Unity of design, essential to, 418. Epic poems of different languages, 419. Derivation of the term *epic*, 419. The plot of an epic, what it should be, 419.
Epigram, the, defined, 423.
Epilogue, the, 421.
Episodes, what they are, 418.
Epitomising, in what it consists, 346.
Epopea, the, 419.
Equivocation, in what it consists, 284. Varieties of, 289.
Erse Language, a branch of Celtic, 38.
Essays, 379. Wide application of the term, 379. Different classes of, 380. Latitude allowed in the conduct of, 380.
Etymology, figures of, 236.

Exclamation (the figure), 260.
Exclamation-point, rules for the use of the, 92—95. Does not always denote the same degree of separation, 93. Use of more than one, 95.
Exordium, the, 386.
Exposition, in what it consists, 354.
Expression, has much to do with beauty of countenance, 222.

F.

Fable, the, 339.
Farce, the, defined, 421.
Feet, what they are, 403. Enumeration of, 403. Primary, 404. Secondary, 404.
Fiction, what it is, 374. May be made the vehicle of good or evil, 375.
Figure, regularity of, a source of beauty, 217; not synonymous with sameness, 217.
Figures, what they are, 235. Four classes of, 235. Of orthography, 235. Of etymology, 236. Of syntax, 237. Of rhetoric, 239, 246; origin of, 240; history of figurative language, 241; most used in the early stages of society, 242; grow less common as a language progresses in refinement, 242; advantages accruing from the use of, 242—244; frequently convey the meaning more forcibly than plain language, 244; rules for the use of, 244—254; not absolutely essential to beauty of composition, 244; should not be the chief object had in view, 255; should spring naturally from the subject, 255; should not be used to excess, 255.
French Language, the source of many English words, 54. Character of the, 59. Its poetry, without rhyme, indistinguishable from prose, 59.
Frigidity, 213.
Frisian Language, its resemblance to English, 45.
Frisians, reasons for supposing that they engaged in the invasion of Britain, 45. Where they lived, 45.
Frontispiece, the, 155.

G.

Gaelic, a branch of Celtic, 38.
Gallicisms, 273.
Gardens, Chinese, 193.
Genius, distinction between it and taste, 181, 182. Universal, 192.
Germanic Languages, offshoots of Gothic, 46.

INDEX. 445

Gestures, 14. Extent to which they were carried on the ancient stage, 15. Decline of their use, 16.
Gothic Language, its two great branches, 46.
Grace, Hogarth's line of, 217. What it is, 221.
Grandeur, see *Sublimity*.
Greek Language, the, English scientific terms borrowed from, 50.

H.

Harmony, in what it consists, 299. Words to be avoided as inharmonious, 800. Requires the writer to avoid repeating a sound, 800. Requires him to avoid a succession of words of the same number of syllables, 801. Depends on th proper arrangement of the parts of a sentence, 301. Carried to greater perfection in the ancient languages than in ours, 304. Danger of paying too much attention to, 302. Requires that the fullest clauses and most sonorous words be reserved for the close of a sentence, 803. Highest kind of, consists in the adaptation of sound to sense, 304.
Head-lines, what they are, 155.
Hebrews, their claim to the invention of letters, 26.
Hemistich, a, what it is, 402.
Hengist and *Horsa*, expedition of, 42. Hengist's stratagem for procuring land, 43.
Heptameter, of what it consists, 404. The regular ballad-measure of our language, 408. Generally written in two lines, 408.
Heroic Line, its character, 410. Used in the Spenserian stanza, 410. Most commonly found in the form of the couplet 411. Constitutes blank verse, 412.
Hexameter, of what it consists, 404.
Hieroglyphics, 21.
Hindoos, their claim to the invention of letters, 26.
Historians, of England, 368. Of America, 869.
History, a, what it is, 368. Essentials of a good history, 368. Style appropriate to, 869.
Hogarth, his line of beauty and line of grace, 217.
Hume, his view of taste, 170.

Humor, in what it consists, 231. Opposed to the pathetic, 232. Its subjects, 232. Not short-lived, like wit, 232. Novelty not essential to it, 232. Enters into every literature, 233. Carried to the greatest perfection in Don Quixote, 233. Distinction between it and ridicule, 233.
Hymn, the, 422.
Hyperbaton, what it is, 239. Enters largely into poetry, 239.
Hyperbole, what it is, 249. Occurs in common conversation, 249. Has its origin in liveliness of imagination, 249. Violent hyperbole, out of place in mere descriptions, 250. May be so extravagant as to render the writer ridiculous, 259.
Hyphen, derivation of the word, 143. What it is used to denote, 143. Rules for its use, 143, 144. Sometimes employed instead of the diæresis, 144.

I.

Iambus, the, 406.
Idyl, the, 423.
Imagery, or *Vision*, 250.
Imagination, defined, 183. Pleasures of, 183; process by which they are excited, 183. Its exuberance in youth fatal to sound criticism, 196. Its pleasures increased by associations, 186. Has had much to do with the origin of figures, 241. Vividness of, apt to betray the young into too great floridity, 264.
Imitation, fidelity of, a source of pleasure to the imagination, 190. Servile, to be avoided, 816.
Index, or *Hand*, for what used, 150.
Induction, the process of, 333.
Infinitive Mood, when to be preceded by the comma, 124.
Infinity, a source of sublimity, 196.
Interjections, the first words, 29. Definition of, 65. To be followed by exclamation-points, 94.
Interrogation (the figure), 250.
Interrogation-point, rules for the, 91. Does not always denote the same degree of separation, 98.
Introduction, importance of an effective, 880. Varieties of, 831, 832. Of an argumentative discourse, 386; modesty, essential to it, 887. Should be accommodated to the discourse that is to follow 887.

Invention, not a division of rhetoric, 164. In what it consists, 325. The most difficult part of composition, 325.
Ireland, originally peopled by Carthaginian colonies, 85.
Irony, 234, 252.
Italian Language, origin of the, 41.
Italics, how indicated in manuscript, 154. For what used, 154. Not to be too freely employed, 154. Their use in the English Bible, 154.

J.

Jeu de mots, 230.
Justice, poetical, 420.

K.

Kassiterides, or *Scilly Isles*, intercourse of the Phœnicians with the, 86. Peopled by Celts, 86.

L.

Lampoon, the, 423.
Language, spoken, 16; its origin, 17; theories as to its origin, 18; the gift of Deity, 19. Written language, 20; its different systems, 21. The Phœnician, written from right to left, 28. Mode of writing the Greek, 28. Gradual development of a system of, 29. English, see *English Language*. Irish, supposed to have been derived from the Phœnician, 85. Celtic, see *Celtic Language*. Effect of climate and atmosphere on, 88. Individual languages affected by the character of those who speak them, 59.
Latinizing, of Johnson and his imitators, 55.
Latin Language, English words derived from it, 54.
Leaders, 152.
Leads, what they are, 154.
Letters (characters), introduced into Greece by Cadmus, 25. First divided into different classes by Thaut, 25. Their invention attributed to Thaut by Sanchoniathon, 25. The honor of their invention claimed by the Indians, 26.
Letters (species of composition), 355. News, 356. Of business, 356. Official, 356. Of friendship, 357. Of condolence, 357. Of congratulation, 357. Of introduction, 358. Style of, 358. Answers to, 358. Manual execution of, 359. Date of, 359. Address of, 860. Subscription of, 361. Folding and sealing of, 365. Superscription of, 366.
Licenses, poetical, 401.
Lyric Poetry, 421.

M.

Machinery, of an epic poem, 419.
Macron, the, 150.
Madrigal, the, 422.
Mannerism, what it is, 270. An excess of it to be avoided, 216.
Maxim, the, 343.
Measures, defined, 404. Varieties of, 404. Iambic, 405; constitute the great body of our poetry, 406. Trochaic, 405 adapted to gay and tender sentiments, 406. Anapestic, 405; adapted to animated sentiments, 406. Dactylic, 406; difficult to write, 407.
Melodrama, the, 421.
Metaphor, what it is, 248. The commonest of figures, 248. Should not be far-fetched, trite, obscure, or inappropriate, 258. Metaphorical and plain language should not be blended, 258. Mixed metaphors, to be avoided, 259. Should not be carried too far, 259.
Metonymy, what it is, 249. Relations on which it is founded, 249.
Metre, long, 407. Common, 407. Short, 408.
Might, actively exerted, the principal source of the sublime, 195.
Mimesis, 236.
Molossus, the, 403.
Monometer, of what it consists, 404.
Motion, when gentle, an element of beauty, 218. When very swift, an element of sublimity, 218. Often vividly represented in composition by peculiar combinations of words, 306.
Music, effect of, increased by associations, 187, 200. When beautiful, and when sublime, 222.

N.

Narration, what it is, 353.
Narratives, what they are, 367. Classes of, 368.

INDEX. 447

Nature, the productions of, a source of pleasure to the imagination, 190.
Norman French, origin of, 41. First introduction of, into England, under Edward the Confessor, 47. Made the court language under William the Conqueror, 48. Source of many English words, 53.
Notes, 366. Of invitation, 366.
Nouns, origin of, 30. Definition of, 62. Common, 62. Proper, 62.
Novel, the, 375.
Novelty, a source of pleasure to the imagination, 191. Different degrees of, 192. Essential to the effect of a pun, 230.
Number, plural, origin of the, 30.

O.

O and *oh*, difference between, 78.
Obelisk, or *Dagger*, 151.
Obituary, the, 369.
Obscurity, a source of sublimity, 197. As opposed to clearness, in what it consists, 284; causes from which it results, 285.
Octometer, of what it consists, 404. Generally written in two lines, 408.
Ode, the, 422.
Omission (the figure), 252.
Onomatopœia, 252. Continued, 305.
Oration, the, 380, 392. Style appropriate to, 393.
Orthography, figures of, 235.
Ossian, why his writings are classed as poems, 59. One of the sublimest of writers, 211. Description of his style, 211.

P.

Paragoge, 236.
Paragraph (character), where used, 150. Meaning of the word, 150.
Paralipsis, 252.
Parallels (character), 151.
Parallels (a variety of composition), 342.
Paraphrase, what it is, 344.
Parentheses, meaning of the word, 136. How indicated in reading, 136. Much used by old writers, 136. In disfavor with modern critics, 136. Rules for the use of, 137—139. Their proper place in a sentence, 137. How to punctuate matter within parentheses, 138. Long, to be avoided, 312.

Parenthetical Expressions, 104. Where generally used, 104. To be preceded and followed by the comma, 104, 106, 107. Examples of, 105.
Parodies, what they are, 226, 421.
Paronomasia, see *Pun*.
Parsing, difficulties in, explained, 66.
Participles, definition of, 64. Number of, 64.
Particles, splitting of, 295.
Pasquinade, the, 423.
Pastoral Poetry, 423.
Patriotism, a source of moral sublimity, 205.
Pauses, should be distributed at proper intervals, 302. Poetical, 415; primary, 415; secondary, 415, 416.
Pentameter, of what it consists, 404. Iambic, constitutes the *heroic line*, 410; its character, 410; used in the Spenserian stanza, 410; most commonly found in the form of the couplet, 411.
Period, meaning of the term, 86. Found in manuscripts of an early date, 86. Rules for the, 87—90. When used to denote the omission of letters, 142.
Peroration, the, of an argumentative discourse, 389.
Personification, 250.
Perspicuity, see *Clearness*.
Phrases, definition of, 69.
Picturesque, the, 193, 194.
Pleonasm, 237.
Plot, the, what it is, 374. Characteristics of a good, 374.
Poetry, what compositions it embraces 400. Features that distinguish it from prose, 401. Varieties of, 419.
Points, punctuation, first use of, 81. To be used independently of reading-pauses, 84. Used to separate words and clauses, 84. Used to indicate the parts of speech, 84. Show to what class a sentence belongs, 85. Indicate sudden transitions, 85. Denote the omission of words, 85. Must be used only when there is a positive rule for so doing, 85. Enumeration of the, 86.
Polysyndeton, 295.
Portuguese Language, origin of the, 42.
Possessive Case, rules for the formation of the, 142.
Precision, derivation of the term, 279 In what it consists, 279. Violated

a want of discrimination in the use of synonymes, 279. Rejects unnecessary words, 281. Often violated by indefinite circumlocutions, 282.
Predicate, what it is, 68. When the comma must be inserted in a compound, 119.
Prepositions, origin of, 80. Defined, 64. List of, 64. List of prepositions that follow certain words, 159. Should not close a sentence, 297.
Prescott, remarks on the style of, 369.
Prologue, the, 421.
Pronouns, adjective, origin of, 81; definition of, 63. Personal, origin of, 81; definition of, 62. Relative, origin of, 32; definition of, 62. Interrogative, definition of, 62. The same pronoun not to refer to different objects in the same sentence, 287.
Propriety, in what it consists, 276. Faults opposed to it, 276. Violated by the confounding of derivatives, 276.
Prose, compositions it embraces, 348.
Prosopopœia, 250.
Prosthesis, 236.
Proverb, the, 345.
Psalm, the, 422.
Pun, the, 230. Novelty essential to its effect, 230.
Punctuation, what it is, 81. By whom invented, 81. Too generally neglected, 82. Prevents misconceptions, 62. Founded on great and definite principles, 83. General principles of, 84, 85, 86.
Purity, in what it consists, 271.
Pyrrhic, the, 403.

Q.

Quantity, of syllables, on what it depends, 402; how indicated, 403; in Latin and Greek, independent of accent, 403.
Quantity-Marks, 150.
Quatrain, the, 407.
Quintilian, his view of the perfect orator, 164.
Quotation-points, of what they consist, 145. By whom first used, 145. For what employed, 145. Not to be used when merely the substance of a quotation is given, 145. How to punctuate matter within, 146. Single, when used, 146.
Quotations, when to be preceded by the colon, 97. When to be preceded by the comma, 124.

R.

Reason, the distinction between man and brutes, 18.
Reasoning, the, in an argumentative discourse, 359.
Reference-Marks, 150.
Regimen, of verbs and prepositions, 68.
Repetition (the figure), 252.
Restrictive Expressions, defined, 105. Not to be separated by the comma from that which they restrict, 105, 110. To be set off by the comma, when they refer to several antecedents themselves separated by that point, 110. Should stand immediately after their logical antecedents, 110.
Review, the, 380.
Revision, the best means of correcting too great floridity, 264. Necessary to the effect of good writing, 315.
Rhetoric, ancient meaning of the word, 163. Its present acceptation, 163. Its province as a science and as an art, 164. To be regarded as a useful and an elegant art, 165. Advantages resulting from the study of, 166—168. Objection to its rules, 168. Source from which its rules are drawn, 169. Figures of, 246.
Rhyme, an unfavorable medium for the expression of sublime ideas, 211. Defined, 402. Principles to be observed respecting it, 413, 414. Rich rhymes, 413. Speaks to the ear, 414. Perfect rhymes, 414. Admissible rhymes, 414. Inadmissible rhymes, 414. Regularity of, important, 415.
Ridicule, in what it consists, 233. To what it may be effectively applied, 233. Its attack covert, 234.
Romance, the, 375. Difference between it and the novel, 375.
Romans, the, their policy in introducing their language into conquered states, 40.

S.

Sanscrit, supposed to be one of the most ancient of languages, 26.
Satire, the, 423.
Satirical Poetry, 423.
Saw, the, 345.
Saxon Language, an offshoot of Gothic, 46.

Saxons, what part of Germany they inhabited, 44.
Scandinavia, emigration of barbarians from, 41.
Scandinavian Language, an offshoot of Gothic, 46.
Scanning, in what it consists, 405.
Science, its relation to art, 165.
Section (character), where used, 150.
Semicolon, meaning of the word, 100. Degree of separation which it denotes, 100. First employed in Italy, 100. When first used in England, 100. Rules for the, 100—102.
Semi-Saxon Writings, 50.
Sense, adaptation of sound to, 304.
Senses, the, rendered acute by constant use, 172. Three of them incapable of awakening pleasure in the Imagination, 188.
Sentences, definition of, 67. Component parts of, 67. Subjects of, 67; how ascertained, 68. Predicates of, 68. Members of, 69. Declarative, 70. Interrogative, 71. Imperative, 71. Exclamatory, 71. Simple, 71. Compound, 71.
Sermons, 893—399.
Shakspeare, his dramatic poems highly irregular, 822; their popularity accounted for, 823.
Side-heads, what they are, 155.
Silence, a source of sublimity, 197.
Simile, the, what it is, 247. Sometimes used without any formal term of comparison, 247. The explanatory, 247. The embellishing, 248. Rules for its use, 256. Should not be founded on faint resemblances, 256. Should not be trite, 256. Should not be founded on local allusions, 257. Should not be drawn from resemblances to trivial objects, 257. Is out of place, when anger, terror, or despair, is the prevalent passion, 258.
Simplicity, essential to sublimity, 208.
Sketches, historical, 868. Biographical, 869.
Smallness, an element of beauty, 219. The idea of, associated with whatever we are fond of, 219.
Smell, a source of pleasure to the imagination only by means of associations, 189.
Smoothness, an element of beauty, 219
Solecisms, 273.
Solitude, a source of sublimity, 197.
Solon, the laws of, how written, 28.

Sonnet, the, borrowed from the Italians, 409. Of what it consists, 409. Arrangement of its rhymes, 409.
Sophism, difference between it and sophistry, 277.
Sound, beauty of, 222. Adaptation of, to sense, 304.
Sounds, inarticulate, 16. Employed in composition to imitate motion, 806; to represent the emotions of the mind, 807.
Spanish Language, the, origin of, 42. Character of, 59.
Speculation, what it is, 854.
Speech, parts of, their origin, 29—33; their number, 62; to be carefully distinguished, 65.
Spondee, the, 403.
Stanzas, what they are, 402. Their variety, infinite, 407. Four-lined, 407. Six-lined, 403. The Spenserian stanza, borrowed from Italian, 408; by whom used, 408; of what it consists, 408.
Statement, the, of an argumentative discourse, 888.
Story, the, 876. Difference between it and the tale, 876.
Strength, in what it consists, 293. Requires the rejection of superfluous words, 293. Requires that proper connectives be used, 293. Requires that the too frequent use of *and* be avoided, 294. Requires the writer to avoid splitting particles, 295. Requires that the important words be so disposed as to make the greatest impression, 295. Requires that a shorter member should precede a longer and a weaker a stronger, 296. Requires that a sentence should not be closed with an unaccented word, 297.
Style, dignified by figures, 243. What it is, 262. Derivation of the word, 262. Varieties of, 263; appropriate to different subjects, 263. The dry, 263. The plain, 263. The neat, 263; adapted to all subjects, 264. The elegant, 264. The florid, 264; two varieties of, 264; best means of correcting too great floridity, 264. The simple, 265. The labored, 265. The concise, 265. The diffuse, 266. The nervous, 266. The feeble, 266. Essential properties of, 270. Forming of, 313 rules for the, 314—316. Must be adapted to the subject, 316.
Sub-heads, what they are, 155.

Subjects, definition of, 67. How to be ascertained, 68. Grammatical, 68. Logical, 68. Logical, when to be followed by the comma, 115. List of, 427—434.

Sublimity, defined, 194. Its principal source, 195. An element in scriptural descriptions of powerful animals, 195. Vastness, one of its sources, 196. Darkness, solitude, and silence, conducive to it, 197. Obscurity, one of its sources, 197. Heightened by disorder, 198. Sounds characterized by, 199. Produced, in sounds, exclusively by associations, 200. The sublime in writing, 201; excludes what is merely beautiful, 201. Moral or sentimental sublime, 204; its sources, 204. Style essential to it, 206; conciseness, one of its essentials, 207; simplicity, one of its essentials, 208. The emotion it excites, short-lived, 209. An unimproved state of society, favorable to it, 210. Rhyme, unfavorable to sublimity in writing, 212. Faults opposed to it, 213. Very swift motion, an element of, 218.

Substantives, what they are, 62.

Syllabication, two systems of, 144. Rules of, 145.

Syllepsis, what it is, 237.

Syntax, principles for correcting false, 156—159. Figures of, 237

Synæresis, 236.

Syncope, 236.

Synecdoche, 249

Synonymes, what they are, 280. Want of discrimination between them violates precision, 279.

T.

Tale, the, 375.

Taste, defined, 170. Various theories respecting it, 170, 171. Common to all men, 171. Possessed in different degrees, 171. An improvable faculty, 172. Its connection with the judgment, 173. Its elements, 174. Its characteristics, 174. Delicacy of, 174. Correctness of, 175. Mutations of, 176. Often vitiated, 176, 177. Diversity of, when admissible, 178. Standard of, 179. Distinction between it and genius, 181, 182. Pleasures of, 183; derived from imagination, 185; increased by associations, 186.

Tautology, what it is, 800. How to correct it, 300.

Technical Terms, to be avoided in composition, 288.

Testimony, argument from, 833.

Tetrameter, of what it consists, 404. Iambic, a favorite measure, 411; its facility of construction, 410.

Teutonic Language, a branch of Gothic, 46.

Texts, choice of, 394.

Thaut, supposed to be identical with Hermes Trismegistus, 25.

Thesis, the, 385.

Thought, essential to effective writing, 326.

Title-page, the, 155.

Titles Running, what they are, 155.

Tmesis, 237.

Touch, incapable of awakening pleasure in the imagination without the aid of sight, 189.

Tract, the, 380.

Tragedy, defined, 420.

Travels, 370.

Travesties, what they are, 226, 421.

Treatise, the, 380.

Tribrach, the, 403.

Trimeter, of what it consists, 404.

Triplet, the, what it is, 402.

Trochee, the, 403.

Tropes, 247.

Type, kinds of, 154.

U.

Unity, in what it consists, 309. Requires that the scene and subject be changed as little as possible, 309. Requires us to avoid crowding into one sentence things that have no connection, 310. Punctuation, no remedy for violations of, 311. Requires the writer to avoid long parentheses, 312. The three dramatic unities, 420.

Unity and Variety, held by some to constitute beauty, 215.

Usage, the only standard of speaking an writing, 274. Present, 274. National, 274. Reputable, 274. Rules with respect to words when usage is divided, 275

Utility, held by some to constitute beauty 215.

V.

Variety, one of the elements of beauty of figure, 217.

Fastness, a source of sublimity, 196.
Verbs, origin of, 31. Defined, 63. Subjects of, 63. Transitive, 63. Intransitive, 63. Finite, 63. Voices of, 63. Transitive and intransitive, to be carefully distinguished, 158.
Verse, of what it consists, 401. Iambic, 404. Trochaic, 404. Anapestic, 404. Dactylic, 404. Blank, see *Blank Verse*.
Verses, what they are, 402. When called *pure*, 404. When said to be *mixed*, 404. Catalectic, 404. Hypercatalectic, 405. Acatalectic, 405.
Versification, what it is, 402.
Vignette, the, 155.
Vision, 250.
Volumes, different sizes of, folio, quarto, &c., 158.
Voyages, 370.
Vulgarisms, to be avoided, 276.

W.

Welsh, its resemblance to Hebrew, 37.

Wit, what it is, 225. How produced, 226 Varieties of, 226—231. Capable of making beauties, as well as blemishes, subjects of derision, 321.
Wonderful, the, a source of pleasure to the imagination, 193. An element in Chinese gardening, 193.
Writing, ideographic system of, 21; used by the Mexicans and North American Indians, 21. Verbal system of, 21; objection to it, 22. Chinese system of, 22 read and understood by other Asiatic nations, 22. Syllabic system of, 23 written languages of which it is the basis, 23. Alphabetic system of, 23; its origin 24; its invention attributed to the Deity to Moses, Abraham, Enoch, and Adam, 24; its invention attributed by the Greeks and Romans to the Phœnicians, 25; different theories as to its invention, 26; known to the Jews in the time of Moses, 27. Present manner of, introduced by Pronapides, 28.

THE END

www.ingramcontent.com/pod-product-compliance
Lightning Source LLC
Chambersburg PA
CBHW022136300426
44115CB00006B/213